大学汉英双语教材系列
袁宪军　主编

Tourism Industrial Economics
旅游产业经济学

王起静　编著

图书在版编目(CIP)数据

旅游产业经济学/王起静编著. —北京:北京大学出版社,2006.1
(大学汉英双语教材系列)
ISBN 7-301-08887-6

Ⅰ. 旅… Ⅱ. 王… Ⅲ. 旅游经济学—高等学校—教材—汉、英 Ⅳ. F590

中国版本图书馆 CIP 数据核字(2005)第 130129 号

书　　　名:	旅游产业经济学
著作责任者:	王起静 编著
责 任 编 辑:	刘胜利
标 准 书 号:	ISBN 7-301-08887-6/G · 1463
出 版 发 行:	北京大学出版社
地　　　址:	北京市海淀区成府路 205 号　100871
网　　　址:	http://cbs.pku.edu.cn　电子信箱: zpup@pup.pku.edu.cn
电　　　话:	邮购部 62752015　发行部 62750672　编辑部 62765014
排　版　者:	兴盛达打字服务社　82715400
印　刷　者:	三河市新世纪印务有限公司
	650 毫米×980 毫米　16 开本　24.75 印张　398 千字
	2006 年 1 月第 1 版　2006 年 12 月第 2 次印刷
定　　　价:	29.00 元

未经许可,不得以任何方式复制或抄袭本书之部分或全部内容。
版权所有,翻版必究

《大学汉英双语教材系列》
编审委员会

主　编
　　袁宪军

编委会成员（按姓氏笔划为序）
　　付耀祖（外交学院教授，中国国际关系学会副会长兼秘书长）
　　杜　江（北京第二外国语学院教授、院长，中国旅游协会常务
　　　　　理事，国际旅游科学院院士）
　　杜厚文（中国人民大学教授、博导，中国世界经济学会副会长，
　　　　　中国人民大学前副校长）
　　金　碚（中国社会科学院工业经济研究所研究员、副所长、博
　　　　　导，中国经营报社社长）
　　袁宪军（北京第二外国语学院教授）
　　韩德昌（南开大学教授、博导，市场营销系主任）

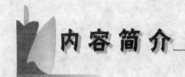

内容简介

此书为大学汉英双语教材系列之一。

全书分为四大部分。第一部分是旅游产业的发展和演变,主要深入探讨了旅游产业的产业特质,并详细介绍了国内外旅游产业的发展历史;第二部分包括旅游产业结构、旅游产业关联度和旅游产业区域结构;第三部分是旅游产业组织结构。这部分是本书的重点,主要用成熟的产业组织理论分析旅游产业的组织结构、旅游企业行为和企业绩效,其中用博弈论分析的旅游企业价格竞争行为是本书的难点。第四部分是旅游产业的政策和发展模式。

总　序

在世界经济、文化走向全球化的21世纪,我们已经进入了一个双语的时代,我们的科学技术、经济文化的进一步发展,急需大批具有较强英语运用能力的专业人才。我们国家从中学到大学的英语基础教育,为培养学生专业的英语运用能力奠定了坚实的基础。为了培养高尖端专业人才,国家教育部制定了在大学实施双语教学的规定,要求大学本科教育阶段应该有相当比例的课程用双语教学。目前,我国大多数高等院校都努力在双语教学上进行尝试,试图创制一些行之有效的双语教学方法和途径。在这些院校中,双语教学大多是采用英语原版教材,而教学则是用汉语进行讲解和解释。当然,采用英语原版教材无疑对我们教学内容的更新、教学方法的改进、教学体系的革新都有颇大影响。然而,采用英语原版教材存在着很多的不利方面。首先,英语原版教材使用的对象是英语作为母语的大学本科学生,而不是作为第二语言的本科学生,我们国家的学生尽管英语水平相对较好,但使用英语原版教材仍然不能达到得心应手的程度。第二,英语原版教材的编写体系,是针对英美国家的教育体制和学生的知识结构编写的,与我们国家有很大差距,不完全适合我们所用。第三,英语原版教材是从国外引进的,课本的售价非常昂贵,不是我们的学生所能负担得起的。基于这些方面的考虑,采用英语原版教材进行双语教学很难在我国的大学推广。也是基于这些方面的考虑,我们组织编写了《大学汉英双语教材系列》,以适应我国大学汉英双语教学的需要。

汉英双语教材的编写,完全是一种新的尝试,没有先例可以参考,更没有编写的程序可以遵循,这对我们确定编写原则造成极大困难。教材的编写者在进行广泛调查和多次讨论之后,达到一致共识:内容上反映该学科的最新发展,形式上方便于教学。另一方面,教材不采用汉英对照的形式,而是选择用英语有利于教学时则用英语,用汉语有利于教学时则用汉语,关键的、重要的术语和词汇则英汉/汉英对照。

  参加汉英双语教材编写的人员,大多为获得博士学位、曾在英美国家留学的中青年学者,有的在编写过程中还到国外搜集材料,请教专家,从2002年开始着手编写到完成长达近四年的时间,有的书稿几经修改,可谓一丝不苟,呕心沥血,竭尽全力。我们对汉英双语教材的尝试,这只是刚刚开始,今后还会陆续推出其他系列。衷心地希望教材的使用者给我们提出宝贵的建议和意见,以便我们改进编写方法,提高汉英双语教材的质量和水平。

  这次出版的《大学汉英双语教材系列》得到了北京市教委的资助和北京大学出版社的极大支持,在此表示诚挚的感谢。

袁宪军

2005年8月于北京

前言
Preface

在西方经济学学科体系中,产业经济学与产业组织学是同义语,是一门发展的相对成熟的学科。但我国学者对产业经济学的研究对象和研究内容的看法尚不统一,一部分学者认为产业经济学就是产业组织学,还有的学者认为,产业经济学的研究对象既然是"产业",就应该不仅研究产业内部各企业之间的关系,还应该研究产业之间的关系及其运动的规律性,所以持这种观点的学者认为产业经济学应该包括产业结构理论、产业关联理论、产业组织理论和产业政策等内容。在本书中,我们认同后一观点。

旅游产业作为众多行业的集合体,是"产业的产业",其本身具有很多特殊的运行规律,本书就是用产业经济学的一般原理来分析特定的旅游产业。全书共分为四大部分,第一部分是旅游产业的发展和演变,主要深入探讨了旅游产业的产业特质,并详细介绍了国内外旅游产业的发展历史。第二部分包括旅游产业结构、旅游产业关联度和旅游产业区域结构。第三部分是旅游产业组织结构。这部分是本书的重点,主要用成熟的产业组织理论分析旅游产业的组织结构、旅游企业行为和企业绩效,其中用博弈论分析的旅游企业价格竞争行为是本书的难点。第四部分是旅游产业政策和发展模式。

双语教材在我国尚属新鲜事物,没有可以借鉴的写作模式,这给本书的作者提出了极大的挑战。在行文过程中,我们根据写作内容灵活地使用中文和英文,使读者能够深入浅出地理解产业经济学的经典理论和旅游产业的运行规律。本书作者怀着极大的热情和美好的愿望,尽自己最大的努力完成了写作。希望此书的出版能为提高我国双语教学水平、推动双语教学的发展做出应有的贡献。但由于作者能力有限,再加上初次尝试双语写作而缺乏经验,书中的不当甚至错误之处在所难免,恳请各位专家和读者批评指正。

全书共分为十二章,各章撰写者如下:第一章,杜长辉;第二、三、四章,李连宇;第五、六、七、十章,王起静;第八、九章,吴延兵、王起静;第十一章,程莲舟;第十二章,王起静、杜长辉。全书最后由王起静统稿并修改。

本书在写作过程中得到了北京第二外国语学院的大力支持和协助,同时北京大学出版社的刘胜利老师和徐万丽老师也为本书的出版付出了大量辛勤的劳动。在此表示感谢。

王起静
2005年11月于北京

目 录

导论 …………………………………………………………………（1）
第一章　旅游产业的产生与发展 ……………………………………（6）
　　第一节　产业和旅游产业 ………………………………………（6）
　　第二节　西方国家旅游产业的发展 ……………………………（15）
　　第三节　中国旅游产业的发展和演变 …………………………（35）
第二章　旅游产业结构 ………………………………………………（47）
　　第一节　产业分类和产业结构 …………………………………（47）
　　第二节　旅游产业结构的影响因素 ……………………………（54）
　　第三节　我国旅游产业结构及优化 ……………………………（57）
第三章　旅游产业关联分析 …………………………………………（67）
　　第一节　产业关联的内涵 ………………………………………（67）
　　第二节　投入产出法 ……………………………………………（70）
　　第三节　旅游产业关联分析 ……………………………………（79）
第四章　旅游产业的区域结构 ………………………………………（83）
　　第一节　旅游产业区域结构的基本理论 ………………………（84）
　　第二节　旅游产业区域结构的内容和影响因素 ………………（105）
　　第三节　旅游产业的空间布局模式和原则 ……………………（112）
　　第四节　我国旅游产业区域结构 ………………………………（120）
第五章　产业组织导论 ………………………………………………（130）
　　第一节　产业组织的产生与发展 ………………………………（130）
　　第二节　产业组织的研究方法 …………………………………（140）
　　第三节　产业组织的 SCP 理论 …………………………………（145）

第四节　企业 …………………………………………………… (146)
第六章　旅游产业市场结构 ……………………………………… (156)
　　第一节　市场结构 ……………………………………………… (156)
　　第二节　旅游产业的市场集中度 ……………………………… (167)
　　第三节　旅游产品差异 ………………………………………… (175)
　　第四节　旅游产业的进入壁垒 ………………………………… (179)
　　第五节　旅游产业的退出壁垒 ………………………………… (187)
　　第六节　我国旅游产业过度竞争的原因分析 ………………… (190)
第七章　旅游企业的价格行为 ……………………………………… (194)
　　第一节　市场行为概述 ………………………………………… (194)
　　第二节　旅游企业的成本加成定价 …………………………… (197)
　　第三节　旅游企业的价格歧视 ………………………………… (200)
　　第四节　旅游企业的两部收费制 ……………………………… (205)
　　第五节　旅游企业之间的价格行为 …………………………… (207)
第八章　博弈论与旅游企业的竞争行为 …………………………… (211)
　　第一节　博弈问题的基本概念及表述方式 …………………… (212)
　　第二节　完全信息静态博弈与纳什均衡 ……………………… (220)
　　第三节　完全信息动态博弈 …………………………………… (238)
　　第四节　旅游企业的价格竞争战略 …………………………… (250)
　　第五节　旅游企业的竞争与合作选择 ………………………… (262)
第九章　旅游企业的一体化与纵向控制 …………………………… (271)
　　第一节　旅游企业的一体化战略 ……………………………… (271)
　　第二节　旅游企业一体化战略的实现途径(1)：并购 ……… (285)
　　第三节　旅游企业一体化战略的实现途径(2)：联合 ……… (293)
　　第四节　旅游企业的纵向控制行为 …………………………… (298)
第十章　旅游产业的市场绩效 ……………………………………… (304)
　　第一节　市场绩效的内涵和评价 ……………………………… (304)
　　第二节　旅游产业市场绩效的衡量指标 ……………………… (305)
　　第三节　旅游产业竞争力分析——以旅游目的地为例 ……… (309)
第十一章　旅游产业政策 …………………………………………… (321)
　　第一节　产业政策概述 ………………………………………… (321)
　　第二节　旅游产业政策 ………………………………………… (339)
　　第三节　世界各国旅游产业政策 ……………………………… (345)

第十二章 旅游产业发展模式的特征和类型 …………………… (361)
  第一节 旅游产业发展模式的特征和类型 …………………… (361)
  第二节 我国政府主导型旅游发展模式的制定和实施 …… (365)
  第三节 我国旅游产业发展中的市场和政府 ………………… (369)
  参考文献 ……………………………………………………… (381)

导 论
Introduction

一、产业经济学的研究对象(The Research Object of Industrial Economics)

在研究旅游产业经济学之前,首先应该清楚产业经济学(industry economics)的内涵。目前,在我国教育部和国务院学位委员会颁发的学科分类目录中,经济学分为理论经济学(theory economics)和应用经济学(applied economics)两大类,产业经济学则属于应用经济学中的二级学科。

产业经济学作为一门独立的学科,它的研究范畴和内容有它的特殊性,与西方经济学有很大的区别。

西方经济学分为微观经济学(microeconomics)和宏观经济学(macroeconomics)两个部分,属于理论经济学。微观经济学以价格理论为核心,研究单个的抽象的经济主体(企业、家庭)在市场上的行为规律。微观经济学的主要研究内容就是企业如何在生产资料市场上获得生产资料,在预算约束下组织生产,以获得利润最大化;同时家庭如何在收入约束下,在产品市场上获得产品以满足效用最大化。微观经济学以人是理性的为假设前提,认为市场上存在着"看不见的手",能够自动调节生产和分配,有效的使产品市场和要素市场出清。因此,政府是不必要干预经济的。但是发生在20世纪30年代的资本主义世界的经济危机,让西方的经济学者清醒地认识到,市场是会失灵的。市场经济不仅需要那只"看不见的手"来指导,更需要政府这只"看得见的手"的宏观调控。因此,以研究整个国民收入的生产、分配和使用为核心的宏观经济学应运而生。宏观经济学主要研究国民生产总值及国民收入的构成与决定、投资理论、消费理论以及由于不均衡所带来的通胀及失业问题。

由以上可以看出，微观经济学研究的是个体经济，宏观经济学则研究的是最终产品的总和及其经济运动。而我们知道，整个经济体系不仅包括个体和总体的经济运动，还包括个体所形成的群体运动，即产业和产业之间的关系。而产业及产业之间的经济关系则是产业经济学所研究的对象。

那么，什么是产业（industry）呢？产业经济学中所说的产业，是指在社会分工的条件下，进行同类产品生产（或提供同类服务）的企业（单位）的集合体。所谓同类生产（同类服务）是指产品（服务）的经济用途相同，或者所使用的原材料相同，或者工艺技术性质相同。产业经济学则是以"产业"为研究对象，研究社会经济活动中不同产业之间的结构、产业内部企业组织结构、产业之间关系结构、产业地区分布结构的变化规律，以及研究这些规律的方法。

关于对产业经济学的研究对象的认识，我国学者尚不统一，有人认为，产业经济学主要是研究企业行为的，主要研究的是如何通过某种组织机制，使各种生产活动与社会对各种商品的需求相协调。产业经济学的主要研究内容是市场结构、企业行为、经济绩效和产业政策。这种观点是把产业经济学与产业组织学的研究范围统一起来了。还有的学者认为，产业经济学的研究对象既然是"产业"，就应该不仅研究产业内部各企业之间的关系，还应该研究产业之间的关系及其运动的规律性，所以持这种观点的学者认为产业经济学应该包括产业结构理论、产业关联理论、产业组织理论和产业政策等内容。在本书中，我们认同后一观点。

二、产业经济学的研究内容（The Research Contents of Industrial Economics）

1. 产业结构理论（The Theory of Industrial Structure）

产业结构理论是西方产业经济理论中的重要内容，主要研究产业之间相互关系及其演化规律的理论。从广义角度说，产业结构重要研究三次产业间的关系。从狭义的概念出发，产业结构主要研究工业内部各产业间的关系。

关于三次产业结构的概念是澳大利亚经济学家费歇尔提出的，他把整个经济分为第一产业、第二产业和第三产业，这是现代产业结构理论中第一次确立的三次产业分类法。此后的一些经济学家在费歇尔研究的基础上，运用大量的统计资料进行分析，得出了一些关于三次产业结构变动的一些规律性的研究成果。比如，英国经济学家克拉克就曾研究过经济发展过程中劳动力在三次产业之间的分布及其转换规律,即随着经济的发展,第一产业的劳动力逐渐地向第二、第三产业转移,这一规律被称为"配第—克拉克定理"。美国经济学家库兹涅茨也广泛收集和整理了20多个国家的资料,深入考察了经济发展中国民收入在三次产业结构间的分布状况及演变趋势。

德国经济学家霍夫曼在研究工业结构之间的关系时,把全部工业分为消费资料工业和生产资料工业,并论证了消费资料产业比重是逐步下降的,而资本资料产业比重是不断上升的,这一过程就是工业化过程,这一结论被称为霍夫曼定理。

研究产业之间的关系时还应该研究产业之间的技术经济联系,产业关联理论就是从技术的角度深入地研究国民经济各个产业、部门之间投入产出关系,使各个产业部门按一定比例进行生产,从而使整个市场有效地出清。美国经济学家列昂惕夫创造了投入产出法,建立大量的数学模型深入研究各个产业、部门之间的投入产出关系,为产业关联理论做出了巨大的贡献。

2. 产业组织理论(The Theory of Industrial Organization)

一般认为,产业组织理论的系统研究发端于20世纪30年代的美国哈佛大学。在此以前,经济学研究和大学的经济学课程中也有一些涉及了股份公司、企业营销、公用事业、金融组织及反托拉斯等的内容,但这些内容并没有形成系统的体系。如果再往前追溯,英国经济学家 A. 马歇尔(A. Marshall)在其1890年出版的经济学名著《经济学原理》一书中,就提出了生产要素不仅有劳动、资本和土地,还有第四种生产要素"组织"。但是,直到20世纪30年代之前,产业组织还没有成为一门具有独立意义的经济学分支学科,而最多只是在一般的经济学中对产业组织的一些问题有所涉及。而且这些内容也没有同经济学的主体框架有机地结合起来。

1933年,美国经济学家张伯仑(E. H. Chamberlin)和英国经济学家琼·罗宾逊(J. Robinson)分别出版了《垄断竞争理论》(The Theory of Monopolistic Competition)和《不完全竞争经济学》(The Economics of Imperfect Competition)。经济学界高度评价这两本书的出版,萨缪尔逊称之为"垄断竞争的革命"。

30年代,在哈佛大学,张伯仑和梅森(Edward. S. Mason)教授开设了产业组织课程。1957年,梅森出版了他自1936年以来的论文集《经济集中和垄断问题》(Economic Concentration and Monopoly

Problem)。1959年,梅森教授当年的博士生贝恩教授出版了《产业组织》(Industrial Organization)一书。这本书被推崇为现代产业组织的经典著作。由于贝恩的产业组织理论体系的基本逻辑是从市场结构推断市场绩效,通常被称为结构主义的产业组织理论,同时也被称为哈佛学派的产业组织理论。

后来,芝加哥学派的经济学家指出,哈佛学派进行的产业组织问题研究,具有明显的经验主义的性质,所揭示的经济关系实际上在很大程度上只是一种相关关系,而未必揭示了内在的因果关系。而且哈佛学派的产业组织理论建立在经验研究的基础之上,缺乏严密理论体系的支撑,虽然利用回归分析技术验证了一些理论,但随着实践的发展,哈佛学派的SCP理论越来越不能很好地解释现实经济中存在的一些现象和问题。1968年施蒂格勒的名著《产业组织》一书问世,标志着芝加哥学派理论上的成熟。

20世纪70年代由于博弈论研究方法的引入,产业组织研究进入了新产业组织理论时代,主要对静态博弈理论、重复博弈和寡占理论、产品差别化、进入壁垒和进入阻止、技术进步与市场结构的动态演变以及信息不对称等问题进行了研究。

3. 产业政策(The Industrial Policy)

产业政策是关于产业发展的政策,它主要包括产业组织政策、产业结构政策、产业分布政策等。

产业结构政策是指政府根据产业结构变动规律的客观要求,通过确定产业的构成比例、相互关系和产业发展序列,为实现产业结构合理化和高度化而实施的政策。产业结构政策的目的是以技术进步来不断促进产业结构的优化,既是现代经济增长的内在要求,又是各国经济发展战略的体现。

产业组织政策是指为实现产业内部企业之间资源配置而制定的政策的总称。其实质是政府通过协调自由竞争与规模经济的矛盾,以维持正常的市场秩序,促进有效竞争的形成。防止大规模企业凭借其垄断地位,通过不正当手段来获取高额利润、抑制竞争。

产业分布政策是指政府根据产业区位理论以及国民经济与区域经济发展的要求,制定和实施的有关产业空间分布、区际经济协调发展的政策总和。产业分布合理化过程的本质是建立合理的地区分工关系的过程。产业布局政策既是产业政策体系中必要的组成部分,又是区域政策体系中很重要的内容。

三、旅游产业经济学的主要研究内容(The Main Research Contents of Tourism Industrial Economics)

旅游产业按照三次产业的划分标准属于第三产业,但旅游产业本身又具有特殊性。从国民经济统计体系来看,旅游产业包括旅游社业、饭店、旅游景区、旅游车船公司等行业。按照产业结构理论和产业组织理论对产业的定义,是否存在旅游产业则是一个值得争论的问题。因此,在研究旅游产业之前需要对旅游产业的概念进行界定。

在承认旅游的"产业"规定性的前提下,则需要研究旅游产业是怎样在产业结构的演变过程中逐渐发展起来的,并需要研究旅游产业与其他产业之间的关系以及旅游产业内部各行业之间的关系,这种关系不仅包括结构演变规律,还包括产业之间的经济技术联系,即产业关联关系。另外,旅游产业的区域结构也是旅游产业研究的重要内容,从更严格的意义上来说,这是属于区域经济学研究范畴,但在本书中也把旅游产业的区域结构纳入进来。

旅游产业内部各产业的市场结构、旅游企业的市场行为以及旅游产业的市场绩效则是旅游产业组织的研究内容。这也是本书的重点。

旅游产业的发展需要相应的产业政策,在制定政策过程中需要正确处理政府和市场之间的关系。通过制订旅游产业政策可以促进旅游产业和其他产业协调发展,并促进旅游产业内部企业之间有效竞争的实现,同时还要促进旅游产业在各地区之间的协调发展。

第一章
旅游产业的产生与发展
(The Initiation Development of Tourism Industry)

第一节 产业和旅游产业(Industry and Tourism Industry)

一、产业和旅游产业(Industry and Tourism Industry)

旅游产业真是产业吗？学术界在这一问题上一直存在着分歧和争论。在权威的《国际标准产业分类》(ISIC)和各国的国民经济行业分类中，很难找到"旅游业"或"旅游产业"这样特定表述的条款，然而在另一方面，"旅游产业"这一名词又频繁出现于政府的政策性和统计性文献之中，在民间的使用更为广泛。我们要了解旅游产业经济学，首先应该对这个问题做出回答。

美国著名学者 Thomas Davison 认为，旅行和旅游（Travel & Tourism)是为了外出经营、娱乐或者私事外出的人的活动，远远不是传统意义上的产业。作为一种力量，它是游客或旅游者支出产生的一种效应。因此，实际上是"支出推动"经济现象，而并非"收入推动"经济现象。为此，他进一步指出："把旅游定义为产业是不正确的，而且这一定义有损旅游的真实状况。旅游是一种社会现象，它既是推动经济进步的推动机，同时又是一种社会力量，旅游更像是一个影响许多产业的部门。"(Thomas Davison,2000)

Thomas Davison 的观点是有一定代表性。传统经济学认为，产业是所有生产相同产品的单个企业的集合，而产品是否相同是根据交叉需求弹性理论中的可替代性来限定的。旅游是一种相差悬殊的经历或过程，不是一种产品。是一种社会现象，而不是一种生产性活动，所有旅游者支出的总和并不是这一组相似企业的收入所得。因此,将旅游定义为产业是不正确的。然而,如果我们考察一下产业的发展历程,就不难发现,旅游作为一种经济现象,确实具有现代产业的基本性质。

产业是随着社会分工的产生而产生,并随之发展的,是历史发展的产物。它以社会经济发展为背景,分工和技术进步为契机。马克思曾经指出,"单就劳动本身来说,可以把社会生产分为农业、工业等大类,叫做一般分工;把这些大类分为种和亚种,叫做特殊分工;把工场内部的分工,叫做个别分工。"(《马克思恩格斯全集》第23卷,第389页)这就说明,产业的分化和发展与分工有着密切的关系,分工的发展形成了许许多多的产业部门。人类从旧石器时代进入新石器时代,在新石器时代实现的畜牧业和农业的分离是人类历史上第一次社会大分工,其直接后果就是产生了人类社会的最初两个产业:农业和畜牧业。随着生产力的不断发展,在原始社会瓦解时期,实现了第二次大分工,形成了手工业和农业的分离。在奴隶社会初期,商业从农业、畜牧业和手工业中分离出来,实现了第三次社会分工,相应地形成了农业、畜牧业和商业等产业部门。从这一发展过程来看,产业由简单到复杂,由落后到先进,从传统产业发展到现代产业,大致经历了两个不同的阶段,即从产业革命开始的工业化阶段和产业的现代化阶段。18世纪下半叶的工业革命,使工业走到了历史的发展舞台,农业的主导地位开始动摇,机器大工业已经形成了社会发展的主导力量。伴随着工业和手工业的分离和工业内部特殊分工的形成,产业部门也迅速地发展起来。

在产业漫长的发展历史中,在不同时期的历史时期和理论研究中,虽然都将其确定为经济学的范畴,但研究的重点不尽相同。在重农学派流行时期,产业主要是指农业。在资本主义工业产生以后,产业曾被用来专指工业,而我们所说的传统的产业概念就是在这个时期形成的。近代以后,随着社会生产力的发展和社会分工不断细化,特别是服务部门得到空前发展,出现了"经济服务化"的现象,导致以经济为中心的全社会各种物质生产活动和非物质生产活动日益紧密地结合起来。作为经济研究对象的产业,范畴外延不断延伸和扩展,于是,凡是有投入产出活动的行为和事业都列入产业活动之内。

由此不难看出,产业是历史范畴,在社会生产力发展的不同阶段,由于社会分工的主导形式转换和不断地向深层发展,以致形成具有多层次的产业范畴。因此,在界定产业时,不能忽视在微观经济与宏观经济之间多层次地形成产业的现象。另外,产业作为一个经济单位并不是孤立存在的,甚至是交叉和部分重叠,从而使全部产业成为一个有机的系统。正因为如此,目前学术界一般是从如下几个方面规定产业这一范畴的:

- 产业是有投入和产出效益的活动单位;
- 产业是处于宏观经济与微观经济之间,从事同类物质生产或相同服务的经济群体。所谓"同类""相同"的含义是指:从需求方面说是指具有相互密切竞争关系的商品或服务;从供给方面说是指生产技术、工艺相近的物质生产和经济性质相同的服务业;
- 产业是与社会生产力发展水平相适应的社会分工形式的表现,是一个多层的经济系统,如部门、行业、业种;
- 产业与产业之间存在着直接或间接的经济联系,整个产业构成一个具有函数关系的经济系统。
- 在实际分析产业问题时,应以一般分工和特殊分工形式所形成的多层产业活动为范围,根据不同的分析目的,对产业进行相应的组合和分类。

综合上述分析可以看出,"产业"作为应用性经济理论中的一个概念,人们对其边界界定的立足点与其说是理论上的严密性,不如说是现实的可用性。换言之,人们在确定"产业"划分的基准——企业某类共同特征时,是可以有选择性的,这种选择性服从于企业市场关系分析和社会再生产过程均衡状态分析的需要。同时,"产业"概念既是一个"集合"的概念,又是一个"细分"的概念,前者指具有某种同一属性的企业的集合,后者则是把国民经济以某一标准划分的产业,这样产业就形成粗细不均的若干层次。

在现实社会中,的确存在着一个为旅游者服务的经济系统,这个系统是凭借旅游资源和设施,为人们的移动消费提供行、住、食、游、购、娱等服务的综合体系。由于存在着旅游需求和旅游供给,也就存在着厂商的活动,同时也就存在着旅游厂商通过旅游供给来满足旅游者消费需求的经济活动。而且,不同的厂商向某一特定市场提供相似的产品和服务,这样各个厂商之间存在着竞争或合作的可能,从而满足了传统经济学中"根据交叉需求弹性理论中的可替代性来限定产品"的基本要求。因此,我们称之为旅游产业是合乎产业质的规定性的。同时,旅游产业的消费趋向性性质,说明它的外延要比一般产业宽泛得多。若用旅游者提供旅游服务或产品这一基准来论,旅游产业既包括旅馆(在我国现行的《国民经济行业分类与代码》中属 K 门类 78 大类)、旅行社和旅游公司(K 门类 80 大类,统称为旅游业)等直接旅游企业以及旅游行业管理部门,也包括旅客交通运输企业(属 G 门类)、零售业(H 门类 64 大类)、餐饮业(H 门类 67 大类)、公共设施服务业(K 门类 75 大类)、娱乐服务业(K 门类 81 大类)、信息咨询服务业(K 门类 82 大类)等等部分为旅游者提供产品或服务的企业。同时,结合旅游的"空间移动"这一基本特点,考虑到上述所有的旅游活动的经济属性是旅游供给和旅游需求相结合的活动,而推动这一结合不断发展的动力正是旅游产业运动,我们就可以把旅游产业定义为"为了充分满足旅游者的消费需求,由旅游目的地、旅游客源地以及两地之间的旅游连结体企业、组织和个人通过各种形式的结合,组成生产和服务的有机整体"(张辉,2002)。

二、旅游产业的行业规定性(The Trade Prescriptions of the Tourism Industry)

旅游行业作为国民经济中诸多产业中的一个新兴行业,与其他行业相比较,具有三个方面的行业规定性:

1. 旅游产业是一个跨地区、跨行业的产业(Tourism as an Industry across Areas and Trades)

从旅游产业的范围来看,它是一个跨地区、跨行业的产业。其地区范围包括旅游客源地和旅游目的地,两地的结合组成了旅游产业的空间体系。如果一个旅游产业空间体系中只有客源地或者目的地,这样的旅游产业是不完整的。两地的经济运动中存在的旅游通道,我们称之为旅游连接体,因此旅游产业内部构造在地域空间上是一个"哑铃经济"的模型(图 1-1),是发生在旅游客源地的诸多经济现象和发生在旅游目的地

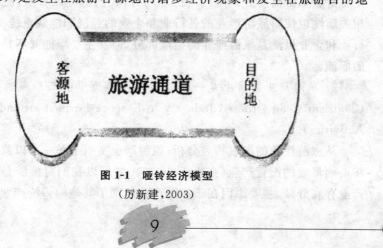

图 1-1 哑铃经济模型

(厉新建,2003)

的众多经济现象,客源地和目的地之间的经济联系体三者之间的矛盾运动(厉新建,2002)。而旅游通道作用的充分发挥,除了旅游者连接旅游需求和旅游供给实现"碰面"之外,政府和政府主导下的旅游规制起着重大的作用,这表明了旅游产业具有宽泛的地区跨越性。

同时,旅游产业的行业范围又是和旅游活动的形式相联系的。旅游产业要满足旅游者从居住地到旅游目的地的全部消费需要,涉及到行、住、游、食、购、娱等多种需要,从满足社会的各个行业如交通运输业、饭店业、景区业、商业、饮食业、娱乐业、旅行社业等行业变成了旅游行业的组成部分。世界旅游理事会在旅游卫星账户(Tourism Satellite Accountant)的统计中,把只要和旅游产业相关的各部门都划入了旅游业的范围中。(图1-2)

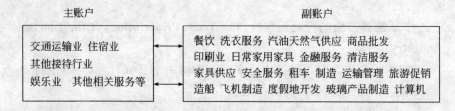

图1-2　世界旅游理事会旅游卫星账户

(资料来源:世界旅游理事会南非旅游卫星账户设计,转引自陶汉军、林南枝,《旅游经济学》,第12页。)

不同的国家和地区在官方统计上对旅游产业所涉及的部门也不相同,在实践操作中也没有一个统一的标准。值得注意的是,虽然这些相关行业在旅游产业运行中承担的作用和各自的功用有所不同,但是在满足旅游者旅游需要方面是相同的。同时,我们也可以看出,旅游产业的相关属性也使得旅游产业的各行业和企业的经济职能缺乏统一性,有的行业和企业虽然是旅游产业的组成部分,但其主要职能并不是旅游经济的职能。

2. 旅游产业实质上是一个以旅游活动为中心而形成的配置产业(Tourism as an Ordered Industry in Essence Formed around Tourism Activities)

从旅游产业的形成特点分析,旅游产业实质上是一个以旅游活动为中心而形成的配置产业(张辉,2002)。之所以我们对旅游是不是一项产业存在分歧,主要原因在于旅游产业区别于其他的传统产业。旅游产业的边界缺乏明确的规定,也没有明确的划分,产业涉及的范围是根据旅游形式的演化进行的。旅游产业所规定的各个行业之所以成为旅游产业的组成部分,在于这些行业和企业都具有为旅游者提供服务的职能。我们也可以说,旅游产业是以旅游活动为中心形成的配置产业,凡是为旅游活动提供直接和间接服务的行业都是这个配置产业的组成部分。

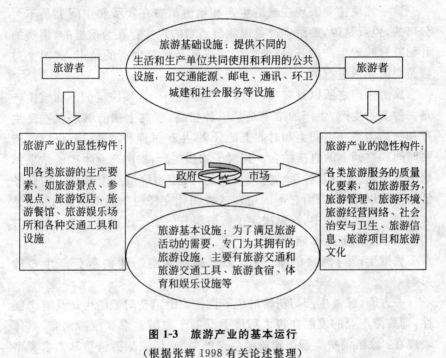

图 1-3　旅游产业的基本运行

（根据张辉 1998 有关论述整理）

3. 旅游产业是一个提供劳务为主的服务行业（Tourism as a Service Industry Mainly Supplying Service）

从产业性质上研究旅游产业,它是一个提供劳务为主的服务行业,它所提供的旅游服务是一种包括直接和间接服务在内的综合性服务。在旅游产业的生产旅游服务体系中,有的服务将价值物化在原有的物品之中,成为一种有形物体来满足旅游者的需要。有的服务并不物化在一个物体之中,而体化在一种活动之中,成为一种无形的产品来满足旅游者的需要（井员哲夫,1986）。尽管旅游产业提供的产品内容和形式千变万化,但是从总体上讲,旅游产业所提供的产品是一种劳务产品。

三、旅游产业生产的性质(The Nature of Tourism Industry)

旅游产业作为具有上述三种产业规定性的行业,同一般的物质生产相比较,具有以下几个特殊性:

1. 旅游生产和消费的同一性(Inseparability of Tourism Supply and Consumption)

这一性质主要表现在旅游生产和旅游消费在实践和空间上是不可分离的,也就是说,旅游生产是以旅游消费的现实存在为前提的,消费的开始就意味着生产的开始,消费的完成就意味着生产的结束,这两个过程是同时同地进行的。

旅游生产之所以具有这一特性,是由其生产性质决定的。物质生产是一种实物生产,生产的结果是某一种物品,客观上就能够形成物品生产和物品消费在空间上和时间上的分离,生产过程和消费过程可以不需要时间和空间上的直接结合。相对于物质生产,旅游产业生产的结果是旅游劳务,它是以某种活动直接出现的,其使用价值必须在一定的服务活动中加以体现,因而它不固定在或者固化在任何物品的对象中,而是体现在一种活动之中,这就决定了旅游服务的生产过程和消费过程在时间上或者空间上是不能分离的。

旅游生产与消费的统一性,必然会对旅游产业的运行产生多种影响:

一方面,旅游生产与消费的统一性使旅游消费对旅游生产具有牵制性,即旅游产业的发展在很大程度上受制于旅游需求和旅游消费,具体表现在:旅游消费类型决定旅游生产的类型,形成旅游消费和需求类型的变化牵动产业变动的现实;旅游消费规模直接决定旅游生产的规模,旅游生产规模直接受制于旅游消费规模的限制等。

另一方面,旅游生产与消费的统一性使旅游产业的生产率具有较大的变动性。一般来说,旅游产业生产率随着旅游者消费时间的长短及全年需求分配的不同有所差异,从而形成旅游生产率的时间波动和周期波动。在这里需要指出的是,需求时间的分布的变化状态和旅游生产率的关系极为紧密,在非需求的高峰时间内,通常有着较多的空闲劳动力与设施,需求增加如果发生在这一段时间,劳动生产率就会有较高的提升;相反,则不能提高劳动生产率。以旅游目的地的短期经济波动为例。所谓旅游目的地的短期经济波动,是指在一个自然年的周期内,由旅客流量的变化所引起的旅游目的地接待数量与最低规模和最大规模之间的矛盾现象。这一矛盾的主要表现形式就是过剩需求和过剩供给,即我们经常说的淡季和旺季。虽然在一个旅游目的地的设施、景区、服务人员的组成是一个常量,在需求充足的环境中基本供给具有一定的弹性空间,景区的合理容量可以超过通常容量的数倍,然而,这种供给的弹性,虽然能够保证向旅游者提供基本的服务,但却不是优质的服务,因为旅游供给方会通过降低每个单位的旅游需求的满足程度来达到接待更多旅游者的目的。

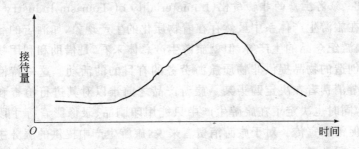

图1-4　旅游目的地短期波动示意图

2. 旅游生产的脆弱性(Fragility of Tourism Industry)

相对于物质部门的生产,旅游生产具有较强的脆弱性。各种自然的、政治的、社会和经济因素都可能对旅游产生过重要影响。虽然这些因素也会对一些物质生产部门的生产产生影响,但其影响的规模、程度和时间都远远不及对旅游生产的影响。

从时间的长短看,这一脆弱性主要表现在两个方面:第一,从长期来看,旅游生产具有周期性,这一周期性和传统的物质生产相比较,表现为周期波动的最高值和最低值差距较大,并且受偶然性的制约;第二,从短期看,即使在较为平缓的时间段内,全年的各个月份、各个月份的不同周、甚至每一周的每一天都会有很大的波动。这一长期和短期的波动,既是旅游生产脆弱性的表现,也是旅游生产向常规生产转变的客观障碍。这些变动在性质上都是非常规的变动,导致了旅游生产缺乏常规生产的科学预测,也就缺乏对旅游生产的宏观控制能力。更重要的是,从根本上说,在影响旅游生产长期和短期经济波动的诸多因素中,大量的因素都是不可控制的因素。

从地域范围上看,旅游生产具有分配极为不均衡的特点。一般来说,一个国家或地区或城市的旅游生产往往集中在某特定的地域范围内,这一范围的生产能力在这一旅游目的地中占据了主导地位。由于旅游时间分布的不均衡,会导致旅游生产能力的过度使用和过度闲置,从而加重了旅游生产的脆弱性。

努力减少旅游生产的长期波动和短期波动是减缓旅游生产脆弱性的主要措施。囿于种种客观条件,人们现在还不能消除旅游生产中的短期波动,然而却能不同程度地减少旅游生产中的长期和短期波动的幅度,达到减缓旅游生产的目的。

3. 旅游生产的非物质化(Immateriality of Tourism Industry)

在旅游生产体系中虽然存在着物质化的生产现象,如酒店的餐饮生产,旅游纪念品的生产等,但就旅游生产总体来看,是借助和利用物质生产所创造的物品提供非物质旅游劳务的有目的的活动。这一特性决定了旅游消费者在决定购买某一旅游产品之前难以对其进行检查和客观评价,同时也决定了在旅游生产中只能用印刷品、录像影音等手段进行旅游促销和宣传。对于旅游消费者来说,旅游生产中提供的服务主要有两种不同类型:一种是经验品,另一种是搜寻品。前者是指只有在旅游者购买了旅游服务,参加了旅游活动之后才能识别其质量和效用的产品,后者是指旅游消费者在购买之前就能够了解和识别其质量和效用的产品。除非旅游消费者经常消费某种旅游服务,大多数旅游服务都属于经验品,从这个意义上说,旅游生产具有非物质化的特性。这种特性首先表现为生产的结果不是物质化的产品,而是非物质化的劳务;其次表现在生产和消费的同一性上,旅游劳务的生产过程也就是旅游劳务的消费过程;再次表现为旅游劳务的产品无库存性,其劳务产品价值的实现与劳务生产和消费同时完成;最后旅游生产的结果具有无转移性和后效性。旅游产品无需经过运输等中间环节即能现场消费,其产品的质量和效用只能在消费过程结束后才能体现出来,这是旅游生产非物质化的具体表现。

第二节 西方国家旅游产业的发展
(A Review into the Development of Tourism Industry in Western Society)

一、蒸汽机时代的旅游业(Tourism from the Age of Steam)

1. 铁路时代(The Age of Railways)

The prospering of western tourism has a very close relation with the development of technology. And practically, two technological developments in the early part of the nineteenth century were to have a profound effect on transport and the growth in travel generally. The first of these was the advent of the railways.

The first railway was built in England in 1825, between Stockton and Darlington. It was to herald a major program of railway construction throughout the world, and a major shift in the facility to travel. We have noted the problems of traveling by road up to that point; and, although traveling by canal had been possible by 1760, this mode was too slow to attract travelers, being used essentially for the carriage of freight. As a means of transport for all purposes, it was to suffer a rapid decline after 1825, when railways made it possible to travel at 13 mph for the first time—at least three miles an hour faster than the fastest mail coaches. In the decade following the introduction of a rail link between Liverpool and Manchester in 1830, trunk routes sprang up among the major centers of population and industry in Britain, on mainland Europe and throughout the world; in the USA, for example, passenger services on the east coast were being built from the 1820s, and by 1869 a transcontinental link was in place. One of the last great rail routes, the Trans-Siberian, was opened in 1903, connecting Moscow with Vladivostok and Port Arthur.

In the UK, after their initial function to serve the needs of commerce, new route emerged linking these centers to the popular coastal resorts such as Brighton, bringing these within reach of the mass of pleasure travelers for the first time. On the whole, however, the railway companies appeared to be slow to recognize the opportunities for pleasure travel offered by the development of rail services, concerning trading instead of providing for the needs of business travelers. Certainly, in the 1840s, the growth of regular passenger traffic was enough to occupy them; between 1842 and 1847, the annual number of passengers traveling by train rose from 23 million to 51 million.

Competition among the railway companies was initially based on service rather than price, although from the earliest days of the railways a new market developed for short day trips. Before long, however, entrepreneurs began to stimulate rail travel by organizing excursions for the public at special fares. In some cases, these took place on regular train services, but in others, special trains were chartered in order to take travelers to their destination, setting a precedent for the charter services by air which were to become so significant a feature of tour operating a century later. As an indication of the speed with which these opportunities were put into place, within twelve days of the rail line to Scarborough opened in 1845, an excursion train from Wakefield was laid on to carry a thousand passengers to the seaside.

Thomas Cook, contrary to popular opinion, was not, in fact, the first entrepreneur to organize tours for the public. Sir Rowland Hill, who became chairman of the Brighton Railway Company, is sometimes credited with this innovation (others have suggested that the first package tour can in fact be traced to a group of tourists taken from Wadebridge to Bodmin to witness a public hanging), and there were certainly excursion trains in operation by 1840.

However, Cook was to have by far the greatest impact on the early travel industry. In 1841, as secretary of the South Midland Temperance Association, he organized an excursion for his members from Leicester to Loughborough, at a fare of one-shilling (the equivalent of five pence) return. The success of this venture—570 took part—encouraged him to arrange similar excursions by using chartered trains, and by 1845 he was organizing these trips on a fully commercial basis.

The result of these and similar ventures by other entrepreneurs led to a substantial movement of Pleasure-bound travelers to the seaside. In 1844, it was recorded that almost 15,000 passengers had traveled from London to Brighton during the three Easter holidays alone, while hundreds of thousands traveled to other resorts to escape the smoke and grime of the cities. The enormous growth in this type of traffic can be appreciated when it is revealed that by 1862 Brighton received 132,000 visitors on Easter Monday alone.

Supported by a more sympathetic attitude to pleasure travel by public authorities such as the Board of Trade, the railway companies themselves were actively promoting these excursions by the 1850s, while at the same time introducing a range of discounted fares for day trips, weekend trips and longer journeys. By 1855, Cook had extended his field of operations to mainland Europe, organizing the first 'inclusive tours' to the Paris Exhibition of that year. This followed the success of his excursions to the Great Exhibition in London in 1851, which in all had welcomed three million visitors.

Cook was a man of vision in the world of travel. The success of his operations was due to the care he took in organizing his programmers to minimize problems; he had close contacts with hotels, shipping companies and railways throughout the world, which ensured that he obtained the best possible service as well as cheap prices for the services he provided. By escorting his clients throughout their journeys abroad he took the worry out of travel for the first-time travelers. He also made the administration of travel easier by introducing the hotel voucher in 1867, which allowed tourists to prepay their hotel accommodation and produced evidence to the hotels that this had been done. In 1873 he introduced the 'circular note', the precursor to today's traveler's cheque, which helped to overcome the problems caused by many different coinages in Europe. The latter was not a totally new concept; a certain Robert Herries set up the London Banking Exchange Company in 1772 in order to issue similar documents, but it was Cook (and later in North America, American

Express) who popularized these ideas, which made travel far more tolerable for the Victorian travelers.

The expansion of the railways was accompanied by a simultaneous decline in the stagecoaches. Some survived by providing feeder services to the nearest railway stations, but overall road traffic shrank, and with it the demand for the staging inns. Those situated in the resorts were quick to adapt to meet the needs of the new railway travelers, but the supply of accommodation in centers served by the railways was totally inadequate to meet the burgeoning demand of this new market. A period of hotel construction began, in which the railway companies themselves were leaders, who established the great railway terminus hotels which came to play such a significant role in the hotel industry over the next hundred years. The high capital investment called for by this development led to the formation of the first hotel chains and corporations.

2. 汽船时代(The Age of Steam Ships)

Just as the technological developments of the early nineteenth century led to the development of railways on land, so was steam harnessed at sea to drive new generations of ships. Here, necessity was the mother of invention. Increasing trade worldwide, especially with North America, required Britain to develop faster, more reliable forms of communication by sea with the rest of the world. Although, as we have seen, ferry services were operating as early as 1761 between Brighton and Dieppe, the first regular commercial cross-Channel steamship service was introduced in 1821, on the Dover-Calais route. The railway companies were quick to recognize the importance of their links with these cross-Channel ferry operators, and by 1862 they had gained the right to own and operate steamships themselves. Soon after, control over the ferry companies was in the hands of the railways the cross-Channel services which rapidly expanded the cross Channel service.

Deep-sea services were introduced on routes to North America and the Far East; the Peninsular and Oriental Steam Navigation Company (later P & O) is credited with the first regular long-distance steamship service, beginning operations to India and the Far East in 1838. This company was soon followed by the Cunard Steamship Company which, with a lucrative mail contract, began regular services to the American continent in 1840. Britain, the first to establish regular deepsea services of this kind, came to dominate the world's shipping in the second half of the century, although it was soon to be challenged by other leading industrial nations on the popular North American route. This prestigious and highly profitable route prospered not only from mail contracts but also due to the huge demand from passengers and freight as trade with the American continent expanded. Later, the passenger trade would be boosted by the flow of emigrants from Europe (especially Ireland) and a smaller but significant number of American visitors to Europe. Thomas Cook played his part in stimulating the package tour market to North America, taking the first group of tourists in 1866. In 1872, he went on to organize the first round-the-world tour, taking twelve clients for 220 days at a cost of some 200—more than the average annual salary at the time.

The Suez Canal, opened in 1869, stimulated the demand for P & O's services to India and beyond, as Britain's Empire looked eastwards. The global growth of shipping led, in the latter part of the century, to the formation of shipping conferences, which developed cartel-like agreements on fares and conditions applicable to the carriage of traffic. The aim of these agreements was to ensure year-round profitability in an unstable and seasonal market, but the result was to stifle competition by price, and eventually led to excess profits which were to be enjoyed by, the shipping companies until the advent of airline competition in the mid-twentieth century.

3. 19世纪末期的其他发展(Other Developments in Late Nineteenth Century)

As the Victorian era drew to a close, other social changes came into play. Continued enthusiasm for the healthy outdoor life coincided with the invention of the bicycle, and cycling holidays, aided by promotion from the Cyclists' Touring Club, which was founded in 1878, enjoyed immense popularity. This movement not only paved the way for later interest in outdoor activities on holiday, but may well have stimulated the appeal of the suntan as a status symbol of health and wealth, in marked contrast to the earlier association in Victorian minds of a fair complexion with gentility and breeding. The bicycle offered for the first time the opportunity for mobile rather than centered holidays, and gave a foretaste of the popularity of motoring holidays in the early years of the following century. As tourism grew in the later years of the century, so the organizers of travel became established institutionally. Thomas Cook and Sir Henry Lunn (whose name is retained in the company Lunn Poly) are two of the best-known names of the period, but many other well-known companies became established at this time. Dean and Dawson appeared in 1871, the Polytechnic Touring Association (the other half of Lunn Poly name) in the following year, and Frames Tours in 1881.

Mention has already been made of the impact of photography on nineteenth-century travel. As the century drew to a close, the vogue for photography was accompanied by the cult of the guidebook. No British tourist venturing abroad would neglect to take a guidebook, and a huge variety of these soon became available on the market. Many were superficial and inaccurate, but the most popular and enduring of those published were those of John Murray, whose Hand-books, appeared from 1837 onwards, and Karl Baedeker, who introduced his first guidebook (of the Rhine) in 1839. By the end of the century Baedeker had become firmly established as leading publisher of guidebooks in Europe.

We have seen how social and, in particular, technological change had begun to make mass travel feasible. In next part we will see how contemporary mass tourism developed, with further advances in technology and, above all, improved standards of living throughout the developed world.

二、20 世纪前 50 年的旅游业(The First Fifty Years of Tourism in the Twentieth Century)

1. 大众旅游(Mass Tourism)

In the opening years of the twentieth century, travel continued to expand, encouraged by the increasing wealth, curiosity and outgoing attitudes of the post-Victorian population, and by the steady improvement in transport. Travelers had become safer from disease and physical attack, mainland Europe was relatively stable politically, and documentation for British travelers uncomplicated—since 1860, passports had generally not been required for travel to any European country. The popularity of French Riviera resorts as places for wealthier British visitors to spend the winter is evidenced by the fact that immediately before World War I some 50,000 UK tourists are estimated to have been wintering on the coast.

Disastrous though it was, the Great War proved to be only a brief hiatus in the expansion of travel, although it led to the widespread introduction of passports for nationals of many countries. The prosperity, which soon returned to Europe in the 1920s, coupled with large-scale migration, meant unsurpassed demand for travel across the Atlantic, as well as within Europe. The first-hand experience of foreign countries by combatants during the war aroused a sense of curiosity about foreign travel generally among less well-off sectors of the community for the first time. These sectors were also influenced by the new forms of mass communication, which developed after the war—the cinema, radio and ultimately television, all of which educated the population and encouraged an interest in seeing more of the world.

Forms of travel also began to change radically after the war. The railway went into a period of steady decline, following the introduction of the motorcar. The vehicles achieved immense popularity in the 1920s for outings to the seaside in licensing regulations governing road transports. For those who could afford luxurious coaches also made an appearance. Coach company Mortorways offered Pullman coaches, generally accommodating fifteen people in comfortable armchairs with tables, buffet bars and toilets. These coaches operated company parts in Europe and North Africa, were used on safaris in East and Central Africa, and even provided a twice weekly service between London and Nice, taking a relaxing five to six days for the trips.

However, it was the freedom of independent travel offered by the private motorcar, which contributed most to the decline of the railways' monopoly on holiday transport. The extensive use of the motorcar for holidaying has its origins in the United States where, in 1908, Henry Ford introduced his popular Model T at a price, which brought the motorcar within reach of the masses. By the 1920s, private motoring was a popular pastime for the middle classes in Britain, and the threat to domestic rail services was clear, although Continental rail services survived and prospered until challenged by the coming of the airlines. In an effort to stem the decline, domestic rail services in Britain were first rationalized in 1921 into four major companies—the London, Midland and Scottish Railway (LMS), the London and North Eastern Railway (LNER), the Great Western Railway (GWR) and the Southern Railway (SR)—and later nationalized following World War II, remaining under public control until again privatized in the mid-1990s.

The arrival of the airline industry signaled the beginning of the end, not only for long-distance rail services but, more decisively, for the great steamship companies. British shipping lines had been under increasing threat from foreign competition throughout the 1920s, with French, German and US liners challenging British supremacy on the North Atlantic routes particularly. The first commercial air routes were initiated as early as 1919 within Europe. The infant service air service were expensive (nearly 16 pounds between London and Paris, equivalent to several weeks average earnings) and uncertain (passengers were warned that forcing landing and delay could occur). It was therefore many years before air services achieved the reliability and low price which could make them competitive with world shipping routes. Pan America Airways introduced transatlantic air service in 1930s (initially using flying boats), but in addition to their expense, the aircraft proved unreliable and uncomfortable by modern standards, and long-distance journeys necessitated frequent stopovers. In the early years, commercial aviation was more important for its mail-carrying potential than for the carriage of passengers. Only with the technological breakthroughs in aircraft design achieved during after the World War II did air services prove a viable alternative to shipping for intercontinental travel.

2. 假日旅游的到来(The Arrival of the Holiday Camp)

Among the major tourism developments of the 1930s, the creation of the holiday camp deserves a special mention. Aimed at the growing low-income market for holidays, the camps set new standards of comfort, offering 24-hour entertainment at an all-inclusive price, were efficient in operation and included child-minding services—a huge bonus for young couples on holiday with their children. This was in marked contrast to the lack of planned activities and the often-surly service offered by the traditional seaside boarding houses of the day.

The origin of these camps goes back to early experiments by organizations such as the Co-operative Holidays Association, the Workers' Travel Association and the Holiday Fellowship (although summer camps for boys such as that run by Joseph Cunningham on the Isle of Man have been dated as early as 1887). However, their popularity and widespread acceptance by the public have commonly been ascribed to the efforts and promotional flair of Billy (later Sir Billy) Butlin. Supposedly Butlin, who built his first camp at Skegness in 1936, met a group of disconsolate holiday-makers huddled in a bus shelter to avoid the rain on a wet summer afternoon. It is thought he was also influenced by a visit to Trusville Holiday Village in Mablethorpe, Lincolnshire, which had been opened and operated successfully by Albert Henshaw since 1924. Butlin determined to build a camp with all-weather facilities, for an all-in price. The instant success of the concept led to a spate of similar camps built by Butlin and other entrepreneurs such as Harry Warner and Fred Pontin in the pre-war and early post-war years. On the Continent, pre-war Germany had introduced the concept of the highly organized and often militaristic health and recreation camp, which enabled many to enjoy holidays who would otherwise have been unable to afford them.

In France, the *villages de vacance* arose from similar political and social influences. The success of this concept of all-in entertainment was later to be copied by hotels, and the hotel with its leisure complex became a popular development in the United States even before the war.

The Youth Hostels Association also stimulated interest in outdoor holidays and healthy recreation in 1929 (the French equivalent opened in the same year), and provided budget accommodation for young people away from home.

3. 海边旅游的兴起(The Popular Movement to the Seaside)

In spite of the rising appeal of holidays abroad, mass tourism between the wars and in the early post-World War II era remained largely domestic. This period saw the seaside holiday become firmly established as the traditional annual holiday destination for the mass of the British public. Suntans were for the first time seen as a status symbol, allied to healthy and time for leisure. Blackpool Scarborough Southend and Brighton consolidated their position as leading resorts, while numerous newer resorts—Bournmouth, Broadstairs, Clacton, Skegness, Colwyn Bay-grew rapidly in terms of both visitors and residential population. Until the Great Depression of the 1930s, hotels and guesthouses proliferated in these resorts. The tradition of the family holiday, taking annually over two weeks in the summer, became firmly established in Britain at this time.

The growing threat of competition from the European mainland was already apparent, for those who chose to take note of it. From the 1920s onwards, the Mediterranean Riviera had begun to attract a summer, as well as a winter, market from the UK, while the resorts of northern France were seen as cheaper and began to offer competition for the popular south coast resorts of Brighton, Hove, Folkestone and Eastbourne. These nearby French resorts, however, were seen primarily as places for short summer holidays, rather than the longer winter stays, which had been popular with wealthy British clientele in the nineteenth century.

三、二战后的旅游业(Tourism Since World War II)

1. 航空业和战后旅游愿望(The Aviation Industry and the Postwar Desire for Travel)

As had occurred after World War I, World War II also led to an increased interest in overseas travel, arising from a desire to see the sites of such battles as those fought on the Normandy beaches and at St Nazaire. The extensive theatre of war had introduced combatants not only to new countries, but to new continents, generating new friendships and an interest in diverse cultures. Another outcome of the war, which was radical to change the travel business, was the advance in aircraft technology which was soon to lead to a viable commercial aviation industry for the first time.

The surplus of aircraft in the immediate post-war years, a benevolent political attitude towards the growth of private sector airlines, and the appearance on the scene of air travel entrepreneurs like Harold Bamberg (of Eagle Airways) and Freddie Laker aided the rapid expansion of air travel after the war. But more significantly for the potential market, aircraft had become more comfortable, safer, faster and, in spite of relatively high prices in the early 1950s, steadily cheaper by comparison with other forms of transport. Commercial jet services began with the ill-fated Comet aircraft in the early 1950s, but already by that time advances in piston-engine technology had ensured that air travel prices would fall substantially. With the introduction of the commercially successful Boeing 707jet in 1958, the age of air travel for the masses had arrived, hastening the demise of the great ocean liners. The number of passengers crossing the Atlantic by air exceeded those by sea for the first time in 1957, and although the liners continued to operate across the Atlantic for a further decade, their increasingly uncompetitive costs and the length of the journey time resulted in declining load factors from one year to the next. The new jets, with average speeds of 800—1,000 kph compared with older propeller-driven aircraft traveling at a mere 400 kph meant that an air traveler could reach a far more distant destination within a given time.

This was particularly valuable for business journeys where time was crucial. The early 1970s saw the arrival of the first super-sonic passenger aircraft, the Anglo-French Concorde. Never truly a commercial success (the government wrote off the huge development costs), it nevertheless proved popular with business travelers and the wealthy. Traveling from London or Paris to New York in three and a half hours, it allowed business people for the first time to complete their business on the other side of the Atlantic and return home without a hotel stopover. The limited range and carrying capacity (100 passengers) of the aircraft, and restrictions against sonic booms over land, acted as severe constraints on operable routes, and the fatal crash near Paris of a chartered Concorde in 2000 led to the withdrawal of the aircraft for an undetermined (at the time of writing) period. It is unlikely that any further supersonic aircraft development will take place for at least twenty years.

2. 包价旅游的发展(The Development of the Package Tour)

The package tour depends on the ability of tour operator to charter aircraft for their clientele, in order to drive down the prices. The purchase of new jets by the large airlines left a large supply of the good, second-hand propeller-driven aircrafts, which were often purchased cheaply by smaller companies to undertake charter operations. These were able for the time to transport holiday tourists to Mediterranean destination both faster than, and almost as cheaply as, trains and coaches. These new charter services soon proved highly profitable. Initially, government policy ensured that charters were restricted to troop movement, but as official policy became more lenient, the private operators sought new forms of charter traffic. The package holiday business resulted from cooperation between these carriers and entrepreneurs in the travel business. Although there are instances of charter fights as early as the 1920s (Thomas Cook, for example, had organized an escorted charter believed to be the first, to take fans from New York to Chicago in 1927 to see the Dempsey-Tunney heavyweight title fight), and the national union of students is known to have been organizing charter flights for its members as early as 1949. Vladimir Raitze is generally credited with establishing the mass charter air movement as we know it today. In 1950, under the horizon Holiday banner, he organized an experimental package holiday trip using a charter flight to Corsica. By chartering the aircraft and filing every seat instead of committing himself to a block of seats on scheduled air services, he was able to reduce significant by the unit cost of his air transport and hence the overall price to his customers. He carried only 300 passengers in the first year, but repeated the experiment the following year and was soon operating profitably. Other budding tour operators copied his idea, and by the early 1960s the package holiday to the Mediterranean had become an established product for the mass holiday market. While the Spanish coastline and the Balearlc Islands received the greatest proportion of these tourists, Italy, Greece and other Mediterranean coastal regions all benefited by the "rush to the sun". Other northern European countries were also soon setting up their own package holiday arrangement to the Mediterranean and began to compete with Britain for accommodation along the Mediterranean coast. In Denmark pastor Eilif Krogager conducted a group of package tourists by coach to Spain in 1950, using his village name Tjaereborg as the company name. In 1962 Tjaereborg Travel moved into the air charter market with the formation of Sterling Airways, which was to become Western Europe's largest privately owned charter airline.

In Britain, difficulties in the economy forced the government to impose stricter control over the purchase of foreign currency. By the late 1960s the foreign travel allowance had been cut to only 50 pounds per person. There was, however, a silver lining to his particular cloud: it encouraged people to take package holidays rather than travel independently and the industry continued to flourish. The limits were relaxed from 1970 onwards, and with further liberalization of air transport regulations, and longer paid holidays, which encouraged a growing number of tourists to take a second holiday abroad each year, a new winter holiday market emerged in the 1970s. Through the more even spread of package holidays throughout the year, operators found it was able to reduce their costs still further, and package holidays prices continued to fall, boosting off seasons demand. It should be recognized, however, that Britain was alone within Europe in impossible currency restrictions during these years. Indeed, exchange controls were not totally abolished in nation for Europeans as the major Mediterranean France until as recently as 1990.

A further technological breakthrough in air transport occurred in 1970, when the first wide-bodied jets (Boeing 747s), capable of carrying over 400 passengers, appeared in service. The unit cost per seat fell sharply, and the result was an increased supply of seats at potentially cheaper fares. This innovation meant that once again the aviation industry had to unload cheaply a number of obsolescent, although completely airworthy, smaller aircraft, and these were quickly pressed into service for charter operations.

3. 向阳光地带的旅游转移(Travel Movement to the Sun)

By the 1960s, it was clear that the future of mass market leisure travel was to be a north-south movement, from the cool and variable climates of North America and northern Europe, where the mass of relatively well-off people lived, to the sunshine and warmth of the temperate to tropical lands in the southern part of the northern hemisphere. These southern countries were also for the most part less developed economically, and offered low cost opportunities for the formation of a tourism industry. The new breed of tourism entrepreneurs involved with packaging tours recognized this trend very early on. Major hotel corporations, too, were quick to seize the opportunities for growth in these countries, and chains such as Sheraton and Hyatt in the USA quickly expanded into Mexico and the Caribbean, as well as into Florida and Hawaii, the states offering the most attractive climates for tourism development. In Europe, British and German tour operators such as Thomson and TUI developed bulk inclusive tours to the Mediterranean and North Africa, and with increasing volume, were able to charter jumbo jets for the first time, bringing prices still lower. As transport costs fell, operators were able to attract a mass market for long-haul travel on chartered jumbo jets.

Florida, boosted particularly by the attractions of Disney World and Miami Beach, has become almost as popular a destination for Europeans as the major Mediterranean destinations.

4. 组合目的地(Identikit Destinations)

The net result of these developments in tourism for the mass markets has been the establishment of destination for particular market segments, which, in all but their locations, are very often remarkably similar. A convention center, for example, may contain a conference building which may be usable for those purposes, which committee rooms, single rooms or twin bedded hotel rooms with private facilities restaurants with banqueting rooms, bars, exhibition space, indoor and outdoor sports facilities and good scheduled transports links. The location may be sports Portsmouth, Basel or Rio—once inside their hotel or conference center, delegates may not even notice where they are.

The larger the mass markets, the less distinctive destinations are likely to be, especially if the destination is small and recently developed. One can find newly built "marina" type resorts with yachting basins, hotel/apartment/villa accommodations, similar restaurants, cafes and shops, and golf, tennis, water sports, folk singers and barbecue nights in any one of a dozen countries around the Mediterranean, the Caribbean, North Africa and the South Pacific. These 'Identikit' destinations are the result of comprehensive market research among various generating markets to find products with guaranteed mass demand. They may be compared with the piecemeal development of resorts two or three generations ago which may have had purely local or domestic attractions.

Not all destinations are similar, of course. While many may be "down-market"in their attraction-that is, they may offer cheap tourism to a large number of people, with the image of great popularity—others may offer an up-market Identikit image, allegedly offering higher quality and thus more expensive services to fewer people. So in the former category we may think of Benidorm, Magaluf, Benitses in the Mediterranean, Miami Beach in Florida, or Seefeld in Austria, while in the latter category we may think of Tahiti, Fiji, Malindi in Kenya, or Barbados. Sandals in the Caribbean, France's Club of Mediterranee etc, have developed many Identikit destinations through the activities of multinational tour companies such as the all-inclusive resorts. Within their establishments the tourists will find a comforting degree of uniformity.

It is important to note, however, that there are exceptions to the rule of the Identikit destination, particularly in the field of the British domestic holiday resort. Recent research by the English Tourism Council has revealed that one of the failings of the English seaside resorts is their failure to project a unique image. Those that have succeeded, notably Blackpool and a handful of other major or minor resorts, have done so through a combination of significant investment and differentiation from other, often similar, resorts.

5. 私家车的大规模出现(Mass Appearance of Private Motoring)

After a slow post-war recovery, standards of living rose steadily in the 1950s and after. Many people could consider buying a motorcar for the first time, even if it were second-hand. For the first time, the holiday masses had the freedom to take to the roads as a family in their own private car, and the popular routes between London and the resorts on the south coast were soon clogged, in these pre-motorway days with weekend traffic.

The flexibility that the car offered could not be matched by public transport services, and both bus and rail lost the holiday traveler. In 1950 some two out of every three holidaymakers took the train for their holidays in Britain. This fell to one in seven by 1970. In this period, private car ownership in Britain rose from 2 million to over 11 million vehicles, while by the end of the 1980s it had risen to some 20 million.

This trend led in turn to a growth in camping and caravanning holidays. Ownership of private caravans stood at nearly 800,000 by the end of the 1980s (excluding static caravans in parks), while 13 million holidaymakers in the UK took their holidays in a caravan. This development has been a cause for some concern, however, the benefits to a region of private caravan tourism are considerably less than most other forms of tourism (owners can bring most of their own food with them, and do not require accommodation), while caravans tend to clog the holiday routes in summer. Both mobile caravans and static caravans on site are something of an eyesore, too.

The switch to private transport led to new forms of accommodation to cater for this form of travel. Britain saw the development of its first motels, modelled on the American pattern, the contemporary version of the staging inn catering for transit passengers. The construction of a new network of motor ways, and other road improvements, brought the more distant resorts closer to centers of population, in some cases changing both the nature of the market served and the image of the resort itself. The ever-resourceful tour operators met the private car threat to package holidays by devising more flexible packages such as fly-drive programs. Hotels, too, spurred on by the need to fill their rooms off-peak, devised their own programs of short-stay holidays tailored to the needs of the private motorists. Demand for hire cars abroad rose, as the overseas holidaymaker was emboldened to move away from the hotel ghettos, and the car rental business benefited accordingly.

6. 战后航运业(The Shipping Business in the Postwar Period)

In the passenger shipping business, hit by rising prices and competition from the airlines, shipping companies were gradually forced to abandon their traditional liner routes in the 1960s. Some companies attempted to adapt their vessels for cruising, though not entirely successfully; vessels purpose-built for long-distance fast deep-sea voyages are not ideally suited for cruising, either economically or from the standpoint of customer demand. Many were incapable of anchoring alongside docks in the shallow waters of popular cruise destinations such as the Caribbean. Companies that failed to embark on a program of new construction, either due to lack of resources or lack of foresight, soon ceased trading. Others, such as the Canard Line, were taken over by conglomerates outside the travel or transport industries. However, many new purpose-built cruise liners, of Greek, Norwegian and later Russian registry, soon appeared on the market to fill the gaps left by the declining maritime powers. These vessels, in spite of their registry, were to be based primarily in the Caribbean or Mediterranean waters. British shipping was not entirely without innovations at this time, however, Cunard initiated the fly-cruise concept in the 1960s, with vessels based at Gibraltar and Naples, where passengers flew out to join their cruise in chartered aircraft.

If the rapid escalation of fuel and other costs during the 1970s threatened the whole future of deep-sea shipping, the ferry services by contrast achieved quite exceptional levels of growth from the 1950s onward. This largely resulted from the increased demand from private motorists taking their cars abroad, influencing particularly routes between Scandinavian countries and Germany, and between Britain and Continental Europe. Growth in demand was also better spread across the seasons, enabling vessels to be in service throughout the year with respectable load factors (although freight demand substantially boosted weak passenger revenue in the winter period). Regular sailings, with fast turnarounds in port, encouraged bookings, and costs were kept down by offering much more restricted levels of service than would be expected on long-distance routes. Hovercraft and jetfoil services were introduced across the Channel, although their success was limited by technical problems and their withdrawal in rough weather.

7. 商务旅游重要性不断增强(The Growing Importance of Business Travel)

The growth in world trade in these decades saw a steady expansion in business travel, individually and in the conference and incentive travel fields, although the recession of the late 1980s and early 1990s caused cutbacks in business travel as sharp as those in leisure travel. As economic power shifted between countries, so emerging nations provided new patterns of tourism generation: in the 1970s, Japan and the oil-rich nations of the Middle East led the growth, while in the 1980s, countries such as Korea and Malaysia expanded both inbound and outbound business tourism dramatically.

Today, business travel of all kinds is of immense importance to the tourism industry, not least because the per capita revenue from the business traveler greatly exceeds that of the leisure traveler. It must be stressed that business travel often complements leisure travel, to spread the effects of tourism more evenly in the economy. A major factor is that business travelers are not generally traveling to areas that are favor by leisure travelers; business people have to go to locations where they are to conduct business, and this generally means city centers, often in cities that have little to attract the leisure tourists. Travel also takes place all year round, with little peaking, and hotel demand occurs between Mondays and Fridays encouraging the more attractively situated hotels to target the leisure market on weekends. Often, spouses will travel to accompany the business traveler, and their leisure needs will have to be taken into consideration; thus in practice it is very hard to distinguish between business and leisure tourism, especially in terms of spend.

Although business travel is more price-inelastic than leisure travel, efforts to cut costs in the world of business today are ensuring that the business traveler no longer spends as freely as formerly. Fewer business travelers now travel first class or business class on airlines, less expensive hotels are booked and there is even a trend to travel on weekends to reduce prices. Companies are buying many more tourism products, particularly air tickets, through the Internet, where they can shop around for the cheapest tickets, and budget carriers are attracting a growing proportion of their business from these travelers. These changes are not seen as short-term trends, and in future any distinction between the two major tourist markets is likely to become less apparent.

8. 会议旅游和奖励旅游的发展(The Conference and Incentive Travel Business)

Conferences and formal meetings have become very important to the tourism industry, both nationally and internationally, with rapid growth each year since the 1960s. The British conference market alone is responsible for the organization of some 700,000 individual conferences each year, the very large majority lasting just one or two days, and as most of these are held in hotels this market is vital to the accommodation sector. Major conferences, such as that of the American Bar Association, which accounts for up to 25,000 delegates each year traveling all over the world have a huge impact on all sectors of the industry, from hotels to the destination itself, which will benefit from expenditure in shops, theatres, night clubs and other centers of amusement. To serve the needs of the largest conferences, international conference centers seating up to 5,000 or more delegates have been built in major cities such as London and Berlin, but the number of conferences of this size is inevitably, limited, and the competition to attract them intense. The logistics of organizing these and other major events are generally in the hands of professional events organizers, most of which in Britain will belong to the Association of Conference Executives (ACE).

Exhibitions also account for another form of business travel. Major international exhibitions can be traced at least as far back as the Great Exhibition, held at Crystal Palace in London in 1851, and World Fairs have become common events in major cities around the globe as a means of attracting visitors and publicizing a nation's culture and products. Many national events are now organized on an annual basis, some requiring little more than a field and marquees or other temporary structures—the Royal Bath & West agricultural show being one example of a major outdoor attraction, held annually in the UK's West Country. As these events have grown and become more professionally organized, so have they, too, become an important element in the business of tourism.

9. 全包价假日旅游(The All-inclusive Holiday Tour)

Mention has already been made of the trend to all-inclusive holidays. As the term indicates, this holiday includes everything—food, alcoholic drinks, water sports and other entertainment at the hotel. The attractions of this form of tourism are obvious—it is seen by tourists as offering better value, because they can pay up front for the holiday, know what their budget will be well in advance, and be unconcerned about changes in the value of foreign currency, or the need to take large sums of money abroad. For the more timid foreign traveler, or those who are concerned about being badgered by local souvenir sellers, and 'beach salesmen', there is the added reassurance that they do not even have to leave the hotel complex to enjoy their holidays. However, there are clearly serious implications for the local economy, as local bars, shopkeepers—and others no longer stand to benefit from filer influx of tourists, while greater profits flow back to the operators in generating countries, who control the leisure site. This form of tourism may be judged far removed from the concept of sustainable tourism, although operators themselves would argue that by keeping tourists in "ghettos" they are in fact helping to reduce the negative impact of tourism on locals.

This form of tourism originated in the Caribbean, and up-market tour operators such as Sandals have promoted these programs very successfully to the US and European markets. However, the concept later moved down-market and became popular in the more traditional European resorts such as those of the Balearic Islands. Further expansion is seen as a direct threat to the livelihood of many in the traditional coastal resorts.

第三节 中国旅游产业的发展和演变
(A Review of the Development of Tourism Industry in China)

如果把托马斯·库克(Thomas Cook)在1841年成立组织的第一次铁路旅游作为现代旅游业的开端,中国无疑是世界旅游舞台的后来者。虽然早在20世纪20到30年代旅游业作为一项经济活动在中国大地上曾经出现过,但那只是昙花一现,并且这个行业基本上是由外国人来控制的,主要服务对象也是在中国的外国人。自1949年中华人民共和国成立到1978年改革开放政策实施之前的近30年中,旅游业被看作是外事活动的组成部分,一直是为政治服务的,并没有真正意义上的经济产业的功能。中国的旅游产业是改革开放政策的产物,没有改革开放,就没今天的旅游产业。从1978年到今天的短短20多年中,中国的旅游产业经历了从崛起到平稳繁荣发展的过程,一跃成为亚洲的旅游大国。进入 21 世纪后,中国政治稳定,经济持续增长,旅游业保持着强劲的发展势头。毫无疑问,随着中国改革开放向纵深的不断深化和发展,作为中国最有活力的产业之一,旅游业将会在中国社会经济发展中取得越来越大的成绩。本节将以时间为经线,以旅游产业所涉及的行业为要素,对中国旅游业发展历史做一简单的回顾。

一、1978年以前的中国旅游业(The Tourism of China before 1978)

1840年以后,帝国主义用坚船利炮打开了中国封建锁国的大门,延续了2000多年的中国传统社会的经济形态开始向近代转变的过程。外国侵略者凭借在中国的种种特权对中国积极地展开以商品输出为中心的侵略活动,形成了以通商口岸为中心的中国近代市场体系。在这一历史背景下,中国的市场结构发生了巨大的变化,传统的旅游业受到西方政治、经济、文化的全面冲击,国人的旅游观念发生了深刻的变化,平民阶层开始逐步进入旅游行业。西方的商人、传教士、学者和冒险家纷纷到中国从事经商、传教和旅游活动。为了适应这种旅游形势的变化,饭店、旅馆等旅游业的重要组成部分逐渐发展和繁荣起来,北京及对外开放的商埠开始出现外资经营的西式旅馆和中西结合式高档旅馆和饭店。

1. 近代中国旅馆业的产生和发展(The Arising and Development of Hotel of China in Modern Times)

中国近代旅馆业是以外国人对华经济入侵、国际贸易和投资的发展以及中国人自身旅游需求的扩大为基础产生和兴起的。一方面,它的起步时间和水平大大落后于西方近代旅馆业,另一方面又受到西方近代旅馆业的发展的影响和促进,并带有浓厚的半殖民地半封建的色彩。外资经营的西式旅馆,大多建在帝国主义列强在中国的租界地或者势力范围之内。1860年英国人Richard在上海建立了上海开埠后第一家外国人经营的饭店Richard Inn。1900年,北京饭店在东单菜市场西隔壁正式挂牌,是北京最著名的闹市区。这些高档旅馆、饭店仅供洋人和清政府的达官贵人享乐。中国平民旅游者,包括文人举子、商人则建立会馆,建设具有地方色彩和风格的羁旅之家。随着中国半殖民地半封建化程度的加深,在旧中国各主要城市和交通枢纽地带,以外国资本为后盾的中小型旅馆多数称为"旅馆"或"酒店"。此时的民族资本也得到一定发展,以民族资本为主体的旅馆多成为"旅社"和"旅店"。中外栈馆共处,旅馆设备设施土洋结合,管理和服务中西交融,不同建筑风格、不同规模的旅馆如雨后春笋,建起中国近代旅馆业的基础和框架。可以说,两次世界大战间的二三十年代既是旧中国经济现代化发展的最好时期,也是中国近代旅馆业发展的黄金时期。

2. 近代中国旅行社业的产生和发展(The Arising and Development of the Chinese Travel Agencies in Modern Times)

在20世纪初,大量外国游客涌入中国,而中国的各界人士也不断出国经商、考察和留学,于是英国的通济旅行社、美国运通银行旅行部等外国机构开始在中国组织旅游,并为出国者代办手续。1923年8月15日,民族资本"上海商业储蓄银行旅行部"正式成立,这是陈光甫先生在自家银行内部设立的旅行部。1927年,陈光甫将设在自家银行的旅行部迁出,正式地打出"中国旅行社"的招牌,这是中国第一家旅行社。

3. 新中国成立以后至改革开放以前我国旅游业的发展(The Development of Tourism after the Foundation of New China and before Reforming & Opening Era)

新中国成立以后,由于在政治、经济、社会等方面的客观原因,在观念上我们并没有认识到旅游业经济性质的一面,没有把它作为一个产业来发展,旅游业发展的主要目的和任务是增进我国与世界各国人民的相互了解和友谊,宣传社会主义。但是在客观上,我国的旅游业通过这一时期的发展,在旅游组织建设、国际旅游市场的开拓等方面积累了一定的经验。

新中国旅游业首先经营的是国际旅游业务,建国后成立的第一家旅行社是厦门的华侨旅行社。华侨旅行社成立之后,在广东省的深圳以及天津、沈阳等十几个城市都建立起了华侨服务社。1957年4月22日,华侨旅行服务总社在北京成立。从此新中国从早期的公费接待少量的观光团,发展到组织华侨、港澳同胞自费回国或到内地观光、旅游、探亲等等。

1955年4月15日,新中国第一家面对外国人的旅行社——中国国际旅行社在北京诞生,在上海、天津等地成立了14家分社。成立之后的国旅,基本的业务是承办除政府代表团以外的所有机关团体单位委托的对外宾食、住、行、游的生活招待,并办理中国铁道部和苏联政府签订的国际铁路旅客联运业务。由此不难看出,中国国际旅行社是适应日益繁重的外宾接待工作而设立的。

1964年6月5日,国务院决定成立中国旅行游览事业管理局,经由全国人大常委会1964年7月22日正式批准。旅游局作为国务院的直属机构,负责全国旅游事业的管理。其主要任务是:负责对外旅行者的旅游管理工作;领导各有关地区的国际旅行社和直属的服务机构的业务;组织我国公民出国旅游;负责有关旅游的对外联络工作和宣传工作等。以中国对外旅行游览事业管理局的成立为标志,我国的旅游事业已开始进入一个新的时期。

在这以后的长达10年的"文化大革命"中,刚刚起步的新中国旅行事业却受到严重的干扰和破坏。一些服务机构被取消,干部职工被下放,使我国的旅游接待事业无法正常进行,处于历史上的萧条、停滞阶段。在这一期间,我国的旅游事业虽然遭受到干扰和破坏,但一直没有间断过,特别是周恩来总理在逆境中给与了极大的关怀,1969年6月,周总理亲自抓旅游工作,提出了"宣传自己,了解别人"的正确方针。1974年经国务院批准,成立了中国旅行社,专门负责接待外国旅游者。

1977年"文化大革命"结束后,我国的旅游业出现新的发展趋势,特别是在1978年底召开的十一届三中全会上做出的全国工作重点转移到社会主义建设上来的战略决策,确定了对外开放、对内搞活的正确方针,并指示要重视旅游业的发展。这使我国的旅游业出现新的生机与活力。

二、1978—2001年中国旅游产业的发展(The Development of Tourism Industry in China Between 1978 and 2001)

中国旅游产业是改革开放的产物,因此中国旅游产业的发展过程也大致遵循改革开放的轨迹。随着改革开放的不断深化,市场经济体制不断建立和完善,旅游产业也获得最适宜的发展空间,成为国民经济各产业中发展速度最快的产业之一。概括地说,在这23年的发展历程中,中国旅游产业也遵循了旅游产业的发展演变的基本模式,经历了发育期和成熟期两个历史时期。1978年至1991年,这是旅游业的发育时期。在这一时期,明确了旅游活动的经济功能,奠定了旅游产业发展的基础。入境旅游迅速崛起,旅游活动日益成为社会经济活动的一部分,旅游产业渐具规模,市场管理体系也逐步成熟,但是旅游业的经营管理都没有脱离计划经济的基本框架。1992年至今,是旅游产业的成长期。在这一时期,确定了旅游产业的产业地位,实现了旅游产业的常规发展,旅游产业的经济贡献日益明显。旅游业形成了入境旅游,出境旅游和国内旅游三个稳定的市场,产业规模不断扩大,产业功能也得到了较好的发挥,促进行业健康发展的政策和措施也在不断出台,中国旅游产业市场经济的框架不断形成,中国不断步入旅游大国发展的行列。

1. 旅游产业的发育期(1978—1991年)：从传统计划经济中脱颖而出（The Developing Period of Tourism Industry [1978—1991]：A Growth Out of the Traditional Planned Economy）

(1) 1978—1980年：现代中国旅游业的起步阶段（The Starting Period of Tourism Industry in Contemporary China[1978—1980]）

我国的旅游产业是改革开放的产物。1978年12月,中共十一届三中全会确定国家的工作重点向社会主义现代化建设转移,我国旅游业也因此进入了新的发展时期。1978年10月至1979年7月,邓小平同志五次专门讲话要求尽快发展旅游业并在旅游业对国家政治经济的积极作用、对改革开放的积极作用以及旅游管理、旅游开发、旅游促销等一系列旅游业的基本认识、基本规律上都作了明确指示。按照邓小平同志的指示,国务院成立了以主管副总理为首的旅游工作领导小组,各地政府也相继成立领导小组,推动了我国旅游业发展的步伐,并在制度建设、行业管理方面等取得很大的成绩。具体表现在：①1979年5月,国务院批准北京等四个城市利用侨资、外资建造6座旅游饭店。同年9月召开的全国旅游工作会议,提出旅游工作要从"政治接待型"转变为"经济经营型",会议还就旅游住宿和旅行社外联权等做出了重要决定。②国务院相继批复国家旅游局《关于开创旅游工作新局面几个问题的报告》、《关于当前旅游体制改革几个问题的报告》,全国旅游工作出现了全新的局面。③1978年3月,中共中央批转《关于发展旅游事业的请示报告》,提出将中国旅行游览事业管理局改为直属国务院的管理总局,各有关省、自治区、直辖市成立旅游局、成立旅游事业领导小组等意见。1978年7月,国务院据此作了批复。④1978年,来华旅游入境人数为180.9万人次,位居世界第48位,其中外国人23万人次。旅游创汇2.63亿美元,位居世界第41位。

这时候的旅游业表现出总体规模较小,结构也比较单一,但旅游接待开始转向旅游经营,旅游业开始朝真正意义上的新产业迈进。

(2)"六五"计划(1981—1985年)时期：入境旅游奠基阶段（The Sixth Five-year-plan Period[1981—1985]：The Establishment Phase of Inbound Tour）

在80年代初期,我国的旅游业和其他行业一样,具有鲜明的计划经济的特征。每年旅游工作会议为本年确定的旅游业的总体目标就是例证。1981年7月,全国旅游工作会议确定"六五"计划旅游业的总体目标是,到1985年接待外国旅游者130万至160万人次,华侨、港、澳、台同胞探亲旅游约 600 万人次,旅游外汇收入 12 亿至 13 亿美元。1982 年 9 月,中共十二大提出了全面开创社会主义现代化建设的新局面、到 2000 年实现中国工农业总产值翻两番的宏伟目标。根据这一目标,旅游管理部门提出:以 1980 年为基数翻两番,到 1990 年接待外国旅游者增至 212 万人次,外汇收入约为 25 亿美元。

为实现上述确定的目标,国家主要采取两项措施:一是适当放宽外联权,给地方一定的外联工作权力;二是逐步发展散客旅游和家庭式旅游。与此同时,国家还出台了旅游发展的基本方针和原则来实现这些目标:①1981 年 3 月,中共中央书记处和国务院常务会议听取了旅游工作会议汇报,提出了今后一个时期发展旅游事业的方针:"积极发展,量力而行,稳步前进";旅游管理体制原则:"统一领导,分散经营";并决定旅游总局要与国旅总社分开,国务院成立旅游工作领导小组。②1984 年是中国经济体制改革深入发展的一年。国务院在向六届人大二次会议提交的《政府工作报告》中提出,今后一个时期,要着力抓好体制改革和对外开放两件大事,这也是关系到旅游事业发展前途的大事。7 月 27 日,中共中央书记处、国务院批准了国家旅游局《关于开创旅游工作新局面几个问题的报告》,提出了加快旅游基础设施的建设要采取国家、地方、部门、集体和个人一起上,自力更生和利用外资一起上的方针和旅游行政部门简政放权等措施。③1985 年 1 月 31 日,国务院批转国家旅游局《关于当前旅游体制改革几个问题的报告》,提出了旅游管理体制实行"政企分开,统一领导,分级管理,分散经营,统一对外"的原则,向各省、自治区、直辖市下放外联权的签证通知权,从而解决了 6 年来旅游系统普遍关心的问题。在这一年的 5 月 11 日,国务院发布了《旅行社管理暂行条例》,这是旅游产业第一部行政法规。上述文件法规的积极贯彻执行,极大地调动了各方面办旅游的积极性,旅游工作开始实现历史上的四个转变:一是从过去主要搞旅游接待,转变为开发、建设与接待并举;二是从只抓入境旅游,转变为入境旅游、国内旅游一起抓,相互促进;三是从以国家投资为主建设旅游基础设施转变为国家、地方、部门、集体和个人一起上,自力更生与利用外资一起上;四是旅游经营单位由事业单位转变为企业化经营。

经过这一段时期旅游产业的发展,旅游产业规模和产业业绩有比较明显的提高,尤其是入境旅游接待设施有很大发展,为旅游业的发展奠定了基础。但是从整体上看,旅游业的发展水平不高,在世界旅游业中所占的比例还是很低。1985 年,全国旅游收入仅占国际旅游总收入的

1.14%，与中国丰富的旅游资源相比很不相称。

（3）"七五"计划时期(1986—1990年)：入境旅游继续发展、国内旅游开始起步（The Seventh Five-year-plan Period[1986—1990]：The Growth of Inbound Tour and the Rising of Domestic Tour)

1985年12月20日，国务院举行第92次常务会议，批准《全国旅游事业发展规划(1986年至2000年)》，会议决定把旅游事业发展规划列入国家的"七五"计划并增加投资，国务院决定成立旅游协调小组。在1986年《国民经济发展"七五"计划》中，国家对"七五"时期国家对旅游工作的规划的目标是：到1990年接待海外游客500万人次（其中外国人300万人次）；外汇收入27至30亿美元，平均年增长率分别为11%和15.7%—18.2%；正式指出了发展旅游业的基本方针是"要大力发展旅游业，增加外汇收入，促进各国人民之间的友好往来"。这是旅游业第一次在国家计划中出现，是旅游产业发展的一个重要标志。这样国家就初步明确了旅游业产业地位并开始形成了旅游行业管理。旅游业的产业地位正式地得到确立。

在此之后，国家先后出台了一系列制度和条例完善旅游行业管理体系。1987年11月14日，国务院批准发布了第二部旅游管理行政法规《导游人员管理暂行条例》。1988年6月，国家旅游局发布《旅行社管理暂行条例施行办法》，总结3年来贯彻实施《旅行社管理暂行条例》的经验，并贯穿了强化管理、严格旅行社管理、支持骨干旅行社发展、鼓励有条件的单位开办旅行社的指导思想。8月，发布《中华人民共和国评定旅游涉外饭店星级的规定》，决定在全国旅游涉外饭店中施行星级评定制度。12月，国务院转发旅游管理体制改革的总体方案，形成了旅游业行业管理的基本框架，进一步明确了行业管理范围权限，明确了旅游部门在这些管理范围实行分级管理。国家还在1990年4月在全国开展了清理整顿旅行社市场的活动，规范市场秩序。这一时期的旅游产业取得了巨大的成绩，但是由于1989年的政治风波，入境旅游市场出现了巨大的波动，凸现了旅游产业对社会政治经济等的强依赖性。

在1988年5月，国务院成立国家旅游事业委员会，同时撤销国务院旅游协调领导小组，这表明国家对旅游业务的监管力度也进一步加大，一些关于旅游发展的主导观念如产业观念、市场观念、形象观念和中央地方两个积极性的观念也得到了认可和增强。

经过以上三个阶段的发展，我国的旅游产业渐渐从传统的计划经济体制中脱离出来，并表现出以下主要的发展特征：①境外需求拉动是旅游产业发展的主要原因。改革开放后的第一轮旅游需求冲击是来源于境外旅游市场,这一巨大的冲击催生了20世纪70年代末刚刚萌发的中国旅游业。这一轮的冲击是一个外生变量,它增长快,密度大,来势猛,与我国实际经济发展水平和居民消费层次存在着相当大的差距,因此我国旅游业在短期很难做出全面的反应来满足这些需求,只好采取适应需求策略,在供给和需求之间尽量寻找弥补缺口的平衡点。在产品的开发组织和产业体系的组建上主要依赖原有的资源自我发展。在这一时期,我国的旅游产业主要以观光接待型旅游为主,以买方市场为主,靠迅速增长的国际旅游市场创造了20世纪80年代中国旅游业高速发展的奇迹。②非常规发展特征明显。这一时期,我国旅游业很明显地表现出初创时期非常规发展的特征,这种特征具体表现为发展旅游的目的主要是赢得外汇收入,入境旅游几乎是旅游业经营的主要内容,国民的合理的旅游需求没有得到重视;旅游业自身的产业体系不健全,服务设施严重不足;产品浅层次开发,产品类型单一;在经营中,市场观念还比较淡漠;在旅游管理体制上,政企不分,行政管理依然是主要的手段;旅游人数增长速度很快;旅游产业在国家和地方经济发展的促进作用还不很明显,虽然在名义上列入国家社会经济发展计划,但是并没有真正确立产业地位。因此在这一阶段,旅游产业"先国际,后国内"的推进型发展模式得到了充分的体现。

2. 旅游产业的成长期(1992—2001年):在市场经济中寻求发展(The Maturing Period of Tourism Industry[1992—2001]:Seeking to Develop in the Market Economy)

20世纪90年代以后,中国的改革开放逐渐深入,市场经济的意识大大加强,市场经济的力量发挥着更加明显的作用,中国旅游业也出现了蓬勃发展的新局面。整个市场格局发生了重大的变化,从原来仅仅有的入境旅游逐渐转化为国际旅游(包括入境旅游和出境旅游)、国内旅游并重,旅游发展从海外市场外生变量的拉动转化为内外市场的拉动。在经济规模上,旅游业也有了质的飞跃,这表现为它对地方经济发展的刺激作用大大增强,变成了与百姓生活息息相关的"家事",发展旅游业成为举国上下普遍关注的热点问题。这个时期的产业政策突出表现在:各地政府对发展旅游的鼓励和支持,各级旅游管理机构纷纷设立,行业管理从上至下形成比较完整的系统;旅游业在各地经济发展中的地位空前提高,成为国家和地方新的经济增长点。其中至关重要的一点是,各地将中央发展旅游业的宏观决策转化为具体的行动,并针对各地旅游发展的要素结构出台了比较完善的政策体系。至此,旅游业获得了跨世纪发展的政策发展的空间。

同时,整个国家的经济改革不断深入,特别是邓小平1992年南巡讲话之后,中国经济进入了发展的快车道。在近10年的时间里,市场意识全面强化,市场经济体制全面建立,旅游产业市场准入障碍基本上扫清,行业内各种所有制形势日益普遍化,市场规则逐渐形成,并探索出一些具有成效的发展旅游业的阶段性模式。在旅游产品上,为适应新的竞争,各地注意深度开发,不断推出新的旅游产品类型,突破原来观光旅游产品占主导地位的形势。产业的发展更大程度表现在产业内部的结构调整和产业素质的提高。同时,这一时期的旅游业真正全面发展的时期,也是产业内部积累的问题逐渐暴露的过程。

(1)"八五"计划时期(1991—1995年):入境旅游有较大发展,国内旅游迅猛崛起(The Eighth Five-year-plan Period[1991—1995]: Great Development of Inbound Tour and Rapid Growth of Domestic Tour)

"八五"计划时期,旅游产业得到进一步的发展,主要表现在以下两个方面:首先,旅游业产业地位进一步提升:1992年6月,中共中央、国务院《关于加快发展第三产业的决定》,进一步明确旅游业是第三产业的重点,各级政府及各有关部门相继把旅游业列入国民经济和社会发展计划中,大多数省、自治区、直辖市已明确提出把旅游业作为支柱产业、重点产业或先导产业来发展。

其次,旅游的行业管理得到了进一步的完善。在1991年年初,国务院批转国家旅游局《关于加强旅游行业管理若干问题的请示》,提出了对各地建立正常的、规范的旅游行业管理秩序的总要求,并要求继续进行治理整顿旅行社工作,进一步整顿旅游价格市场。5月,国家旅游局与国家物价局联合制定《旅游涉外饭店客房租价最低限价的规定》。1992年,国务院批准设立12个国家旅游度假区,国家旅游局制定《旅游行业对客人服务的基本标准》。1993年,为了加强对国内旅游业的指导和管理,国务院办公厅批转了国家旅游局《关于发展国内旅游业的意见》,将"搞活市场,正确引导,加强管理,提高质量"作为今后一个时期的国内旅游发展方针。同年,中国国内旅游协会成立。1994年,国家对国有企业进行了股份制试点。在这一环境下,部分旅游企业集团获得了国有资产管理局授予的国有资产管理权。1995年,国家继续大抓国内旅游,对旅行社实行了质量保证金制度,还成立"全国旅游标准化基础委员会",发布一个国家标准和两个行业标准。

这一时期旅游产业发展取得的主要成绩有：国际旅游业跃上新台阶，创汇进入世界前十名；国内旅游迅猛崛起；旅游产品更加丰富多彩，旅游促销形成系列工程；在旅游产品结构性优化迈出关键步伐，以山水风光、文物古迹、民俗风情为特征的传统产品加快更新改进，普遍充实了新的游览内容，由一般观光、单纯观光向主题观光、参与性观光发展，并提高产品的档次和品位，开始了度假产品、专项产品的开发，12个国家级度假区、54个省级度假区和一批环城市度假设施已初具雏形。在这一时期，国家已经态度鲜明地把旅游业当作主要经济产业来办，多方面探索旅游经济发展的客观规律，并根据旅游市场需要一定提前量、一定规模和声势的客观规律，提出了1993—1997"五年促销计划"，增强了市场促销工作计划性和主动性，有利地促进了主题旅游产品的开发。政府主导发挥了良好的作用。在市场方面，国家坚持把"海外抓促销、国内抓建设"作为发展旅游的战略思想，使旅游市场整体促销有了实质性的提高，形成了一年一个主题、年年出现新高潮的新局面。如1992年的友好观光年，1993年的山水风光年，1994年的文物古迹游，1995年的民俗风情游等。

(2)"九五"计划时期(1996—2000年)：产业基础夯实、为21世纪积蓄后劲阶段（The Ninth Five-year-plan Period[1996—2000]：The Laying of a Firm Foundation of the Industry and the Amassing of Stamina for the 21st Century）

在"九五"时期，旅游产业在国民经济中的地位进一步提高，主要表现在：

一方面，在1998年12月召开的中央经济工作会议上，房地产业、信息业和旅游业被确定为国民经济新的增长点。在这一会议精神的引导下，先后有24个省、自治区和直辖市结合自己的实际情况，把旅游业作为支柱产业、重点产业、先导产业来发展，并不同程度地加强了"政府主导"的力度。在1998年，全国旅游总收入占GDP比重达到4.32%。

表1-1 我国各个省、直辖市对旅游产业的定位

地区	产业地位的说明	地区	产业地位的说明
北京	第三产业中的支柱产业	湖北	支柱产业
天津	第三产业中的重点产业	湖南	支柱产业
河北	第三产业中的重点产业	广东	支柱产业

续表

地区	产业地位的说明	地区	产业地位的说明
山西	支柱产业	广西	第三产业中的支柱产业
内蒙	第三产业中的先导产业	海南	支柱产业
辽宁	先导产业	重庆	支柱产业
吉林	第三产业中的重点产业	四川	支柱产业
黑龙江	支柱产业	贵州	支柱产业
上海	新的经济增长点	云南	支柱产业
江苏	支柱产业	西藏	支柱产业
浙江	支柱产业	陕西	支柱产业
安徽	支柱产业	甘肃	支柱产业
福建	支柱产业	青海	
江西	第三产业中的支柱产业	宁夏	第三产业中的重点产业
山东	支柱产业	新疆	支柱产业
河南	支柱产业		

（资料来源：何光玮：《新世纪 新产业 新增长》，P161，中国旅游出版社，北京。）

另一方面，国家出台了一系列措施来改善对旅行社的经营管理。1996年10月15日，国务院第205号令，颁布新的《旅行社管理条例》。按照这一新的条例，1997年顺利实现了由一、二、三类旅行社向国际旅行社、国内旅行社的转变。1998年，按照国务院机构改革的部署，国家旅游局保质保量按时完成机构改革，进一步提高干部"四化"水平和机关工作效率，并如期完成了与经济实体的脱钩工作。同年，国家旅游局制定《中国优秀旅游城市》检查标准，对自1995年以来开展创建中国优秀旅游城市工作的75个城市进行了验收，其中54个城市荣获第一批"中国优秀旅游城市"称号。这一工作改善了我国旅游业的发展环境，促进城市向国际化、现代化方向发展，为旅游业跨世纪腾飞积蓄了后劲。在1999年，对外经济贸易部和国家旅游局联合发布《中外合资旅行社试点暂行办法》，进一步开放旅行社市场，开始允许外资旅行社按照中外合资或其他的所有制形式有步骤地在中国开办旅游业务等。

这一时期我国旅游产业发展的成绩主要表现为：入境旅游、国内旅游和出境旅游三个市场平衡发展的局面开始形成，"朝阳产业"的优势和作用得到充分显现；主题促销为主的海外市场宣传成效卓著。1996年，我国首次推出中国度假休闲游。1997年，第二次举办中国旅游年，江泽民主席亲自在新年致辞中宣布旅游年开幕，当时适逢香港回归和党的十五大召开等重大历史事件,旅游业抓住这个历史机遇,积极对外宣传促销,使海外旅游者的旅游行程丰富多彩。1997年4月,PATA年会、交易会在我国举行。国务院总理李鹏在年会开幕式上向世界旅游界全面阐述了我国政府发展旅游业的政策和举措。1998年,举办了华夏城乡游,同年还举办了中国国际旅游促销会,成为亚太地区规模最大的国际旅游交易会。1999年,我国旅游宣传的主题是生态环境游。在1999年5月1日至10月1日,我国政府成功举办了"99'昆明世界园艺博览会",这是本世纪末规模最大、为期最长的一次国际展览盛会。1999年8月30日至9月1日,国家旅游局和世界旅游组织联合举办了"中国生态旅游可持续发展及市场促销研讨会"。2000年举办的"神州世纪游"是我国迈向21世纪的旅游促销主题,是中国旅游业以崭新的风貌、昂扬的气概,迎接新世纪更大发展的一个重大举措。国家旅游局重点推出"中国的世界遗产——21世纪的世界级旅游景点"的主题产品,并将结合全国60多项国际性文化、体育盛事进行包装组合,形成一批全新的旅游产品推向市场。

经过以上几个阶段的发展,中国的旅游产业成为国民经济中的一个崭新的产业。这一时期中国旅游产业凸现了产业地位日益明显、国民旅游全面发展、行业管理进程加快、旅游产品结构和市场结构呈现多元化等特点。

复习思考题:

1. 如何理解旅游产业的概念?如何理解旅游产业的行业规定性?
2. 旅游产业生产具有哪些特征?
3. 西方国家旅游产业大体经历了哪几个阶段?战后西方旅游业出现了哪些发展趋势?
4. 我国旅游产业经历了哪些发展阶段?每一阶段有什么特点?

第二章
旅游产业结构
(The Structure of Tourism Industry)

产业结构既可以解释为某个产业内部的企业关系,也可以解释为各个产业之间的关系结构。一般说来,狭义的产业结构理论只研究产业之间的关系结构,而广义的产业结构理论还包括研究产业内的企业间关系的产业组织理论(Theory of Industrial Organization)。有关产业组织的内容后面将专门介绍,本章不涉及这部分内容。本章研究的产业结构指的是广义的产业结构理论,并在此基础上结合旅游产业的特殊性做进一步研究。首先,通过研究产业结构演进的原因和条件,归纳产业结构演变的规律;其次,从动态、均衡的角度对一定经济发展阶段上产业结构的合理化问题进行探讨;最后,结合旅游产业自身的特点,研究旅游产业链条上各个部门之间的关系。

在研究产业之间的结构关系时,有两种形式:一是研究产业之间比例关系及其演变规律的形式,即产业发展形态理论。本章的产业结构研究指的是这种形式。二是利用投入产出经济学研究产业之间投入、产出联系的形式,即产业联系理论——关联度分析。由于涉及到数学模型,较为复杂,所以产业联系理论在后面单列一章详细说明。

第一节 产业分类和产业结构
(Classification and Constitution of Industry)

一、产业和产业分类(Industry and Industrial Classification)

产业是按社会分工而从事物质产品生产或提供劳务的一切经济活动群体的总称。研究产业结构,首先要将产业按照一定的方法分解、归类,然后进一步研究他们之间的比例关系和相互联系。因此,产业分类是产业结构概念和产业结构研究的基础。由于研究产业结构的角度不同,产业分类也呈现多样化的特点。

1. 三次产业分类法(Three Stages of Industrial Classification)

所谓三次产业分类法就是根据社会生产活动历史发展的顺序对产业进行划分。产品直接取自自然界的部门称为第一次产业(Primary Industry),对初级产品进行再加工的部门称为第二次产业(Secondary Industry),为生产和消费提供各种服务的部门称为第三次产业(Tertiary Industry)。

三次产业分类法是西方产业结构研究中最重要的分类方法之一。第一次产业、第二次产业这两个名词最早流行于 20 世纪 20 年代的新西兰和澳大利亚。当时把农业、畜牧业、渔业、林业和矿业称为"第一次产业",把制造业称为"第二次产业"。1935 年新西兰奥塔哥大学教授阿伦·格·费希尔(A. G. B. Fisher)鉴于第一次产业和第二次产业没有涵盖全部经济活动,提出了第三次产业的概念,把除了第一次产业和第二次产业以外的所有经济活动统称为第三次产业。1940 年英国经济学家和统计学家科林·克拉克(C. G. Clark)在其著作《经济进步的条件》(The Conditions of Economic Progress)中继承并发扬了费希尔的三次产业分类法,运用了其研究经济发展与产业结构变化之间的规律,从而开拓了产业结构理论的新领域,并使得三次产业分类法广泛流传。

2. 联合国标准产业分类法(U. N. Standard Industrial Classification)

联合国标准产业分类法是联合国为了统一世界各国产业分类而制定的标准产业分类法。2002 年,联合国颁布的《全部经济活动的国际标准产业分类》(International Standard Industrial Classification of All Economic Activities, ISIC)把全部国民经济分为若干个部门,各项下面包含小项,并对各项都规定了统计编码。

This classification was acknowledged by the Statistical Commission in March 2002.① (以下只列示了部门大项)

A—Agriculture, hunting and forestry

B—Fishing

C—Mining and quarrying

---

① 英文版摘自 2002 年联合国最新《全部经济活动的国际标准产业分类》。资料来源:http://unstats.un.org/unsd/cr/registry/regcst.asp

D—Manufacturing

E—Electricity, gas and water supply

F—Construction

G—Wholesale and retail trade, repair of motor vehicles, motorcycles and personal and household goods

H—Hotels and restaurants

I—Transport, storage and communications

J—Financial intermediation

K—Real estate, renting and business activities

L—Public administration and defense, compulsory social security

M—Education

N—Health and social work

O—Other community, social and personal service activities

P—Activities of private households as employers and undifferentiated production activities of private households

Q—Extraterritorial organizations and bodies

A standard classification of economic activities is arranged so that entities can be classified according to the activity they carry out. The categories of International Standard Industrial Classification of All Economic Activities (ISIC) at the most detailed level (classes) are delineated according to what is, in most countries, the customary combination of activities described in statistical units. The groups and divisions, the successively broader levels of classification, combine the statistical units according to the character, technology, organization and financing of production. Wide use has been made of ISIC, both nationally and internationally, in classifying data according to kind of economic activity in the fields of population, production, employment, gross domestic product and other economic activities (Source: United Nations). ISIC is a basic tool for studying economic phenomena, fostering international comparability of data and for promoting the development of sound national statistical systems. Thus, despite the word "industrial" in its name, ISIC is not just a classification of industries.

联合国产业分类法和三次产业分类法保持着稳定的联系，其分类的十个大项,可以很容易地组合为三部分,从而同三次分类法相一致。

标准产业分类法对全部经济活动尽可能详尽地进行划分并使之规范化,因此它不仅对于各国的国民经济统计有很高的可比性,而且便于进行各种分析和研究,有广泛的实用性。在研究产业之间联系时使用的投入产出表的编制也是以联合国标准产业分类法为基础的。我国国家统计局发布的经济行业分类标准基本上是参照联合国标准产业分类法制定的,不过根据我国的实际情况做了一些必要的调整。

3. 资源集约度产业分类法(Resource Intensity Classification)

所谓资源是指投入生产活动的生产要素总和,如自然资源、劳动、资本技术等。根据不同的产业在生产过程中对资源依赖程度的差异,将产业划分为劳动密集型产业、资本密集型产业和技术密集型产业。这种划分方法明确了不同产业在利用资源上的显著特征,有助于从资源合理配置上来考虑确定相应的产业结构。

• 劳动密集型产业

在生产要素的配合比例中,是劳动力投入比重较高的产业,这是相对资金技术密集型产业而言的。在社会发展过程中,随着生产的发展,科学技术的进步,资本有机构成的提高,出现劳动密集型和资金技术密集型两种不同的产业类型。劳动密集型产业中物化劳动消耗比重较低,活劳动消耗比重较高。例如,机械工业、纺织工业和旅游产业属于劳动密集型产业。

• 资本密集型产业

资本密集型产业在生产要素的配合比例中,是资本(资金)投入比重较高的产业。例如,重工业、钢铁、汽车、机器制造和石油化学工业属于资本密集型产业。

• 技术密集型产业

又称知识密集型产业,指在生产要素的投入中需要使用复杂先进而又尖端的科学技术才能进行生产的产业,或者在作为生产要素的劳动中知识密集程度高的产业。例如,计算机产业既是技术密集型产业,又是劳动密集型产业。

除以上几种分类方法之外,还有其他许多产业分类方法。如按产业是处于增长或衰退状态可将产业分为朝阳产业(Sunrise Industry)和夕阳产业(Sunset Industry)。Sunrise industry is an industry growing quickly and expected to be increasingly important in the future. Sunset industry is an industry growing slowly or declining. 旅游业就属于典型

的朝阳产业。

另外还有生产结构分类法。生产结构产业分类法是指研究再生产过程中的产业之间的比例关系和相互联系的产业分类法。生产结构产业分类法中最具代表性的是霍夫曼分类法。霍夫曼为了研究工业化及其阶段,把工业产业分为三大类:消费资料产业(Consumption Goods Industries);资本资料产业(Capital Goods Industries);其他产业。由于旅游产业和这种分类方法没有太大关系,在此不做过多介绍。

二、产业结构的演进理论(Evolution Theory of Industrial Structure)

产业结构,是指社会再生产过程中,国民经济中各产业之间的生产技术经济联系和数量比例关系。产业结构演进理论主要研究经济发展过程中产业结构演变的特点及其规律,考察产业结构变化与经济发展过程的内在联系,并在此基础上体现出相应的产业结构政策的含义。产业结构理论研究的内容主要包括:第一,研究在一定的经济发展阶段,各个产业之间在量上的比例关系,结构不合理首先反映在各产业在量上的比例关系不合理。第二,研究各产业之间在质上的逻辑联系,即在分工基础上,各产业间的前后关联关系。在经济运行过程中,表面松散的各企业之间有其内部的逻辑联系,这种联系可在投入—产出表中直观地表现出来。主导产业是在特定的经济时期中,前项和后项的系数关联很高的产业,它是具有很大发展前途的产业。第三,考察产业结构高度与经济发展阶段的互动关系。产业结构高度化是指一个国家的产业结构随着经济发展的过程,所达到的阶段和层次,包括新技术的应用、各产业能力的不断提高、产业之间的更新换代。产业结构高度化的一个标志是第一产业下降,第二、三产业占有生产要素和产出能力的增加。

产业结构演进是指产业结构本身所固有的从低级到高级的变化趋势。

1. 李斯特产业结构阶段论(List's Stage Theory of Industrial Structure)

李斯特(1789—1846),在19世纪40年代,在其著作《政治经济学的国民体系》中提出经济学应是国民经济学,应研究怎样激发、增长和保护整个国家的生产力;认为经济发展有五个阶段,原始未开化时期、畜牧时期、农业时期、农工业时期和农工商时期。

2. 马列主义的再生产理论与两大部类增长规律(Marxist-Leninist's Theory of Reproduction and Growth Law of Two Major Departments)

马克思的社会再生产理论论述了两大部类之间的关系和生产资料优先发展规律。按实物形态划分,社会总产品分为生产资料和消费资料,社会生产相应分为两大部类:生产资料的生产,称为第 I 部类;消费资料的生产,称为第 II 部类。按价值形态划分,社会总产品由三部分组成:不变资本价值(C),可变资本价值(V)和剩余价值(M)。社会资本扩大再生产的实现条件,是第 I 部类 1 年内所生产的生产资料必须多于两大部类 1 年内所消耗的生产资料,以便第 2 年有多余的生产资料用于扩大再生产,可用公式表达为 I(C+V+M)>I(C)+II(C),也可简化表达为 I(V+M)>II(C)。这个公式在政治经济学中,被表述为生产资料的优先增长,这是我国建国以来集中力量优先发展重工业的主要理论依据。

3. 配第—克拉克定理(Petty Clark's Law)

英国科学家科林·克拉克在威廉·配第的基础上,深入分析研究就业人口在三次产业中分布结构的变动趋势后,得出了关于产业结构与劳动力分布关系的演变规律,即配第—克拉克定理。其主要结论是,随着经济的发展和人均国民收入水平的提高,劳动力首先由第一产业向第二产业移动;当人均国民收入水平进一步提高时,劳动力便由第二产业向第三产业移动。劳动力在产业间的分布状况为:第一产业将减少,第二、三产业将增加。人均国民收入水平越高的国家,农业劳动力在全部劳动力中所占的比重相对来说越小,而第二、三产业中劳动力所占的比重相对来说越大;反之,人均国民收入水平越低的国家,农业劳动力所占的比重相对越大,而第二、三次产业劳动力所占比重相对越小。These statistics are consistent with Petty-Clark's Law, which states that as an economy develops, its structure evolves from primary to secondary to tertiary (services).

4. 霍夫曼定理(C. Walther's Law)

1931 年德国经济学家霍夫曼(Walther Hoffmann)在《工业化的阶段和类型》(Growth of Industrial Economies)中提出了著名的霍夫曼定理。霍夫曼对工业产业结构的研究,是根据近二十个国家按时间序列的数据分析工业中消费资料产业和资本资料产业的比例关系,即消费资料产业的净产值与资本资料产业的净产值之比。这就是所谓的"霍夫曼系数"。随着工业化的进程,霍夫曼系数(消费资料产业净产值/资本资料产业净产值)呈现不断下降的趋势,这就是"霍夫曼定理"。

霍夫曼还根据霍夫曼系数的变化趋势,把工业化过程分成四个阶段:

- 重化学工业化过程。即工业结构由以轻工业为主转向以重化学工业为主的过程。
- 高加工度化过程。即工业结构由以原料工业为中心转向以加工、装配工业为中心的发展过程。
- 技术集约化过程。即工业主体结构经历由劳动密集型向资本密集型,最终向技术密集型工业转化的发展过程。
- 支柱产业的形成。支柱产业就是在特定经济时期和特定产业结构中对整个产业的发展贡献最大的产业。支柱产业一般具有广大的市场、很高的增长率、很强的产业关联度、大规模的产出能力、很高的利润率等五大特征。

工业化不仅是工业部门比重不断上升的过程,而且是工业部门内部结构不断变化的过程。霍夫曼从理论和经验上证明,工业化过程一般要经历三个阶段,第一阶段是消费品工业(如食品工业、纺织、烟草、家具等,相当于轻工业)居主导的阶段;第二阶段是资本品工业(如冶金、化工、机械、汽车等,相当于重工业)加速发展并逐步赶上消费品工业的阶段;第三阶段是资本品工业居主导的阶段。

5. 库兹涅茨理论(Kuznets' Theory)

库兹涅茨在继承克拉克研究成果的基础上,对产业结构的演变规律作了进一步探讨,阐明了劳动力和国民收入在产业间分布结构演变的一般趋势。他认为:大多数国家农业劳动力减少的趋势没有停止;工业化达到一定的水平以后,第二次产业不可能大量吸收劳动力;第三次产业的相对国民收入(=该产业的国民收入的相对比重/该产业的劳动力的相对比重),从时间序列分析来看,一般表现为下降趋势,但劳动力的相对比重是上升的。这说明第三次产业具有很强的吸收劳动力的特性,但是,劳动生产率的提高并不快。特别值得提起的是,第三次产业是这三个产业中规模最大的一个,无论从劳动力的相对比重、还是国民收入的相对比重上看都占一半以上。

根据库兹涅茨定理,第三次产业具有对劳动力的强吸附特性,故常常被称为吸纳劳动力的大蓄水池。如果从投入产出的效果来看,每投入

100万元可提供就业的岗位：重工业是400个，轻工业是700个，第三产业是1000个。这也符合库兹涅茨所说当工业化达到一定的水平以后，第二产业将不能吸纳大量的劳动力，第三产业的吸纳能力远大于第二产业，而且我国第三产业占CDP的比重与发达国家相比还有很大差距。据统计，发达国家第三产业占GDP的比重为50%—60%，而我国的第三产业仅占GDP的30%左右，所以发展的空间很大。据资料表明，如果不考虑第三产业单位增加值吸纳劳动力数量的变化，第三产业增长速度每提高1个百分点，则可多增加劳动就业人数200万人左右。如果我国第三产业比重能达到发展中国家的平均水平，则可增加数千万就业岗位。因此充分发挥第三产业门槛低、投入少、容量大的特点，将为绝大多数下岗失业人员提供一个迅速实现再就业的渠道。鉴于中国人多、劳动力资源丰富和资本短缺的基本国情，要解决就业问题，第三产业应为再就业的主攻方向。

第二节 旅游产业结构的影响因素
(Influential Factors of Tourism Industrial Structure)

一、旅游产业结构(Structure of Tourism Industry)

旅游产业结构是指旅游经济内各产业部门、各地区以及各种经济成分和经济活动的各环节的构成及其相互比例关系。主要包括旅游产业行业结构、地区结构、所有制结构、产品结构以及组织结构。其中旅游产业的地区结构和组织结构有单独章节讲述，所以在本章重点谈旅游产业的行业结构、所有制结构和产品结构。

应从以下几个方面理解旅游产业结构的内涵：第一，旅游产业结构反映的是旅游经济各个产业之间的生产、技术、经济联系。旅游产业是一个综合性很强的产业，在旅游经济内部，每一个经济活动都是以其他产业的经济活动为基础的，一个产业经济规模的变化必然导致与其相联系的其他产业规模的变动。第二，旅游产业结构是社会资源在旅游产业体系中配置的结果。从这一点上说，旅游产业结构是一个静止的状态，但这种静止只是一种相对的、短期的状态，同其他任何一种产业一样，资源配置的流向总是在不断的变化中。所以从长远来看，旅游产业结构永远处于动态的变化中，不存在一成不变的产业结构状态。第三，产业结构总是与特定的旅游产业政策相互作用。在完全的市场导向中，市场失效带来资源配置的无效从而导致产业结构的不合理。因此，在世界范围内,政府一定程度的干预经济,实行特定的产业政策,带来产业结构的调整。产业结构状态就是当前产业结构不合理的现状与国家产业政策之间的矛盾运动的结果。

二、旅游产业结构的影响因素(Influential Factors of Tourism Industrial Constitution)

1. 社会生产力发展水平的影响(Influence of Social Productivity Developmental Level)

市场力量使社会资源流向资源配置效率最大的行业和部门,社会生产力发展水平越高的国家和地区,市场机制发挥的作用越充分,资源流向就越趋于合理,各行业间的比例关系就越科学、合理。

2. 旅游产业发展模式的影响(Influence of Tourism Industry Developing Mode)

从旅游产业成长的协调机制来看,旅游产业发展模式可以分为市场型和政府主导型。在市场型模式中,旅游产业主要由市场这只"看不见的手"自动调节产业资源配置,旅游产业的成长侧重于产业内部的自均衡,在没有较大的经济性和非经济性外力影响下,各行业之间的比例关系在短期内不会有较大波动,相对于平缓。政府主导型的发展模式是以政府规划或者通过指定产业政策来干预旅游产业的成长与演进,政府通过调整产业内部各部门之间的比例关系达到一定的经济目标。

3. 旅游需求对旅游产业结构的影响(Influence of Tourism Demands on the Industry Structure)

需求决定供给,旅游需求的形式与规模的变化带来行业结构的调整。As has been noted, tourism is a very unusual product in which consumers must physically go to the place of production—the 'tourism factory'—to acquire the product, and the travel element is a part of the product itself. Frequently, the economic conditions prevailing in the destination are quite different from those in the generating area, particularly in international tourism and on long-haul visits. Thus it is not just economic variables affecting tourists in their home areas that will have an effect on demand. Table 2.1 provides a form of classification of the economic variables likely to affect tourism demand:

Table 2.1 Sources of Economic Influence on Tourism Demand

Generating area economic variables (Group A)	Destination economic variables (Group B)	Link variables (Group C)
Personal disposable income levels	General price level	Comparative prices between generator and destination
Distribution of incomes	Degree of supply competition	Promotional effort by destination in the generating area
Generating area economic variables (Group A)	Destination economic variables (Group B)	Link variables (Group C)
Holiday entitlements	Quality of tourism products	Exchange rates
Value of currency	Economic regulation of tourists	Time/cost of travel
Tax policy and controls on tourist spending		

The group A variables are those which act specifically on demand by all intending travel and tourism consumers in a generating area, regardless of their destination. They are largely concerned with overall constraints on the ability of buyers to enter tourism markets at all-constraints such as income and time at their disposal, and the degree of government permission for them to be tourists.

Group B variables define the economic attractiveness, all else being equal, of a tourism destination to consumers, wherever they may come from. These variables may be product-related or supply-related. Since there is competition between, as well as within, destination areas, conditions in a number of competing destinations will functionally act together, through substitution effects, to influence tourism demand.

Group C variables are in many ways the most interesting, emanating from the specific link between one generating area and one destination. That is, they will act only on demand for that destination from the one generating market. Once again, a link cannot be considered in isolation, but consumers are likely to take into account the link variables of several links, to competing destinations, include frontier crossing (perhaps measured by a quantified dummy variable) as a tourism demand constraint.

4. 产业政策的影响(Influence of Industrial Policies)

即使在市场经济高度发达的国家,政府也不会采取完全放任自流的产业态度,产业政策的实施既有长期的、中长期的、也有短期的。短期产业政策解决目前出现的急待解决的产业不合理状况,中长期产业政策是要在短期合理的基础上达到长期产业行业结构均衡。无论是短期的还是长期的产业政策的实施,都会影响到旅游产业内各行业之间不同的比例关系。

General economic policies, and those which may be directed at other sectors of the economy, may have substantial indirect effects on tourism. For example, business expenditure or 'fringe benefits' taxes may reduce demand for business travel and hospitality services through reduced tax deductibility; measures to control interest rates alter the marginal profitability of travel and tourism ventures. The directness of effects and their degree of influence are not necessarily correlated, as economy-wide policies may in the end have more pervasive influences throughout every channel of economic activity.

A government's general tourism policies are likely to reflect a range of objectives: economic, environmental, social/ educational/ diplomatic and so on. Almost always, the non economic policies have considerable economic implications for tourism, particularly if equity or normative judgments are involved. Increasingly, policies are likely to be composite, addressing economic as well as non economic issues.

第三节 我国旅游产业结构及优化
(The Structure and Optimization of Tourism Industry in China)

一、旅游产业结构优化的含义(Significance of Tourism Industry Optimization)

产业结构优化是指通过产业结构调整,使产业结构效率、产业结构水平不断提高的过程。旅游产业结构的优化是指通过一定的产业政策对旅游产业进行适度调整,使各个产业结构要素实现协调发展,保持符合产业发展规律和内在联系的比例关系,确保旅游产业持续、健康、稳定,促进旅游产业在国民经济中的比重不断加大,并满足社会和旅游者不断增长的需求的过程。它包括产业结构的合理化、高度化。

1. 合理化(Rationalization)

旅游产业结构的合理化,是指在现有技术水平上通过对旅游产业各种不同的结构要素的协调,使之有较强的相互转换能力,有较好的互补关系及和谐的配合,从而实现整个旅游产业的协调运行。

旅游产业结构的合理化是旅游产业各种不同的结构要素由不合理向合理发展的过程,要求建立起各结构要素之间最优的比例关系。旅游产业结构的合理化是一个阶段性的概念,不同的旅游业发展阶段有不同的、具体的合理化目标。例如:在我国刚刚开放入境旅游时,接待设施严重缺乏,旅游产业结构合理化的重点是加快旅游涉外饭店建设;而到目前我国旅游业经过20多年的积累和发展,旅游饭店已经有相当大的规模并出现相对过剩的局面,因此,在当前旅游产业行业结构中,合理化的一个目标就是要抑制饭店投资过热。阶段性的特点说明旅游产业结构变动中的随机协调,即在旅游产业结构的演变过程中,既要考虑其发展的动态规律性,使产业结构的变化具有适应性;同时又要考虑旅游业结构演变中的非常规性,加强旅游产业结构中的随机协调,从而在动态和随机的不均衡中促进旅游产业结构的协调。

旅游产业结构合理化又是一个动态的、相对的概念,是一定历史条件和旅游产业经济发展到一定阶段上的合理化,并随着旅游产业经济的发展将旅游产业结构不断推向更高阶段的合理化。

旅游产业结构合理化包括两个层次:一是宏观结构的合理化,即旅游产业的发展必须与国民经济整体发展相适应,与第一、第二产业发展的要求相协调,能够促进我国整体经济结构的调整。二是旅游产业内部各要素的合理化,与旅游经济发展相适应,平衡旅游市场供需矛盾,满足不断增长的旅游需求。三是旅游产业发展的区域合作与协调通过区域合作,共同开发,相互带动,相互促进,形成合理的产业布局。

2. 高度化(Upgrading)

旅游产业结构高度化,是指旅游产业结构在合理化的基础上,充分利用科技进步和社会分工的优势,使产业结构不断地向资源深加工、产出高附加值的方向发展,从而不断提高旅游生产要素的综合利用率,不断提高旅游经济效益。影响旅游产业结构的高级化主要有三个因素。一是旅游需求拉动。从需求决定供给的角度说,旅游需求不断地由低级形态向高级形态发展,势必要求旅游产业结构满足这种需求。例如,在20世纪80

年代,旅游对我国广大居民来说还属于奢侈品,旅游类型主要是短线的观光旅游。表现在旅行社行业中,规模小,很少甚至没有在组团社以外的旅游区设立分支机构,采取低级的客源地组团社—目的地接待社这种业务关联方式。进入90年代后半期,我国居民收入和休闲时间增加,旅游需求转变为长线的、板块式的度假旅游。反映在旅行社行业中,网络化兴起,一些有实力的旅行社在各旅游城市广设门市网点,有些触角已经伸及海外市场。二是竞争促进。市场经济是一个追求"优胜劣汰"的机制。

3. 合理化与高度化的关系(Relationship Between Rationalization and Upgrading)

旅游产业的合理化是高度化的基础。旅游产业结构高度化必须以旅游产业结构合理化为基础,只有实现了合理化,才能达到高度化。因为,产业结构高度化是相对稳定的,而产业结构合理化是经常性的,只有当产业结构实现了合理化,其结构效益积累到一定水平之后,才能推进旅游产业结构向高度化发展。

旅游产业结构合理化与高度化是相互渗透,相互作用的。旅游产业结构要实现高度化,必须先实现合理化。但是旅游产业结构的发展水平越高,其结构合理化的要求也就越高,即高层次上的合理化。因此,旅游产业结构合理化也是一个动态发展的过程,即不断调整旅游产业部门关系,调整其关联作用的过程,而这一过程本身就是旅游产业结构向高度化发展的过程。

二、旅游产业行业结构[1](Constitutions of Tourism Industry)

1. 旅游产业行业结构(Constitutions of Tourism Industry)

旅游产业的行业结构是指旅游产业在经济运行过程中所形成的各个行业、部门之间的比例关系以及相互作用关系。它是旅游产业的最基本的结构,包括旅游交通、旅游游览和旅游住宿、旅游餐饮、旅游购物、旅行社、娱乐等部门(见表2-2)。这些部门按递进关系横向构造旅游产品形成旅游的产业链,满足旅游者在旅游活动中的行、食、住、购、娱等基本

---

[1] 在旅游产业的行业结构方面,国内外学者对于旅游产业和旅游业这两个基本定义存在着分歧。一般旅游学著作都是把旅游产业和旅游业等同起来,在行业构成上旅游业的构成也是旅游产业的构成;但也有的学者认为旅游产业和旅游业是两个既有区别,又有联系,分别属于不同层次的概念(王兴斌,2000),也有旅游学者认为旅游产业不仅包括旅游业,而且旅游业仅仅是旅游产业的核心部分(张陆,2001)。本书对旅游产业的定义并不是从其行业构成上来规定的,而是根据旅游具有"空间移动(Movement of Person)"这一根本属性来定义的。

的旅游需求。它的形成是社会分工发展的结果,是伴随着人的消费方式的转变,逐渐从服务行业中脱离出来,通过社会的进一步分工而形成的新型行业。

旅游产业行业结构不仅是宏观旅游经济的运行结果,而且是旅游产业宏观控制与管理的对象。旅游产业结构的运行过程实质上是人们自觉依据旅游经济活动的内在的要求调整过程,它的合理状况不仅反映了人们对旅游经济的规律的认识程度,也反映了整个社会对旅游经济的控制能力。

表2-2 旅游产业行业结构构成图

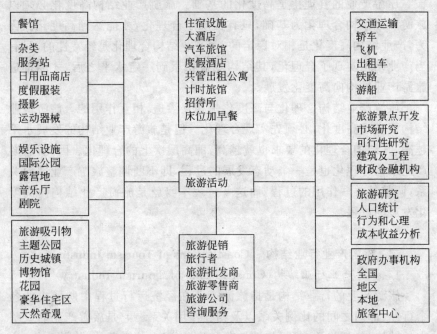

(资料来源:魏小安、王大悟,1998 转引自唐留雄,2002)

2. 旅游产业行业结构的优化(Optimizing the Structure of Tourism Industry)

旅游产业行业结构优化是在旅游经济运行中不同经济职能的行业或部门所形成的内在联系和数量比例关系。旅游产业行业结构既是社会分工的结果也是社会资源在旅游各行业、部门之间分配的表现形式,还是旅游生产内在比例关系在旅游各行业、部门间的具体反映。

旅游产业是一个相关性强、覆盖面广的产业。狭义的旅游产业是包括食、住、行、游、购、娱六大要素部门,但是从实现旅游交易持续发生来看,涉及旅游者经历中任何一个环节所需产品和服务都会影响下一次旅游经历的实现,因此更应注重与旅游者直接关联度不是那么高的的行业部门。所以优化旅游产业各行业部门结构首先要树立"大旅游"的概念。"大旅游"不仅包括六大要素,凡是向旅游者提供相关服务和产品的部门都应包含在内。

优化旅游产业结构要使与旅游产业关联度最高的六大要素部门保持相互协调,比例合适,既包括不要有瓶颈制约的供给不足的要素部门,又包括不要有"一枝独大"单个产业要素供给过剩的部门。任何一个产业都存在上下游部门链条,保持链条的畅通是这一产业良性运转的前提。旅游者旅行经历的位移性、时间性强的特点使得保持各部门的链条畅通更为重要。旅游车船不能满足旅游者从一个目的地到另一个目的地位移的实现,就不能说实现了旅游产品。同时旅游业又有明显的季节性制约导致产业需求弹性较大。拿一个饭店的投资规模来说,在旅游旺季,最大接待人次是500间客房,淡季为100间,那么饭店是建成大型饭店还是建成中型饭店?建成大型饭店能满足旺季旅游者的住宿要求,但在淡季房间的闲置带来大量沉淀成本和维修费用。建成中型饭店却又丧失了旺季盈利机会。

从旅游的六大要素来说,目前我国的旅游购物处于最薄弱的环节。发达国家的旅游购物一般会占到旅游总收入的30%,2001年我国的旅游购物只占20%。而旅游购物作为"无限"花费,在旅游产业的构成要素中有可挖掘的经济效益的潜力。世界上许多旅游发达的国家和地区都十分重视发展旅游购物。旅游购物所占比重的增加也是旅游产业结构优化的表现。

三、旅游产业所有制结构(The Structure of Tourism Industry Ownership)

旅游产业所有制结构是旅游产业经济运行过程中,各种所有制成分在旅游产业经济中的构成、地位及其相互作用。

1. 我国旅游产业所有制结构的现状(The Current Situation of the Ownership Composition of Travel Industry in our Country)

(1) 多种所有制成分并存。目前我国旅游产业所有制形式包括国有经济、集体经济、私营经济、个体经济和外商投资经济五种成分,形成了多种经济成分共同发展的格局。

(2) 旅游产业中国有经济成分占主体地位。

(3) 各经济成分在不同的产业中所占的比重是不同的,有轻有重。在中国旅游饭店和相关旅游住宿业结构中,尽管自 1987 年以来国有旅游涉外饭店企业数和客房数量在全国旅游涉外饭店中的比重呈下降趋势,但是国有资产至今仍然居于绝对多数份额的地位。

2. 所有制结构的优化思路(Thought of the Optimization of the Ownership Composition)

(1) 加快产权制度改革,建立以股份制为代表的现代企业制度

所有制结构的合理化不仅表现在各种经济成分有适当的比例关系,还内在要求各种经济成分支配社会资源的有效性。而在目前我国国有资本占绝大比例的一些产业中,产权关系不明晰、所有者缺位、激励机制和约束机制弱化等现实是制约产业发展的一大障碍,也是困扰所有制结构合理化的一大难题。以股份制为代表的现代企业制度要求产权明晰、责权明确,首先有利于吸收各种经济成分,改变国有资产"一枝独大"的不合理局面,其次保证了各种所有制类型的资产有人负责,有激励机制和约束机制双重刚性制约。

上市公司的发展是我国旅游业开拓资本运营的新方式,对推动旅游业发展的作用也日益突显。一是上市公司按照现代企业制度规范组建和运营;二是对旅游业的各类经济资源在新的层面上进行组合,有利于优化产业结构;三是股市上募集资金有助于缓解局部短缺局面,同时为国有经济成分的资本拓宽了投资渠道,有利于所有制结构的优化。

(2) 促进民营经济发展壮大(Promoting the Development of Private Economy)

旅游产业作为第三产业并非是关系国家命运安全的产业,根据国家"有进有退"、"有所为有所不为"的产业政策,吸引大量民间资本进入旅游行业,对优化我国旅游产业结构所有制结构,弥补旅游发展资金缺口,促进旅游产业的发展意义重大。

吸引民营经济进入旅游产业首先要创造一个对民营企业来说更为有利的发展环境。目前在许多领域还存在对民营经济的歧视性政策。首先要放宽民营企业所进入的领域,允许外资进入的领域都应对民营企业放开,真正享受国民待遇。其次完善相关配套措施,尤其是完善对民营企业在注册、税收、金融、收费服务、国际贸易等方面的政策。再次是改进服务,减少审批手续和行政干预。

目前在不同的旅游各产业内,民营经济的渗入程度是不同的。旅行

社行业民营资本的发育程度是最高的,由于所需要的资金少,进入障碍主要是政策性壁垒,国家旅游局逐步放开对旅行社行业的政策性歧视后可以预计民营经济成分在旅行社行业所占比重还会有更大的发展空间。饭店行业由于所需资金数额巨大,相对于国家鼓励开办合资饭店来说,对民营经济的开放要晚,但是近几年由于旅游业整体发展态势的良好,我国民营经济的发展壮大使之看好旅游市场这一投资领域,民营经济在饭店业中的比重上升很快。在旅游产业的三大支柱行业中景区、景点业中民营经济成分的比重是最低的。这与人们传统观念中根深蒂固的思想是分不开的,认为景区、景点属于国家资源,所有权属于全国人民,民营资本介入是搞私有化,损害了全国人民的共同利益。其实在目前我国政策允许的范围内,民营资本介入的只是景区景点的经营权领域,还远远没有触及所有权。而且近年来不乏大型民营资本介入景区景点的经营开发,通过探索新的治理模式,形成良好的发展态势,把保护和开发很好的结合起来的成功范例。

(3) 处理好流量和存量的关系,通过改变两者的比例达到所有制结构的优化。(Handling Properly the Relationship Between the Flow and the Reserved in Order to Optimize the Ownership Structure Through Modification of Their Proportion in Traveling Industry)

旅游产业的存量是指现有旅游产业的总资产,流量是指今后新注入的资产。在旅游产业中,存量结构突出地表现为国有经济成分比重过大,优化所有制结构可以通过增加新的经济成分这种流量加大非国有经济的相对比重的方式,还可以通过把原有国有经济成分这种存量以合适的方式退出,减少国有经济的相对比重的方式。经过近20年的摸索,我们已经探索出几种有效的退出的方式:(1)外部自然人或法人买断。即自然人、法人、集体用现金或其他财务杠杆买断企业中国有成分的全部产权,实现民营化。(2)内部职工买断型。对于那些资产存量较少,债务负担较轻的企业,内部全体或部分职工以现金或政府认可的有价证券买断所有权,企业可以转换为股份有限公司或有限责任公司。(3)引进法人资本和社会资本重组企业,促使股权结构多元化。(4)国有经济成分不变,不再增加国家对企业的政策性投资,使国有经济成分的比重逐步减少。

四、旅游产业的产品结构(Product Constitution of Tourism Industy)

1. 我国旅游产品结构现状及存在的问题(The Current Situation and Existing Problems of the Traveling Product Structure)

我国旅游产业经过20多年的发展,旅游产品结构已经形成了一定的结构体系。从整体旅游产品类型来说:(1)类型比较齐全,观光旅游、度假旅游、探亲访友旅游、专项旅游等旅游产品已经具备了一定的市场供给能力,能够满足不同的旅游消费者的需求。(2)特别是传统的观光型旅游已经进入成熟期。(3)新兴旅游产品异军突起,以满足不同旅游者需求的多样化、个性化。如:探险旅游、体育健身旅游、修学旅游等。(4)旅游产品更加注重环境保护因素,突出地表现为近年来蓬勃发展的生态旅游、农业旅游。

从各旅游行业部门提供的单项旅游产品来说,各单项旅游产品种类比较齐全,基本能满足不同层次的旅游消费者的需要。比如旅游饭店行业,我国星级旅游饭店接近八千家,从一星级到五星级,饭店提供的住宿设施和服务,类型多样;此外还有非星级的社会住宿业,为更经济型的旅游消费者提供更为广阔的选择。在旅行社行业,虽然我国目前依然采用国内社、国际社的水平分工体系,但在提供的旅游产品上,可以提供外国旅游者的来华旅游、中国公民的出境游以及国内旅游。在旅行社的产品类型上,既有小到代办票务、安排食宿;又有大到整条旅游线路的设计、旅游者的接待游览。在景区景点业,有传统的以自然旅游资源为吸引力的名山、大川、峡谷、森林;有以人文旅游资源为吸引力的园林、洞窟、寺庙;还有近几年兴起的以娱乐性、趣味性为主的主题公园等等。

我国旅游产品虽然呈现出多种多样的发展趋势,但在产品结构和产品深度上还存在许多问题。首先,旅游产品大多停留在表层开发,属于初级产品;其次,旅游产品文化内涵挖掘不够,大量的人文旅游资源特别是人造景观的开发停留在浅层次的开发上;再次,旅游产品结构在门类上表现出不同区域的雷同,景区景点开发中的无序性,导致大批旅游景点倒闭,加剧了区域间不合理的、低层次的竞争。

2. 优化我国旅游产品结构的思路(Thought on the Optimization of the Traveling Product Structure in our Country)

(1)提高旅游产品的升级换代(Progress in the Upgrading of Traveling Product)

随着旅游产业的发展,旅游市场的不断成熟,旅游需求呈现多样性、个性化的趋势。原有的单一以观光旅游为主的旅游产品结构体系不再适应旅游消费需求的发展趋势。观光旅游实际上处于多种旅游产品的较低层次，对一个旅游目的地的自然旅游资源条件依赖程度比较大，在产品开发方面可以不做大的文章。而作为旅游产品较高层次的度假旅游、专项旅游开发商在产品设计、产品定位、产品开发上有较高的要求。从产业的角度讲，度假旅游、专项旅游的附加值比较高，对旅游目的地的经济效益更加突出。旅游产品的升级换代应该从两个层面上展开：一是由单一以观光旅游产品向多层次产品结构转变，多层次结构应该包括传统的观光产品，还应该包括度假旅游产品、特色旅游产品、专项旅游产品、生态旅游产品。特别是生态旅游产品，符合旅游业可持续发展的需要，顺应了国际化发展趋势，更应大力倡导。二是单一旅游产品本身也要不断提高档次，丰富产品内涵，不断开发特色旅游项目。只有那些文化内涵丰富、富有浓郁地方特色、民族风情的、参与性强的旅游产品才能满足旅游者不断提升的旅游需求，才有更加广阔的发展空间。

（2）加强宏观调控，科学规划旅游产品开发(Strengthening Macro Adjustments and Controls and Programming the Development of Traveling Product Scientifically)

旅游开发主管部门在旅游资源开发中要加强规划引导，对那些资源丰富、有独特开发价值、品位高的旅游产品要着眼于长远，充分考虑当前旅游发展趋势，结合当地、当时开发能力，力求出精品；对那些目前虽然有开发价值，但开发难度较大的旅游产品项目，不能急于开发；对那些虽然有特色，但对生态自然环境有较大破坏作用的旅游项目，要谨慎开发；对那些地方政府单纯从短期经济效益出发，盲目抄袭，简单雷同的旅游项目，要严格把关，拒绝审批。

（3）提升旅游产品的文化内涵(Improving the Cultural Connotation of Traveling Product)

无论是整体旅游产品，还是单项旅游产品，丰富的、独特的文化内涵是保持产品具有生命力、吸引旅游者的内在动力。首先，旅游产品的文化内涵是人们赋予的，它与旅游资源的丰富程度没有必然的联系。例如，我国的深圳属于一个旅游资源相对贫乏的城市，但是深圳的"欢乐谷"，"锦绣中华"等旅游产品每年吸引大量的旅游者前往，这与旅游产品所内涵的文化因素是分不开的。其次，展现旅游产品的文化内涵，容易陷入一个文化虚假化的误区。我国西部少数民族地区，为发展旅游业，吸引旅游者，开发本民族的风情表演，这原本是一个蕴涵丰富文化内涵的旅游产品。但是作为表演形式的产品，常年累月的重复和演出者的职业化使得风情表演原汁原味的民族特色日渐消退，旅游者感受到的只是一种商业性的演出。保持以演出为表现形式的文化性旅游产品的持久生命力是目前比较难以解决的问题。再次，文化性旅游产品要注意如何向旅游者传递的问题。文化性旅游产品之所以吸引旅游者，是因为它的"新"、"奇"、"异"。不同的旅游者对文化内涵的理解受制于他的文化背景、生活阅历以及知识丰富程度。因此传递文化内涵时，要照顾不同旅游者的需要。

复习思考题：
1. 如何理解产业结构和旅游产业结构的内涵？
2. 根据不同的产业结构演进理论，分析产业结构具有什么样的演进趋势。
3. 影响旅游产业结构的因素有哪些？旅游需求如何对旅游产业结构产生影响？
4. 我国旅游产业结构存在哪些问题？如何对其进行优化？

第三章 旅游产业关联分析
(The Analysis of the Relevancy of Tourism Industry)

第一节 产业关联的内涵
(The Connotation of Relevancy of the Industry)

产业关联理论由美国经济学家瓦西里·列昂惕夫（Wassily Leontief,1906）首先提出。产业关联理论是借助投入产出表等对产业之间在生产、交换、分配上的关系进行分析的一种方法。旅游产业关联分析是用投入产出表分析旅游产业与相关产业之间的关联关系的一种方法。

一、产业关联概念(Concept of Relevancy of the Industry)

1. 产业关联(Relevancy of the Industry)

在一般的经济活动过程中,各产业都需要其他产业为自己提供各种产出,以作为自己的要素供给;同时,又把自己的产出作为一种市场需求提供给其他产业进行消费。在经济活动中,各产业之间存在着广泛的、复杂的和密切的技术经济联系。这种技术经济联系在产业经济学中也被称之为产业关联。

2. 旅游产业关联(Relevancy of Tourism Industry)

在旅游活动中,旅游产业与其他产业或部门之间存在的技术经济联系构成旅游产业关联。旅游的产业特性决定了旅游产业与其他产业的关联程度较高,一项旅游活动的完成需要多个产业的密切配合。因此,旅游产业与其他产业之间存在着密切的关联关系,具体表现在:

- 产品和服务关联

旅游业以其他相关产业或部门提供的产品或服务为依托,如交通运输部门、住宿部门、餐饮业等。由于旅游活动在客观上涵盖了"吃、住、行、游、购、娱"六要素,这一特点就决定了它包容的物质产品内容非常丰富,进而决定了旅游活动可以直接带动和推进相关社会生产活动的不断深化和发展,这种高度的关联带动功能,使得旅游业无可取代地占据了一个产业群体的核心地位。在这个核心地位中,旅游业就好比一个晶体的晶核,对与之关联的建筑、交通、饭店、餐饮、娱乐、商贸、工艺美术以及工农业的许多行业都能起到直接或间接的带动作用。

- 生产技术关联

科技是第一生产力。科学技术运用于旅游产业,同样会对旅游经济的发展产生巨大的推动力。如网络发展,信息技术革命,旅游业营销、旅游资源开发利用等通过新的生产技术,以更快的速度向前发展。

- 投入产出关联

旅游业消耗其他产业部门的生产产品和服务,因此形成"投入"、"产出"关系,即以货币为媒介的等价交换。

- 劳动就业关联

旅游业是劳动密集型产业,为社会提供大量就业机会。由于旅游活动涉及到"吃、住、行、游、购、娱"等诸多行业,也就能在多种行业范围中创造和提供更多的就业机会。据统计,旅游业自身就业人数在1000万左右,带动就业人口比例为1:5左右,提供机会多,就业成本低,国家投入不大,经济效益显著。因此,从扩大就业,发展经济,稳定社会等积极意义方面着眼,旅游业无疑可以成为新的经济增长点。

- 投资关联

旅游业的发展,要通过相关产业部门的协调发展来实现,这就需要一定数量的投资。旅游业要发展,需要进行必要的旅游投资,对旅游基础设施,如道路交通和饭店宾馆的投资,必定带动相关产业如建筑行业的发展。这就是旅游投资乘数效应。旅游业具有较高的经济效益和较强的国际竞争力。旅游业是一个融劳动密集型产品、资金密集型产品、技术密集型产品于一体的综合性行业,因而在商品经济由低到高的发展过程中,可以在各个阶段同时并存,寻求发展,参与竞争。中国旅游资源不仅非常丰富,且大多得天独厚;同时,作为一个人口大国,我国还有丰富的劳动力资源。依照国际间对外贸易形成和发展的基本依据——比较利益原则看,一个国家所生产的成本最低和资源拥有量最丰富的商品必然是对外贸易中比较利益最大的商品,那么与其他产业相比,中国旅游业确实是国际市场上发展潜力最大、竞争能力最强、创汇条件最优的产业之一。

二、产业关联方式（Ways of the Relevancy of Industry）

目前的产业关联方式可分为以下几种：

1. 前向关联与后向关联（Forward Relevancy and Afterward Relevancy）

发展经济学家赫希曼在《经济发展战略》中论述了产业关联在不同经济发展战略选择中的重要作用。前向关联是指某一产业的产品在其他产业中的利用而形成的产业关联。后向关联是指某一产业在生产过程中需要从其他产业获得投入所形成的依赖关系。二者会形成一种动力，以促进相关产业发展。旅游产业需要交通运输部门、通讯部门、信息技术部门等产业提供产品和服务，因此，相关部门的发展影响旅游业的成长，表现为后向关联性较强。

2. 单向关联与多向关联（Undirectional Relevancy and Multiple Relevancy）

单向关联是指一系列产业部门间，后面的产业部门直接消耗前一个产业部门生产的产品或服务，而后续产业部门生产的产品或服务并不为前一个产业部门服务。如橡胶厂生产的橡胶被轮胎厂加工成车轮，之后成为装配汽车的原配件，最终制造出汽车。多向关联是指各产业部门之间生产的产品和服务在产业之间循环消耗。旅游产业既存在单向关联也存多向关联，其中单向关联占主体。正确认识旅游产业的单向关联和多向关联，有助于提高旅游资源利用效率和旅游经济效益。

3. 直接关联与间接关联（Direct Relevancy and Indirect Relevancy）

直接关联是指具有直接的投入产出关系的各产业之间的联系；间接关联是指两个产业部门不发生直接的产品或服务联系，通过其他产业部门的中介才有关联。根据投入产出表计算直接消耗系数和资金消耗系数，分析制定产业发展规划。由直接消耗系数和资金消耗系数反映产业之间直接关联和间接关联关系。前向、后向、单向、循环关联中相邻两个产业之间的联系都是直接关联。

三、产业关联效应（Effect of the Relevancy of the Industry）

在产业链条上，大部分单位既是供给者，又是市场的需求者。作为供给者，它通过向其他产业提供要素的投入，来确立自己在产业链中的地位;而作为需求方,则通过对其他产业产出的消费,来显示其在产业链中的作用。在产业经济学中,可以利用关联系数对某个产业的直接关联效应进行分析。

设 $X=(X_{ij})n \cdot n$ 为中间投入矩阵。其中,X 的第 i 个行向量,即为 i 产业作为供给者对其他产业的投入;而 X 的第 j 个列向量就是 j 产业作为需求方从其他产业所获得的各种收入。

前向关联效应的计算公式为:

$$Lf(i)=(\Sigma X_{ij})/X_i \quad (i=1,2,\cdots,n)$$

式中:$Lf(i)$ 是第 i 项产业前向关联指数,X_{ij} 为 i 产业对 j 产业提供的中间投入,X_i 为 i 产业的全部产出。

后向关联效应的计算公式为:

$$Lb(j)=(\Sigma X_{ij})/X_j \quad (j=1,2,\cdots,n)$$

式中 $Lb(j)$ 为 j 产业的后向关联指数,X_j 为 j 产业的全部产出,X_{ij} 为 j 产业从 i 产业获得的中间投入。

第二节 投入产出法(Input-Output Method)

一、投入产出法(Input-Output Method)

投入产出法,是由美国经济学家瓦西里·列昂惕夫创立的。Since he was a young man growing up in St. Petersburg, Wassily Leontief devoted his studies to input-output analysis. When he left Russia at the age of nineteen to begin the Ph. D. program at the University of Berlin, he had already shown how Leon Walras's abstract equilibrium theory could be quantified.① But it was not until many years later, in 1941, while a professor at Harvard, that Leontief calculated an input-output table for the American economy.② It was this work, and later

---

① 列昂惕夫的"投入产出分析"的理论基础和所使用的数学方法,主要来自于瓦尔拉斯的"一般均衡模型"(瓦尔拉斯在《纯粹政治经济学要义》一书中首次提出(1874年))。因此,列昂惕夫称投入产出模型是"古典的一般均衡理论的简化方案"。

② 1941年列昂惕夫出版了《美国经济结构,1919—1929》一书,详细地介绍了"投入产出分析"的基本内容。到1953年又出版了《美国经济结构研究》一书,进一步阐述了"投入产出分析"的基本原理和发展。

refinements of it, that earned Leontief the Nobel Prize in 1973.[①] Throughout his life Leontief campaigned against "theoretical assumptions and nonobserved facts"[②] According to Leontief too many economists were reluctant to "get their hands dirty" by working with raw empirical facts. To that end Wassily Leontief did much to make quantitative data more accessible, and more indispensable, to the study of economics.

1. 投入产出法(Input-Output Method)

投入产出法,作为一种科学的方法,是研究经济体系(国民经济、地区经济、部门经济、公司或企业经济单位)中各个部分之间投入与产出的相互依存关系的数量分析方法。其中投入是指产品生产所消耗的原材料、燃料、动力、固定资产折旧和劳动力等生产性消耗;产出是指产品生产出来后的分配去向、流向。

投入产出法主要是通过编制投入产出表、建立相应的线性代数方程体系(即投入产出模型),综合分析和确定国民经济各部门之间错综复杂的联系,分析重要的宏观经济比例关系及产业结构等基本问题。其中投入产出表是指反映各种产品生产投入来源和去向的一种棋盘式表格。投入产出模型是指用数学形式体现投入产出表所反映的经济内容的线性代数方程组。

通过编制投入产出表和模型,能够清晰地揭示国民经济各部门、产业结构之间的内在联系。特别是能够反映国民经济中各部门、各产业之间在生产过程中的直接与间接联系,以及各部门、各产业生产与分配使用、生产与消耗之间的平衡(均衡)关系。正因为如此,投入产出法又称为部门联系平衡法。

目前,投入产出分析已经拓展到经济研究领域的各个方面,如为编制经济计划,特别是为编制中、长期计划提供依据;分析经济结构,进行经济预测;研究经济政策对经济生活的影响;研究某些专门的社会问题,如污染、人口、就业以及收入分配等问题。此外,投入产出法还可以推广应用于各地区、国民经济各部门和各企业等类似问题的分析。当用于地

---

① 列昂惕夫由于在"投入产出分析"研究中做出的卓越贡献,于1973年获得第五届诺贝尔经济学奖。

② It is the title of a speech Leontief delivered as president of the American Economic Association, 1970-1971.

区问题时,它反映的是地区内部之间的内在联系;当用于某一部门时,它反映的是该部门各类产品之间的内在联系;当用于公司或企业时,它反映的是其内部各工序之间的内在联系。

2. 投入产出法的基本特点(Basic Characters of Input-Output Method):

- 它从国民经济是一个有机整体的观点出发,综合研究各个具体部门之间的数量关系(技术经济联系)。整体性是投入产出法最重要的特点。
- 投入产出表从生产消耗和分配使用两个方面同时反映产品在部门之间的运动过程,也就是同时反映产品的价值形成过程和使用价值的运动过程。
- 从方法的角度,它通过各系数,一方面反映在一定技术和生产组织条件下,国民经济各部门的技术经济联系;另一方面用以测定和体现社会总产品与中间产品、社会总产品与最终产品之间的数量联系。其中两个最重要的系数是:
  直接消耗系数:单位总产品生产中消耗劳动对象和生产性服务产品的数量。中间产品与总产品之间的数量联系正是通过它表现出来的。
  完全消耗系数:单位最终产品的生产中对其他部门提供的总产品或中间产品的全部消耗量。这里所谓全部消耗量除直接消耗外,还包括通过以前各生产阶段中其他中间产品所转移过来的同类的间接消耗在内。最终产品与总产品之间的数量联系正是通过它表现出来的。
- 数学方法和电子计算技术的结合。

二、投入产出表和投入产出分析(Input-Output Table and Input-Output Analysis)

投入产出表(input-output table)又称里昂惕夫表、产业联系表或部门联系平衡表,是反映国民经济各部门间投入与产出关系的平衡表。理论上,投入产出表所反映的是部门之间的联系,是生产技术经济联系。因此,表中(见表3-1)第一部分(即表示中间产品的部分)是投入产出表的核心部分,即所反映的主要是部门之间的生产技术联系。[①] 国民经济每个部门既是生产产品(产出)的部门,又是消耗产品(投入)的部门。投入产出表是以所有部门的产出去向为行、投入来源为列而组成的棋盘式表格,主要说明两个基本关系。一个关系是,每一部门的总产出等于它所生产的中间产品与最终产品之和,中间产品应能满足各部门投入的需要,最终产品应能满足积累和消费的需要。另一个关系是,每一部门的投入就是它生产中直接需要消耗的各部门的中间产品,在生产技术条件不变的前提下,投入决定于它的总产出。投入产出表按计量单位可分为实物型和价值型两种,实物型是以实物量单位编制的,价值型是以货币单位编制的。按时间划分,有统计和计划投入产出表。按性质划分有静态和动态,平衡和优化投入产出表。按内容划分,有产品、固定资产、生产能力、投资和劳动消耗等投入产出表。编制投入产出表是进行投入产出分析的前提。

表 3-1 投入产出表

	$1, 2 \cdots, n$ 中间产品	最终产品 Y	总产品
物质消耗 $1, 2, \cdots, n$	$X_{11} \cdots X_{n1}$ $\vdots$ $X_{n1} \cdots X_{nn}$	Y_1 $\vdots$ Y_n	X_1 $\vdots$ X_n
净产值 LM	$N_1 \cdots N_n$		
总产值	$X_1 \cdots X_n$		

投入产出分析研究经济系统各个部分(作为生产单位或消费单位的产业部门、行业、产品等)之间表现为投入和产出的相互依存关系的经济数量分析方法。Input-output analysis shows the extensive process by which inputs in one industry produce outputs for consumption or for input into another industry. 投入产出分析从一般均衡理论中吸收了有关经济活动的相互依存性的观点,并用代数联立方程体系来描述这种相互依存关系。其特点是:在考察部门间错综复杂的投入产出关系时,能

---

① 它也反映经济联系,特别是在价值形态表的条件下,因为这时表中各元素受价格和各种结构变动的影响。

够发现任何局部的最初变化对经济体系各个部分的影响。The matrix devised by Leontief is often used to show the effect of a change in production of a final good on the demand for inputs. Take, for example, a 10 percent increase in the production of shoes. With the input-output table, one can estimate how much additional leather, labor, machinery, and other inputs will be required to increase shoe production.

Most economists are cautious in using the table. The reason is that it assumes, to take the shoe example, that shoe production requires the inputs in the proportion they were used during the time period used to estimate the table. Therein lies the rub. Although the table is useful as a rough approximation of the inputs required, economists know from mountains of evidence that proportions are not fixed. Specifically, when the cost of one input rises, producers reduce their use of this input and substitute other inputs whose prices have not risen. If wage rates rise, for example, producers can substitute capital for labor and, by accepting more wasted materials, can even substitute raw materials for labor. That the input-output table is inflexible means that if used literally to make predictions, it will necessarily give wrong answers.

Early on, input-output analysis was used to estimate the economy-wide impact of converting from war production to civilian production after World War II. It has also been used to understand the flow of trade between countries. Indeed, a 1954 article by Leontief showed, using input-output analysis, that U.S. exports were relatively labor-intensive compared to U.S. imports. This was the opposite of what economists expected at the time, given the high level of U.S. wages and the relatively high amount of capital per worker in the United States. Leontief's finding was termed the Leontief paradox. Since then, the paradox has been resolved. Economists have shown that in a country that produces more than two goods, the abundance of capital relative to labor does not imply that the capital intensity of its exports should exceed that of its imports.

At the time of Leontief's first work with input-output analysis, all the required matrix algebra was done using, as inputs, hand-held calculators and sheer tenacity. Since then, computers have greatly simplified the process, and input-output analysis, now called "inter-industry analysis", is widely used. Leontief's tables are commonly used by the World Bank, the United Nations, and the U.S. Department of Commerce.

三、投入产出模型(Input-Output Model)

是指用数学形式表示投入产出表所反映的经济内容的线性代数方程组。它是由系数(变量)的函数关系组成的数学方程组构成,而"直接消耗"等系数的计算和函数关系的确定,是依据投入产出表及其平衡关系式来确定。投入产出模型的建立分两步进行:先依据投入产出表计算各类系数,再依据投入产出表的平衡关系,建立投入产出模型。

1. 系数计算(Ratio Calculation)

(1) 直接消耗系数(Direct Consumption Ratio)

指某一个部门生产单位总产出需要直接消耗各部门产品和服务的数量,也称为投入系数。它反映该部门与其他部门之间直接的技术经济联系和直接依赖关系。

直接消耗系数又称投入系数,其经济含义是生产单位 j 产品所直接消耗的 i 产品的数量。依据投入产出表中的数据,将各产业部门的总产品去除它所消耗的各种投入要素量。直接消耗系数的计算公式为:

$$a_{ij} = x_{ij} / X_j \ (i, j = 1, 2, \cdots, n)$$

用矩阵表示,为:

$$A = Q X^{-1}$$

其中,

$$A = \begin{pmatrix} a_{11} & a_{12} & \cdots & a_{1n} \\ a_{21} & a_{21} & \cdots & a_{2n} \\ \vdots & \vdots & \vdots & \vdots \\ a_{n1} & a_{n1} & \cdots & a_{nn} \end{pmatrix}; \quad Q = \begin{pmatrix} a_{11} & a_{12} & \cdots & a_{1n} \\ a_{21} & a_{21} & \cdots & a_{2n} \\ \vdots & \vdots & \vdots & \vdots \\ a_{n1} & a_{n1} & \cdots & a_{nn} \end{pmatrix};$$

$$X^{-1} = \begin{pmatrix} 1/X_1 & 0 & \cdots & \cdots & 0 \\ 0 & 1/X_2 & \cdots & \cdots & 0 \\ 0 & 0 & 1/X_3 & \cdots & 0 \\ \cdots & \cdots & \cdots & \cdots & \cdots \\ 0 & 0 & 0 & \cdots & 1/X_n \end{pmatrix}$$

矩阵 A 为直接消耗系数矩阵，反映投入产出表中各产业部门间技术经济联系和产品之间的技术联系。直接消耗系数是建立模型最重要、最基本的系数。

（2）完全消耗系数（Full Consumption Ratio）

完全消耗系数是指增加某一个部门单位总产出需要完全消耗各部门产品和服务的数量。完全消耗系数等于直接消耗系数和全部间接消耗系数之和，它是全面揭示国民经济各部门之间技术经济的全部联系和相互依赖关系的主要指标。

完全消耗系数用公式表示：

$$b_{ij} = a_{ij} + \sum b_{ik} a_{kj} (i,j = 1,2,\cdots,n)$$

其中，b_{ij} 为完全消耗系数，表示生产单位 j 产品所直接和间接消耗 i 产品数量之和（$i,j=1,2,\cdots,n$）；a_{ij} 为直接消耗系数；$\sum b_{ik} a_{kj}$ 为间接消耗系数，其中 k 为中间产品部门，是通过 k 种中间产品而形成的生产单位 j 产品对 i 产品的全部间接消耗量。

用矩阵表示：

$$B = (I - A)^{-1} - I$$

其中，

$$A = \begin{pmatrix} a_{11} & a_{12} & \cdots & a_{1n} \\ a_{21} & a_{21} & \cdots & a_{2n} \\ \vdots & \vdots & \vdots & \vdots \\ a_{n1} & a_{n1} & \cdots & a_{nn} \end{pmatrix} ; \quad Q = \begin{pmatrix} a_{11} & a_{12} & \cdots & a_{1n} \\ a_{21} & a_{21} & \cdots & a_{2n} \\ \vdots & \vdots & \vdots & \vdots \\ a_{n1} & a_{n1} & \cdots & a_{nn} \end{pmatrix}$$

旅游产业与相关产业有着密切的联系，这些联系既包括直接联系，也包括间接联系。完全消耗系数反映一个部门的生产与其他部门发生的经济数量关系，比直接消耗系数更全面地反映部门内部和部门之间的技术经济联系。因此，分析旅游产业的完全消耗系数对于正确理解旅游经济和旅游产业结构十分重要。

2. 投入产出分析的运用（the Application of the Analysis of Input-Output）

The purpose of this set of exercises is to provide three more examples of the Leontief Input-Output Model in action.

The input-output model requires that the economy in question be divided into sectors. Each sector produces goods or services except for the open sector, which only consumes goods and services. A production vector x lists the output of each sector. A final demand vector (or bill of final demands) d lists the values of the goods and services demanded from the productive sectors by the open sector. As the sectors strive to produce enough goods to meet the final demand vector, they make intermediate demands for the products of each sector. These intermediate demands are described by the consumption matrix. This matrix is constructed as follows.

The description of the economy begins with a collection of data called an input-output table (or an exchange table) for an economy. This table lists the value of the goods produced by each sector and how much of that output is used by each sector. For example, the following table is derived from the table Leontief created for the American economy in 1947. (See References 1 or 2 for the complete table.) For purposes of this example the data from the 42 sectors has been collected into just 3: agriculture, manufacturing, and services. Of course, the open sector is also present.

表 3-2 Exchange of Goods and Services in the U.S. for 1947
(in billions of dollars, 1947)

	Agriculture	Manufacturing	Services	Open Sector
Agriculture	34.69	4.92	5.62	39.24
Manufacturing	5.28	61.82	22.99	60.02
Services	10.45	25.95	42.03	130.65
Total Gross Output	84.56	163.43	219.03	

Reading the table is straightforward; for example, in 1947 the agriculture sector spent 84.56 billion dollars for the inputs it needed. These inputs were divided among the sectors as follows: 34.69 billion dollars of agricultural output was consumed by the agriculture sector itself, 5.28 billion dollars of manufacturing output was consumed by the agriculture sector, etc.

To create the consumption matrix from the table, divide each column of the 3 × 3 table by the Total Gross Output for that sector. The result is the Table, which appears on the following page.

The matrix with entries taken from this table is the consumption *matrix* C for the economy.

$$C = \begin{bmatrix} .4102 & .0301 & .0257 \\ .0624 & .3783 & .1050 \\ .1236 & .1588 & .1919 \end{bmatrix}$$

	Agriculture	Manufacturing	Services
Agriculture	.4102	.0301	.0257
Manufacturing	.0624	.3783	.1050
Services	.1236	.1588	.1919

For the 1947 economy, the final demand vector d is the column of the table associated with the open sector:

$$d = \begin{bmatrix} 39.24 \\ 60.02 \\ 130.65 \end{bmatrix}$$

The equilibrium levels of production for each sector may now be calculated. These equilibrium levels are the production levels which will just meet the intermediate demands of the sectors of the economy plus the final demands of each sector. If x is the desired production vector, x must satisfy

$$x = C_x + d$$

This equation may be solved for x to find that

$$x = (I - C)^{-1} d$$

where I is the identity matrix.

In the example,

$$(I-C)^{-1} = \begin{bmatrix} 1.7203 & .1006 & .0678 \\ .2245 & 1.6768 & .2250 \\ .3073 & .3449 & 1.2921 \end{bmatrix}$$

and thus

$$x = (I-C)^{-1} d = \begin{bmatrix} 82.40 \\ 138.85 \\ 201.57 \end{bmatrix}$$

第三节 旅游产业关联分析[①]
(The Analysis of the Relevancy of the Tourism Industry)

应用投入—产出法对旅游业进行分析的前提是：旅游者的消费流向不同的行业，旅游者在每个行业中的花费(Y_i)可以看出该行业的最终需求的增加，将 Y 作为该行业的最终需求，分别计算出每一部分旅游花费引起的各个部门产出的改变量(X_i)，将每个行业的旅游消费引起的各部门产出的改变量(X_i)相加，就是旅游业对整个国民经济的影响。

为此，对目前最新的《1992年中国投入—产出表》按照旅游研究的需要重新进行了行业划分，并计算了直接消耗系数和完全消耗系数。在此基础上，得出了中国旅游业的直接投入结构和完全投入结构，并进一步探讨哪些部门是对旅游业提供产品和服务投入的部门，及其相应的比重，研究旅游业发展到一定阶段时，需要哪些产业及多大规模作为支撑条件。本节从定量角度验证了一个重要论断：旅游业与工业化之间存在着必然联系，并进一步指出，旅游业产业与重化学工业化及其相应的发展阶段是密切相联的。也就是说，一个国家的经济在发展到重化学工业化或相应阶段时，才会出现旅游业产业化现象。

表 3-3 的第一列为按照《1992年中国投入—产出表》重新划分后的部门，第二列为与之相对应的旅游者花费，第三列为 1995 年海外旅游者和国内旅游者花费中各部分所占的比重，第四列为在 1995 年海外旅游者花费 87.33 亿美元和国内旅游者花费 1375.5 亿元人民币情况下，海外旅游者和国内旅游者用于每个国民经济部门的消费，即每个国民经济部门的最终需求的增加量(Y_i)。

表 3-3　旅游消费所对应的国民经济部门

国民经济部门	旅游消费内容	旅游者花费的比重		旅游者花费额	
		国际	国内	国际(亿美元)	国内(亿元)
公用事业	市内交通、游览	7.3	9.2	6.38	126.55
居民服务业	住宿、娱乐	23.6	20.5	20.61	281.98
饮食业	餐饮	19.0	18.4	16.59	253.09
商业	商品销售	18.8	17.4	16.42	239.34

---

① 本节内容节选自闫敏《旅游业与经济发展水平之间的关系》，《旅游学刊》1999 年第 5 期。

续表

国民经济部门	旅游消费内容	旅游者花费的比重		旅游者花费额	
		国际	国内	国际(亿美元)	国内(亿元)
航空客运业	航空交通	17.1	12.3	14.93	169.19
铁路客运业	铁路交通	1.9	7.6	1.66	104.54
公路客运业	公路交通	1.5	3.7	1.31	50.89
水上客运业	海运内河交通和其他	2.6	3.0	2.27	41.27
邮电通讯业	邮电通讯	2.9	0.7	2.53	9.63
	其他	5.3	7.2	4.63	90.04

注：旅游消费中的"其他"部分，由于其去向没有明确的统计，且所占比重较小，在后面的研究中暂且忽略。

一、直接投入(Direct Input)

按照投入-产出原理，最终需求部门每增加的单位收入，都是在国民经济各部门的直接投入下取得的。这里以 1992 年投入-产出表国民经济各部门间的直接消耗系数为依据，计算在海外旅游者花费和国内旅游者花费分别为 87.33 亿美元和 1375.5 亿元人民币的情况下，分别需要国民经济各部门直接投入的产品和服务的价值量。计算的过程为：$I_i = A_i \times Y_i$，其中：I_i 为第 i 部门的直接投入价值量，$i=1,2,\cdots 9$，分别为邮电通讯业、商业、饮食业、铁路客运业、公路客运业、水上客运业、航空客运业、公用事业和居民服务业，Y_i 为旅游者用于第 i 个部门的花费，A_i 为第 i 个部门的直接消耗系数。

直接投入总和 $= \sum_{i=1}^{9} I_i$，即，将海外旅游者和国内旅游者花费按照表 3-3 的结构分解，作为旅游业直接相关部门最终需求的增加量，将每个部门最终需求的增加量与该部门的直接消耗系数相乘，得出国民经济各部门为满足该部门最终需求的增加而需要的投入量，将国民经济各部门为满足每个旅游业相关部门最终需求的增加所增加的投入量相加，得出为满足旅游者消费所需直接投入的产品和服务的价值量(见表 3-4)。

可以看出，为满足海外旅游者 87.32 亿美元的消费，国民经济各部门的直接投入为 369.1 亿元人民币，其中食品制造业投入的比重最高，占到各部门总投入的 14.1%，其次是交通运输设备制造业，占到直接投入的 13.0%，石化和化工工业排在第三位，占到 12.7%，农业占到 9.0%，商业为 8.8%，这 5 个部门的投入占到直接投入的 57.6%，其余的 24 个部门仅占到 42.4%。

为满足国内旅游者 1375.5 亿元人民币的消费,国民经济各部门需提供 658.2 亿元人民币的中间投入作为直接投入,其中食品制造业仍是最大的直接投入部门,占到直接投入的 14.0%,石化和化学工业排在第二位,占到 13.7%,交通运输设备制造业有所下降,为第三位,占到 12.0%,农业为第四位,占到 9.1%,商业为第五位,占到 8.8%,这 5 个产业同样占到直接投入的 57.6%。

国际旅游和国内旅游对各产业直接投入结构的要求基本没有大的差别,对国际和国内旅游业直接投入最大的部门依次是食品制造业、石化和化学工业、交通运输设备制造业、农业、商业、货运业等 6 个产业,它们对旅游业的直接投入分别约占到国民经济各部门对旅游业直接总投入近 60%。

表 3-4 国民经济各部门为满足旅游者花费所提供的直接投入

(单位:亿元人民币)

部门	海外旅游者花费要求其他部门投入		国内旅游者花费要求其他部门投入		合计占该部门总产出的比重
	价值量	比重	价值量	比重	
农业	33.3	9.0	59.8	9.1	1.02
采掘业	5.8	1.6	12.9	2.0	0.85
食品制造业	52.0	14.1	91.8	14.0	3.54
纺织业	6.1	1.7	10.0	1.5	0.42
缝纫及皮革制品业	1.9	0.5	3.1	0.5	0.33
木材加工及家具制造业	2.9	0.8	5.3	0.8	1.69
电力及蒸汽、热水生产和供应业	7.5	2.0	12.0	1.8	1.11
石油化工及化工工业	9.8	2.7	18.0	2.7	2.36
建筑材料及其他非金属矿物生产业	46.7	12.7	90.3	13.7	2.34
金属冶炼、压延加工和金属制品业	11.4	3.1	22.6	3.4	1.34
机械工业及机械设备修理业	8.8	2.4	17.7	2.7	0.58
交通运输设备制造业	9.6	2.6	19.0	2.9	0.70
电气、电子、通讯和仪器仪表设备	9.2	2.5	15.2	2.3	0.88
其他工业	7.0	1.9	12.1	1.8	2.43
建筑业	4.6	1.2	7.9	1.2	0.24
货运业	18.2	4.9	32.4	4.9	2.92
邮电通讯业	3.6	1.0	6.1	0.9	3.81
商业	32.6	8.8	58.2	8.8	1.64
饮食业	0.0	0.0	0.0	0.0	0.00
铁路客运业	1.1	0.3	2.1	0.3	1.98
公路客运业	1.1	0.3	1.9	0.3	0.91
水上客运业	1.1	0.3	2.0	0.3	3.78

续表

部门	海外旅游者花费要求其他部门投入		国内旅游者花费要求其他部门投入		合计占该部门总产出的比重
	价值量	比重	价值量	比重	
航空客运业	0.4	0.1	0.7	0.1	1.08
房地产业	9.3	2.5	15.8	2.4	3.60
公用事业	5.6	1.5	9.6	1.5	3.05
居民服务业	12.0	3.3	20.7	3.1	3.82
文教卫生科研事业和行政机关	5.8	1.6	10.6	1.6	0.39
金融保险业	13.7	3.7	21.3	3.2	2.04
合计	369.1	100.0	658.2	100.0	

注：①在《1992年中国投入-产出表》中的基本流量表里，没有对饮食业的产出情况进行调查，因此该项为空白，这在一定程度上造成结果上的误差，这一点以后不再说明。

②由于数据所限，"合计占该部门总产出比重"一项对应的是1992年各部门总产出量，因此只能作为粗略估计结果，实际值应当略低于上述结果。

资料来源：根据"直接消耗系数表"计算。

从部门产出的角度来看，交通运输设备制造业是对旅游业贡献最大的部门，它总产出的8%左右都提供给旅游业，其次是食品制造业、邮电通讯业、水上客运业、房地产业、公用事业和居民服务业，总产出中约有3%的产品和服务直接提供给旅游业，再次是电力及蒸汽热水生产和供应业、石油化工和化学工业、其他工业、货运业、铁路客运业、金融保险业等，对旅游提供的直接投入占该产业总产出的2%左右。这一结论与旅游业是一个"投资少，见效快"的观点有很大的差距。一般认为，旅游业直接消费的都是第三次产业部门的产品和服务，不会对国民经济结构产生压力，但从上述的结论来看完全不是这样。在旅游业的背后，需要石化和化学工业、交通运输设备制造业和农业这样基础性产业的大量投入。

直接投入引起的国民经济各部门的产出扩大将对继续引起各部门投入的再扩大，形成旅游业对国民经济各部门的间接影响（indirect）和引致影响（induced）。这需要从旅游业完全投入的角度来研究旅游业对国民经济各部门的影响。有兴趣的读者可以阅读闫敏的《旅游业与经济发展水平之间的关系》(《旅游学刊》1999.5)。

复习思考题：
1. 理解产业关联和旅游产业关联的内涵。
2. 什么叫投入产出法？投入产出法在测算旅游产业关联中如何使用？

第四章
旅游产业的区域结构
(Location Structure of Tourism Industry)

旅游业的发展离不开一定的地域空间,旅游产业区域结构的状况及变化是研究旅游经济发展的重要依据。旅游产业的布局是通过对旅游产业区域结构的研究,掌握旅游产业布局的原则,分析影响旅游产业区域布局的因素,探寻旅游业合理布局的内容和方法,促使旅游产业布局的合理化。旅游经济在区域内长期稳定的协调发展,关键在于旅游资源的合理配置和旅游产业各要素空间配置的合理化。事实证明,旅游经济的增长,不仅是在数量上的扩张,也是经济结构的转换过程,实现产业结构合理化的调整过程。旅游产业区域结构的调整,将对未来的旅游经济增长起着重要的作用。

对旅游产业空间结构的研究是从对旅游资源和旅游现象的描述转向对旅游地土地利用和区划研究,注重旅游业空间效应和旅游业的空间联系。目前,旅游产业区域结构的研究重点在于旅游业可持续发展和区域协调发展。传统的旅游业空间结构研究成果主要集中在以下几个方面:第一,旅游资源与旅游现象的分布及其区划工作。旅游学的研究在初期是对旅游业空间结构的初步研究,也就是对旅游资源和旅游现象的空间分布的描述。第二,旅游产业区域开发的研究。它往往与旅游资源的研究联系在一起,在旅游资源评价的基础上,进行开发条件的研究,最后回到旅游资源的开发上。第三,旅游产业区域规划的研究。它是旅游业发展到了一定规模以后,在较大范围内出现了竞争,在特定区域内开始的对以后旅游业的发展规模、速度、类型等进行一种超前计划的研究活动。区域规划的研究对象包括了旅游点、旅游线路、旅游区三个层次的由点到线到面构成的空间系统的建设和调控。

本章在对旅游产业区域结构基本理论阐述的基础上，对我国旅游产业区域结构的现状进行了描述，并对我国旅游产业区域结构合理化提出了对策。在本章最后，以西部旅游大开发为案例分析了旅游区域结构的协调与发展。

第一节 旅游产业区域结构的基本理论
（Basic Theories of Location Structure of Tourism Industry）

一、旅游产业区域结构的概念（Concept of Location Structure of Tourism Industry）

旅游产业区域结构是一定时期和一定区域范围内旅游业发展水平的相对差异程度的静态表现，从内涵上看，包括旅游企业及其发展的空间分布；在外延上看，包括旅游业空间要素的全部表现。旅游产业区域结构是旅游业布局和区域旅游业发展的直接后果，在旅游产业发展的不同阶段上，表现出不同的空间格局特色。所以旅游产业区域结构只是区域旅游业发展在一定阶段上的静态表现，是在旅游业不断发展中逐渐成熟的。

一个国家的旅游经济发展和旅游产业布局离不开一定的地域空间。只有对旅游产业各要素在地域空间上进行合理的配置和布局，才能实现旅游产业生产力的合理组织，最终实现旅游经济的效率目标与空间目标的和谐统一。

旅游产业区域结构是指旅游产业各要素在空间上的组成、分布及其相互关系，即从区域角度所反映的旅游资源、旅游交通、旅游市场等旅游产业要素的形成、数量、规模及相互关系和比例关系，简称旅游产业的生产力布局。旅游产业区域结构实质上是研究旅游生产力在空间上的分布与组织，也就是如何通过科学合理的布局使得生产能以较少的投入获得较大的收益的问题。

二、旅游产业区域结构的理论基础（Theoretical Basis of Location Structure of Tourism Industry）

（一）区位理论（Theory of Location）

区位理论，西方称之为"区位论"，是一种生产布局的理论，其宗旨是人类社会经济活动的空间法则，即社会经济活动（客体）在空间中的分布、运动、关联等。区位理论研究的实质是生产的最佳布局问题,即如何通过科学合理的布局使得生产能以较少的投入获得较大的收益。

1. 区位理论的产生与发展 (Derivation and Evolution of Location Theory)

区位理论并不是贯穿人类历史发展的整个过程,而是随着社会经济的发展,在生产和经营过程中逐渐形成的。资本主义工业革命以后,随着竞争的日益激烈,产品的运输成本和劳动力成本在很大程度上决定产品在市场上的竞争力,于是生产的最佳区位的选择就成为市场竞争中获胜的重要条件,于是产生了区位理论。

从区位理论思想的产生到现在,已经有了近三百年的发展历史,大致可以分为四个阶段:萌芽时期、古典理论时期、近代理论时期和现代理论时期。

在萌芽时期,区位理论还没有被作为一个独立的理论进行专门的研究,而仅仅是作为生产过程中的一个影响因素,在研究中加以关注。如1767年英国的斯秋阿特(J. Steuart)在《政治经济因素》一书中探讨地域分工时,就涉及了区位论的一些问题。

古典区位理论时期,又可称为微观研究阶段,因为研究的对象大多是单个的工业企业,追求单项的区位决策,反映的是静止、局部的均衡状况。代表人物有德国的农业经济学家杜能(von Thünen)。在他的第一部研究区位理论的著作《孤立国对于农业及国民经济之关系》(简称《孤立国》, *The Isolated State*, 1826)中对农业生产的空间布局模式进行了研究,并提出了他的农业生产圈层模型。

In 1826, von Thünen, an educated landowner in northern Germany, published a treatise, *The Isolated State*, which became one of the founding works in spatial economics and location theory. In this work, von Thünen gave a predictive model of rural development around an idealized isolated urban center, imposing several simplifications in an attempt to focus on some of the fundamental processes at work in settlement patterns and rural economic activity. It is presently a regular component of introductory economic geography courses. Despite criticisms for over-simplifications, it has persisted in geographic, economic, and rural development curricula.

到了近代区位理论时期,研究比古典区位理论时期更加宏观,考虑的因子更加复杂,并且在进行分析时大量引入了微观经济学的分析方法。此时的区位理论已从追求局部均衡发展到了追求一般,立足于一定的地区或城市,着眼于市场的扩大和优化。

现代区位理论是对系统进行连续而非间断的研究,强调合理地利用有限的资源和空间,促进区域间的动态平衡发展。它利用多种成本因素进行综合分析,既包括各种经济性成本要素,也包括其他的非经济性的成本要素(如制度、文化、心理、军事等因素),又借用计量学的方法,使用数学模型对区位问题进行预测性的分析,如美国的著名经济学家库兹涅兹(Kuznets)利用投入—产出模型对影响生产布局的投资、就业和货币的变动情况进行预测分析,对预定地区的未来发展进行规划。

在区位理论发展历程中,廖什的市场区位论(Location of Industry)和克里斯泰勒的中心地理论(Central Place Theory)是对旅游产业区域布局极具影响力的研究成果。

2. 市场区位论(Location of Industry)

(1) 理论假设(Theory Assumptions)

- There is an uneven distribution of natural resources on the plain. Raw materials are concentrated in specific sites.(自然资源非均匀分布,原材料集中在特定区域)
- The size and location of markets are given at fixed points on the plain.(市场范围和市场区位在特定地点)
- There are fixed locations of labor where wage rates are fixed and labor is immobile and unlimited.(劳动力区位是固定的,工资水平固定、劳动力稳定并且不受限制)
- The area has a uniform culture, climate and political system.(区域有统一的文化以及统一的环境政策体系)
- Entrepreneurs minimum costs of production.(企业:产品成本最小化)
- Perfect competition exists.(适者生存,优胜劣汰)
- Costs of land, structures, equipment and capital do not vary regionally.(区域内的土地、结构、设备和资本成本不变)
- There is a uniform system of transport over a flat surface.(运输的统一系统)

(2) 基本概念(Some Concepts)

- Factory or Plant

The factory or plant is an individual building or premise that produces manufactured goods. A company may own several factories, probably in different locations. The industry comprises many factories, or plants, and a number of independent companies. Industrial location is primarily concerned with the site of a single factory, rather than the whole industry, although the location of the industry is in itself a locational factor. The concepts of site and situation play separate roles, although we may use the word site in relation to location when we are really looking at the situation of the factory.

- The Site of a Factory or Group of Factories

The site of a factory, or group of factories, is the actual physical location, or block of land. There are some basic locational constraints for the site, such as a plentiful supply of flat land, access to transport, power and water, availability of labor, and capital and finance facilities. Almost all cities will possess appropriate industrial sites and these will be zoned by councils.

It is therefore the situation, or the relative location, in relation to other factories and the industry that is important. Like agricultural and central place location theories, Weber makes assumptions that simplify reality, but unlike these other theories, he does not assume an equal distribution. Rather he assumes that raw materials are unequally distributed in fixed locations.

(3) 基本内容(Main Contents)

Location of industry is concerned with the least cost location, so that again transport costs are a crucial element in the location decision. A German economist, Alfred Weber devised the theory of industrial location, in 1909. In the early part of the industrial revolution factories developed in areas that were already producing manufactured goods. These were the places where woollen textiles were produced in farmhouses on farms that bred the sheep. The shift was from the farmhouse to a mill, in the same area. By chance many of these textile mills were on coalfields, so that when the shift from water powered to steam coal powered mills occurred, the transition was in the same place. The same thing happened as steel production was also shifted from local forges to coal powered mills. The early industrial revolution saw mills and factories develop on coalfields, and remain entrenched there for more than a century.

By the end of the 19th century, these raw material locations were losing their ascendancy. At the beginning of the industrial revolution roads were in poor quality and slow. Canals were rapidly constructed to move heavy industrial materials, but nowhere did these form a really convenient network.. It was the development of railways into extensive networks by the end of the 19th century that enabled industrial location to free itself from raw material sites. This trend continued with roads and vehicles in the twentieth century, but water transport and especially the sea, remained dominant for long distance transport of industrial goods. Weber's analysis came at the point where railway networks had developed to their ultimate extent. He was therefore concerned with the balance of location between raw material site, the market for manufactured goods, and transport.

In the first instance we consider whether to locate an industry in the raw material or market location. If there is no weight loss or weight gain in production, you site your factory at either location, because the transport costs are the same each way. The diagram on the handout illustrates how isocheims of equal cost distance are constructed around each site, thereby creating intersection points of equal but higher values, termed soapiness.

As transport costs are not identical for raw material and manufactured goods a relative weighting must be calculated. Weber did this with a material index, whereby the relative weight gain or loss is calculated.

If the product is a pure material its index will be 1. If the index is less than 1 the final product has gain weight in manufacture, thus favoring production at the market place. The weight gain is most likely to come from the addition of ubiquitous materials, like water, that we can expect to occur anywhere. Such a product would be a drink, soft drinks or beer, where a small quantity of usually dried materials are added to water and bottles to make a much heavier and more fragile final product. Most products lose weight in manufacture, such as a metal being extracted from an ore. Thus their material index will be more than 1, thus favoring the raw material site.

The significance of the material index is in calculating precisely the difference between the unit transport costs of raw materials and finished products. The number of the index is used to calculate a relative weighting, which is then applied to the spacing/radius of the isocheims. The locational triangles on the handout are small examples of the weighting of more than one material.

While the drawing of isocheims and isodapanes is very straightforward for 2 sites, it is in adding a number of material sites and markets that the spatial model both increases in complexity and begins to provide a useful method for calculating the least cost location. As well as weight loss or gain the material index and weighting of transport costs can also take account of loss or gain in transport, of features such as perishability, fragility and hazard.

(4) 旅游市场区位理论与传统市场区位理论的区别（Discriminations of Location Theory in Tourism Market and Traditional Market）

传统意义上的区位理论，是针对物质资料生产的区位理论，在进行旅游产业区域结构分析中就可能会出现"失灵"的现象。这主要是由以下几个方面的原因造成的：

• 旅游业的生产具有不可转移性（Unchangeability of Tourism Production）

旅游业是以旅游资源为依托，无论是人文旅游资源还是自然旅游资源一般说来均是不能移动的，旅游者只能到旅游资源所在地进行消费。因此，旅游产业研究的区位是大致确定的，即不存在旅游资源的运输费用影响旅游生产布局的问题。

• 旅游需求的不确定性（Uncertainty of Tourism Demand）

旅游产品的无形性使得对旅游市场的需求进行预测十分困难。因此，市场对旅游区位的影响表现出不确定性。因为即使是相同的旅游资源和旅游产品对于不同的旅游者来说也可能会产生不同的吸引力，有主观原因如旅游者的兴趣爱好、性格特征、文化背景、知识结构、审美观、职业等,也有家庭和个人的经济状况、个人周围人际关系、流行时尚等客观原因。所以,由于影响旅游需求的因素复杂多样,从而旅游区位的市场具有不确定性。

- 旅游产业的综合性和强关联性(Integrity and Strong Relevance of Tourism Industry)

由于旅游产业具有综合性和强关联性,所以进行旅游生产布局不仅要从旅游业自身特点出发,还要从区域角度全面考虑。旅游的内容除了传统意义上的"食、住、行、游、购、娱"六大要素外,还需要交通、园林、文物、环境等其他相关部门的配合。旅游业是关联性强、带动性强的行业。据世界旅游组织测算,旅游业每投资 1 元钱,相关行业就增收 4.3 元;旅游业每直接就业 1 人,社会就可以新增 5 个就业机会。传统的区位理论所研究的对象没有如此巨大的关联网,因而在理论的研究上对产业关联性的考虑不够,所以要真正实现区域旅游发展的目标,要从旅游业及其配套服务这两个方面来思考,探索出适应旅游业独特发展个性的区位理论。

3. 中心地理论(Central Place Theory)

Central Place Theory(中心地理论)was originally published in 1933 by a German geographer Walter Christaller(克里斯泰勒)who studied the settlement patterns in southern Germany. Central Place Theory (CPT) is an attempt to explain the spatial arrangement, size, and number of settlements.

(1) 理论假设(Theory Assumptions)

- Consumers are evenly distributed across a market plane.(按照市场水平,消费者是均匀分布的)
- Each good sold has its own optimal market-area size, expressed as the radius of a circular market area.(每个业绩不错的销售都有其理想市场区域范围,表现为市场半径)
- A firm selling a given good co-exists with a firm that sells goods with smaller optimal market area.(一家商品销量很好的厂商和一个产品的理想市场规模稍小的厂商)
- It is possible for a new firm to enter and serve any unsupplied area.(新企业可以自由进入)

(2) 基本观点(Basic Idea of the Central Place Theory)

In the flat landscape of southern Germany Christaller noticed that towns of a certain size were roughly equidistant. By examining and defining the functions of the settlement structure and the size of the hinterland he found it possible to model the pattern of settlement locations using geometric shapes (usually triangles and hexagons). Christaller examined the factors, which caused variation or deviation from his and other settlement hierarchy models. It is now possible to incorporate factors, which cause the variation in the regular geometry of CPT in the neural network modeling framework.

Christaller noted three different arrangements of central places:

- 市场原理 marketing principle ($K=3$ system)
- 运输原理 transportation principle ($K=4$ system)
- 管理原理 administrative principle ($K=7$ system)

Christaller found that the number of settlements at any level in either of these hierarchies is directly related to which hierarchy it is.

In a $K = 3$ system for each of the largest settlements in the hierarchy there are on average 3 proximal settlements of the next size down in the hierarchy, for each of these again there will be on average 3 proximal settlements of the next size down in the hierarchy and so on down the hierarchy to the smallest sized settlement. Christaller noted that this type of hierarchy prevailed where it was most important for society to ensure equal provision of goods and services.

Examining the pattern using hexagons Christaller found that central places emerge at the center of a hexagon, containing six lower-order settlements. If transportation costs are to be minimized Christaller found that by rotating and enlarging the hexagon that central places emerged where there are 4 proximal settlement of a given size. Finally, for administration purposes Christaller believed the need for 7 proximal settlements of the highest order to drive the creation of the central one into the next order in the hierarchy.

There are various interpretations of Christaller's CPT. Often too much is read into the 3 main systems he studied. The key is the fractal type nature of settlement hierarchies. In the interpretation I've outlined above using proximity K could attain any integer value. It is quite possible that the value of K could be calculated for sub areas of Europe and would be helpful in creating EU population surfaces.

Since delivered price is composed of store price and transport cost, a consumer living further pays more. Therefore, a seller serves consumers who live within a range where cheaper delivered price provides. The range shows average maximum distance from the store to consumers willing to purchase. Therefore, the distribution of store location and its market area is shown. Although the stores are distributed with maximization of the size of those market areas, an uncovered area exists. To cover all of areas with the maximum size of each market area, the shape of borders between market areas must be hexagonal.

(3) 中心地理论的应用(Application of CPT)

Applying the central place theory, many studies have been done regarding to establishments and retail viability. For instance, in his article, Shonkwiler (1996) summarized important knowledge already established by other researches.

- Average transportation costs per purchase are lowered by multipurpose shopping trips.
- The consumer might find it desirable to shop at multiple locations on a single trip.
- Not only population but demographic characteristics, socioeconomic structure, potential expenditures, and shopping behavior are the most important factors to explain spatial clustering.
- Although a major tenet of central place theory was that producers tend to locate as far as possible from competitors, firms may recognize the advantages of agglomeration and the benefit of centrality that result from adjacent location.
- The development of central places depends on factors such as transport costs, expenditure shares for relevant goods and the

cost characteristics of stores.

- Planning commissions continue their efforts on industrial recruitment while the pursuit of other development strategies such as retail-sector expansion may be overlooked.

Moreover, in his statistical analysis of rural retail business, Shonkwiler (1996) concludes, "retail business interdependencies exist and minimum demand threshold values for various retail sectors are sensitive to the presence or absence of other type of retail firms."

Additionally, in his regression analysis to rural communities, Mushinski (2002) concludes "incorporating explicit geographic interdependence between establishments in a place and sources of supply and demand in neighboring areas" exists, and is "particularly significant on the supply side." Moreover, "outlying establishments tend to reduce the number of establishments in a place, which underlines the importance of spatial competition in retail development."

（4）旅游产业中心地理论（The Central Position Theory of Tourism Industry）

由于旅游业与其他物质生产行业不同，旅游产业也就有其独特的中心地理论。意大利罗马讲师马里奥蒂在《旅游经济学讲义》中第一次提出旅游中心地理论，指出吸引旅游者参观游览的是当地的自然资源、风土人情等自然吸引力以及由外部的设施、饭店、娱乐等组成的派生吸引力共同形成的旅游吸引力，由此形成了旅游中心地。

在旅游中心地的研究中，首要的问题是如何界定旅游中心地。丰富的旅游资源和便利的交通条件是旅游地成为区域旅游中心的两个必要条件。此外，根据一定的标准判断某个特定的旅游地是否为该地区的旅游中心地。例如，旅游地人均旅游收入与周边地区人均旅游收入的比例以及客源市场消费的该旅游区提供的旅游产品等。

对旅游地的影响范围起决定性作用的因素是旅游地资源的吸引力。此外，旅游产业的配套服务设施、旅游服务组织的完善程度、旅游者旅行成本的高低等因素也会对旅游地的市场范围产生影响。

4. 旅游区位理论的应用（Application of Tourism Location Theory）

区位论是关于人类经济活动空间及其空间组织优化的理论。旅游产业区域结构研究旅游在空间上的变化，其实质是旅游产业各部门在一

定区域内的布局及配置过程,其项目选址、旅游路线安排等都存在区位优化问题。旅游区位理论的研究侧重于以下 5 个方面:

- 旅游资源开发的最优区位选择(Best locational selection of the exploitation of tourism resource)
- 旅游交通与旅游路线(Travel transportation and tourism products)
- 旅游企业的规模、市场定位以及选址的确定(The scale, market positioning and address selection of travel services)
- 不同的旅游区域间相互协调关系(Cooperation of tourism regions)
- 旅游开发的区域分析与区域模型研究(Research on regional analysis of tourism exploitation and regional model)

(二) 地域分工理论(Theory of Division of Labor)

1. 地域分工理论的起源和发展(Derivation and Evolution of Division of Labor Theory)

(1) 亚当·斯密(Adam Smith)的绝对优势理论(Absolute Advantages)

地域分工理论(Theory of Territorial Division of Labor)起源于亚当·斯密(Adam Smith)的《国民财富的性质和原理》(The Wealth of Nations)。他把劳动分工理论扩展到空间层面,提出了绝对优势理论(Absolute Advantages)。The early logic of the absolute advantages theory was that free trade could be advantageous for countries which were based on the concept of absolute advantages in production. Adam Smith wrote in *The Wealth of Nations*, "If a foreign country can supply us with a commodity cheaper than we ourselves can make it, better buy it of them with some part of the produce of our own industry, employed in a way in which we have some advantage." (Book IV, Section ii, 12)

The idea here is simple and intuitive. If our country can produce some set of goods at lower cost than a foreign country, and if the foreign country can produce some other set of goods at a lower cost than we can produce them, then clearly it would be best for us to trade our relatively cheaper goods for their relatively cheaper goods. In this way both countries may gain from trade.

(2) 大卫·李嘉图(David Ricardo)的比较优势理论(Theory of Comparative Advantage)

继亚当·斯密之后,大卫·李嘉图(David Ricardo)提出了比较优势理论(Theory of Comparative Advantage)。The original idea of comparative advantage dates to the early part of the 19th century. Although the model describing the theory is commonly referred to as the "Ricardian model", the original description of the idea can be found in an Essay on the External Corn Trade by Robert Torrens in 1815. David Ricardo formalized the idea using a compelling, yet simple, numerical example in his 1817 book titled, *On the Principles of Political Economy and Taxation*. The idea appeared again in James Mill's *Elements of Political Economy* in 1821. Finally, the concept became a key feature of international political economy upon the publication of *Principles of Political Economy* by John Stuart Mill in 1848.

大卫·李嘉图认为,任何区域都有其相对有利的条件,即相对优势或比较优势,如果各区域都生产并输出具有比较优势的商品,输入相对劣势的商品,这样各地区的资源都得到充分有效的利用。大卫·李嘉图的思想被视为地域分工关系的规范。Because the idea of comparative advantage is not immediately intuitive, the best way of presenting it seems to be with an explicit numerical example as provided by David Ricardo. Indeed some variation of Ricardo's example lives on in most international trade textbooks today.

In his example Ricardo imagined two countries, England and Portugal producing two goods, cloth and wine, using labor as the sole input in production. He assumed that the productivity of labor (i. e., the quantity of output produced per worker) varied between industries and across countries. However, instead of assuming, as Adam Smith did, that England is more productive in producing one good and Portugal is more productive in the other; Ricardo assumed that Portugal was more productive in both goods. Based on Smith's intuition, then, it would seem that trade could not be advantageous, at least for England.

However, Ricardo demonstrated numerically that if England specialized in producing one of the two goods, and if Portugal produced the other, then total world output of both goods could rise! If an appropriate terms of trade (i.e., amount of one good traded for another) were then chosen, both countries could end up with more of both goods after specialization and free trade then they each had before trade. This means that England may nevertheless benefit from free trade even though it is assumed to be technologically inferior to Portugal in the production of everything.

As it turned out, specialization in any good would not suffice to guarantee the improvement in world output. Only one of the goods would work. Ricardo showed that the specialization good in each country should be that good in which the country had a comparative advantage in production. To identify a country's comparative advantage good requires a comparison of production costs across countries. However, one does not compare the monetary costs of production or even the resource costs (labor needed per unit of output) of production. Instead one must compare the opportunity costs of producing goods across countries.

A country is said to have a comparative advantage in the production of a good (say cloth) if it can produce cloth at a lower opportunity cost than another country. The opportunity cost of cloth production is defined as the amount of wine that must be given up in order to produce one more unit of cloth. Thus England would have the comparative advantage in cloth production relative to Portugal if it must give up less wine to produce another unit of cloth than the amount of wine that Portugal would have to give up to produce another unit of cloth.

All in all, this condition is rather confusing. Suffice it to say, that it is quite possible, indeed likely, that although England may be less productive in producing both goods relative to Portugal, it will nonetheless have a comparative advantage in the production of one of the two goods. Indeed there is only one circumstance in which England would not have a comparative advantage in either good, and in this case Portugal also would not have a comparative advantage in either good. In other words, either each country has the comparative advantage in one of the two goods or neither country has a comparative advantage in anything.

Another way to define comparative advantage is by comparing productivities across industries and countries. Thus suppose, as before, that Portugal is more productive than England in the production of both cloth and wine. If Portugal is twice as productive in cloth production relative to England but three times as productive in wine, then Portugal's comparative advantage is in wine, the good in which its productivity advantage is greatest. Similarly, England's comparative advantage good is cloth, the good in which its productivity disadvantage is least. This implies that to benefit from specialization and free trade, Portugal should specialize and trade the good in which it is "most best" at producing, while England should specialize and trade the good in which it is "least worse" at producing.

Notice that trade based on comparative does not contradict Adam Smith's notion of advantageous trade based on absolute advantage. If as in Smith's example, England were more productive in cloth production and Portugal were more productive in wine, then we would say that England has an absolute advantage in cloth production while Portugal has an absolute advantage in wine. If we calculated comparative advantages, then England would also have the comparative advantage in cloth and Portugal would have the comparative advantage in wine. In this case, gains from trade could be realized if both countries specialized in their comparative, and absolute, advantage goods. Advantageous trade based on comparative advantage, then, covers a larger set of circumstances while still including the case of absolute advantage and hence is a more general theory.

2. 地域分工理论(Theory of Division of Labor)

一般认为,地域分工理论由静态比较优势原理、动态比较优势原理和区域主导产业理论三部分组成。

(1) 静态比较优势原理(Static Comparative Advantage Theory)

静态比较优势理论也称静态地域分工理论,它解释了各区域要素禀赋比率和需求偏好状态下的分工和贸易方向。各区域专业化发展具有比较优势的产业部门通过交换,均能获得比较利益。静态地域分工理论确立了分工原则:在要素禀赋比率基础上形成比较优势原则。区域差异是构成地域分工的主要来源,各个区域要素禀赋各不相同。其中,自然禀赋是区域差异的基础,虽然人为因素可能使某些自然要素的区域差异发生变化,但对要素的空间分布差异影响不大。若利用禀赋好、资源相对丰富的要素生产产品则容易处于有利地位;反之,若利用禀赋差,相对稀缺的要素生产产品,则可能处于不利地位。因此,各地区应该多利用本地区资源丰富的条件,以发挥各自的禀赋优势。例如,在旅游产业生产力布局中,应重点开发旅游资源丰富的地区,在旅游需求旺盛而旅游资源不足的旅游地则可采取适当建造人造景观的方法。要素禀赋区域差异的另一方面是劳动力和资本区域间的不完全流动性。一般说来,区域间劳动力和资本的收益差异与区域之间的空间距离成反比,即空间距离越大,劳动力和资本流动的成本和风险就越大。例如,客源地离旅游目的地越远,人们的语言、文化背景、风俗习惯以及行为的差异就越大,这种差异在一定程度上造成了人们外出旅游的心理障碍。

The static theory does not consider a dynamic change in comparative advantage or disadvantage of industries over the course of several decades. The theory overlooks the face that additional resources can be made available to the trading nation because they can be created or imported. 随着时间的延续,各区域的经济都在增长,并非是各要素等比例的数量扩张,而是经济规模的扩张。这就反映出静态地域分工理论的局限性。随着经济发展,各区域间的产业结构也随之发生变化,区域的比较优势就由静态转变为动态。

(2) 动态比较优势原理(Dynamic Comparative Advantage Theory)

动态比较优势原理认为:区域比较优势并不是一成不变的,而是可以随着条件的变化而转变的。随着经济发展以及由此产生的区域要素禀赋的变动,新兴产业不断产生和发展,区域产业系统或产业结构不断扩张也更趋成熟。The comparative advantage in a particular industry can be created through the mobilization of skilled labor, technology, and capital. In addition to the business sector, government can establish policies to promote opportunities for change through time. Such a process is known as dynamic comparative advantage. When government actively involved in creating comparative advantage, the term industrial policy applies. Industrial policy is the initiation of a strategy to revitalize, improve, and develop an industry. Proponents maintain that government should enact policies that encourage the development of emerging, 'sunrise' industries (such as high-technology). This requires that resources be directed to industries in which productivity is highest, linkages to the rest of the economy are strong (as with semiconductors), and future competitiveness is important. Presumably, the domestic economy will enjoy a higher average level of productivity and be more competitive in world markets as a result of such policies. 所以,虽然有些产业在初期时还比较弱小,在市场竞争中没有比较优势;但是如果它对区域经济的发展具有重大意义,就应加以扶持。经过一段时间的努力,产业增长越过了增长曲线上的转折点,即可转化成具有比较优势的产业,在竞争中处于有利地位。

因此,在进行旅游空间布局时,可以选择那些旅游业所占比重暂时较小,但具备发展前景的城镇作为重点加以培育,使之发展成旅游中心城市。例如,绍兴市在20世纪80年代末旅游业所占GDP的比重还比较小,但绍兴具有丰富的旅游资源和良好的外部条件。1997年绍兴市旅游业总收入占全市GDP的10.25%,旅游业发展成为支柱产业,为绍兴市的经济发展做出了重要贡献。

(3) 区域主导产业理论(Theory of Regional Leading Industry)

在区域发展过程中,各个产业在区域产业系统中的地位不同,其中一个或几个产业居于主要地位,构成区域的主导产业或主导产业群。现代区域经济的成长过程,实质上是产业部门的发展过程。优化区域产业结构就是正确选择区域的主导产业,确定其发展规模和速度,协调区域主导产业和其他非主导产业的关系,提高本区域与外区域在经济上的互补性和区域产业间的关联度。

区域旅游的空间布局涉及到旅游产业结构的调整和优化。旅游地若选择旅游的空间布局作为其主导产业,则应优先发展它,使其带动区域经济发展的辐射力不断增加,并发挥旅游的强关联性,带动关联产业发展,并尽可能地延长产业链,提高产业整体素质。

3. 地域分工与区域经济协调发展（Harmonious Expansion Between Division of Labor and Regional Economy）

区域经济协调发展，是在市场机制和中央政府的协调下充分发挥区域优势，使区域间形成相互依赖、合理分工、共同发展的经济统一体。它既是一种发展观，又是一种资源配置方式。从静态角度考察，区域经济协调发展就是在既定的要素供给条件下，如何在各区域配置生产要素，实现整体利益最大化。地域分工能通过发挥各区域的比较优势，提高资源利用率，实现空间合理布局。例如，对区域内旅游资源丰富的地区进行合理的开发规划。从动态发展角度来看，区域经济协调发展作为一种空间资源配置方式，应该能够不断调整地区资源配置结构，使其适应经济发展所产生的要素供给结构以及需求变动，提高区域竞争力，缩小地区间差异。例如，西部大开发，有助于启动国内需求市场，调整我国旅游产业结构，发挥西部资源优势，缩小和东部的差距。

（三）增长极理论（Growth Pole Theory）

增长极理论（Growth Pole Theory）最初由法国经济学家弗朗索瓦·佩尔鲁克斯（F. Perroux）于50年代提出，1955年他在《增长极概念的解释》中正式提出"增长极"的概念。增长极理论的出发点是抽象的经济空间，而不是普通意义上的地理空间。其主要思想是：区域经济的发展是非均衡的，并且存在极化趋势。经济增长并非同时出现在每个区域，它以不同的强度首先出现在一些增长点或增长极上，然后通过不同的渠道向外扩散，最终带动相关区域的经济发展。

由于某些主导产业部门或有创新能力的大企业在核心区或大城市的聚集，导致资本与技术高度集中，形成规模经济，通过自身增长迅速对邻近地区产生强大扩散作用的"增长极"，可带动相邻地区的共同发展（Krakover, 1987）。增长极理论的本质是通过区域内部的发展形成增长的中心，并通过扩散作用，带动相关区域的经济发展。

The main ideas of the growth pole theory can be concluded as follows:

- Economic activity and development do not necessarily spread evenly and equitably throughout the land—the natural tendency is toward polarization.
- The pole is not a city, but a grouping of propulsive enterprises, generating spread effects, which are likely to be in a city, but

which could also be in a mining or plantation area.
- The banality of geographic space is rejected for analytical purposes and replaced by a general concept of economic space.
- The investment that occurs in propulsive enterprises is not induced but is based upon innovations and the expectation of profit in the future.

The core idea of the growth pole theory is that economic development, or growth, is not uniform over an entire region, but instead takes place around a specific pole. This pole is often characterized by a key industry around which links industries development, mainly through direct and indirect effects. The expansion of this key industry implies the expansion of output, employment, related investments, as well as new technologies and new industrial sectors. Because of scale and agglomeration economies near the growth pole, regional development is unbalanced. Transportation, especially transport terminals, can play a significant role in such a process. The more dependant or related an activity is to transportation, the more likely and strong this relationship. At a later stage, the emergence of a secondary growth pole is possible, mainly if a secondary industrial sector emerges with its own linked industries.

The growth pole concept, which was thought to solve most development problems, was used extensively in the 1960s. However, it failed to live up to expectations because it only works in situations where industries are natural-resource based, and the propulsive region, among other areas, does not.

（四）旅游地生命周期理论(Destination Area Lifecycles)

旅游地生命周期理论是加拿大学者布尔特在研究旅游目的地或旅游吸引物的发展周期时提出的描述旅游地发展阶段的理论。Butler (1980) describes the progress of destinations or attractions through a 'growth-peak-decline' cycle in a model of tourist destination development called the Destination Area Lifecycle. The model describes a cycle of evolution, with destination areas moving through six distinct stages(即探索、参与、发展、巩固、停滞、衰落或复苏六个阶

段). The characteristics of the destination, in terms of the nature of the tourism industry, the level of local involvement, the consequences of tourism, and the attitude of local people, are different at each stage. Each stage is also characterized by different perceptions of the destination by tourists, and of tourism by local people.

- 探索阶段(Exploration Stage)：是旅游地发展的初期阶段，这一阶段的特点是由于旅游地的可进入性和基础设施较差，游客数量少，主要是探索旅游者。旅游商业行为还很有限。
- 参与阶段(Involvement Stage)：是旅游市场逐渐形成阶段，这一阶段的特点是游客量开始持续增加，并形成一定的旅游市场和旅游淡、旺季，旅游增长率稳步上升，并拉动旅游地旅游设施的建设和发展。
- 发展阶段(Development Stage)：是旅游市场快速发展阶段，其特点是旅游市场迅速形成而扩展，游客量保持持续的高增长，旅游地的旅游设施不断完善和提高，旅游地的形象和知名度逐渐扩大。但该阶段存在一些隐患，如旅游设施的过度使用，超过旅游承载力而与当地居民发生冲突等等，必须进行区域旅游规划。
- 巩固阶段(Consolidation Stage)：是旅游地逐步进入成熟阶段，尽管游客总量继续增长，但增长率已有所下降。旅游地的经济社会发展已同旅游业发展密切相关，旅游设施的使用出现饱和状态。
- 停滞阶段(Stagnation)：是旅游地已进入完全成熟阶段，其特点是游客总量已达到最大值，旅游环境容量已达到最大限度，出现不良竞争行为，旅游市场开始萎缩，旅游带来的各种经济、社会和环境问题逐渐显现出来。
- 衰落或复苏阶段(Decline or Rejuvenation Stage)：是指旅游开始衰落，游客总量开始减少，一些旅游地开始开发新的旅游资源以吸引新的游客市场，旅游市场竞争剧烈。如果在这一阶段没有切实有效的措施使旅游地进入复苏期，则旅游地很可能被新的旅游地所削弱或替代。

The six stages are described in Table 4.1 and illustrated in Figure 4.1.

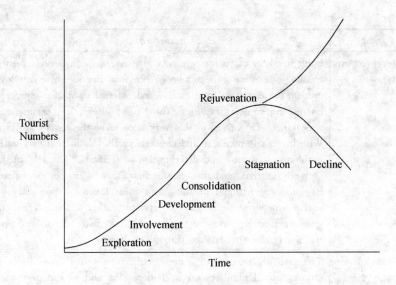

Figure 4.1 Destination Area Lifecycle

Table 4.1 Destination Area Lifecycle (adapted from Cooper, et al, 1993)

Stage	Characteristics
Exploration stage	Small numbers of adventurous visitors are attracted by the unspoilt natural beauty or culture at the destination. Numbers are small due to poor access and facilities. At this stage, the attraction of the destination is that it is as yet unchanged by tourism, and contact with local people will be high. Visitors seek to merge with the local community. The host community welcomes tourism. There is limited commercial activity in tourism.
Involvement stage	By the stage, local initiatives to provide for visitors and to promote the destination have begun. This results in increased and regular numbers of visitors. A tourist season and market area emerges, and pressure may be placed on the public sector to provide infrastructure. Tourists display a high level of interest and sympathy with local life. A harmonious relationship exists between tourists and the host community. There is increased involvement of the community in commercial tourist facilities and services.

续表

Stage	Characteristics
Development stage	Large numbers of visitors are now arriving; at peak periods perhaps equaling or exceeding the number of local inhabitants. The control over tourism passes out of local hands, and external companies emerge to provide up-to-date facilities that may alter the destination's appearance. However, in this very success lie the roots of failure. With increasing numbers and popularity, the destination may suffer problems of overuse and deterioration of facilities. The relationship between tourists and the host community is more formalized. Regional and national planning and control become necessary, in part to ameliorate problems, but also to market to the international tourist-generating areas as visitors become more dependent upon travel arrangements booked through the trade.
Consolidation stage	The rate of increase of increase of visitors has now declined, although total numbers are still increasing and exceed permanent residents. The destination is now fully fledged, with all the major franchises and chains represented, and there is an identifiable recreational business district (RBD). Economic, social and environmental problems emerge.
Stagnation	Peak numbers have been reached and the destination is no longer fashionable. It relies on repeat visits and business use of its extensive facilities, and major efforts are needed to maintain the number of visits. The destination may have environmental, social and economic problems. Residents may express concern about the loss of economic opportunities and initiate actions to redress problems.
Decline	By this stage, the destination has become dependant on a smaller geographical catchment for day trips and weekend visits. There is withdrawal of foreign-owned business; property turnover is high; and tourist facilities, such as accommodation, are converted for other uses.
Rejuvenation	This involves deciding on new uses, markets, and distribution channels, thereby repositioning the destination. Changing the attraction is a common response. Similarly, some destinations capitalize on previously unused natural resources, such as winter sport, to extend the season and attract new markets. These facility developments often reflect joint public/private sector ventures to seek new markets and invest in the destination, to reach a cycle/recycle pattern.

第二节　旅游产业区域结构的内容和影响因素
(Contents and Affection Factors of Location Structures of Tourism Industry)

一、旅游产业区域结构的内容(The Content of Location Structures of Tourism Industry)

旅游产业区域结构一般包括各旅游要素的区域结构和综合旅游经济区域结构。旅游要素的区域结构包括旅行社区域结构、旅游饭店区域结构、旅游交通区域结构、旅游商品区域结构、旅游资源区域结构、旅游市场区域结构、旅游客源地区域结构,旅游投资区域结构等等。它反映的是旅游要素的空间分布与布局、功能分区以及要素与区域间的空间联系等等。

旅行社区域结构(Location Structure of Travel Agents)是指不同性质、规模的旅行社在各区域的分布情况以及区域内各旅行社之间的协作关系。

旅游饭店区域结构(Location Structure of Hotels)是指由于旅游资源的分布及旅游市场需求的特点而形成的旅游饭店分布格局。其中旅游资源的分布对旅游饭店在区域内的分布具有决定性的作用。旅游饭店的发展速度和规模应当适度,分布应当合理,等级应当适合旅游需求的发展,建筑风格应当与周围的环境相匹配。

旅游交通的区域结构(Location Structure of Transportation)受旅游资源与旅游客源分布的影响。一般情况下,旅游城市和旅游景区景点周围的旅游交通分布的规模、水平、密度都高于其他地区。

旅游商品的区域结构(Location Structure of Tourism Goods)不仅受旅游资源的分布影响,而且同各地区旅游商品生产,特别是名优土特产相关,因而形成不同地区的特色旅游商品。

旅游市场区域结构(Location Structure of Tourism Market)是对国际和国内不同区域的旅游市场的需求进行研究,针对不同区域市场的需求特点、规模及水平,因地制宜,开发与之相适应的旅游产品。旅游市场区域结构反映了旅游客源的分布及其需求变化特征,它对各旅游供给因素特别是旅行社、旅游饭店、旅游交通的合理布局具有重要的影响。

旅游投资区域结构(Location Structure of Tourism Investment)是

指资金在各旅游区的流动及配置,它取决于不同地区经济的发展速度、资源特征、经济政策等特点。旅游投资要以有限的资金投入取得较高的综合经济效益,因而提高资金利用率对旅游投资区域结构具有重要意义。

旅游资源区域结构(Location Structure of Tourism Resources)是以旅游吸引力为主的旅游资源的空间配置,以旅游资源自身的性质、特点、规模、数量为划分依据,是旅游产业区域结构的基础。旅游资源区域结构研究的是旅游区的特点与构成,通过运用区域区划理论分析旅游区的特色与发展方向,明确各旅游区的开发重点以及塑造旅游形象,探讨旅游区的总体构成及相互之间的联系,形成既有层次又浑然一体的旅游总体形象。

二、影响旅游产业区域结构的因素(Influencing Factors of Location Structures of Tourism Industry)

1. 旅游资源(Tourism Resources)

旅游资源是旅游产业形成发展的内在因素,是旅游产业存在和发展的基础。旅游资源的丰富程度决定着旅游产业的分布特点、区域产业结构的特征和类型,从而决定着旅游投资的方向和比重以及旅游开发的次序。一般说来,各国政府在进行旅游业布局时,首先考虑的是各地区旅游资源状况,从中择优进行投资开发。

From the earlier definitions and consequent discussion, two main problems immediately appear:

- As there is frequently a mismatch between producer and consumer perceptions of what constitutes the tourism 'product', there may be conflict in ideas of which resources are properly involved.
- Many of the resources likely to be in demand for tourism are public goods, or even free resources.

It may be argued that in today's world there are really very few, if any, free resources left (virtually any human activity makes demands on this world such that someone at sometime will have to pay for it), undoubtedly the demand for tourism involves a substantial amount of public goods. These may be defined as existing facilities which are under-utilized, where an individual may make use of them without reducing the amount of the facilities available to others. This is a situation of zero opportunity cost. If a family takes a camping vacation by car at an off-season period, they may use the road network, public or national parks, beaches, and they may 'consume' scenery by looking at it or taking photos, without impinging in any way on other people. Of course, if the same family were to travel in peak season, there might be considerable opportunity costs, from traffic congestion, overcrowding at destinations and spoilt views.

Travel and tourism suppliers will also use combinations of the same scarce resources that other producers use. There have been various attempts and tourism, which are summarized in figure 4.1.

Figure 4.2 demonstrates that tourism frequently is built upon a basis of free resources, with a mixture of publicly and privately used scarce resources superimposed. Thus there is a combination to form what tourists may perceive as the 'production' they are consuming, and what suppliers are producing.

Some writers have use the terms **resource-basis and user-orientation** to identify types of tourism product, particularly destinations and their attractions. Resource-based products tend to be those oriented ones are more widely spread and are likely to have been created specifically for tourist use.

Examples of resource-based products could be: mountains, exotic wildlife in its natural habitat, or Roman ruins; and of user-oriented products: sports stadium or convention centers. However, most successful tourism products are neither entirely of one type nor the other. For downhill skiing, a mountain requires specific tourist-oriented capital investment in runs, lifts and lodging as well as the natural slope, and a successful convention center benefits from being located in a scenically or culturally interesting place.

由此可见，旅游资源是影响旅游区域布局的重要因素。然而，旅游资源却不是影响旅游区域布局决策的唯一条件。例如：我国西部地区地域辽阔、民俗风情浓郁，具有独具特色的旅游资源，但由于对旅游产业

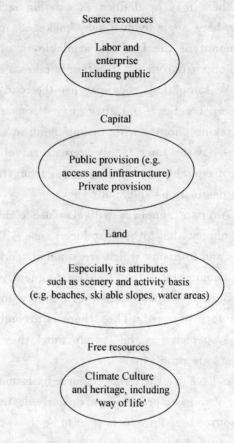

Figure 4.2 Significant Resources for Travel and Tourism Scarce Resources

的重视不足以及交通不便等因素,在决定投资和开发规划上没有得到足够的重视,所以,与东部地区相比,旅游业发展比较落后。

2. 地理位置、交通和信息条件(Geographical Position, Transportation Conditions and Information Conditions)

(1) 地理位置(Geographical Position)

地理位置(Geographical Position)是指地表上某一事物与其他事物的空间关系。由于任何事物都具有各不相同、各具特点的地理位置,所以,各个事物具有不同的地域性。地理位置对旅游布局具有重要意义。优越的地理位置往往对发展旅游是有利的,在旅游地域布局中常常起着主要作用。例如,我国东部沿海地区,虽然旅游资源并不很丰富,但是由于有利的地理位置,旅游产业发展起步早,已经形成了一定的规模。

地理位置分为数理地理位置、自然地理位置、政治地理位置和经济地理位置。

- 数理地理位置是利用地球表面的经纬网或地理坐标来确定的。用经纬网确定的位置也叫做绝对位置或天文位置。例如，北京位于北纬 39°56′，东经 116°20′。
- 自然地理位置是指地表上某一事物与周围自然事物的空间关系，即与周围的陆地、海洋、山脉、河流等自然地理事物的空间关系。例如：北京位于华北大平原的东北部，东临渤海湾。
- 政治地理位置是指一国与邻国以及国家集体之间的空间关系。邻国的对外政策、国力、经济状况、国与国之间的边界关系以及国家集团之间的相互关系等，都对另一国的经济发展、产业分布和经济地域的发展产生重要影响。例如：日本的经济状况、国力以及对华政策等对日中旅游产生重要影响。
- 经济地理位置是指某一事物与具有经济意义的其他事物的空间联系。例如：某一国家、地区或城市与主要航线、港口、主要交通路线、主要交通枢纽的空间关系，与主要客源市场的空间关系等。

(2) 交通条件(Transportation Conditions)

交通条件是指一个国家、地区、城市或居民点与外界进行人员来往(客运)和物资交流(货运)的方便程度。交通条件主要通过交通路线、交通工具和港站、枢纽的设备状况反映出来。Tourism, by definition, includes traveling from one place to another using some form of transport. In the history of tourism, transport was often the critical element in the growth of tourism generally, and the development of destinations specifically. Destinations cannot develop successfully without efficient transport links to the generating markets. The provision of transport services and infrastructure at the destination is equally important. Domestic and international tourism is dependent upon the maintenance and improvement of airport terminals, harbors, and road and rail systems. Besides transport infrastructure, a range of other infrastructure services must be provided to support both the local community and tourists.

交通在旅游业发展中起着先导作用,发达而又便利的交通条件在旅游业布局中常常具有关键的意义。旅游业的发展首先是在交通枢纽地区,尤其是拥有国际口岸的城市,是旅游者的聚散地,因而也是旅游者集中的地区。随着旅游资源丰富地区交通条件的改善,逐渐对旅游者产生了吸引力。例如,上海市位于长江出海口,是国际、国内重要的水上运输枢纽,重要的国际航空港,又是铁路枢纽,交通条件十分优越。因此,上海的旅游业发展有着得天独厚的便利条件。我国西部地区拥有丰富的旅游资源,然而由于远离主要客源市场,交通条件较差,没有或很少有铁路、航空路线等与其相连,旅游业发展受到影响。

(3) 信息条件(Information Conditions)

信息条件是指传递情报的设施和方便程度。在旅游产业区域结构中,信息条件是一个新的术语,是影响旅游产业分布和经济地域发展的一个新的条件因素。例如,SARS过后,我国旅游业在国内旅游与出境旅游快速反弹,甚至速度超过业内人士预计,但是入境旅游却恢复很慢。原因之一是国外新闻媒体很少报道有关中国政府抗击"非典"所取得的成功,因此,国外游客对来华旅游还存在相当程度的恐惧心理。由此看来,信息传递是否通畅也是影响旅游业发展的一个重要因素。此外,在传统旅游业受到"非典"严重影响的时候,旅游电子商务以及网络会议等新兴的旅游形式异军突起,取得良好的成绩。在当今电子信息产业日益发达,世界经济网络化、集团化的发展中,信息条件在旅游产业区域经济发展中的作用将越来越重要。

3. 经济条件(Economic Condition)

经济条件是旅游产业区域结构产生和发展的物质基础,对旅游业发展起着促进或制约作用。发达的经济条件能为旅游业发展提供所需的基础设施、交通运力和高素质的人力资源,从而提高旅游产业的经济效益和社会效益。因此,在旅游业的布局中,区域经济条件也是需要认真考虑的重要因素。经济条件主要包括区域的经济基础和发展状况、市场条件以及资金条件三个方面。

(1) 区域的经济基础和发展状况(Basic and Developmental Conditions of Regional Economy)

我国地大物博,各区域的经济基础和发展水平各不相同。例如,我国东部沿海地区经济发展较快,集中了我国大部分工业企业、重要港口和一批大城市,如上海、广州等。交通发达,科技发展也高于内陆地区。因此,东部具有十分有利的经济条件。旅游产业区域发展必须在原有的经济基础上,改变其劣势,充分利用已有的条件发挥自己的优势。而不能脱离区域经济发展的实际,盲目开发不符合区域经济条件的旅游项目。

(2) 市场条件(Market Condition)

市场经济作为社会经济运行的方式和社会资源配置机制,是一种以市场为导向的经济,要求一切经济活动都以市场为轴心,按照市场经济规律对社会经济活动进行调节和控制。旅游经济也是市场经济的一部分,因此,必须遵循市场经济的规律。首先,从需求角度看,一个地区旅游业的规模和水平表现在对旅游客源市场的拥有程度,而客源地的数量、社会经济发展水平和游客出游率等,都决定着该地区旅游经济的发展速度和规模。其次,从供给角度看,一个地区的旅游市场大小还取决于旅游产品供给和旅游服务水平的高低。它不仅决定着该地区旅游市场接待规模,也决定着旅游市场的发育程度和旅游经济效益。因此,在考虑旅游区域布局时,一方面要考虑不同地区、不同发展阶段的旅游客源市场的对象、范围及变化趋势,从而把握旅游市场的容量大小;另一方面,又要根据旅游需求,合理布局旅游资源的开发和旅游产品的供给,从而形成合理的旅游区域定位,为合理的旅游区域布局提供依据。

(3) 资金条件(Investment Condition)

任何旅游区域的发展都离不开资金的保证。我国东部地区旅游产业起步早、发展快、资金充裕,在区内如何合理地投放资金进行区域开发是他们面临的主要问题。而对于西部旅游产业相对落后的区域,资金短缺成为影响其旅游产业发展的重要因素。因此,在旅游产业区域开发过程中,必须认真分析资金筹措措施,研究资金的合理投向,从而为旅游产业区域发展计划提供科学依据。

4. 社会条件(Social Condition)

社会条件是旅游产业区域形成和发展的社会基础。随着经济的迅速发展和社会化进程的加快,社会因素在旅游产业区域发展中起着日益重要的作用。社会条件主要包括政策条件和政治环境两个方面。

(1) 政策条件(Policy Condition)

首先,管理体制对旅游产业区域发展产生影响。管理体制分为计划经济和市场经济两种。在计划经济管理体制下的旅游产业区域发展是以政府规划或者通过制定产业政策来干预旅游产业成长与演进的管理体制。市场经济管理体制则是以竞争为主要目的来推动旅游产业区域经济发展的模式。政府对旅游产业发展的影响不是直接的,而是通过市场这只"看不见的手"间接调节旅游产业在各区域间的资源配置。

其次,经济政策和法律、法规是政策部门的重要调控手段之一。运用经济政策和法律、法规能加快旅游资源的优化配置,促进旅游经济在数量扩张、结构转换和水平提高等方面同时发展,实现旅游经济的良性循环,有利于旅游经济布局的合理化,减少地区间差异,实现总体效率与空间平等的统一。旅游业是以市场为导向的经济产业,如果没有国家从政策和法律、法规等方面给予宏观指导与调控,旅游业不仅不能快速地发展,而且也不能得到健康地发展。因此,在考虑旅游区域布局的同时,一方面要从旅游经济总体发展的需要来制订有利于旅游区域布局合理化的产业政策和法律、法规,引导旅游区域布局的合理化;另一方面,又要根据现有的产业政策及法律、法规合理地进行旅游产业的区域布局,从而促进旅游经济健康、持续地发展。

(2) 国内外政治条件(Civil Political Condition)

任何一个国家旅游产业的发展都需要良好的国内和国际政治环境。否则,如果一个国家或地区的国内政局不稳或者与其他国家或地区的国际关系紧张,那么这种局势将对旅游产业的发展产生十分不利的影响。例如,印度尼西亚的巴厘岛屡次发生恐怖主义的自杀性爆炸事件,严重损害了当地旅游业的发展。

总之,以上4个方面的因素对旅游产业区域布局的影响和作用是相互关联的,因此,必须综合考虑。每一种因素虽对旅游业布局都会产生影响,但各因素的复合作用更为重要。而且,这些因素并非一成不变,而是随着经济的发展,各方面条件的改善,它们对旅游地区布局的影响也在变化。

第三节 旅游产业的空间布局模式和原则
(Space Layout Model and Principle of Tourism Industry)

一、旅游产业的空间布局模式(Space Layout Model of Tourism Industry)

旅游产业的空间布局模式是指根据旅游地在空间上的布局特点具有不同的模式。旅游产业的空间布局要因地制宜,归纳起来主要有增长极布局模式、点轴布局模式和圈层布局模式三种。

1. 增长极布局模式（Growth Pole Layout Model）

增长极布局模式是指重点开发某个旅游地，使其发展规模和发展潜力超过其他旅游地，成为区域旅游中心，即增长极。然后，通过增长极的极化作用，促进区域旅游中心发展，为旅游地的空间扩散做准备。在增长极布局模式中，主要的旅游企业和接待服务设施都集中在区域旅游的中心，旅游地则作为旅游者进出的集散地和开展旅游活动的依托基地。

佩尔鲁克斯（F. Poerroux）提出增长极理论以后，各国规划人员已成功地将其应用于实践。但增长极的选择和培育受主观因素影响较大，一些脱离实际情况、一厢情愿选择的增长极，虽接受大量投资但往往仍不能实现预定目标。所以，增长极的选择要遵循一定标准。具体说来，区域旅游增长极应具备以下几个条件：

- 具备旅游开发条件。旅游地本身要具备一定的旅游资源、经济基础、基础设施以及相对客源地而言合适的区位。
- 产生集聚经济的能力。增长极所在的旅游地不仅要集聚大量相关的旅游服务企业，而且要具有吸引投资、集聚投资和人才的能力，使旅游地进入自循环良性发展的阶段。
- 合适的自然社会环境。良好的自然生态环境、社会风气、效率和法治观念，有助于形成吸引旅游者和旅游投资的旅游环境并促进增长极的发展。

区域旅游开发处于起步阶段时宜采用增长极布局模式，推动增长极形成，并通过增长极自身的发展以及它对其他旅游地的辐射作用推动整个区域旅游业的发展。

2. 点轴布局模式（Point-Axis Layout Model）

点轴布局模式是指旅游开发应沿着一定的方向进行，有意识地选择交通线作为区域开发的纽带和客流运输的生长轴，重点开发区域中心旅游地和位于生长轴上或附近的旅游地。

例如，杭州市旅游业经过"六五"、"七五"和"八五"计划的发展，1996年旅游业增加值已占 GDP 的 5.9%，成为杭州市的支柱产业，形成了以杭州市区为主体，年接待海外旅游者 1000 人次以上的各类景点 110 余处，旅游接待网络初步形成。根据杭州未来旅游业发展的需要，杭州市指定的 1998—2010 年旅游业发展规划提出：以杭州西湖为核心，千岛湖为次中心，以钱塘江、富春江、新安江为轴线，构筑多层次、多元化、多功能的旅游网络。

生长轴的选择往往不止一个,因而需要对生长轴进行等级评价。首先,集中力量开发较高等级的旅游地和生长轴,随着区域旅游业的发展和经济实力的增强,开发重点逐步转移到级别较低的旅游地和生长轴。

例如,黄山旅游区以黄山作为区域旅游中心,规划了黄山—太平湖—九华山、黄山—潜口—歙县、黄山—休宁—齐云山三条生长轴。现阶段以前两条生长轴为重点发展对象,继续扩大黄山旅游区的规模和吸引力。

点轴布局模式中,点(中心旅游地)无疑居于主导地位,但生长轴对新增长极的形成和老增长极的兴衰也会产生重要影响。生长轴实质是依托城镇的旅游产业开发带。

3. 圈层布局模式(Circle-layer Layout Model)

圈层布局模式是以中心城市(城镇)为核心,各旅游地分布在由内向外扩展的圈层中,形成市场—资源共轭型的旅游地体系。进行圈层布局的区域应具备以下条件:

- 具有规模大、辐射力强的增长极或中心旅游地——旅游城市或大型旅游城镇。
- 中心旅游地位于区域中心或附近位置,其他旅游地在区域内大致均匀分布。
- 中心旅游地要具有吸引地带。
- 基本形成交通发达的城镇体系。
- 旅游网络化,不仅要形成旅游接待网络,还要形成资金、人才、信息、物质等方面的流通网。

以北京市旅游布局为例,形成以北京市区为中心,从北京市综合的自然、经济、文化、交通和区位出发,合理配置北京周边旅游地的互补资源,发挥接待服务优势,构筑都市中心区、边缘区、腹地区三圈组合的都市旅游空间开发结构。

二、我国旅游产业区域布局的原则(Principles of Regional Layout of China Tourism Industry)

从我国旅游经济区域发展不平衡的现状以及不同地区旅游资源和社会经济发展的差异性出发,实现我国旅游区域布局合理化应抓好以下几个方面。

1. **突出重点,带动周边**(Give Prominence to the Key Points, Pull the Circumference)

"突出重点"即使在全国和各省范围内,借助旅游资源的优势,面向市场,形成一批在旅游市场特别是国际旅游市场上具有强大吸引力的旅游目的地。目前,我国旅游业经过十多年的高速发展,初步形成了一部分旅游经济的"增长点"。因此,旅游区域布局应按照突出重点的原则,加强对重点旅游区、旅游城市及旅游路线的建设和发展。应重点对目前在国际上已具有一定知名度的旅游区的配套建设及旅游度假区进行开发。通过重点建设一批融观光、度假及文化娱乐为一体的旅游区,形成一定的产业规模,增强对国内外游客的吸引力。加快对重点旅游城市的配套建设,特别是对改革开放以来形成的旅游中心城市的建设,进一步深度开发,提高综合接待能力,充分发挥旅游中心城市的作用,增强对周边地区的辐射功能,成为全国旅游创汇的基地。例如,全国要重点开发和建设一批具有发展潜力、经济效益好的旅游精品,开展多种专项旅游,增强旅游产业发展的后劲。

2. **合理分工、优势互补**(Rational Division of Labor, Having Complementary Advantages)

从区域旅游经济的发展看,我国旅游经济的发展不仅存在区域差别,而且各区域之间在发展阶段、规模及水平上也存在着差距。因此,旅游区域布局必须遵循合理分工、优势互补的原则,根据各区域间旅游经济的发展水平及区位状况,进行合理的分工和布局;一方面,各地区应根据自身的旅游资源优势和区位条件,按照旅游市场需求开发出与经济发展相适应的旅游产品,与有关地区联合,形成合理的分工和布局;另一方面,在注意突出各自的优势和特色时,要强调互补互济,形成各地区之间资源互补、市场互补,促进生产要素的流动和有效利用,提高旅游经济的整体效益。

3. **遵循点轴式发展规律**(Fellow the Point-axis Development Law)

点轴式系统模式是根据发展轴和中心地理论提出的,体现了社会经济空间的有效形式。所谓点轴式发展,就是以建设国际化旅游城市为依托,形成优先发展的"增长点",再经过辐射扩散作用,以"点"到"轴",进一步发展旅游区,带动整个区域的旅游经济向前发展。遵循点轴式发展原则,首先要加快国际化旅游城市的建设,在目前的重点旅游城市中,有选择地建设一批具有国际化标准和功能的旅游城市,形成旅游经济"增长极"。然后,依托这些"增长极"的辐射扩散作用,不断向周围地区扩散,并形成旅游网络,带动相关地区旅游经济跳跃式地发展,从而促进全国旅游经济网络的形成和旅游业的大发展。例如,2001年底全国评选的138个"中国优秀旅游城市"以及在此基础上创建的"中国最佳旅游城市",旨在提高旅游城市的综合素质,全面优化城市旅游业发展,形成旅游区域经济的"增长点",通过乘数效应,向周围地区扩散,带动区域旅游经济健康发展。

4. 积极发展区域间的合作(Regional Tourism Cooperation)

An increasing trend in international tourism is the desire of tourists to visit more than one destination on a trip to a long-haul (over 1500 miles) tourism region. Multiple tourism-destination development which allows the creation of regional tours and multi-national circuits is only one element of regional cooperation in tourism development. Others include:

- Joint promotion and marketing;
- Tourism facilitation including liberalization policies for passport and visa requirements;
- Currency regulation, immigration and customs controls;
- Collection of uniform tourism statistics;
- Investment incentives and regulations for local and foreign investors;
- Transport system policies for landing rights, charter flights, and overland international crossing;
- Standardization and regional classification of tourism facilities;
- Coordination of health and medical requirements;
- Conservation and preservation programs for natural, historical and cultural resources;
- Personnel and manpower training;
- Foreign assistance (aid) programs;
- International representation on foreign markets.

旅游产业是开放型的经济产业,因此必须实行对外开放,积极寻求国际合作。一方面,要按照旅游经济的内在联系,以区位理论为指导,加强各地区之间的联合和协作,逐步形成具有一定规模、水平且各具地方特色的区域旅游网络,提高区域旅游业的整体竞争能力;另一方面,要积极发展国际区域合作,参与国际市场竞争,要顺应当前国际经济区域一体化的趋势,打破国界约束,寻求更大范围内的区域合作,增强我国旅游业在国际旅游市场上的联合竞争能力,为我国进一步开拓国际旅游市场拓展途径。例如,应积极参与并组建亚洲地区旅游协调网络,促进亚洲区内各国的协调与合作,推动亚洲旅游业更大发展。

5. 坚持可持续发展原则(Sticking to the Sustainable Development Principles)

The concept of sustainable development emerged in the mid-sixties. However, the term was first used in the Brundtland report titled *Our Common Future*, prepared by the World Commission on Development and Environment in 1987. Sustainable development brings together the apparently contrasting concepts of economic development and environmental conservation.

The sustainability development approach implies that the resources for development are conserved for indefinite future as well as present use. Sustainable development is defined as 'development that meets the needs of the present without compromising the ability of future generations to meet their own needs'.

The concept of sustainability has been further elaborated since then, notably in Agenda 21 of the Global Conference on Environment and Development, popularly known as the Earth Summit, which was held in Rio De Janeiro in 1992. Item three of the Rio Declaration states that 'the right to development must be fulfilled so as to equitably meet developmental and environmental needs of present and future generations' (United Nations, 1992). Figure 4.3 illustrates the cornerstones of sustainable development.

What is sustainable tourism development? Sustainable tourism development is intended to reduce the tension and friction created by the interaction between the tourism industry, visitors, the environment, and host communities. The meaning of sustainable tourism development includes some aspects as follows:

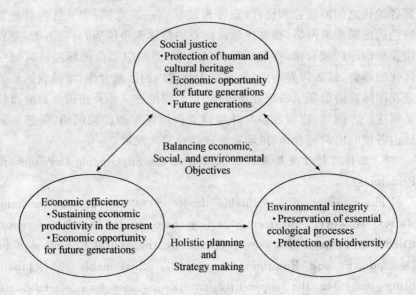

Figure 4.3 Illustrates the Cornerstones of Sustainable Development.

- Sustainable tourism development implies that the resources for tourism be conserved, and often enhanced, for both present and continuing future use and enjoyment by residents and visitors.
- Tourism development must be compatible with the society and culture of the tourism destination.
- Sustainable tourism development meets the needs of the host population for improved living standards.
- The expectations of increasing numbers of tourists must be satisfied in a way that the destination continues to attract tourists. Simultaneously, tourists respect and protect the environments and host communities they visit.
- Tourism resources must be properly maintained, and often can be improved through the application of conservation measures and the development of appropriate visitor facilities and services. This approach brings benefits to a destination on a permanent basis. In fact, sustainable tourism can be an important justification and help to pay for the conservation of

certain resources.
- Tourist attractions, facilities, services, and infrastructure must be planned, located, designed, and managed in an environmentally and culturally sensitive manner, so that they do not congest, pollute or degrade the environment, or create social problems.
- Local communities participate in planning tourism in their areas, and benefit directly from tourism.

Sustainable tourism development recognizes limits to growth, takes a long-term view of economic activity, and questions uncontrolled economic growth. It supports the long-term viability and quality of both human and natural resources, with an approach aimed at establishing the appropriate nature and scale of tourism development. The realization of it requires the application of long-term planning and implementation of mechanisms and strategies to manage tourism. Sustainable tourism development embraces a community-oriented approach, encouraging community involvement and participation. The various definitions of sustainable tourism emphasize three important features:

- **Quality** Sustainable tourism involved providing quality experiences for visitors, while improving the quality of life of the host community and protecting the quality of the environment.
- **Continuity** Sustainable tourism ensures the continuity of the natural resources upon which it is based, and the continuity of the culture of the host communities.
- **Balance** Sustainable tourism balances the needs of the tourism industry, supporters of the environment, and the local community. It emphasizes the mutual goals of and cooperation among visitors, host communities, and destinations.

第四节 我国旅游产业区域结构
(Location Structure of China Tourism Industry)

我国旅游产业区域结构存在着东部、中部和西部三个梯级,梯级之间级差较大。西部地区属于旅游冷点地区,旅游业处于起步阶段。该地区旅游资源丰富,民族文化特色浓,对外国旅游者很有吸引力。但由于经济发展水平低,基础设施与劳动力素质比东部差,远离口岸城市,发展国际旅游的成本高,经济效益较低。中部地区属于旅游温点地区,该地区旅游业已经形成一定的基础,不仅旅游资源潜力大,旅游吸引力不断增强,而且经济技术和交通条件也比西部好,因而旅游业已呈现不断增长势头。东部地区是旅游热点地区,经济技术发达,基础设施、人力资源条件好,交通便利。

虽然从旅游资源来说,中、西部并不亚于东部,甚至更富有特色,然而由于历史和自然的因素,中西部经济基础比较薄弱,旅游基础设施建设缓慢,地理位置离口岸城市较远,交通又不太畅通,限制了旅游业的快速发展。要改变这种不平衡状态,我国旅游业的布局应在以东部为主体的同时,逐步向西推进。

一、我国旅游产业区域结构的现状分析(Analysis of Existing Circumstance of China)

我国各地区旅游业自改革开放以来有了较大发展,但在发展规模和发展速度上差异较大。目前,我国旅游业区域结构大体上表现为以下三种格局。

1. 以东南沿海地区为主体的区域格局(Regional Pattern: South-Eastern Areas Remaining Dominant)

旅游产业作为国民经济的重要力量,必然以现有的社会经济条件为依托。沿海地区凭借得天独厚的政策优势、区位优势和经济优势快速发展,带动中国旅游业区域格局形成了以北京为龙头,以长江三角洲和珠江三角洲为重点,深圳、厦门、汕头和珠海4个经济特区、14个沿海开放城市和海南岛的总体格局。东南沿海地区是我国对外开放的窗口,经济发展快、交通便利,因此,成为我国旅游业地区布局的重点地区。沿海地区的旅游业不仅发展速度快,而且经济效益和社会效益比较显著。目前，沿海地区旅游业已经形成规模，逐步实现了从依靠数量型增长向效益型发展的转变。

2. 七个旅游重点地区的确立（Building Up Seven Important Tourism Regions）

"七五"期间，我国确定了北京、上海、江苏、浙江、广东、广西、陕西七个重点旅游地区。其中，包括广西、陕西这两个内陆地区。这是因为两个地区的旅游资源各具特色，同时也为将来向西北和西南的发展奠定基础。从我国旅游业总体发展战略考虑，旅游业区域格局以东南沿海为主体，同时渐进式向西部内陆推进。1999年，全国旅游外汇收入排在前列的依次为：广东、北京、上海、福建、江苏、浙江、云南、辽宁、陕西、山东、天津、广西。实践证明，这七个重点旅游地区已成为我国旅游业的创汇基地，其旅游外汇收入约占全国旅游外汇收入总额的84％。

3. 新的旅游重点地区的兴起（The Springing Up of New Important Tourism Regions）

随着经济的发展，交通条件的改善，对外开放步伐的加快，一些新兴的旅游地区正在异军突起。

- 随着台湾市场的不断扩大，位于东南沿海的福建省旅游业迅速发展。1992年以来，福建省接待海外旅游者人次、旅游外汇收入不断上升，成为继广东、北京、上海之后的第四位旅游外汇收入超过亿美元的省份。
- 位于我国东部的辽宁省旅游业发展速度也很快，旅游外汇收入已进入全国前十名。虽然辽宁省接待海外旅游者的数量不是很多，但1992年的旅游外汇收入已经突破1亿美元大关，超过7个重点地区中的广西、陕西和浙江。1999年，辽宁省的旅游外汇收入居全国第八位，成为新的旅游热点地区。
- 位于我国南端的海南省，虽然旅游业起步较晚，旅游基础设施较薄弱，但积极利用对外开放所享有的特殊政策带动该省经济和旅游业发展腾飞。海南岛对旅游资源进行了合理的开发，使旅游业成为该地区经济发展的主体产业之一。

总而言之，目前我国旅游业的区域格局基本是：以东南部沿海地区为主体；中部内陆地区相对薄弱；西部地区虽然拥有丰富的旅游资源，但由于受社会历史条件、经济发展、交通运输等各种条件的限制，发展较慢。这种旅游产业区域发展不平衡的现状将在较长时期内存在。

二、我国旅游产业区域结构存在的问题（Problems of Location Structures in China Tourism Industry）

1. 旅游资源开发不尽合理,存在旅游业区域间矛盾（Unreasonable Explication of Tourism Resources, Has Contradiction Between Tourism Industry Regions）

旅游业空间开发的合理性,反映着区域旅游业发展的水平和可持续发展的程度。从旅游业的布局现状来看,旅游资源丰富的地区同时也是旅游市场发育较完善地区的集聚。这种布局特征在旅游业发展的初期,可以取得良好的经济效益,保证旅游业的顺利发展。但旅游业发展到了扩展阶段以后,这种格局就显示出了弱点,即大量的旅游资源不能被充分利用。从旅游业发展的区域关系来看,目前已经有了一定的旅游业区域矛盾。首先是区域旅游业的"冷热不均"矛盾,一些旅游热点地区,游人如织,特别是到了旅游旺季,人满为患,甚至超过了当地环境的承载力,形成了旅游的"热点"和"热线"。相反,另一些旅游地却门庭冷落车马稀,形成了旅游的"冷点"和"冷线"。其次是区域旅游业利益矛盾在旅游业区域竞争中的客观存在,出现了旅游地之间争夺开发投资、开发项目以及争夺客源的现象。

2. 对旅游产业的全面建设重视不足（Attaching Less Importance to Complete Construction of Tourism Industry）

旅游业综合性强,涉及面广,是一个复杂的大系统。系统的存在和发展受到自然、经济、社会、文化、历史等因素构成的整体旅游环境的影响和制约,这就需要旅游规划工作者从大旅游、大系统工程的角度来制订区域旅游规划。一些由旅游部门主持制订的区域旅游规划仅从部门出发,而不是从整个社会的角度来思考问题,忽略对整体旅游环境的研究和规划。我国的区域旅游规划带有浓厚的计划经济色彩,不适应当前市场经济条件下的新形势。旅游规划只强调旅游接待人数、创汇额、货币回笼量、增长速度等经济指标,对提高和改善旅游业综合经济效益的研究则显得相对不足;规划的指令性强,重点建设项目多采用政府投资方式,对市场在配置资源、引导社会资金投资旅游业方面所起的作用认识不全面。区域旅游规划早期主要关注对旅游资源的评价和开发规划,现在已转向旅游业发展的各个方面,研究范围比较全面。但部分区域旅游规划或套用省级规划甚至更高级别规划的编制方法,侧重于宏观战略研究,规划内容过于具体,却对事关全局的旅游业空间布局这个关键问题重视和解决不够,未能提出符合当地具体情况的旅游业空间布局结构。

3. 对旅游区域结构相关制约条件的研究不够(Under-research of Correlative Restrict Condition of Location Structures of Tourism Industry)

旅游业具有强关联性,它的发展能在很大程度上带动相关产业发展。但同时也应该看到旅游业的发展要受到相关产业发展的制约。根据"短边"理论(指水桶的盛水量不由最长的桶边决定,而是由最短的桶边决定),真正影响区域经济发展速度的因素往往不是积极因素而是消极因素。部分区域旅游规划忽视这一原则,提出要超前或超常规发展旅游业,而较少考虑区域内相关产业的支持配套能力,导致区域旅游规划落后于形式,或规划能得以实现而区域经济效果却不理想。

总之,我国在旅游区域结构中存在以上情况,导致旅游资源的空间配置不合理,甚至资源浪费。因此,要对我国旅游业区域结构进行调整、优化。

三、优化我国旅游产业区域结构(Optimization of China Location Structures of Tourism Industry)

优化旅游产业区域结构也就是要使旅游产业区域结构合理化。旅游产业区域结构合理化是指旅游产业各要素在空间配置上从不合理到合理发展的过程。随着旅游经济和旅游需求的变化,旅游产业发展的初始阶段所形成不合理的区域结构需要进行适度调整,使得各种旅游要素在旅游产业之间形成合理的空间配置和有效利用。研究旅游区域经济结构,合理布局旅游产业生产力,不仅对充分发挥各地旅游资源优势,促进旅游经济的协调发展具有十分重要的意义,而且对制定合理的区域旅游经济发展战略和旅游产业地区政策也具有重要的意义。

1. 促进旅游资源充分、合理地开发(Accelerating Complete and Reasonable Exploitation of the Tourism Resources)

我国旅游资源丰富,分布广泛,且区域特色明显,为旅游业发展提供了良好的基础。首先,我们必须在旅游资源种类的选择上进行结构调整,重点开发生态旅游资源和少数民族文化旅游产品,改变旅游资源开发不平衡的现状。其次,是要保证旅游资源开发的合理性。一方面保证旅游业的经济效益,争取合理的旅游资源开发项目;同时,要保证旅游资源开发和其他资源开发的有机结合,发挥旅游开发的带动作用,促进区域经济全面发展。另一方面,促进旅游业的协调发展,使旅游产业和环境、社会发展相互促进,共同发展。

2001年4月11日下发的《国务院关于进一步加快旅游业发展的通知》明确提出了"规划建设一批国家生态旅游示范区、旅游扶贫试验区、旅游度假区"(简称"三区")的工作任务。积极推动"三区"联动,形成滚动式发展格局,促进旅游产业区域结构合理化。通过生态旅游示范和旅游扶贫试验区的建设,使西部地区扬长避短,发挥其资源优势,规避其技术落后之短,逐步打破交通设施等基础设施的瓶颈制约,在产品结构上与中部、东部优势互补,共同发展。

2. 优化旅游资源空间布局(Optimization of Space Layout of Tourism Resources)

随着我国旅游业的发展,旅游资源的空间分布点将逐渐增多。我国旅游业发展的初期,是以旅游资源密集地区为主的旅游布局。到20世纪90年代,随着我国旅游业的发展进一步深入,各地旅游资源开发的热情高涨,旅游开发的条件也渐渐成熟,形成了大量新型的旅游目的地。另外,一些还未被开发的颇具特色的旅游资源,也开始显现其价值,旅游业的布局逐渐趋于平衡。旅游业发展在空间上的变化表现为由集中开发转向全面开发,由不平衡布局转向平衡布局。不仅以旅游资源密集、开发条件较好的地区为旅游业的主体,也要加快其他地区旅游业发展的步伐,形成各种独具特色的旅游地,调整旅游的空间配置,优化资源配置。

3. 加强区域旅游经济的联合与发展(Strengthen the Union and Development of Regional Tourism Economy)

首先,要加强与周边国家,特别是东南亚地区在旅游项目开发、客源市场促销、旅游线路开发等方面的合作,大力推进边境旅游的发展。其次,要加强东部与西部之间的合作,将西部的旅游资源优势与东部省市的资金、技术、市场、人才等优势形成互补联合。最后,要做好西部的联合,云南、贵州、四川、重庆、西藏等省(区)市联手合作,资源共享,客源互动,促进相互投资,开展联合宣传,利用各自优势联合开发出国旅游线路,吸引更多的旅游者;把各自的旅游景区通过旅游交通、民航、旅行社等部门的联合,连成跨省旅游大环线,共同开拓国内外市场。

4. 推进特色旅游产品的建设(Boost Construction of Characteristic Tourism Products)

首先,继续抓紧抓好旅游规划工作。根据国家的宏观区域规划,推进和完善主要旅游地和旅游业的发展规划。同时,尽快把各地的旅游发展规划落实到具体的项目规划上,认真抓好重点旅游景区的规划设计工作,严格把关,确保质量,加强对规划实施和项目建设的管理,搞好对旅游资源和生态环境的保护,避免低水平、近距离重复建设,杜绝破坏性开发行为,实现旅游业的可持续发展。其次,集中力量开发建设一批世界级的、有强烈震撼力和吸引力的特色旅游产品。21世纪旅游业的竞争将越来越激烈,没有特色的旅游产品将无法站稳脚跟,必须开发特色鲜明、有规模、高水平的旅游产品。积极实施"三区"开发战略,加快建设旅游创新工程。为优化旅游产品结构,提升旅游开发档次,突出旅游带动功能,应根据各地的旅游资源和自然生态情况,重点规划建设一批生态旅游示范区、旅游扶贫试验区,争取建设新的国家旅游度假区。

5. 大力发展旅游电子商务,实现旅游产业信息化(Developing E-tour, Realize Information Reform of Tourism Industry)

当代的世界是信息的世界,要跟上世界网络经济发展的新浪潮,必须积极推动旅游产业信息化,建立高效能的专业旅游网站,推行旅游网络化。旅游电子商务不仅提高了业务透明度和工作效率,降低了边际成本,而且体现了旅游产品本身个性化、信息化、时令化等特性。旅游电子商务像张无形的大网,把各区域间的旅游供应商、旅游中介联系在一起。旅游目的地、旅行社、旅游饭店以及诸如银行、商店、娱乐、租车业等旅游相关行业,可借助同一网站招徕更多的顾客。新兴的"网络旅游公司"将原来市场分散的利润点集中起来,提高资源的利用效率,成为旅游行业的多面手。这种建立在优势互补基础上的新运行机制,由于各方面的经营投入与利益获取有着不同的侧重点,很快将形成银行、旅游中介商、旅游产品生产者、旅游者四方得利的共赢局面。旅游电子商务能促进各行业间交叉联合,打破区域界限,促使旅游业的发展改变过去仅仅依赖规模经济扩大的旧模式,走向系统经济的新水平。

四、西部地区旅游业的区域结构(Location Structures of Tourism Industry in Western Areas)

国家实施西部大开发战略为西部发展提供了良好的机遇,西部地区充分利用这个时机,结合当地资源丰富的优势,大力发展区域经济。旅游业是综合性的产业,它所具有的创汇创收和促进经济发展的功能和作用在西部地区日益显现。作为新兴产业,西部旅游业发展迅速,旅游产品的结构调整取得了一定成果,国际国内旅游都呈现出蓬勃强劲的势头。甚至一批具有独特旅游资源的边远贫困地区,通过开发当地的资源

也走上了稳定脱贫致富的道路。然而,西部旅游业的发展还存在以下约束:

1. 旅游交通结构不合理(Unreasonable Tourism Transportation Structure)

由于地理位置偏远,西部地区离主要客源地较远,加上西部铁路、公路、航空运输网络稀疏,运输能力十分有限。旅游城市与旅游景区之间也缺少快捷便利的交通工具。较差开发旅游地区的可进入性制约了旅游资源的开发和市场的拓展。此外,西部缺少像北京、上海、广州等航空口岸城市,国际旅游者进出西部地区都必须途经东部、中部航空口岸城市转行,增加了旅游的时间和成本,从而降低了对国际旅游者的吸引力。

2. 旅游基础设施结构不合理(Unreasonable Tourism Infrastructure Structure)

良好的旅游基础设施是旅游产业发展的物质基础,因为旅游吸引力不仅来自于旅游资源本身的审美价值,也来自于其可进入性。然而,由于开发程度低,缺乏资金支持,相当一部分饭店、餐饮、旅游交通及景区景点配套设施不完善。改革开放以后,西部地区极为落后的基础设施状况虽然有了显著改善,但与旅游产业蓬勃发展的要求相比差距仍然很大。例如,陕西省内铁路营业里程平均每平方公里0.013公里,低于湖北、河南等中部相邻省份。贯通南北的干线铁路还没有打通,一些铁路长期处于超饱和状态。陕西省的公路网络也较不完善,全省公路密度只有21公里/百平方公里,平均密度比东部少13公里。西安市与周边城市之间的公路交通大通道还未形成。全省高等级的公路只有332公里,二级公路2469公里,在全国排名第24位。上述状况严重制约了陕西省旅游业的发展。

3. 旅游企业分布结构不合理(Unreasonable Distribution Structure of Tourism Services)

表4.2 西部各地区旅行社和职工个数(2002年底)

地区	旅行社个数			旅行社职工人数		
	国际旅行社	国内旅行社	合计	国际旅行社	国内旅行社	合计
重庆	23	181	204	2033	3078	5111
四川	49	420	469	3425	5611	9036
贵州	12	111	123	724	1540	2264
云南	37	374	411	3697	6483	10180

续表

地区	旅行社个数			旅行社职工人数		
	国际旅行社	国内旅行社	合计	国际旅行社	国内旅行社	合计
西藏	20	20	40	537	209	746
陕西	34	247	281	2872	3186	6058
甘肃	27	173	200	1409	1674	3083
青海	11	78	89	543	934	1477
宁夏	7	43	50	237	427	664
新疆	39	193	232	1735	1943	3678

（资料来源：《2003年中国统计年鉴》）

表 4.3　各地区星级饭店数（2002年底）

地区	重庆	四川	贵州	云南	西藏	陕西	甘肃	青海	宁夏	新疆
星级饭店数	109	294	82	560	49	178	125	39	35	190

西部地区的旅游业起步晚，旅游企业规模小而且分散，普遍缺乏竞争力。1997年，全国旅游企业固定资产净值为1530亿元，而西北地区5省旅游企业的固定资产净值只有44亿元，仅占全国总额的3%。西部在全国范围内形成网络化经营的大型企业或企业集团数量很少，旅游企业大多是单体经营。受到产业特点的影响，这些单体经营的旅游企业不可能形成规模经济，因此很难降低经营成本。尽管在有些地方也形成了区域性的旅游集团，例如陕西旅游集团、云南旅游集团等，但它们主要是通过行政资产划拨的方式直接组成的旅游集团，作为地方旅游局的直属企业，而不是真正意义上的旅游集团。

4．西部各省旅游收入分布不合理（The Unreasonable Distribution of Traveling Income in the Western Provinces）

表 4.4　西部地区十省（或直辖市）1997—2002年旅游外汇收入

（USD million）

省（或直辖市）	1997年	1998年	1999年	2000年	2001年	2002年
重庆	105	66	97	138	163	218
四川	79	84	97	122	166	200
贵州	44	48	55	61	69	80
云南	264	261	350	339	367	419
西藏	32	33	36	52	46	52
陕西	225	247	272	280	309	351

续表

省(或直辖市)	1997年	1998年	1999年	2000年	2001年	2002年
甘肃	28	30	37	55	45	54
青海	3	3	4	7	9	10
宁夏	1	1	2	3	3	2
新疆	71	82	86	95	99	99

(资料来源:《2003年中国统计年鉴》)

云南省和陕西省是西部的旅游大省,海外游客接待规模和旅游创汇收入进入全国前10名。在90年代以前,云南省还是一个旅游基础设施落后、旅游产业规模弱小的边疆省份,而在"九五"的前4年,云南省国际旅游收入年均增长速度超过20%,大大高于全国12.7%的年均增长速度。截止到1999年底,云南省接待海外旅游者人数居全国第6位,旅游外汇收入居全国第7位,拥有涉外旅游饭店数居全国第2位。旅游业已成为有力促进云南省社会经济全面发展和快速增长的主导产业。然而其他省区旅游业发展却相对落后,排在全国20位以后。特别是宁夏、青海、西藏和甘肃排在最后,列居全国倒数后四名。

总体而言,西部地区旅游业起点低,水平落后,产业规模小,从业人员少,经济效益低,旅游产品开发处于初期阶段。西部应通过10—15年努力,把旅游业建设成西部经济增长的战略支撑点,并进一步成为西部各省区(市)的支柱产业;使西部融入国际社会,成为中国乃至世界重要的生态旅游、文物古迹和民俗风情游的目的地。

西部旅游开发应坚持政府主导与企业自主经营相结合,强调区域联动和资源共享;以旅游中心城市和王牌景区景点为依托,坚持据点式开发和点轴式开发结合,走精品路线。在自然风光游的基础上大力开展生态旅游,在保护文化多样性的基础上大力开展民俗风情游,在严格保护的基础上发展文物古迹游。

西北区将重点发展历史文化遗迹游和特种旅游。西南区重点发展民族风情游和生态旅游。青藏高原区大力培育旅游市场,以青藏铁路的修建和川藏、滇藏公路的改造为契机,加强旅游基础设施建设,建设并推出"茶马古道"产品。

西部各省要利用自己的资源优势,加快旅游基础设施建设,加强生态环境保护和建设,积极调整西部地区旅游区域结构,加强区域间合作,促进西部地区旅游产业的共同发展。

复习思考题:
1. 什么叫旅游产业区域结构?
2. 市场区位论的基本内容是什么?旅游市场区位论与一般市场区位论有什么区别?
3. 中心地理论的基本内容是什么?谈谈其在旅游产业中的运用。
4. 旅游地生命周期理论有哪几个阶段?每个阶段有哪些特征?
5. 影响旅游产业区域结构的因素有哪些?分析旅游资源对旅游产业区域结构的影响。
6. 根据旅游产业区域布局理论,我国旅游产业区域布局应该采取什么样的模式?
7. 我国旅游产业区域布局中存在哪些问题?如何对其进行优化?

第五章
产业组织导论
(Introduction to Industrial Organization)

从本章开始,我们将用成熟的产业组织理论对旅游产业进行分析。本章主要清晰界定产业组织经济学的研究内容、研究方法、理论体系,辨析产业组织经济学与产业经济学以及传统经济学之间的关系,指出在本书中主要涉及的产业组织主要问题,并结合旅游产业研究提出相应问题的研究意义。

第一节 产业组织的产生与发展
(The Initiation and Development of Industrial Organization)

在导论中我们已对产业经济学的研究对象、方法和理论体系做了简单介绍,本章着重研究产业组织理论,也就是西方的产业经济学。需要说明的是,西方的产业经济学和我国的产业组织是一个概念,都是研究产业内部企业之间关系的学科。我国理论界关于产业经济学的概念界定是从日本引进的,即包括产业结构、产业组织和产业政策等内容。这里把产业组织作为重点介绍,一方面是因为产业组织在西方学术体系中作为独立学科具有重要地位,另一方面则是因为它对于研究具体产业内部的企业之间的竞争与垄断关系、竞争与协作关系具有重要意义。

一、产业组织的概念 (The Concept of Industrial Organization)

虽然对于产业的研究由来已久,但是产业组织,即西方的产业经济学的概念却是一个新兴事物。The term "industrial economics" appears to have crept into the literature in the early 1950s. Before the economic analysis of industry was not recognized as a distinctive branch of economics in many quarters, there are many names similar to the industrial economics, such as 'economics of industry', 'industry and trade', 'business economics', 'commerce' and 'industrial organization'. Among these names, 'industrial organization' is the most frequently encountered term and is still a common used term in the United States. 因此,在本篇中,产业经济学和产业组织是同义词,在以后的内容中不做区分。

在产业经济学研究领域中对产业或产业经济学缺乏一个可以被理论界普遍接受的统一概念,这一方面反映出对产业经济学研究对象和范围缺乏统一认识,另一方面也反映了对产业经济学研究方法缺乏统一认识。The editorial introduction to the American Economic Association's *Readings in Industrial Organization and Public Policy*, published in 1958, indicates that at that time:

... the field of industrial organization and public policy has neither a well-defined content nor precise boundaries. Some [graduate] courses emphasize the organization and characteristics of industrial markets in general and of some markets in particular. Others are designed to show the relationship between industrial markets and price theory and to modify and extend that theory in the light of the facts of industrial organization. Still others are concerned primarily with public policy issues. With little attention given to an analysis of market organization or price theory...

在介绍产业组织概念之前,必须要清楚产业(industry)的概念。Industry is strictly a group of sellers of close-substitute outputs (or service) who supply a common group of buyers. 在产业组织经济学的研究中,"产业"是指生产同一类产品(或提供同一类服务)的生产者(企业)的集合。而所谓"同一类产品(或服务)",则是指具有可替代性的产品(或服务)。产业组织经济学就是研究各产业内企业之间的关系,主要研究厂商、产业和市场的组织形式,即以一种什么样的结构存在,这种市场结构是如何影响市场运行过程中企业的行为以及市场绩效的。

产品的相互可替代性是划分不同产业的主要标志,即同一产业的产品虽不完全相同,但却可以替代。从产业组织经济学中"产业"的角度来看,本书中所讲的旅游产业根本不存在,因为我们这里所说的旅游产业包括旅行社、旅游饭店、旅游景区景点和旅游车船公司。旅行社提供的是旅游线路的设计和旅游过程组织的服务,旅游饭店提供的是住宿餐饮服务,旅游景区景点提供的是旅游资源,而旅游车船公司提供的则是交通运输服务。很显然,这四种服务相互之间不可替代。因此,把旅行社、旅游饭店、旅游景区景点和旅游车船公司包括在一个旅游产业中不符合产业组织中关于产业的定义,也就是说,从产业组织的角度来讲,旅游产业这个概念不应该存在或者说这个定义不具有科学性。这个问题在旅游学界曾经引起过争鸣,有人认为根本不存在旅游产业的说法,旅游产业是旅行社产业、旅游饭店产业、旅游景区景点产业和旅游车船公司产业的综合。但不可否认的是,一个完整的旅游产品的提供是由旅行社、饭店、旅游景区和旅游车船公司等共同提供的,它们都是旅游整个过程中不可缺少的重要环节,正是这些不同产品的有机结合才促成了旅游过程的圆满完成。而且多年来无论从理论上还是从实践上我们一直把旅游作为一个"产业"来发展。因此,在研究旅游产业组织问题之前,我们先澄清这样一个问题:在谈到整体问题时,我们把旅游作为一个产业;在研究具体问题时,我们则分别对旅行社、饭店、旅游景区景点和旅游车船公司来进行研究。

为了能更好地理解"产业"及"产业组织"这两个概念,我们需要对一些概念进行辨析。

1. 产业和市场(Industry and Market)

A market is conveniently defined as a closely interrelated group of sellers and buyers. Market includes all the sellers in any individual industry, and all the buyers to whom they sell. 也就是说,市场即包括卖方也包括买方,是卖方和买方、供给和需求的有机结合,只有供求相等时市场才处于平衡状态。而产业的划分是从供给方也就是卖方做出的。从卖方的角度看,市场是产业的综合。把市场划分为不同的产业是为了研究不同产业的市场结构以及产业中的企业行为和绩效。由于不同类产品之间的不可替代性,使得把市场作为一个整体来研究没有什么意义。但在研究问题时我们通常把产业结构和市场结构视为同义词,也就是说:We regard the terms "industry structure" and "market structure" as the similar term in meaning, so we often make no distinguish of the two terms.

2. 产业组织和微观经济学(Industrial Organization and Micro-Economics)

一般认为,产业组织是基础经济学特别是微观经济学向产业经济领域的延伸,因此在研究内容和研究方法上二者有许多相似之处。但产业组织作为一门独立的学科在近几十年的飞速发展,又使其与微观经济学有很大差别。

从研究对象上看,微观经济学和产业组织经济学都研究厂商。但微观经济学主要分析单个经济主体在局部范围内所受到的主要制约因素,这些制约因素在何种条件下,按照何种方式以达到均衡状态,单个经济主体如何取得最大的利润或经济利益,以及最大的经济效益与均衡状态的关系。而产业组织经济学则是研究同一个产业内部各个厂商之间的关系,研究的是企业群体的行为。微观经济学把厂商当作一个黑箱,忽略了企业内部的生产过程和组织过程。而产业组织经济学则探究了企业的本质和企业边界的决定,深入研究了企业内部的行为,拓展了经济学研究空间。

从研究方法上看,微观经济学更注重规范研究,而产业组织经济学则是规范研究和实证研究的结合。

二、产业组织的发展历史(The Development History of Industrial Organization)

1. 产业组织产生之前(The Antecedents of Industrial Organization)

一般认为,产业组织经济学的系统研究发端于20世纪30年代的美国哈佛大学。其实产业组织理论的渊源可以追溯到亚当·斯密。亚当·斯密在《国富论》中提出市场自发调节自由竞争的市场机制以及劳动分工理论。这两个理论都谈到了在市场经济体制下厂商的市场行为。这一论述对西方经济学和产业组织理论都产生了直接影响和重大作用。

英国经济学家 A. 马歇尔(A. Marshall)则被视为产业组织理论的创始人。马歇尔在他与夫人共著的《产业经济学》(Industry and Trade)一书中,第一次把产业内部的结构定义为产业组织。随后,马歇尔在1890年出版的经济学名著《经济学原理》(Principles of Economics)一书中,就提出了生产要素不仅有劳动、资本和土地,还有第四种生产要素"组织"。这里的组织包括企业内部的组织形态、产业内部的组织形态、产业之间的组织形态和国家组织形态。马歇尔在《经济学原理》中专门分析了分工的利益,产业向特定区域集中的利益、大规模生产的利益、经营管理专业化的利益、收益递减和收益递增等许多现代产业组织理论的主要概念与内容。马歇尔之所以把组织作为第四生产要素,是因为他在分析研究上述问题时触及到了规模的经济性问题。马歇尔认为组织作为一种生产要素存在是因为组织与规模经济即收益递增有关。马歇尔发现,随着组织规模的扩大,企业产品的生产成本不断下降,市场占有率不断提高,企业在产业中或市场中的垄断势力不断增强,而垄断势力的增强又必将阻碍竞争,这种竞争与规模经济之间的冲突被称为"马歇尔冲突",并成为产业组织理论研究的核心问题。面对竞争与规模经济之间的冲突,以及如何使规模经济与竞争活力保持某种程度的均衡,马歇尔本人未能提出令人信服的观点和解决办法。

马歇尔的研究对产业组织经济学的产生有着重大的影响。此后,一些经济学的研究和大学的经济学课程中也有了一些涉及股份公司、企业营销、反托拉斯法等内容,但这些内容都没有形成系统的体系。也就是说,直到20世纪30年代之前,产业组织经济学还没有成为一门具有独立意义的经济学分支学科。

2. 产业组织的产生(The Birth of Industrial Organization)

产业组织经济学的产生得益于几部经济学著作:

伯利和米恩斯(Berle & Means)于1932年出版的《现代股份公司和私人财产》(The Modern Corporation and Private Property)。该书推动了用经济学理论来理解企业制度的研究,可以说是对作为产业组织研究基础的厂商理论所进行的早期系统论述。

1933年,美国经济学家张伯仑(E. H. Chamberlin)和英国经济学家琼·罗宾逊(J. Robinson)分别出版了《垄断竞争理论》(The Theory of Monopolistic Competition)和《不完全竞争经济学》(The Economics of Imperfect Competition)。经济学界高度评价这两本书的出版,萨缪尔逊称之为"垄断竞争的革命"。In the mainstream of microeconomic theory perfect competition model is based upon marginal analysis, however, if there were prevalent increasing returns in industry, how could an equilibrium position that satisfied the conditions of the perfect competition model be achieved at the individual firm level? E. H. Chamberlin and J. Robinson have answered the question separately almost at the same time by using the downward-sloping individual firm's demand curve.

In the perfect competition model, there are so many small sellers and buyers to produce or to buy a single identical product in the same industry that none of sellers or buyers can influence the price through changing the production or the quantity of purchase but to accept the price determined by the supply and demand curve in the market. However, the perfect competition market does not exist in more realistic market situations. Many firms are large and multi-product and produce in more than one industry and sell in more than one market. Product differentiation is universal in the industry and many of which are not close substitutes. In order to solve the actual question, Chamberlin and Ronbinson develop the imperfect competition in the early 1930s to regard the structure of market, not the industry, as determinants of business and industrial behavior. Chamberlin argue that the real market is neither pure competition nor pure monopoly, but a mixture of competition and monopoly. In the industry, the products produced by the different firms are similar but not the same and they can substitute but can not substitute perfectly, so every firm has a certain degree market power but has not pure monopoly power and every firm confronts a downward-sloping demand curve but not a horizontal demand curve.

可以看出,在《垄断竞争理论》中,张伯伦对竞争和垄断的概念以及竞争与垄断的关系进行了新的解释和论证。他认为,在现实经济中,竞争和垄断不是截然分开的,实际的市场既不是纯粹竞争的,也不是纯粹垄断的,而是竞争和垄断的混合。竞争和垄断的混合,其根源就在于产品差别。由于产品的差别性使得任何一种产品的生产者(或卖者)都可能拥有对自己产品的垄断性,因此每一个生产者都可能成为垄断者;另一方面,每一种产品又都会受到替代产品的竞争,因此每一个生产者之间又都是竞争者。而琼·罗宾逊在《不完全竞争经济学》中则论证说,由于在现实的经济中,竞争本身使得市场成为不完全的,而不完全的市场又导致不完全竞争。传统的经济学总是首先分析完全竞争,而把垄断竞争当作一个特例。而她的《不完全竞争经济学》则先分析垄断,而把完全竞争当作一个特例。

垄断竞争理论出现之后,产业组织课程开始走进大学课堂。The first courses in industrial organization were started in Harvard in the early 1930s under Chamberlin and Mason(梅森)。Chamberlin's work in the courses gave the definition and classification of more realistic market including oligopoly(寡头垄断) and monopoly-competition(垄断竞争)。1938 年,以梅森为中心,由贝恩(Joe S. Bain)、凯尔森(C. Kaysen)、麦克尔(J. W. Mckie)、麦克海姆(J. Markham)和艾得曼(M. Addman)等人组成了一个产业组织研究小组,以案例研究的方式,分析若干行业的市场结构。1939 年,该产业组织研究小组出版了第一批有关产业的集中度资料。1957 年,梅森出版了他自 1936 年以来的论文集《经济集中和垄断问题》(*Economic Concentration and Monopoly Problem*)。

从以上的论述中可以看出,产业组织理论研究的重点就是不完全竞争的市场结构。The imperfect competition model, compared with perfect competition model, focused on that both the business conduct and the business performance of firms are dependent upon the structure of the market. This view is the basis of the market structure-market conduct-market performance(市场结构—市场行为—市场绩效) paradigm, which began to develop in the 1930s but probably reached its peak during the1960s after the publication of Bain's major work on industrial organization in 1959. 贝恩是梅森教授在哈佛大学的博士生,他是产业经济学的最重要的创始人。贝恩教授的著作《产业组织》一书是现代产业组织经济学的经典著作,由于贝恩的产业组织理论体系的基本逻辑是从市场结构推断市场绩效,通常被称为结构主义的产业组织理论。同时由于贝恩的著作是基于哈佛大学一批产业经济学家的研究成果的基础之上,代表着哈佛大学产业经济学家的学术观点,因此贝恩的产业组织理论也被称为哈佛学派的产业组织理论。

后来,谢勒(Frederic M. Scherer)出版了《产业市场结构和经济绩效》(*Industrial Market Structure and Economic Performance*)一书中,对产业组织经济学作了系统地论述,特别是论述了"基本情况—市场结构—行为—绩效"的关系,最终形成了哈佛学派的"结构—行为—绩效"分析范式,对后来的产业组织理论的发展产生了重要的影响。

哈佛学派的产业组织理论是以新古典学派的价格理论为基础,在承袭了前人一系列理论研究成果的同时,以实证研究为主要手段,把产业分解成特定的市场,按结构、行为、绩效三个方面对其进行分析,构造了一个既能深入具体环节、又有系统逻辑体系的市场结构(Structure)—市场行为(Conduct)—市场绩效(Performance)的分析框架,简称 SCP 分析框架。

贝恩利用 SCP 分析框架,对市场结构的影响因素如产业集中、产品差别化、进入壁垒、规模经济性以及市场结构和市场绩效之间的关系作了很多研究,并得出结论认为高集中度的市场结构会产生垄断性的市场行为,进而导致不良的市场绩效,特别是资源配置的非效率。因此有效的产业组织政策首先应该着眼于形成和维护竞争的市场结构。哈佛学派的这种主张,对战后以美国为首的西方发达市场经济国家反垄断政策的开展和强化都曾产生过重大的作用。

3. 产业组织的发展(The Development of the Industrial Organization)

尽管哈佛学派建立的"结构—行为—绩效"分析范式奠定了现代产业组织经济学的基础,形成了一个独立的经济学分支学科,但是,许多经济学家指出,在这一分析范式下进行的产业组织问题研究,具有明显的经验主义的性质,所揭示的经济关系实际上在很大程度上只是一种相关关系,而未必揭示了内在的因果关系。而且哈佛学派的产业组织理论建立在经验研究的基础之上,缺乏严密理论体系的支撑,虽然利用回归分析技术验证了一些理论,但随着实践的发展,哈佛学派的 SCP 理论越来越不能很好地解释现实经济中存在的一些现象和问题。尤其是在 70 年代后期,很多学者认为由于在哈佛学派理论的指导下,美国实行了世界上最严厉的反垄断政策导致美国一些优势产业的国际竞争力不断下降。而且大型法托拉斯事件所带来的巨额的诉讼费用和大量的时间消耗,也使人们对结构规制的效益产生怀疑。因此,放松政府规制可以促进竞争效果的观点被越来越多的人所接受。所以,从 20 世纪 70 年代后期开始,围绕反垄断政策的放松,批判和反对结构主义理论的产业组织观点受到了瞩目。其中,最有影响的就是芝加哥学派的产业组织理论和鲍莫尔等人的可竞争市场理论。

The industrial economists in Chicago argue that the structure-conduct-performance paradigm may provide a far less suitable analytical framework for large diversified enterprises than for small firms assumed to operate under perfect or near-perfect market conditions. The behavior and performance of small firms may be strongly influenced by the exogenously determined structure of the market, but the influence of market structure on the large multi-product firms' conduct and performance is questionable. For example, firms can transform the structure of the market through technical innovation, product differentiation and merge. That is to say, conduct and performance can change or determine the market in turn. Hence, the structure-conduct-performance framework is weakened in two important points: 1) the conduct of large firms may change market structure; that is, the assumed chain of causality is reserved. 2) discretion in the formation of business goals further wakens the dependence of market performance upon market structure.

芝加哥学派的代表人物是施蒂格勒(J. S. Stigler)、德姆塞茨(H. Demsetz)、布罗曾(Y. Brozen)、波斯纳(R. Posener)、科斯(Ronald H. Coase)和威廉姆森(O. E. Wiliamson)。芝加哥学派强调市场机制自发作用的有效性和市场价格的调节作用,更强调严格的理论分析和对各种理论进行经验证明,把产业组织理论视为是价格理论的扩展。1968年施蒂格勒的名著《产业组织》一书问世,标志着芝加哥学派理论上的成熟。芝加哥学派认为,即使市场中存在着某些垄断势力或不完全竞争,只要不存在政府的进入规制,长期的竞争均衡状态在现实中也是能够成立的。即使市场是垄断的或是高度集中寡占的,只要市场绩效是良好的,政府规制就没有必要。芝加哥学派特别注重集中及定价结果是否提高了效率,而不是像哈佛学派那样只看是否损害了竞争。在芝加哥学派看来,高集中市场中长期出现高利润,只能说明该市场中大企业的高效率经营。因为不是建立在高效率经营基础上的高利润率水平,会招致其他企业的大量进入,而使利润率很快降至平均水平。因此,芝加哥学派对哈佛学派的SCP分析框架进行了猛烈的抨击,认为与其说是存在着市场结构决定市场行为进而决定市场绩效这样的因果关系,倒不如说是市场绩效或市场行为决定了市场结构。

芝加哥学派的主要代表人物科斯(Ronald H. Coase)关于企业与市场关系的理论奠定了现代厂商理论的基础,使交易费用成为产业组织经济理论的重要概念。1985年新制度学派产业组织理论的代表人物威廉姆森(O. E. Wiliamson)出版了《资本主义经济制度:企业、市场和关联合约》,以科斯的理论观点为基础,对交易费用经济学的理论体系、基本假说、研究方法和研究范围作了系统的阐述,建立了比较系统的新制度经济学派的产业组织理论。

鲍莫尔(W. J. Baumol)等人在芝加哥学派理论基础上又发展出可竞争理论。该理论认为,良好的生产效率和技术效率等市场绩效,在传统哈佛学派理想的市场结构以外仍然是可以实现的,而无需众多竞争企业的存在。它可以是寡头市场,甚至是垄断市场。只要保持市场进入的完全自由,只要不存在特别的进出市场成本,潜在竞争的压力就会迫使任何市场结构条件下的企业采取竞争行为。在这种环境条件下,包括自然垄断在内的高集中度的市场结构是可以和效率并存的。沉没成本是可竞争理论的核心概念,沉没成本的大小决定了企业从市场退出的难易程度。

4. 新产业组织理论(New Industrial Organization,NIO)

按照法国经济学家泰勒尔(Jean Tirole)的说法,20 世纪 70 年代,产业组织经济学进入了一个新的发展时期,即新产业组织理论时期,而此前的产业组织理论则被认为是传统产业组织理论。很多经济学家认为,所谓新产业组织理论(NIO),是指 20 世纪 70 年代以后出现的以分析企业策略性行为为主旨的,与以往有着根本不同的产业组织理论。新产业组织理论区别于传统产业组织的首要标志,也是其对产业组织研究的最大贡献,在于理论研究方法的统一,即博弈论已经成为新产业组织理论研究的统一方法,其中非合作博弈理论及其分析方法又无疑居于统治地位。也正因为如此,新产业组织理论得以克服作为传统产业组织理论基础的结构—行为—绩效范式的诸多缺陷,其基于正统寡占模型的一系列分析及其成果,使产业组织理论的发展得以成功地实现了向正统经济学的回归。新产业组织理论研究主要集中于六个方面:静态博弈理论、重复博弈和寡占理论、产品差别化、进入壁垒和进入阻止、技术进步与市场结构的动态演变以及信息不对称。

博弈论被引入产业组织研究极大地促进了产业组织理论的发展。将博弈论引入经济理论中,意味着传统的由市场机制决定的瓦尔拉斯均衡开始受到怀疑。企业可以通过许多非市场的制度安排来解决传统的市场问题。产业组织的博弈受到了经济学家的高度重视,是产业组织理论(更严格地说应该是产业组织理论研究方法)的重大发展。

5. 总结(Summary)

尽管产业组织研究发生了理论革命,理论研究方法的统一似乎也导致了产业组织理论向正统经济学的回归,但是产业经济学毕竟是一个经验性分析的领域,应用性的优劣也从来都是检验一种产业组织理论价值的首要标准。因此,虽然新产业组织理论所构建的理论体系是传统产业组织理论所无法比拟的,但其发展远没有达到足以完全取代传统产业组织理论的地步。即使是结构—行为—绩效理论遭到来自各方的批评,仍然有其广阔的应用空间。影响企业行为及其福利效应的因素极其广泛和复杂,着重于策略性行为分析的新产业组织理论无论其说服力如何,也只是揭示了其中一部分因素;结构—行为—绩效范式所注重的市场结构及其有关产业基本性质对企业行为的影响,也不会因为其分析方法本身的缺陷而被否定。而且在经验性分析领域,20世纪80年代以来经验性研究的复兴也表明结构—行为—绩效范式对于推动产业组织经验性研究的作用仍然优于其他分析范式。

总之,新产业组织理论和传统产业组织理论都是当代产业组织理论体系的组成部分,区别两者谁居于主流地位并不重要。新的和传统产业组织理论的融合是当代产业组织学发展的趋势。因此,本书在分析旅游产业组织时,既用到传统产业组织的SCP理论分析旅游产业的市场结构、企业行为和市场绩效,又用到新产业组织理论的研究方法博弈论来研究旅游企业博弈行为。

第二节 产业组织的研究方法
(The Methodology in Industrial Organization)

一、产业组织研究方法的演变(The Development of Methodology in Industrial Organization)

1. 产业组织产生之前(Antecedents of Industrial Organization)

The emphasis of the historical development of the economic analysis of industrial activity is the methodological division that existed between the mainstreams of English economic thought and the Historical and Institutional Schools in Germany during the late nineteenth and early twentieth centuries. The former has been characterized by the behavioral assumptions which use mathematical tools in relatively long and complex chains of reasoning and a high degree of abstraction from the events of the real world to enable the generalization to be achieved.

The Historical School questioned the assumed universality of the behavioral assumptions maintained by some English economists, however, argued that economic analysis should be based upon empirical investigations, so the theory and analysis are not absolute or universal but relative.

The methodological differences between the two divergent thoughts were reconciled by Marshall(马歇尔) in his distinguished books *Principles of Economics* and *Industry and trade* which may be regarded as two of the early textbooks in industrial economics.

Marshall, however, was not an indiscriminate empiricist who believed in collecting factual information for its own sake. His methods provided for the interplay between induction and deduction.

Induction, aided by analysis and deduction, brings together appropriate classes of facts, arranges them, analyses them and infers from them general statements or laws. Then for a while deduction plays the chief role: it brings some of these generalizations into association with one another, works from them tentatively to new and broader generalizations or laws and then calls on induction again to do the main share of the work in collecting, sifting and arranging these facts so as to test and 'verify' the new law.

Marshall integrated the methods of analysis originating from divergent schools of thought, however, many of his contemporaries of successors didn't agree with that, so the microeconomic theory which is within the received English tradition separate from, and often in conflict with, industrial economics with its strongly institutional antecedents. In mainstream of English economics, the perfect competition model based on the marginal analysis, however, the Oxford economists who established an industry research group questioned the validity of the marginal principles underlying received price theory and also about the validity of inductive empiricism and the particular methods of empirical investigation and interpretation used by them. The gap between the traditional microeconomics was still big in that time.

2. 产业组织产生之后(The Methods after the Industrial Organization)

19世纪30年代产生了以哈佛学派为代表的产业组织经济学。哈佛学派的研究范式是结构主义,即市场结构决定企业行为,进而决定市场绩效。这一时期产业经济学研究的一个主要特点,就是利用计量经济学的方法对产业层面上的数据做了大量的计量分析,验证了结构—行为一绩效理论。可以说,这一时期的研究方法是以实证分析法为主。

During the 1960s and 1970s the gulf between mainstream of English economics and the industrial economics has been narrowing. There are two reasons for the trend: one is a growing awareness of the need to explore the wider implications of their findings for economic analysis and to become more explicitly involved in the process of theory formulation among empirical researchers. Andrews, the editor of *Journal of Industrial Economics*, indicates:

Economics needs a workable theory of the behavior of the individual business. I venture to suggest that this approach will only be found through empirical work on actual businesses... If we wish to theorize fruitfully about individual businesses, we must find out what are the facts about their behavior and then construct a general theory especially in order to take account of those faces.

The main industry economists agree with the view of Andrews:

Although I have depended strongly upon received economic theory for concepts and hypotheses... the present work is definitely not one in a priori price theory. The emphasis is directly on empirical study concerning issues raised by such theory, or on the implementation, application and critical testing of such theory.

The other reason is during 1960s and 1970s there has been a new emphasis placed on the formal empirical testing of hypotheses as a means of establishing that theories are 'acceptable'. The testing techniques have the beneficial side effect of helping to bring these two divergent schools of thinking closer together. On the one hand, this new emphasis is leading economists working in the mainstream of microeconomic theory to enter certain of the traditional areas of empirical research within industrial economics; on the other hand, it is forcing the traditional industrial economist to clarify the objectives of his empirical research and to subject his techniques of investigation to more critical analysis.

3. 产业组织的发展(The Development of the Industrial Organization)

哈佛学派受到芝加哥学派抨击的一个主要原因是芝加哥学派认为哈佛学派的研究大都是建立在经验主义研究的基础之上,本身缺乏一个系统的理论框架,是没有理论的。芝加哥学派以价格理论为基础,建立起自己的理论框架。因此,芝加哥学派更注重规范研究和理论研究,而经验主义研究则趋于衰落。

尤其是博弈论的兴起推动了产业组织理论的发展。博弈论是以人的理性和无限精确的计算能力为理论假设前提的,并有许多博弈论模型来研究产业组织的行为和策略选择。博弈论使产业组织的研究进入了一个飞速发展的时期。

但由于博弈论的假设前提不符合实际——因为人是有限理性的,而且其运算能力也不是无穷的——这种假设前提限制了博弈论在产业组织中的进一步发展。尤其到了九十年代经验研究的重新兴起,使得对企业层面数据的实证研究再度兴起。

二、产业组织的研究方法（The Methodology in Industrial Organization）

在熟悉产业组织经济学研究方法的演变脉络之后,我们继续讨论目前在产业组织研究中被普遍使用的研究方法。

1. 规范研究和实证研究(Normative Analysis & Positive Analysis)

所谓规范研究(Normative Analysis),是一种依靠分析判断、逻辑推理的方法。它回答所研究的经济现象"应该是什么样",从已有的价值判断标准出发,进行严密的分析判断与推理。比如说在产业组织理论中,分析产业组织之间相互影响、相互制约的内在本质,并发现带有普遍性的规律,用的就是规范研究方法。

实证研究法(Positive Analysis)主要是指经验性归纳方法,它回答所研究的经济现象"是什么",并对大量的实际资料进行分析,以总结出带有规律性的结论。哈佛学派中的"结构—行为—绩效"研究框架就是通过对大量的案例进行分析和对数据的计量分析总结出来的基本观点。

2. 理论研究和经验研究(Theoretical Analysis & Empirical Analysis)

从产业组织研究方法的演变中可以看出,理论研究和经验研究一直都是交替居于重要地位,而不能同时发挥作用,这和人们对理论研究和规范研究的错误认识有关。There was once a popular misconception that industrial economics forms part of applied economics, in contrast to received microeconomics, which is treated as a branch of theoretical economics. This confusion arises from identifying empirical investigation with applied economics and from identifying processes of logical deduction from generalized premises with economic theorizing. Empirical investigations in industrial economics place the development and refinement of economic theory among their principal objectives. In addition, the ultimate purpose of theorizing, by whatever method it is undertaken, is to interpret and predict in actual situations in the real world. Applied economics is the logical extension of any theoretical economics and is the ultimate justification for it.

理论研究是指在特定的框架内对事物进行理论上的演绎、推理和归纳，而经验性分析则指的是运用数据和实际资料的经济学研究。产业组织经济学研究中具有浓厚的经验性研究色彩，人们对理论研究和经验性研究容易作出区分，但却常常将经验性研究方法与实证研究方法相混淆。事实上，从研究对象属于已经发生了的事件的角度来说，大多数经验性研究可以说是实证研究，但毕竟还有部分经验性研究因为涉及到价值的判断而实质上属于规范研究的范畴。同样，对于实证研究来说，其既可以是理论研究，也可以是经验性研究。

3. 博弈论(The Theory of Games)

博弈论又称对策论，主要研究决策主体的行为在发生直接的相互作用时，人们如何进行决策以及这种决策的均衡问题。Except where monopoly is assumed and the possibility of entry is assumed away, theoretical research in industrial economics today employs the tools of non-cooperative game theory. Modeling typically begins with the specification of the extensive form of a game: a description of which players move when, the actions and information available at each move, the probabilities of any random events to be chosen by "nature", and the functions determining each player's payoff. Some information may be private; each firm may know only its own cost function, for instance. Other information may be common knowledge; all firms may know the market demand function, for instance, and also know that all other firms have this same information as well.

产业组织是研究厂商行为的学科，由于厂商的行为是相互作用的，其收益函数不仅取决于自己的选择，还依赖竞争对手的选择。博弈论则为分析寡头市场行为及策略冲突提供了标准工具和统一的方法。如在分析厂商的进入与退出、定价行为和合谋策略时，就广泛使用了非合作博弈、不完全信息博弈、重复博弈的理论和方法等。

第三节 产业组织的 SCP 理论
(SCP Theory of Industrial Organization)

虽然哈佛学派的 SCP 理论曾经遭遇过来自芝加哥学派以及新产业组织理论的挑战,但在与这些学派的抗争之中,结构主义理论一直保持着旺盛的生命力,并始终作为产业组织理论的主要内容而存在。本书在介绍产业组织理论时也是以哈佛学派的结构主义理论为主要内容,并吸收芝加哥学派、可竞争市场理论以及新产业组织理论。

企业是市场经济的主体,但不同的企业在市场中的行为及其经营绩效是不同的。那么,what is the general determinants of the market conduct and performance of enterprise? This is the critical question for analyzing the market conduct and market performance. From the casual observation, common-sense judgment, and formalized economic theory, we can make a conclusion that there are two main sorts of determinants. The first is the market structure or the industry structure which has great determining influence on the market performance, so different market structure may lead to different performance. The second is market conduct of enterprises, including price-making, entering and quitting, strategy-making, policy-making and so on. Generally market structure determines the enterprise's conduct and in turn determines the market performance. This is the distinguished theory named SCP in the industry organization.

市场结构—行为—绩效是产业组织的研究范式。The structure-performance model hypothesizes that particular types of market structure are associated with particular types of market behavior and performance. 这种研究范式可用图 5-1 表示:

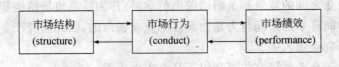

图 5-1 SCP 框架

哈佛学派的观点认为结构、行为、绩效之间的关系是单向的,即市场结构决定市场行为,进而决定市场绩效。但芝加哥学派则认为三者的关系是双向的,市场行为和绩效不仅受市场结构的影响,而且通过提高市场绩效,改变厂商的行为,还可以改善市场结构。

结构—行为—绩效(structure-conduct-performance,SCP)的分析范式完全是建立在新古典经济理论的基础上的,长期以来一直是传统产业组织理论研究的核心。这一理论从理论和实证方面揭示了市场结构、企业行为和市场绩效之间的关系,并指出市场结构通过影响企业行为而决定市场绩效。That is to say, market structure and the market conduct are the primary determinants of the performance of enterprises. If we want to improve the enterprises or market performance, we must rationalize the market structure leading to the rational enterprise conduct. According to this theory, before we measure and appraise the market performance, we should identify, describe, and classify the different types of structure and conduct in the real market and world, and determine what kind of structure type will be the effective structure and will acquire the best performance. In addition, we should establish some meaningful pattern of casual or determining relationship between structure and conduct as well as between the structure and the performance.

由于"结构—行为—绩效"理论范式可以将产业组织的主要内容包容在一个简洁的框架中,所以尽管产业组织经济学的发展已经突破了这一分析范式,但它至今仍然是产业组织经济学体系的主体逻辑构造(参见图 5-2)。

第四节 企业(Firm)

企业是产业的细胞,是产业和市场的主体。产业经济学是研究产业内部企业之间的竞争和垄断的关系的学科,作为联系市场结构和市场绩效的中间环节的市场行为是由具体的企业做出的,因此研究产业经济学要从研究企业入手。

对于企业的研究主要从以下几个方面入手:

- 厂商理论的发展
- 什么是企业?

- 为什么企业是以现有的规模存在？
- 企业是如传统经济学所认为的追求利润最大化的主体吗？
- 传统经济学企业利润最大化目标是否可行？

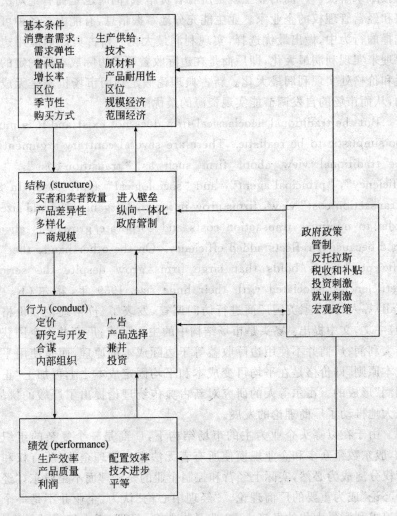

图 5-2 "结构—行为—绩效"理论范式示意图

（资料来源：《产业组织经济学》，P10，金碚编著，经济管理出版社。）

一、厂商理论的发展（The Development of Firm Theory）

In traditional neoclassical theory a firm is a profit-maximizing entity that operates very mechanically. All members of the neoclassical firm work imperfect harmony, with full information, and always to the utmost of their ability. 新古典主义的厂商理论认为,厂商是一个"原子"式的"经济人",一切组织和经营管理问题,都能通过购买生产要素或支付报酬来解决。厂商的业主就是所有者资本家,同时也是拥有绝对决策权和经营管理权的企业家。业主能充分地掌握信息,有能力在各种可供选择的行为中,做出最优选择,实现利润最大化。新古典厂商应用边际原理来实现利润最大化,即厂商是在边际收益等于边际成本所确定的产量和价格处实现利润最大化。新古典理论假定利用市场机制是无成本的,从而市场的自发调节能实现资源的最优配置。

But the traditional neoclassical firm does not exist and it is much too simplistic to be realistic. There are several contrary argument to the traditional view about firm such as "transition-cost", "X-efficiency", "principal-agent", and "sociological" approaches. In the "transaction-cost" view, firms grow in internal organization and size in order to minimize transaction costs and corporate growth is always good because it reflects added efficiency. On the other hand, the "X-efficiency" view holds that large firms grow despite the serious inefficiencies associated with their huge size. 1939年,霍尔(R. L. Hall)等人对38家英国厂商进行访问调查,发表了《价格理论和价格行为》一文,文中提出:寡头是市场结构中的主要形式;厂商并不企图获得最大利润;厂商并不使用边际收益等于边际成本的原理,而是使用平均成本原则,即价格是在平均可变成本和平均固定成本之上再加上"正常利润"形成的。霍尔等人的研究对新古典传统理论提出了严峻的挑战,极大地推动了厂商理论的发展。

由于在以寡头企业为主的市场结构下,厂商是一个复杂的组织结构,股东数量众多和企业规模使所有者无法亲自管理企业,所有权和经营权分离成为必然,实际上经营和控制企业的是经理而不是股东,"经理中心论"成为重要的厂商理论。"经理中心论"认为,企业并不是一个完全追求利润最大化的经济人,企业是由股东、经理、工人组成的结合体,各类人员的利益目标是相互冲突的。经理是实际控制和经营企业的最高决策层,在满足股东一定的利益要求之后,就可以偏离利润最大化目标,追求自身效用最大化。其中有代表性的是:鲍莫尔(W. J. Baumol)在1959年出版了《企业行为、价值而后增长》一书,提出了"最大销售收入"模型;马里斯(R. Marris)在1963年发表《经理型企业模型》一文,提出"最大增长率"假说;威廉姆森(O. Williamson)在1963年发表了《经理决断和企业行为》一文,提出"经理效用函数"理论,都表明了"经理"中心论的思想。

西蒙(H. A. Simon)于1955年发表的《合理选择的行为模型》提出了新的厂商理论。西蒙认为,厂商最高管理层的任务是:确定厂商的目标,尽可能地协调厂商的目标和各群体目标之间的冲突,以做出决策。决策过程遵循的是"令人满意"的原则,即厂商不是完全理性和追求利润最大化的,而是"有限理性"的。

目前,在厂商理论中居于主导地位的是由科斯、威廉姆森提出的现代厂商理论。现代厂商理论提出了交易费用的概念,认为市场和企业是两种配置资源的方式,都存在交易费用。企业对市场的取代是因为在一定程度上企业可以节约交易费用。

二、什么是企业(What Is the Firm?)

1. 企业的性质(The Characteristics of the Firm)

In defining the "firm", three main characteristics deserve emphasis: (1) collectivity of people in an organization; (2) action by superior-subordinate direction, and (3) continuity over time due to incomplete contracts among those in the organization.

(1) 群体性(Collectivity of People in an Organization)

The collectivity characteristic of the firm implies a group of people working together in some way. The group may be small or large in which all people are supposed to be on the same team. 与企业不同的是,市场强调的是个体行为,比如说市场上的每个消费者通常都是自行决策,而没有像企业团队中每个成员那样协作。

(2) 科层制(Action by Superior-subordinate Direction)

The firm is characterized by some degree of hierarchy, in which superiors with authority give direction to subordinates. 这里并不是说企业内部决策都是下级服从上级,都是集权的,其实企业内部许多决策都是通过民主程序完成的。与企业的这种上级对下级的领导不同,在市场中各个主体的行为都是自愿的而且是自由的。

(3) 不完全契约的连续性(The Continuity Over Time Due to Incomplete Contracts)

There is continuity to a firm that arises from the incomplete "contracts" that hold the firm together. In the market, contracts are usually completed, ending with the market transaction itself. But the firm's contracts are incomplete because the managers and employee have continuing relationships with their firms.

从以上对企业性质的分析,我们可以对许多关于企业的定义进行综合,给企业一个相对完整准确的定义:a firm is a coalition among owners of separately owned resources (including labor) whose value as a team exceeds the sum of the market values each could get separately.

2. 公司(Corporation)

在所有的企业类型中,公司是最重要的一种,它与私有制和合伙制企业有很多不同之处。The law grants certain powers, privileges, and liabilities to the corporation, as if it were an entity separate from the stockholder-owners.

The following figure sketches the hierarchy of a simple corporate.

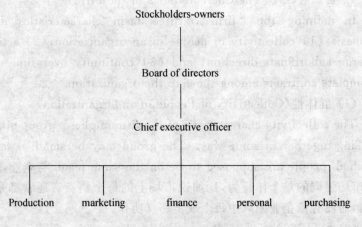

图 5-3　公司组织结构图

From the figure, we can see the stockholder-owners in command and they elect a board of directors to represent their views. The board meets only infrequently and does not make daily decisions. However, the board hires and fires managing officers according to how well they serve the owners' interests. In practice, the managers, not the stockholder-owners, control most major corporations. The usual election procedure is for management to nominate a slate of candidates and then ask the stockholders for proxies, that is, permission to use the stockholders' votes on behalf of this slate for candidates. In short, the managers select and control the board. Indeed, managers themselves hold a majority of seats on the boards of many of corporations. However, stockholders have the option of buying or selling stock to reward or punish the manager, so the managers have to consider the stockholders benefit. The threat of a "takeover" is today the main way in which the capital market could urge managers to act in the owners' interests. A takeover occurs when an acquiring firm buys enough stock to gain ownership control of a target firm and then replaces the old directors and management staff with new blood. The acquiring firm could then remove the bad management, improve decision-making, and thereby increase the earnings of the target firm to make money from the takeover.

  The takeover threat is not a fully effective means of controlling management, however. First, there are information problems. 例如，有的企业业绩不好并不是因为经营管理不善，而是因为其所处的行业不景气，即使企业被接管也不可能有更高的回报，这将降低接管者的积极性。Second, rewards to acquiring firms are severely limited by competition among acquires. 如果经营不善的企业被接管之后真能获得高收益，在接管者之间就会产生激烈的竞争，从供给和需求的角度来看，就是接管的需求增多了，而接管的供给没变，那么接管的价格就要提高，接管者会发现接管的收益不能补偿接管成本甚至给自己带来损失，这也会打消接管者的积极性。Third, managers of prospective target firms can engage in defensive tactics to protect themselves against takeover threats. 一般情况下，被接管企业在面临接管时都要誓死抵抗（除了和接管者达成协议同意接管）或在企业章程中规定一系列章程以增加被接管的难度，如毒丸计划、金色降落伞、银色降落伞等。[①]

三、企业为什么存在(Why Do Firms Exist?)

  与计划相比，市场配置资源这种方式具有很高的效率。那么，为什

---

 ① 相应内容可参见有关收购、兼并的内容，这里不详细阐述。

么人类的一切经济活动不能完全依靠市场来解决呢,为什么会有企业存在呢?科斯在《企业的性质》一书中对这个问题做了深刻的解释。科斯认为,企业和市场都是资源配置的方式,每一种资源配置的方式都有相应的成本。市场配置资源的成本主要包括搜寻成本、交易双方提出要求、讨价还价、签订合同、交货检验搜寻等方面,这些成本都是为了完成一定的交易而产生的,科斯把其称为交易成本。而企业配置资源的成本主要表现在企业内部的管理成本。由于现实中存在的信息不对称、资产专用性以及契约的不完全性等多种原因,在一定程度上用企业代替市场配置资源,以企业内部的行政命令来代替市场中的自由契约可以节省交易成本。当企业规模达到一定程度,企业内部的管理和协调成本大于依靠市场进行交易的成本时,则企业的规模不能继续扩张。企业合理的边界在于企业内部的管理成本和市场的交易成本相等的地方。企业之所以存在是因为市场交易是有费用的,企业是对市场的代替。

企业的优点(The Firms' Benefits)主要表现在以下三个方面:

1. 团队内部的专业化生产(Specialization in Teams)

专业化生产可以提高效率是经济学的鼻祖亚当·斯密早在1776年出版的《国富论》中就提到的观点。其实在市场中也存在着分工,只是在企业内部的分工是在团队之间进行的。团队的组成人员长期在一起劳作,彼此非常熟悉,可以很好地配合,这是团队内部的专业化生产优于市场内部的专业化生产的主要原因。

2. 交易费用的节约(Transaction-cost Economizing)

In 1937 Ronald Coase(科斯) advanced the theory that the firm has significant advantages in being able to carry out some transactions more cheaply than the market. Coase identified the costs of negotiating agreements and determining appropriate prices as the chief costs of market-mediated transactions.

Oliver Williamson(威廉姆森) has argued " that the modern corporation is mainly to be understood as the product of a series of organizational innovations that have the purpose and effect of economizing transactions costs." He stresses three dimensions along which transactions may vary: asset specificity, uncertainty, and frequency. Asset specificity refers to the fact that some assets are of value only or mainly to a specific firm, while other assets are not "specific" to the firm because they have value elsewhere as well.

Uncertainty means that circumstances continually change, precluding certainty about the future. Frequency means the extent to which transactions are often repeated or consolidated into long-term contracts. The firm saves on transaction costs because it curbs the protracted bargaining that arises from asset specificity. It facilitates the adaptability necessary to cope with uncertainty, and it reduces the frequency of transactions.

Because of the asset specificity, uncertainty, and frequency, the transaction costs through market is much more than through firm. By internalizing transactions involving specific assets, the firm can minimize bargaining costs because all gains and losses at stake will then likewise be internalized to the firm. With the stakes internalized, there is, in a sense, nothing more at stake to cause wasteful barging.

3. 资本的形成(Enlarged Capital Formation)

Unlike proprietorships or partnerships, corporations can sell shares of company ownership in the form of common stock or preferred stock. Moreover, "limited liability" protects these shareholders. 这种方式有助于资本的形成。

四、企业的目标(The Objective of a Firm)

企业的经营目标或经营动机与企业的行为,如价格策略、营销等有密切的关系,因此企业经营目标已成为企业的一个重要问题。在前面我们曾谈到过市场结构决定企业行为,其实结构不能单独决定企业行为。The combination of structural conditions and firm motivation determines conduct. Moreover, variance in structure itself probably promotes some variances in motivation.

In traditional theory, profit maximization motivates all firms in all market settings. The hypothesis of firm profit maximization rests on three assumptions concerning "the firms": 1) single-minded purpose; 2) rational or forced choice of objective; 3) the adherence to operational rules of optimality.

(1) single-minded purpose. This assumption infers that no matter how big and diverse the firm happens to be, all its owners and employees work as one to achieve its objective.

(2) Rationality. The assumption of rationality implies a goal of profit maximization.

(3) Operational rules. There is technical rule in maximizing profit: Expand production and promotion as long as added revenues exceed added costs; cut back whenever the resulting reductions in costs exceed the reductions in revenues, that is to say, the maximizing profit is at the point where the marginal revenue equals marginal cost.

随着理论研究的深入和实践的发展,利润最大化目标遭遇了多方的批评。All criticism may be gathered under three broad labels designating focuses of attack: (1) realism in process; (2) managerialism; (3) behaviorialism.

"Realism in process" accepts the assumptions of single-mindedness and rational choice but reject the notion that $MR=MC$ is an adequate operational objective for business people. Business people cannot maximize profits by this rule alone, even they wanted to. There are still some questions left unanswered such as: What costs and revenues are supposed to be included in this calculation?

"Managerialism" doubt that the typical firm is run for the single-minded pursuit of the owners' interests. They argue that in most large corporations the owners and managers are not the same people and they are not driven by the same objectives. This make the assumption irrational and establish more goals other than profit maximization. Oliver Williamson's theories of managerial utility assume that for tax and other reasons managers are interested in executive jets, liberal expense accounts, and other emoluments or perquisites as well as personal income and company profits. 威廉姆森指出,由于多种原因,经理人员除追求正常的个人收入和利润之外,可能还有雇员或职工规模、可随意支配的费用额(交通费或招待费等)、管理者个人"名声"以及其他好处。

"Behaviorialists" deny that profit maximization is typical of business for reasons that blend "realism in process" and "managerialism". They believed that humans engage in "satisficing" rather than maximizing behavior and that human rules of daily operation reflect this.

第五节 旅游产业组织理论的主要内容
(Main Contents of Tourism Industrial Organization)

本书研究的重点是旅游产业组织。根据前面的介绍可以看出产业组织理论经过几十年的快速发展,已成为一门学科体系完善,内容丰富,研究水平较高的学科。本书以旅游产业作为研究对象,主要是研究旅游产业组织之间的竞争与协作关系。在研究过程中,主要是利用哈佛学派的 SCP 理论,并结合芝加哥学派的理论和研究方法以博弈论来研究旅游产业的市场结构、企业行为和市场绩效。

在第六章,我们主要介绍旅游产业市场结构。重点介绍市场结构的衡量指标、各种市场结构类型,并通过产业集中度的计算、旅游企业市场份额的变化、产品差别化程度以及旅游产业进入和退出壁垒的研究,来判断旅游产业市场结构类型。根据市场结构与市场绩效的关系,即合理的市场结构才能产生良好的市场绩效,来优化旅游市场结构。

第七章主要讨论旅游企业的价格行为。旅游企业价格行为一类是以攫取消费者剩余、增加超额利润为目的的价格行为,如成本加成定价法、价格歧视、两部收费制等;另一类是以排挤竞争对手、改变或维持市场结构,追求长期利润为目的价格行为,如掠夺性定价与限制性定价。

第八章主要讨论博弈论与旅游企业的竞争行为。在介绍了博弈论的基本概念与基本内容后,主要运用博弈论的知识分析了旅游企业的价格竞争行为、旅游企业的竞争与合作行为等。

第九章讨论了旅游企业的一体化与纵向控制行为。主要内容包括旅游企业的横向一体化、纵向一体化、混合一体化,以及旅游企业的兼并与联合、纵向控制等内容。

第十章介绍了市场绩效的基本概念与衡量指标,并用竞争力评价体系对我国旅游产业竞争力进行测评。

这几章的主要目的是用比较成熟的产业组织理论解释旅游产业中出现的各种现象,进一步深入分析旅游产业在发展过程中各类企业的市场行为,促进合理市场结构的形成,并探索改善旅游产业经营绩效的策略。

复习思考题:
1. 如何理解产业和产业组织?
2. 从产业组织的发展历史来看,产业组织大体经历了几个发展阶段?每个阶段的核心思想和政策主张是什么?
3. 产业组织研究的基本内容有哪些?

第六章 旅游产业市场结构
(The Market Structure of Tourism Industry)

本章主要讲解市场结构的衡量指标,包括市场集中度、产品差别化和进入退出壁垒。根据市场结构的衡量指标定义四种市场结构类型,指出产业组织研究的重点是垄断竞争和寡头垄断市场,并将其与传统的完全竞争和完全垄断市场进行比较。着重分析旅游产业的市场集中度、旅游企业市场份额的变化趋势、旅游产品差别化以及旅游产业进入和退出壁垒,分析一段时期内饭店业的过度进入以及难以退出的原因,判断我国旅游产业市场结构类型,并提出促进市场结构优化的合理建议。

第一节 市场结构(Market Structure)

What is the meaning of market structure? According to Webster's Dictionary, "structure" means "form, or manner of building". In industry organization, market structure refers to the organizational characteristics of a market; and for practical purposes we emphasize those characteristics which determine the relations of sellers in the market to each other, of buyers in the market to each other, of the sellers to the buyers, and of sellers established in the market to other actual or potential suppliers of goods, including potential new firms which might enter the market. In other words, market structure for practical purposes means those characteristics of the organization of a market which seem to influence strategically the nature of competition and pricing within the market. 从以上的定义可以看出,所谓市场结构

是指厂商之间市场关系的表现和形式,包括买方之间、卖方之间、买卖双方之间以及市场内已有的买卖双方与正在进入或可能进入市场的买卖双方之间在交易、利益分配等方面存在的竞争关系。产业组织经济学所研究的是生产同类产品(严格地说是生产具有密切替代关系的产品)的生产者在同一市场上的集合,这些生产者之间的关系结构是用来描述在某一特定市场或产业中经营的厂商所面临的环境。

The purpose to research the market structure is to identify the market power of firms in the industry. Market power is the ability to influence market price and/or subdue rivals. The firm's ability to influence market price mostly determined by market structure, however, the ability to subdue rivals refers to market conduct.

经济学中把市场结构分为四种类型:完全竞争型(perfect competition)、完全垄断型(perfect monopoly)、垄断竞争型(monopoly competition)、寡头垄断型(oligopoly)。其中传统的微观经济学所涉及到的理论模型主要包括完全竞争型和完全垄断型,而在现实生活中更为普遍的市场结构类型则是垄断竞争型和寡头垄断型,而这两种类型则是产业经济学所研究的重点。完全竞争型和完全垄断型市场结构虽然在现实生活中并不常见,但作为纯理论模型,却是研究垄断竞争和寡头垄断型产业的基础。因此首先应该研究完全竞争型市场结构和完全垄断型市场结构。

表 6-1 基本市场结构的主要特征

市场结构	卖方		买方	
	进入壁垒	数量	进入壁垒	数量
完全竞争	无	很多	无	很多
垄断	有	一个	无	很多
买方垄断	无	很多	有	一个
双边垄断	有	一个	有	一个
寡头	有	少数	无	很多
买方寡头	无	很多	有	少数
垄断竞争	无	很多	无	很多

(资料来源:《产业组织经济学》,P113,金碚。)

一、完全竞争型(The Perfect Competitive Model)

1. 完全竞争模型的基本假定(The Basic Assumption of Perfect Competitive Model)

完全竞争模型是对现实世界的高度抽象,是建立在一系列的假设前提之上的,即在完全竞争市场中有大量的买者和卖者,每个买者和卖者都是价格接受者;每个厂商所生产的产品都是同质的,相互之间可以代替;资源是可以自由流动的,可以在产业之间自由进入和退出,也就是说进入和退出壁垒为零;所有的市场参与主体都是完全信息的拥有者。Perfect competition is defined by four main structural conditions:

第一,大量的买者和卖者。There is a very large number of small buyers and sellers. Each buyer and each seller is so small to the total market that none of buyers individually can affect product price by altering their volume of purchases and none of sellers individually can affect their level of output. At a given price, any firm can sell what it wants to sell, however, the industry demand is definite.

第二,同质产品。The product of any seller must be a perfect substitute for the product of another seller. That is to say, the product is homogeneous or standardized and the consumers have no preference among all firms.

第三,资源的自由流动。Perfect competition requires that productive resources be freely mobile into and out of markets. The productive resources include land and capital besides crude materials and other resources. Although in the short-run, land and capital seem to be immobile, in the long run, the two factors are variable and perfectly mobile.

第四,完全信息。Perfect competition requires that all market participants have full knowledge of the economic and technical data relevant to their decision making. Buyers must be aware of the price and product offerings of sellers. Sellers must know product prices, wage rates, materials costs, and so on.

2. 完全竞争市场的均衡(The Balance of Perfect Competitive Market)

市场均衡是由市场供求曲线决定的。在以上几个假设前提的基础上,可以得出每个厂商所面临的需求曲线(demand curve)是水平的,即在给定的价格水平上厂商可以销售任意的产量,其价格弹性(price elastic)无穷大。但整个市场的需求曲线却是向下倾斜的。Demand refers to the quantity or product that would be purchased at various possible prices during some given period of time, holding all determinants of demand other than product price constant. Demand can refer to (1) the demand of an individual buyer, (2) the demand of all buyers in the market taken together, or (3) the demand facing an individual seller in the market.

市场的供给曲线则是向上倾斜的,即价格越高,企业向市场提供的产品数量越多。市场的均衡产量和价格是由供给和需求曲线的交点决定的。市场均衡产量是产业中所有厂商的产量之和。而每个厂商的产量则可以根据边际收益(marginal revenue)等于边际成本(marginal cost)的原则确定。Marginal revenue is the change in total revenue attributable to the sale of one more unit of output. In the purely competitive market the additional sale of one unit or output always adds to total revenue an amount that just equals the price because the price is constant according to the firm's demand horizontal curve. Hence, price and marginal revenue are equal. Marginal cost refers to the addition to total costs due to the additional production of one unit of output. We can make some conclusions that (1) since price equals marginal revenue for the perfectly competitive form, the principle of $MR=MC$ can be expressed by the principle of $p=MC$; (2) the supply curve for the firm is identical to its marginal cost curve above the AVC (平均可变成本)curve. 此时,平均成本以上的边际成本曲线是厂商的供给曲线,而价格边际收益曲线则是厂商所面临的需求曲线,所以厂商根据 $MR=MC$ 的原则确定产量和价格,其实也是依靠厂商的供给和需求曲线的交点决定的,这与市场均衡的确定原理相一致。另外,市场向上的供给曲线就是每个厂商供给曲线在水平上的加总。

3. 完全竞争市场的福利和效率(The Welfare and Efficiency of Perfect Competitive Market)

传统经济学认为完全竞争市场可以实现稀缺资源的最优配置,完全竞争市场具有最理想的福利和效率特性。

(1) 福利

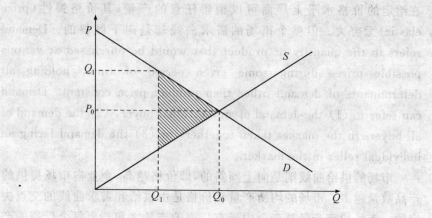

图 6-1 完全竞争型市场

- 消费者剩余（Consumers' Surplus） The demand curve indicates the benefit society gains from the production of the good both at the margin and overall. The price indicates the benefit of the last unit good called marginal benefit because that is the amount consumers would be willing to pay for the last unit. Area indicates the total benefit because that is the amount people would be willing to pay for the entire quantity. The difference between what they are willing to pay and what they actually pay is triangular area, which is like a gift and which accordingly is called consumers' surplus.
- 生产者剩余(Suppliers' Surplus) The supply curve represents society's cost of producing goods both at the margin and overall. 生产者剩余就是可以从生产者收入中扣除但生产者仍愿意生产的产品的最大额,它是指生产者所获得的超过平均利润的超额利润。

消费者剩余和生产者剩余之和被称为社会总剩余。由图 6-1 可以看出,任何偏离完全竞争均衡都会使社会总剩余缩小,其损失的数额就是图 6-1 中的阴影部分。

（2）效率(Efficiency)

生产和分配的最优效率被称为帕累托效率(Pareto Optimality)。Pareto optimality is a situation where no one can be made better off without making someone else worse off. Pareto optimality includes two aspects:

- 生产效率(Production Efficiency)　Production efficiency refers to that in purely competitive market firms will be forced by competition to adopt the most efficient, lowest cost technologies available and to operate at the low point on their long-run average cost curves.
- 分配效率(Allocative Efficiency)　Whenever free and voluntary exchange occurs with no adverse third-party effects, at least one person is made better off and no one is made worse off. Exchange or market processes can therefore move society from inefficiency to efficiency.

（3）平等(Equity)

Equity generally means some "equitable" distribution of income or "equal opportunity." Equity and efficiency are separable in the theoretical sense that efficiency can be achieved regardless of whether or not the income distribution is "equitable" or "just". 虽然完全竞争市场不能带来完全的市场公平，但长期利润的消失可以促进公平的实现。

（4）技术改进(Technological Improvement)

完全竞争市场中，每个厂商可以在给定价格水平下销售任意数量的产品，而且从长期来看每个厂商的经济利润为零，因此厂商没有动力改进技术，增加科研投资。所以从这一点来说，完全竞争市场在促进技术进步方面并不理想。

4. 评价标准(The Standard of Evaluation)

评价一个市场是否属于完全竞争市场可以从结构、行为、绩效三个方面进行评判。

（1）结构标准(Structural Norms)

- The number of traders should be at least as large as scale economies and industry life cycle permits.
- There should be no artificial inhibitions on mobility and entry.
- Where appropriate, there should be moderate and price-

sensitive qualities differentials in the products offered.
- Buyers should be well informed about prices, qualities, and other relevant data.

(2) 行为标准(Conduct Criteria)
- Some uncertainties should exist in the minds of rivals as to whether price initiatives will be followed.
- Firms should strive to achieve their goals independently, without collusion.
- There should be no unfair, exclusionary, predatory, or coercive tactics.
- Inefficient suppliers and customers should not be shielded permanently.
- Sales promotion should not be misleading.
- Persistent, harmful price discrimination should be absent.

(3) 绩效标准(Performance Criteria)
- Firms' production operations should be efficient.
- Promotional expenses should not be excessive.
- Profits should be at levels just sufficient to reward investment, efficiency, and innovation.

二、完全垄断市场(The Pure Monopoly Market)

1. 完全垄断市场特征(The Characteristic of Perfect Monopoly Market)

The structure conditions for pure monopoly are just the opposite of those for perfect competition.

第一,一个供给商。Instead of a large number of relatively small sellers, there is just one seller.

第二,产品差别化。Instead of a standardized product, identical across all sellers, the product may be said to be perfectly differentiated because the monopolist's offering has on close substitutes.

第三,进入受限。Instead of free entry for newcomers, entry is

blocked in the case of pure monopoly.

Under these conditions, the demand facing the individual seller and the market-wide demand are one and the same.

2. 垄断市场的均衡(The Balance of Monopoly Market)

The monopolist facing a downward-sloping demand curve, which is the monopoly's demand curve and also the market demand curve. The rule that $MR=MC$ for maximizing the profit in purely competition market can also be applied in monopoly market, but the result is different at all. In purely competition market, the individual demand curve is the same as the marginal revenue curve, however, the downward-sloping demand of the monopolist generates a downward-sloping that lies below the demand curve.

三、垄断竞争市场(The Monopoly Competitive Market)

Different market structures cause variations in the ways individual sellers view their demand and individual buyers view their supply. In perfect competitive model sellers confront horizontal demand curve and have no power to influence price, however, in monopoly market there is only one firm who has a down-sloping curve which also is a market-wide demand curve as well. The monopolist's power is reflected in the wide range of price options offered by this demand curve.

Between these two extreme cases is an intermediate situation of "rivalry" among a limited number of sellers. There are two demand curves which exist on the assumption the firm may concern its rivals' behaviors. If the firm assumes that when it changes the price the rivals will follow, there will be a followship demand (FD) curve. If the firm makes the assumption that rivals in the market do not follow the price changes, there will be a nonfollowship demand (NFD) curve. The elasticity of this NFD curve is much greater than that of FD curve. If rivals do not follow the price changes, a firm can win customers through cutting price and lose customs through raising price. A firm confronting FD and NFD curves has some power over price, but not as much as a monopolist.

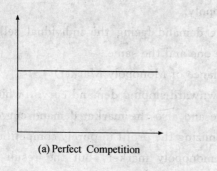
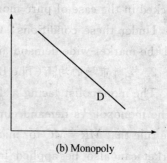

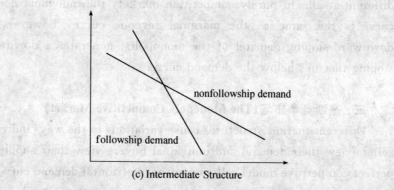

图 6-2 市场结构的需求曲线的比较

There are two important measures of market power suggested by Abba Lerner and Joe Bain. The Lerner index(勒纳指数)measures the divergences between price and marginal cost that may result from the exercise of market power.

Lerner index =(price－marginal cost)/ price

Under perfect competition there is no divergence between price and marginal cost, so the Lerner index is zero. In monopoly model, however, firm can make price over marginal cost and the gap between price and marginal cost is large, so the Lerner index is larger than that in perfect competition. It should be emphasized that in no case could the index exceed a value of one, so its theoretical range is from zero to one.

There is one question about Lerner index, that is marginal costs usually cannot be estimated. The question limits its application in practice. Another question is that Lerner index is a measure of actual conduce—a measure of the exercise of power rather than its mere existence. A value of zero may exist in a monopoly market if the monopolist chose to keep price low close to marginal cost for some reasons, rather than to raise price and maximize profit.

In order to solve this problem, Bain develop Bain index which focuses directly on the excess profit. In perfect competition the excess profit is zero, however, a firm with some degree of monopoly power will have positive excess profit. Bain index was induced from accounting profit which equals to the total revenues surplus total current costs and depreciation, that is

$$\pi = R - C - D$$

where R = total revenues

C = total current costs

D = depreciation

Bain deducts from accounting profit an assumed cost of investors capital, that is:

$$\pi = R - C - D - IV$$

where I = the rate of return that could be earned on alternative (normal profit) investments

V = the total value of the owners' investment

Bain index = π/V

The bigger the excess profit is or the higher Bain index is, the more monopoly power a firm has.

The source of market power is another important issue of market structure, which includes several aspects such as product differentiations, barriers to entry, sellers or buyers concentrations and so on. These sources of market will be discussed in detail in the next section.

四、寡头垄断市场(Oligopoly Market)

寡头市场基本的特征是少数几家大规模的厂商占据了整个行业或行业的大部分产出。它们生产的产品可能是同质的，如钢铁、铝、水泥、石油等行业的产品，也可能是有差别的，如汽车、飞机制造、铁路设备、家用电器等行业的产品。

寡头市场存在较高的进入壁垒,这是少数厂商能够占据绝大部分市场份额的必要条件。构成这种进入壁垒的主要是因为这些行业存在规模经济。规模经济的存在使得大规模生产占有强大的优势,大企业不断壮大,小企业无法生存,最终形成少数厂商激烈竞争的局面。此外,在某些情况下,行业内的厂商刻意构筑起较高的进入壁垒以阻止其他厂商的进入。这种现象的出现主要是因为厂商数目较少,厂商之间的串通比较容易。

与别的三种市场结构不同的是,寡头市场的厂商存在着相互依存的关系,这是寡头市场最突出的特点。由于寡头行业中厂商数量少,一个厂商在采取某种行动时必须考虑其他厂商的反应,因为这种反应会对该厂商的决策产生影响。在完全竞争市场,厂商的行为是完全独立的,根本没有必要去考虑其他人的反应。在垄断市场,垄断厂商垄断了整个行业,也根本不存在会对它的行为产生反应的对手。在垄断竞争市场,虽然厂商之间也存在一定程度的相互依存性,但由于厂商数量众多,每家厂商都只占很小的市场份额,因此其他厂商的反应可以忽略不计。

寡头市场的这种相互依存关系给寡头厂商的决策带来很大程度的不确定性。例如,当一家旅游寡头厂商决定降低其产品的价格以扩大销售量时,显然会严重影响其他厂商的销路,其他厂商不会无动于衷。但是,对手究竟会如何反应是无法完全预料到的。因此,寡头厂商在做出决策时,只能将对别的厂商反应的估计和猜测考虑在内,所以寡头市场的运行具有相当大的不确定性。寡头市场的这种特性使寡头理论分析具有较大的难度,特别是对其均衡价格和均衡产量的决定很难得出完美、确定的结论。为了更好地分析寡头厂商之间的关系,现代经济学发展出很多有力的工具,博弈论是其中最具有代表性的一种,我们将在后面的章节简要介绍博弈论并对旅游企业的竞争行为进行讨论。

在 SCP 理论中市场结构是决定企业行为和市场绩效的主导因素,如何衡量市场结构,并判断旅游市场结构类型是优化旅游市场结构的起点。

There are many factors that influence the structure of industry. The degrees of seller concentration(卖方集中度), the degree of buyer concentration(买方集中度), the degree of product differentiation(产品差别化) and the barriers to entry and exit(进入和退出壁垒) may generally be considered the four primary characteristics of market structure. They are the aspects of market organization which most clearly and systematically influence market conduct and performance throughout all industries. In addition there are numerous other characteristics of industry which also influence market behaviors. 在本章以下的几节中,我们分别介绍旅游产业的市场集中程度、产品差别化以及进入和退出壁垒。

第二节 旅游产业的市场集中度
(Concentration of the Tourism Industry)

一、集中度(Concentration)

在讲述卖方集中度之前,首先要知道集中度的含义。Concentration seems to refer mainly to the ownership or control of a large proportion of some aggregate of economic resources or activity either by a small proportion of the units which own or control the aggregate, or by a small absolute number of such units. 集中度指的是某种经济资源或活动的绝大部分被较小比例的单位或较小数量的单位所拥有或控制。这里所说的经济资源或活动通常用资产、收入、产品的价值以及所雇佣的劳动力来衡量。But in this book we will emphasis on the concentration of business assets and of business sales or income.

需要说明的是,集中度不是指产业内或市场内资源或活动被拥有或控制的一种量的方面的状态,因此,我们不能把产业或市场分为简单的两种情况,即集中或不集中。Here the degree of concentration maybe precisely expresses a continuous range of ownership or control of the resources or activity in the industry instead of concentration. The degree of concentration refers to both the number and the size distribution of the units which own or control a given economic aggregate (such as sales or assets), the size of each (sales or assets) being measured by the proportion of the aggregate it owns or controls.

二、旅游产业卖方集中度(Seller Concentration)

Seller concentration refers to the number and market shares of firms producing goods or services for a particular market. There are many different measures of seller concentration which are different according to :(1) the concentration index used;(2) the size variable used in the concentration of the concentration index. Concentration indices may be grouped into absolute and relative concentration measures. The most commonly used absolute measure is the concentration ratio（集中度比率）and Herfindahl index（赫佛因德指数），however, the measures of relative concentration including Lorernz curve（洛伦茨曲线）and Gini Factor（基尼系数）record the degree of inequality in the share of firms producing for a given market.

1. 集中度比率（Concentration Ratio）

Concentration ratio records the percentage of an industry's size accounted for by a given number of the largest firms in that industry. 在这里我们举几个例子来说明集中度比率（concentration ratio）是怎样衡量卖方市场的集中程度的。假设旅行社产业的所有服务是由4家最大的旅行社提供的,而饭店产业的所有服务是由12家最大的饭店提供的,也就是说旅行社产业中产品的生产集中在更少数的几家厂商生产,那么旅行社产业的卖方集中度比饭店产业的要高。再比如,如果旅行社产业和饭店产业都有12家厂商,而旅行社产业中最大的4家厂商提供全行业中90%的服务产品,而饭店产业中最大的4个厂商只提供60%的服务产品,我们说旅行社产业的卖方集中度要比饭店产业的要高,因为旅行社产业中的更多的产品生产集中在了最大的4家厂商。上面这两个例子中的旅行社和饭店产业都有相同的地方,一个是所提供的产品的总量相同,而提供产品的厂商数量不同;另一个是提供产品的厂商数量相同,但所提供的产品总量在各自产业中所占的比例不同,这种情况下可以简单地判断出来哪个产业的集中度更高。

但有时对两个产业集中度高低的比较需要从绝对和相对两个方面进行判断。如果A产业有10个厂商,其中最大的4个厂商也就是最大的40%的厂商提供了全产业50%的产品,而B产业有100个厂商,最大的20个厂商也就是20%的厂商提供了全产业50%的产品,判断这两个产业集中度的高低就要从两个方面来判断,而且会得出不同的结果。从绝对量上看,A产业中只有10个厂商,而其中最大的4个就提供了50%的产品,而B产业中有100个厂商,而其中最大的20个厂商提供了50%的产品,这说明A产业中产品的生产更集中在少数几个生产者手中。而从相对量指标来看,B产业中仅20%的厂商就提供了全行业中

50%的产品,同样比例的产品的生产在B产业中集中在了相对较少的厂商手中,则B产业的产业集中度比A产业的高。

一般情况下,我们会使用相对集中度比率来测量产业集中度。In the course of analyzing, we usually use the index of Four-firm concentration ratio,(CR4)(四厂商集中度)which records the percentage of the goods or services owned by the biggest 4 firms in the industry and Eight-firm concentration ratio(CR8)(八厂商集中度)which records the percentage of the goods or services owned by the biggest 8 firms in the industry. 贝恩曾根据CR4和CR8的比例对产业的垄断和竞争类型进行了划分。(参见表6-2)

表6-2 贝恩对产业垄断和竞争类型的划分

类型	CR4	CR8	产业内企业总数
极高寡占型	75%		20—40家
高度集中寡占型	65%~75%	85%以上	20—100家
中(上)集中寡占型	50%~65%	75%~85%	企业数较多
中(下)集中寡占型	35%~50%	45%~75%	企业数很多
低集中寡占型	30%~35%	40%~45%	企业数很多
原子型			企业数极多,不存在集中现象

根据集中度的概念,我们可以简单分析一下我国旅行社、旅游饭店的卖方集中度情况。表6-3是国旅、中旅和青旅三大旅行社从1980年至1988年按照接待人数的市场占有份额计算的集中度比率。从表中可以看出,随着我国旅行社的发展,从1980年至1988年的9年间,我国旅行社的市场集中度比率是逐渐下降的。就旅行社业而言,在1978年中国对外开放以前,全国只有中国国际旅行社总社、中国旅行社总社以及它们在主要省会城市设立的分支机构。这些旅行社从成立之日起就一直从事以政治目的为主的对外接待工作,基本不具备企业的性质。中国实行对外开放政策以后,国旅和中旅的主要任务转变为接待自费来华的旅游者,但直到1985年《旅行社管理暂行条例》颁布以前,中国的旅行社仍然具有很强的事业单位性质。1980年,中国青年旅行社总社在北京成立,从此开始了中国旅行社行业寡头垄断的局面。根据国家旅游局有关规定,全国只有国旅、中旅和青旅三家总社拥有旅游外联的权力,它们之间具有相对明确的业务分工。中国国际旅行社主要接待外国来华的

旅游者，中国旅行社主要接待港澳同胞和来华旅游的海外华人，而中国青年旅行社则以来华旅游的青年旅游者作为主要接待对象。1980年，这三家旅行社接待的来华旅游者约占到全国有组织接待人数的80%（参见表6-3），其余20%由其他政府机构组织接待。

表6-3　1980—1988年主要旅行社旅游接待情况

年 份	主要旅行社接待人数占有组织接待人数的比例			
	国旅	中旅	青旅	合计
1980	18.8	59.9	0.9	79.6
1981	17.2	56.1	1.8	75.1
1982	16.6	47.4	1.3	65.3
1983	16.0	45.3	1.4	62.7
1984	16.0	33.0	1.9	50.9
1985	15.6	25.7	1.7	43.0
1986	14.0	18.3	2.4	34.7
1987	13.3	22.4	3.3	39.0
1988	12.1	25.4	3.4	40.9

（资料来源：《中国旅游统计资料汇编》1978—1985；《中国旅游统计年鉴》1986，1987，1988）

　　随着中国旅游业的进一步发展，为适应中国旅游业发展的新形势，国家旅游局于1984年将旅游外联权下放，允许更多的企业经营国际旅游业务，并授予它们业务经营所必需的签证通知权。这一举措对中国旅行社业的发展起了积极的促进作用，旅行社业在全国范围内迅速发展起来。到1988年底，中国的旅行社猛增至1,573家，并由此彻底打破了中国旅行社业寡头垄断的局面。1984年以后，国旅、中旅和青旅接待人数占全国有组织接待人数的比例由1980年的79.6%下降为1988年的40.9%。

　　从1988年开始，旅行社市场集中度进一步降低，截止到1995年，我国旅行社的CR3市场集中度已降到20.9%，基本上属于低集中寡占型的市场结构（见表6-4）。因此，总体上来说，我国旅行社的市场集中度比率是不断下降的，目前已属于低集中寡占型或者是集中型。

表 6-4　三大旅行社市场份额变化(1988—1995)

年份	CITS	CTS	CYTS	合计接待人数	有组织接待人数	CR3
1988	526217	1103949	147295	1777461	4349045	40.9
1989	137776	843129	99836	1080741	3228164	33.5
1990	110238	1064605	135171	1310014	4251941	30.8
1991	487926	1065918	155933	1709837	4963052	34.5
1992	646901	962326	149918	1759145	6326400	27.8
1993	740652	820192	140354	1701198	7012756	24.3
1994	810186	619409	224808	1654443	7639100	21.7
1995	846515	477417	305201	1629753	8026000	20.3

资料来源：中国旅游统计年鉴(1989—1996 各期)；转引自《旅游经济学》，P257。

旅行社一向被认为处于整个旅游产业的龙头地位,我国旅行社普遍存在着"小、散、弱、差"的状况,企业规模小,实力弱。以 2001 年为例,每家旅行社资产平均 394.4 万元,营业收入平均 560 万元,利润平均 12.2 万元。整个旅行社行业缺乏具有较强实力的龙头企业,目前国内最大的国旅、中旅、中青旅 3 家旅行社所占市场份额不足 20%,因此说我国旅行社行业属典型的分散竞争的市场结构。而世界旅行社发展趋势是大的旅行社在行业中所占份额不断扩大,目前英国旅行社业已形成航空2000、航空旅行社及托马斯 3 个旅行社经营商垄断 80% 市场份额的局面。

从全国饭店市场的总情况来看,饭店市场的产业集中度还远远低于垄断竞争的标准,尚处于较为充分的竞争态势,或者说市场静态壁垒较弱。但是从一些细分市场如高星级饭店市场来看,产业集中度已经开始构成了壁垒。在高星级饭店市场上,从 1982 年香港半岛集团接管北京建国饭店开始,一批国际饭店集团就相继进入中国市场,并逐步向全国拓展。目前,假日集团已经管理了国内 25 家饭店,成为在中国饭店市场上占有率最高的国际饭店集团。在中国管理饭店较多的国际饭店集团还有万豪、香格里拉、仁达屋、希尔顿、凯悦等,这些饭店集团所管理的饭店多数集中在旅游热点城市和大都市,并正在向旅游温点城市和地区性中心城市扩张。

上海新亚(集团)有限公司是以饭店业和餐饮业为主营业务的企业集团,从新亚集团的第一支柱产业——饭店业来看,在其全资所有、统一管理的 22 家饭店中,新业汤臣大酒店、海仑宾馆、扬子江大酒店、建国宾馆等四星级以上标准的饭店占全市同类型企业的 20%左右。在地理位置上,新亚集团所属饭店基本处于上海市内环线以内的主要商务中心区。如果再把规模更大的上海锦江以及华亭、文华、东湖等另外几家大型饭店集团纳入考察范围,那么无论是用 C8 法,还是用 C4 法,我们都可以得出这样的结论:上海市饭店市场集中度已经表明该区域产业市场进入垄断竞争态势,并分别对潜在进入者和在位厂商构成结构性壁垒。

2. 赫佛因德指数(Herfindahl Index)

Herfindahl index is calculated by squaring and summating the share of market size accounted for by every firm producing for the market. 用公式表示赫佛因德指数为:

$$HI = \sum_{j=1}^{n}\left(\frac{X_i}{X}\right)2 \quad j=2,3,\cdots,n$$

式中,x 代表产业总规模,下标 i 表示第 i 个厂商,n 为产业中厂商总数。从以上公式可以看出,产业内部企业的规模越是接近,且企业数量越多,HI 指数越接近于 0。当所有企业规模相同时,HI=0;当一个产业中只有一家企业时,HI=1。HI 指数对规模较大的前几家企业(通常称为上位企业)的市场份额比重的变化反映尤为敏感。

Herfindahl index takes into account the number and shares of all the firms producing for the market in which it is different from the concentration ratio. The concentration ratio only records the level of seller concentration at one point on the cumulative concentration curve. Therefore, when comparing the level of seller concentration in different markets the ranking will alter according to the point on the concentration curves selected for the comparison, provided that the concentration curves for the different markets intersect. In order to overcome this potential deficiency, we can use the Herfindahl index to describe the whole industry concentration. 由于 HI 指数在市场集中度的研究中是一个综合反映产业内企业规模分布的指标,因此,20 世纪 80 年代以后,在美国该指标作为最主要的市场集中度指标而被广泛使用。

3. 洛伦茨曲线和基尼系数(Lorernz curve & Gini Factor)

Lorernz curve shows the cumulative percentage of market size accounted for by various percentages of the number of firms producing for the market, cumulated from the smallest. 洛伦茨曲线描绘的是市

场占有率与市场中由小到大企业的累计百分比之间的关系。如图6-3,横轴表示从最小企业开始企业数量的累计百分比,纵轴表示的是这些企业的销售额占市场销售额的百分比。洛伦茨曲线反映产业内部全部企业的市场规模和分布情况。当某一特定的产业内所有企业的规模完全相同时,洛伦茨曲线与图中的45°曲线重合。当企业规模不完全相同时,洛伦茨曲线在45°曲线以下。洛伦茨曲线越是偏离45°曲线,说明企业规模分布越不均等。

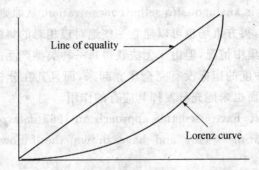

图6-3 The Lorenz curve as an indicator of relative seller concentration

Gini Factor is defined as the area under the Lorenz curve divided by the area under the line of equality. 基尼系数等于洛伦茨曲线图的均等分布线与洛伦茨曲线之间的面积与均等分布线右下方三角形面积的比值。即:

$$基尼系数 = \frac{均等分布线与洛伦茨曲线之间的面积}{均等分布线以下的三角形面积}$$

由于均等分布线与洛伦茨曲线之间的面积是均等分布线右下方三角形面积的一部分,因此基尼系数的取值区间为[0,1]。厂商分布越不均匀,基尼系数越大。当一个产业内只有一家企业时,基尼系数为1;如果所有厂商规模相等,洛伦茨曲线与45°曲线重合,基尼系数为0。

洛伦茨曲线和基尼系数两个指标在一定程度上可以反映出市场的相对集中度,可以反映出某一特定市场上所有企业的规模分布状况。但是,它们具有一定的局限性。这两个指标是相对集中的度量而不是绝对集中的度量,这会导致具有相同洛伦茨曲线和基尼系数的两个产业的市场结构是不一样的,比如一个产业有两家厂商,每个厂商提供50%的产品,另一个产业有100家厂商,每个厂商提供1%的产品,可以看出,在这两个产业中产品的生产是均匀分布的,即两个产业的洛伦茨曲线和基尼系数都相同,但是这两个产业的市场结构是完全不同的。再比如当两条不同形状的洛伦茨曲线所围成的面积大小相等时,可以得到相同的基尼系数。相同的基尼系数可以与不同的企业规模分布情况相对应。

三、买方集中度(Buyer Concentration)

Buyer concentration refers to the number and size distribution of firms purchasing a particular type of product, service or material. Therefore, it is analogous to seller concentration. 从原则上来说,像卖方集中度一样,买方市场也可以建立一些绝对或相对的集中度指标以反映买方市场的集中情况,但由于无法获得每一种类型产品的采购情况和数据,买方集中度的指标没有完全建立起来,而且其在分析市场结构和市场绩效的方面也未能充分发挥其应有的作用。

Guth *et al.* have used this approach on 1963 data relating to the US manufacturing sector and have drawn the following tentative conclusions:

- Overall, the general level of buyer concentration was substantially lower than the level of seller concentration.
- Substantial differences existed in the pattern of buyer concentration across industries.
- In general there was only a weak positive industry-by-industry relationship between buyer and seller concentration ratios, but in some industries concentration ratios were substantial for both buyers and sellers.

以上研究说明在某一特定的产业中,买方力量可能对企业行为和市场绩效产生巨大的影响。如果这是事实,对买方集中度以及其对市场行为和绩效产生的影响将会得到越来越多的关注。

In fact, the tourism industry is affected by both monopoly and monopsony features, although more accurately it is a situation of oligopolist and oligopsonist behaviour. On the one hand there are clearly atomistic clients, who interact with travel agents; the latter are composed of both small and competitively acting agents and large agencies having market power. At the other hand, there are relatively competitive suppliers of services of varying sizes providing a limited capacity. Large travel intermediaries act oligopolistically with espect to individual clients or to smaller agents when functioning as wholesalers. Large hotel chains can deal directly with clients using brand recognition or with intermediaries; when the latter have sufficient size, it can be assumed that the relationship, while not atomistic, is fairly competitive. Smaller or single site hotels may deal with smaller agents in a relatively competitive framework, but face monopsonistic behavior when interacting with large intermediaries controlling large tourist volumes.

第三节 旅游产品差异
(Product Differentiation)

一、产品差异度的概念(The Concepts of Product Differentiation)

Product differentiation refers in some sense to an imperfection in the substitutability to buyers of the outputs competing sellers in an industry, or to the fact that buyers have developed preferences for certain seller outputs over others. That is to say, product differentiation means the products sold within the same market are not regarded by buyers as perfect substitutes. 对于产品差异度概念应以对产业的理解为基础。We have earlier defined an industry as a group of outputs which are sold to a common group of buyers and which are, to these buyers, close substitutes for each other but relatively distant substitutes for all other outputs. The outputs included in a single industry are thus initially defined as close substitutes, and as the poor substitutes for all other outputs in the economy.

That the different seller outputs included in the same industry have close substitutability results from the fact that they are all varieties of the same sort of goods or services with the similarity in form or function and fulfilling the same sort of specific wants or needs of buyers. Conversely, that the different seller outputs included in different industries have distant substitutability results from the reason of different sorts of goods fulfilling different wants or needs of buyers.

A second feature of the market structure is the presence of both homogeneous and heterogeneous goods. Both in the airline and hotel business, there is a gradation of products from basic to luxury. In practice, one can adopt a small discrete classification of levels of products and consider the services within classes as relatively interchangeable or substitutable; yet it is important to recognize individual client preferences as having some distinguishing effects, particularly at the higher class of product. Because of fixed capacity, inventories cannot be accumulated to satisfy later demand. Yet the problem is a multi-period problem within which some inter-period substitution is possible. Furthermore, across different seasons the demand and the perceived value of the products vary greatly. A further complication is the degree of substitutability across regional or national boundaries. In summary, there is probably sufficient size of supplies and demands in most categories (across time, location and classes of service) that one can consider this to be homogeneous within each cell, but substitutable to a degree between "adjacent" cells.

2. 产品差异度的衡量(The Measure of Product Differentiation)

Generally, we use the "cross-elasticity of demand" between different outputs to measure the product differentiation. Cross-elasticity of demand is defined in terms of responsiveness of the sales volume of one output to a small change in the price of the other output, strictly as the ratio of the percentage change in the amount buyers demand of output A to the percentage change in the price of output B which induces the change in the demand for A, the price of A being held unchanged. 交叉弹性就是指保持 A 产品价格不变，B 产品价格每变动 1%，消费者对 A 产品需求变动的百分比。The cross-elasticity between different outputs in the same industry is finite (maybe infinite) and perceptible, however, the cross-elasticity of demand between outputs in different industries will be very small, or approach zero. 不同产品之间的交叉价格弹性可以反映有关产品或产业间的替代性和互补性，替代性越强，竞争性越强。

$$交叉价格弹性 = \frac{A\text{生产者提供的}A\text{产品的数量变动百分比}}{B\text{产品价格变动的百分比}}$$

从以上公式可以看出,如果 B 产品价格降低(或提高),A 产品需求的数量增加(或减少),即交叉价格弹性为负,表明 B 和 A 具有互补性。如果 B 产品价格降低(或提高),A 产品需求的数量减少(或增加),即交叉价格弹性为正,则表明 B 与 A 之间具有替代性。一般来说,交叉弹性越高,B 和 A 之间的替代性越强,竞争性也越强。

In general, all the outputs included in the industry are at least close substitutes to buyers, but they are not necessarily perfect substitutes. The condition that all buyers regard the outputs of all sellers as identical and have no preference for one compared to others is very scarce, however, the cross-elasticity will be finite and perceptible.

3. 产品差异的原因(The Source of Product Differentiation)

导致产品差异性的原因是多方面的,任何能影响到消费者在竞争产品之间的选择的因素都可以成为产品差异性的来源。

• 质量或设计的差别(The Differences in Quality or Design)

The most obvious sources of product differentiation are differences in quality or design among competing outputs. 产品用途虽然基本相同,但不同企业产品的质量、设计、包装等方面有所不同,将导致消费者在质量、设计方面产生偏好。这一源泉是产品差别化的基础。

• 消费者对产品的不了解(The Ignorance of Product)

The ignorance of buyers regarding the essential characteristic and qualities of the goods they are buying is another source of product differentiation. 对于消费者来说,有些产品是他们经常购买的,如一些日用消费品、食品等,这些产品在性能和包装方面比较简单,消费者可以通过直接的接触或品尝来了解产品的基本属性。而对于一些性能、成分、构造等比较复杂的商品来说,消费者无法通过简单的接触深入了解商品的特性,那么为了保证所购买商品的品质,消费者只能选择那些具有知名品牌的产品和企业。而产品的品牌依靠消费者的主观印象和心理上的认同,良好的品牌是建立在企业过去所销售产品的业绩和可信度的基础之上的,或建立在企业是否能够以一种较好的业绩保持在产业中。The reliance on seller or product reputation by ignorant consumers is a further important source of the existence of preferences favoring some seller outputs as compared to others.

旅游产品具有特殊性质,它不像有形商品那样,作为一种实物可供事先观察、检验甚至试用或退换;它也不像家居生活那样,要对同一种必需品经常地、反复地购买和使用。旅游产品是一种无形产品,是各方面服务要素的连续组合,是花钱买到一个新鲜的经历,是一种事后获得效果、不能重复而又弹性极大的享受型消费。因此,旅游者对旅游产品的不了解就成为旅游产品差异的一个重要原因。

• 销售者的促销和广告(Sales-promotion Activities and Advertising of Sellers)

The persuasive sales-promotion activities of sellers, and particularly by advertising are important sources of product differentiation. The advertising and most of the sales-promotion activities aim at building a product differentiation based on a knowledge of the relative designs, qualities, and the prices of competing outputs. 促销活动和广告行为对消费者的选择偏好产生很大的影响,许多品牌的建立都是通过利用各种媒体多次反复地宣传自身产品在性能、设计、包装、价格方面与其他同类产品之间的差别,从而使消费者在选择上倾向于本公司的产品。

4. 产品差别化的意义(The importance and Implications of Product Differentiation)

研究产品差别化的重要意义在于它能够影响企业的行为和市场绩效,这也是把产品差别化作为市场结构的一个重要方面的原因。在微观经济学中我们假定市场是完全竞争,在完全竞争市场中有大量的厂商和消费者,每个厂商都只是价格的接受者,而不是价格的制定者。任何一个厂商只要把价格稍微提高一点,他就会立即失去所有的顾客,而当其他厂商降低价格时,如果某一厂商为留住消费者也必须降低价格。在完全竞争市场中,厂商之间只能进行价格的竞争和销售量的调整,因此完全竞争市场可以把价格压低到等于厂商边际成本的程度,从而可以实现消费者福利最大化,而非价格竞争是不允许的。这主要是因为在完全竞争市场中消费者对生产者所生产的产品没有任何的偏好,决定消费者选择的唯一因素就是价格。但在现实生活中,我们看到更多的却是产品之间在性能、功效、包装、设计、营销、售后服务等许多方面存在着差别,而价格也并不是消费者选择所购买产品的惟一决定因素。

从产品差异可以看出企业建立品牌的重要性,但目前我国旅游企业的品牌意识还比较差,与国外知名旅游企业相比还处于劣势地位。在旅行社领域,我国没有日本交通公社、美国运通、英国托马斯·库克那样的名牌企业,最有条件的国、中、青三大集团的品牌功能极度分散化。在饭店领域,我国也没有马里奥特、雅高、希尔顿、凯悦这样的名牌公司,惟一的锦江集团仅名列世界最大旅馆联号的第97位。而在景点领域,只有深圳华侨城、杭州宋城等极少企业进行过主题公园品牌化的探索,远不能同迪斯尼公司那样的名牌比拟,绝大部分资源品位极高的旅游地仍处于低级经营阶段。

但在某些区域市场上,我国旅游企业的品牌功能正在得到强化。那些拥有知名品牌的饭店企业如上海锦江集团、新亚集团、广州花园饭店等,在特定的细分市场上已经拥有了相对垄断的市场地位,从而对潜在的竞争者造成了品牌壁垒。而那些定位于全国旅游市场的大型旅游集团如中旅系统、招商国旅、民航饭店委员会等也正在借助其内在的行政隶属关系和旅游营销网络整合自己的饭店资源。一旦这些企业建立起全国性的市场网络,其品牌优势将会对进入者造成更大的市场壁垒。现在,尽管来华入境旅游者、合资大企业中高级商务人员仍然是大型饭店的重要客户群体,但是国内旅游者、商务散客的群体数量与品牌偏好正在与日俱增,并且他们的需要更加多样复杂。

第四节 旅游产业的进入壁垒
(Entering and Quitting Barriers of Tourism Industry)

一、进入壁垒的概念(The Concept of Entry Barriers)

Entry is merely a shorthand way of saying that a firm new to the market has begun to offer a product or service that is a close substitute for products or services of firms already in the market. The new-comer may be established in another market and may merely imitate the sellers already in the market entered. 作为一个已在某个产业中生存的企业随时都面临着潜在企业进入的威胁。潜在企业的进入就意味着要和在位企业争夺现有的利润,而由于各种各样的原因,潜在的企业进入现有的产业可能会遇到许多障碍,这种阻止潜在企业进入现有企业的障碍就被称为进入壁垒。Entry involves two conditions—motivation and ability. For motivation, the prospects of eventually earning a substantial profit must be good. In ability, the potential entrant must be capable of making the attempt. Any factor that reduces the motivation and ability of potential entrants despite established firms' excessively high profits may be called a barrier to entry.

Barrier to entry is a major market power which is useful in explaining conduct and performance. Barrier to entry also helps to explain variances in observed concentration, because high barriers tend to be associated with high concentration. The concept is useful, moreover, in assessing public policy, for not all barriers are "naturally" or technologically determined. Some are artificial and due to human manipulation.

The condition of entry may be measured on a numerical scale by defining the advantage of established over potential entrant sellers in a certain systematic way, namely, as the largest percentage by which established sellers can persistently elevate their prices above the minimized or competitive average costs of production and distribution (plus average costs of sales promotion) without inducing new sellers to enter the industry.

进入壁垒也是市场结构中的一个重要组成部分，与市场集中度与产品差别同列为市场结构中的重要组成部分。但三者之间有不同之处，市场集中度与产品差别描写的是产业内部企业与企业之间的关系，表示的现有产业内部企业之间的竞争态势。而进入壁垒则反映的是现有企业和潜在企业之间的竞争能力的转化关系。如果说市场集中度和产品差别化是一段时间内产业结构的静态反映，那么进入壁垒则是产业结构的动态反映。

二、旅游产业进入壁垒的源泉（The Source of Barriers to Entry in Tourism Industry）

1. 旅游产业的规模经济壁垒（Large-scale Production）

The first sort of barriers to entry is large-scale production in the industry. Large-scale refers to the production ability that can acquire the biggest profit or the lowest cost. That is to say, that when a firm can acquire large-scale economy it must be large enough to supply a significant fraction of industry output in order to gain the best ratio of unit selling price to unit sales-promotion cost. An entry firm will encounter two situations: 1) because of the entry firm's addition to total industry output cannot be offset by the established firm's cutting in the output, the total output in the industry will be larger than before, so the price of the goods will decrease and the profits will decrease too. This will hinder the entry firm to enter because the profit is so little due to the decreasing price. 2) It is difficult for a new comer to acquire a sufficient market share to sustain optimal-scale production, and thus has costs above the minimum level, reflecting inefficiencies of smaller-scale production. In either situations, established firms can generally raise prices above minimum average costs, by some amount depending on the importance of the scale economies.

旅行社规模经济通常是指旅行社因其经营规模扩大而导致单位成本减少,具体表现为接待规模的扩大或者组团规模的扩大两个方面。旅行社规模经济可以分为内部规模经济和外部规模经济,内部规模经济是指随着经营规模的扩大,使单位接待成本下降,收益上升;外部规模经济是实现内部规模经济的外部条件,如市场容量的扩大、旅游经济一体化的发展、交通条件的改善和旅行社融资的方便等等。旅行社规模经济与规模不经济表现为团队规模经济、产品规模经济和企业规模经济三个层次。团队规模经济是同一路线产品的组织与接待的经济性,它是旅行社规模经济的基本形态;产品规模经济则是旅行社开发一个新产品所形成的经济性,它是企业实现规模经济的最低界限;企业规模经济是旅行社通过各种形式的联合或战略联盟所形成的经济性,它是实现规模经济的组织保证。

企业规模或所生产的产量与产品成本之间的关系可以用图 6-4 表示。

由图 6-4 可以看出,只有当旅行社的规模达到 SAC_2 时,旅行社的单位成本才降到最低点。如果新进入的旅行社由于在进入产业之后不能快速达到一定的市场份额,不能充分享受到规模经济所带来的经济性,相对于产业内部的在位旅行社来说,是在较高的成本基础上经营的,同时也使得新进入的旅行社在一种不利的地位上经营。

对于饭店业也存在规模经济问题。在短期内,受刚性接待能力的约

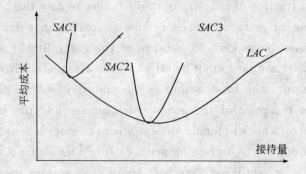

图 6-4 企业规模与成本的关系

束,饭店业追求规模经济是有一定限度的,因为饭店不能调整房间数目;在长期内,旅游目的地的饭店在位者也不会大大增加其生产能力,因为如果所有的饭店都扩大其生产能力,将会导致产品供给大大超过市场需求,饭店规模的扩张很可能会出现规模效益递减或规模不经济。饭店追求规模经济还会受到季节性限制。由于饭店产品具有不可储存性的特点,也不能进行空间转移,饭店产品价值实现只能限定于特定的旅游目的地之中,在这种情况下,饭店规模经济的视线不只取决于旅游目的地的全年总需求,更取决于这种总需求的时间分布状态。

规模经济壁垒的高低,主要取决于两个因素:一是市场容量的大小;二是实现规模经济所必需的生产量的大小,也就是最小经济规模(minimum efficient scale),最小经济规模与我们下面将要谈到的必要资本量壁垒有很大关系。一个特定产业的市场容量较大且仍继续不断扩大时,就越容易吸引潜在企业的进入,进入壁垒较低。当前我国正处于经济高速发展时期,人均收入水平保持着较快的增长,人们对旅游产品的需求日趋旺盛,旅游产业的市场容量也逐渐增大,那么相对于其他产业来说,旅游产业的规模经济进入壁垒就较低。

如果达到规模经济所必需的生产量较小,进入企业在一个很低的产量就可以达到规模经济并达到最低的成本,则产业的进入壁垒较低。关于最小经济规模对规模经济进入壁垒的影响在下面的必要资本量进入壁垒中讲述。

2. 必要资本量壁垒(Capital Cost Barriers)

As we have said above, minimum efficient scale(MES) has great relation with the capital cost barriers. Minimum efficient scale, MES as defined, will in part determine the total capital outlay required for efficient entry. Generally speaking, a large MES necessitates a large capital cost outlay. Besides the MES, the prices of equipment and construction materials can also determine the capital cost. The more capital an industry needs, the more costs the entrant firm will burden. Especially when an entrant firm borrow large amount of money to establish a new firm, it will burden much interest. The deterrence of the capital cost barrier depends on the nature of the potential entrant as well as the nature of the industry. If the prime potential entrant is already a large firm or it has large capital, the enormous capital costs will pose no problem.

必要资本量壁垒是指新企业进入市场所必须投入的资本。在不同的产业，必要资本量随技术、生产、销售的特性的不同而表现出很大的差异。必要资本量越大，筹资越不容易，筹资所负担的利息成本也就越大，新企业在实力较弱或筹资能力较低的情况下进入市场的难度就相对较大，进入壁垒也就越高。一般来说，在一些重化工企业，新企业进入市场所需要的必要资本量往往较大，必要资本量进入壁垒越大；而对于旅游产业，由于产业所需的资本必要量并不是很大，尤其是旅行社业，往往三五个人，几台电脑就能组成一个旅行社。旅行社产业资本进入壁垒低是旅游产业竞争激烈、进入过度、市场集中度低的一个重要原因。

相比旅行社而言，饭店的资本进入壁垒较高。饭店企业在获取资金时所遇到的障碍主要由以下因素引起：一是现在城市中新建饭店的地价、建筑、内外装修、家具、人员工资等方面的刚性支出越来越高；二是除20世纪80年代初中期外，政府历来把"楼、堂、馆、所"作为限制性投资领域，在银行受政府控制程度较深的体制下，饭店企业想从金融市场上获得资金是相对困难的；三是相当一批国有中小型饭店负债比例过大，缺乏持续发展力量。尽管已经有部分民营经济介入中国饭店业，但是在现有政治、经济体制和财务管理制度下，民营经济的有限资金很难盘活庞大的国有存量资产的"空壳"。

3. 产品差别化壁垒(Barriers Caused by Product Differentiation)

Product differentiation is an important aspect of the market structure, and at the same time, it also can become a barrier to entry. Established firms may enjoy a product-differentiation advantage over potential entrants, because of the preference of buyers for established firms and products when compared with new ones. In consequence of this advantage, potential entrants may not be able to secure selling their products at high price as the established firms do; thus the established firms can enjoy some margin of profit than the entrants or the entrants have to incur sales-promotion costs per unit of output greater than those established firms. The advantage of product-differentiation may clearly give established firms the power to elevate their prices by some amount above their minimal average costs without making it attractive for new firms to enter the industry.

The possible sources of product-differentiation barriers to entry include several aspects: 1) the accumulated preferences of buyers for established brand names and company reputations; 2) the exclusive control of superior product designs by established firms, through patent protection; 3) the ownership or control of favored systems of distributive outlets by established firms. 在产品差异化明显的产业，在位企业因为有良好的信誉，或拥有某项专利技术，或拥有庞大的营销网络和客户群体，并已通过持续的广告使在位企业的产品受到了消费者的青睐。在位者与进入者之间消费者偏好的不同是进入壁垒的重要方面，消费者更愿意选择在位企业产品的这种差异使得进入企业即使有能力进入，也不能使消费者转移到自己的产品上，这就意味着企业在进入之后的一段时间内不能获得市场，只能获得很少的利润甚至是亏损。

另外还有两种壁垒与进入壁垒非常相似，即消费者转移成本（customer switching costs）和进入分销渠道的能力（poor access to distribution channels）。Customer switching costs are one-time costs buyers must bear when they switch from one supplier to another, particularly from established firms to entrants. 对于消费者来说，由一种已经比较熟悉的产品转向新的产品会包括许多方面的转移成本，比如说搜寻成本、试错成本、风险成本等。也就是说，消费者要更换消费对象，那么他首先要在众多新进入企业中选择一家企业的产品，在这个过程中消费者要进行一系列的活动，包括搜集信息、对比价格、与卖方进行讨价还价，最后根据利益最大化原则确定哪一家企业的产品最适合自己消费，这就是所谓的搜寻成本。在搜寻的过程中，消费者可能要不断地尝试新产品,那么每一次选择的失误都会给消费者带来试错成本。另外,选择新产品是有风险的,比如说新产品可能会给消费者带来物质或精神上的损失,这些就是风险成本。Poor access to distribution channels refers to that normal distribution channels for a product are already filled by the established firms in the market. 比如说我国旅行社产品中大部分都被国旅、青旅和中旅占领了。

4. 绝对费用壁垒(Absolute Cost Advantage Barriers)

For any given level of output, established firms can produce and market their wares at a lower cost per unit than newcomers. If there exist absolute cost advantage barriers, the established firms can obtain prices above their costs, however, the potential entrants could not cover costs and so would not enter the market. The absolute cost advantage barriers include the followings: 1) control of superior production techniques by established firms, either by patents or by secrecy; 2) exclusive ownership by established firms of superior deposits of resources required in production; 3) inability of entrant firms to acquire necessary factors of production (management services, labor, equipment, materials) on terms as favorable as those enjoyed by established firms; and 4) less favored access of entrant firms to liquid funds for investment, reflected in higher effective interest costs or in simple unavailability of funds in the required amounts. 5) distribution channels controlled by the established firms and so on. 绝对费用壁垒使新企业在进入市场时的生产成本总是高于在位企业,即使新企业选择一个能达到规模经济的产量,其成本与在位企业相比仍处于劣势。

制度性/政府行为壁垒。这一壁垒主要是由制度环境和政府的行为与不行为导致的。比如政府计划部门和行业主管部门的产业政策抑制资金、技术、人才等要素对饭店业的进入,设置较高的技术和服务标准门槛,限制政府部门、社会团体、国有企事业单位对饭店产业的集团消费,区域保护主义通过地方政府的行为限制外地饭店集团对本地区的进入,以稳定为导向的政治目标取代或部分取代企业的效率目标,执法和行政人员在饭店市场的寻租活动等等,都会构成显性和隐性的饭店市场壁垒。

5. 其他壁垒(Other Barriers to Entry)

前面我们谈到的四类进入壁垒都是从结构的角度或技术的角度来

谈的,其实有时在位企业实行的某些策略性壁垒或者说行为壁垒(behavioral barriers)更值得我们关注,因为结构性壁垒或技术性壁垒往往在一段时间内是相对不变的,而行为壁垒则是可以随时调整的。Behavioral barriers are those purposely erected by incumbents to reduce the possibility of entry. For example, established firms will maintain a larger production ability than its normal production to deter that if the entrants enter indeed they will increase production quantity quickly and acquire the biggest market fraction. There are so many behavioral barriers such as collective boycotts, collective aggregated rebates, exclusive dealing, and predatory pricing. These behavioral barriers will be explained in the chapter of market conducts.

In addition, there are various legal barriers to entry including patent licensing, chartering, and franchising regulations administered by local, state, or federal government authorities.

三、各种进入壁垒的相对重要性(The Relative Importance of Barriers)

上面列举的各种进入壁垒的重要性是不一样的,许多产业经济学家通过对制造业相关数据进行分析得出了有关进入壁垒相对重要性的结论。Through analyzing the manufacturing industries during the late 1940s and early 1950s, Bain concluded that product differentiation was the most important entry barrier and the capital cost requirements barrier is coming close behind. Economies of scale were judged to rank in the third, however, absolute cost barriers seemed to be rather inconsequential except in some industries.

The results of recent survey conducted by Karakaya and Stahl differ from Bain's. The following table reports the results for the six barriers in the surveys:

From the following table, we can see that the cost advantages of incumbents outrank product differentiation in importance. Government policy ranks last especially for consumer goods markets as compared to industrial goods markets. Product differentiation is a more important barrier for consumer goods than for industrial goods.

Percentage of Corporate Executive Respondents Who Considered Market Entry Barriers Important		
Entry Barrier	Consumer Markets(%)	Industrial Market(%)
1. Cost advantage of incumbents①	83	83
2. Capital requirements	78	76
3. Product differentiation②	70	62
4. Customer switching cost	70	69
5. Limited distribution	56	55
6. Government policy③	45	55

Source: F. Karakaya and M. J. Stahl, "Barriers to Entry and Market Entry Decisions in Consumer and Industrial Goods Markets," *Journal of Marketing* (April 1989), p. 85. It should be noted that Karakaya and Stahl distinguish between early entry (e.g., first movers) and late entry. These are the results for late entry.

第五节 旅游产业的退出壁垒
(Barriers to Exit of Tourism Industry)

从大量的产业组织文献中可见,人们似乎热衷于对进入壁垒的研究,而对退出壁垒的研究相对较少。但事实上,退出壁垒也有十分重要的研究价值,特别是我国当前正处于经济结构调整时期,对退出壁垒的研究就显得更加重要。本节在弄清退出壁垒的概念的基础上,将着重讨论旅游产业退出壁垒的决定因素和退出壁垒的度量问题,并讨论进入壁垒与退出壁垒的关系。

一、退出壁垒的决定因素(The Factors of Barriers to Exit)

For many businesses, there are also barriers to exit which increase the intensity of competition in an industry because existing firms have little choice but to "stay and fight" when market conditions have deteriorated. 退出壁垒是指现有企业在产业(市场)前景不好,企业业绩

---

① Cost advantage of incumbents, including in this category absolute production costs as well as economies of scale.
② Product differentiation of incumbents due to brand allegiances.
③ Government policy, such as licensing requirements or regulations.

不佳时准备退出该产业(市场),但由于受多种因素的阻碍,资源难以转移出去,这些阻碍现有企业退出产业(市场)的因素,就构成退出壁垒。因此,退出壁垒也称退出障碍。退出壁垒由以下要素构成:

1. 沉淀成本(Sunk Cost)

e.g. the Expense Associated with Writing-off Items of Plant and Machinery, Stocks and the Goodwill of a Brand. 许多资产具有专用性,用以生产特定的产品。企业要退出原有产业,很难将这些资产转为他用,生产其他的产品,也难以将这些资产以公平的价格卖给其他生产同类产品的企业。这就成为企业的沉淀成本。例如,某旅游目的地企业为吸引游客,购买了价值10亿元的专用设备,当年投产,计划在10年内补偿投资,每年偿还1亿元。但过了5年后,该旅游企业发现这个旅游项目的前景不好,便考虑退出,转入其他新兴产业。那么,如果未补偿的5亿元设备能按原价转卖,这家企业至少还能完全收回固定资产投资。但是,如果这些专用性较强的设备因旅游市场的竞争不能转卖或只能以很低的价格出售,甚至不得不废弃,这5亿元的投资就不能收回。这些不能收回的投资就是"沉淀成本"(sunk cost)。沉淀成本越大,企业就越想维持原来的生产经营,努力收回未得到补偿的投资,因此,退出产业的障碍就越大。沉淀成本具有较为广泛的内涵,这里所说的沉淀成本概念不仅适用于各种机械、装置、建筑物等固定性设备,也适用于为特定的旅游服务项目而购入、租赁的用地,还适用于库存等流动资本,更适用于旅游企业信誉等无形资产。所以,沉淀成本适用于所有的企业有形、无形资产,这些都构成了旅游企业的退出障碍。

2. 违约成本和企业信誉损失(The Loss of Business Reputation and Consumer Goodwill)

A decision to leave a market can seriously affect goodwill among previous customers, not least those who have bought a product which is then withdrawn and for which replacement parts become difficult or impossible to obtain. 如果旅游企业退出原有产业,就不能履行原先签订的合同,企业就必须承担违约成本。同时,企业退出产业往往被视为竞争能力不足,这会造成企业信誉损失。其他企业可能因此不愿与这家企业签订新的合同,也会增加企业融资的难度,提高融资成本。这些因素都会阻碍旅游企业退出原有产业。

3. 行政法规壁垒(Barriers of Regulations)

在我国,对于国有性质的旅游企业,企业退出原有产业会造成一部分职工失业,增加社会负担,一些政府部门从保持社会政治安定的角度考虑,在一定的时期内不允许企业退出产业。此外,一些地方政府出于本位主义,维持地方利益的目的,尽管某些旅游项目处于严重过剩、过度竞争状态,也可能会阻止企业退出产业。事实上,这种现象在我国具有一定的普遍性。

4. 市场发育不完善而造成的退出壁垒(Barriers to Exit Caused by Undevelopment of Market)

A market downturn may be perceived as temporary and could be overcome when the economic or business cycle turns and conditions become more favourable. 旅游企业退出原有产业通常需要生产要素转卖和产权交易,但在缺乏生产要素市场和产权交易市场正常运作机制的情况下,旅游企业就难以寻找生产要素和产权交易伙伴,实现交易,从而阻碍企业退出产业。

二、退出壁垒的度量(Measurements of Barriers to Exit)

对于退出壁垒的度量问题,至今还没有这方面的比较成熟的研究成果,但至少可以从"生产能力过剩度"和"亏损企业率"这两个指标来度量退出壁垒。

1. 生产能力过剩度(Surplus Ratio of Production Ability)

在正常情况下,大多数产业的生产能力利用率应该在70%—80%以上,即生产能力过剩度应在20%—30%以下。如果旅游产业的生产能力过剩度高于30%,意味着该产业中有相当一部分企业生产能力闲置。如果不存在退出壁垒,这些企业应该考虑退出该产业而去投资其他产业。但由于退出壁垒的存在,即使企业的生产设备在相当程度上处于闲置状态,企业也无法退出产业。因此,我们可以通过生产能力过剩度这一指标来衡量退出壁垒,即生产能力过剩度越高,退出壁垒也越高。

2. 亏损企业率(The Rate of Loss Firms)

造成旅游企业亏损的原因是多方面的,如该产业处于夕阳产业,市场需求减少;产业内企业过于"拥挤",造成过度竞争;政府对企业实行严格的价格管制,强制企业实行低价政策等等。在市场经济条件下,企业不能长期处于亏损状态,否则就要破产倒闭。这就客观上会促使亏损企业退出原有产业而去投资赢利率较高的产业,但由于各种退出壁垒的存在,企业即使亏损,也不能退出产业。在市场竞争的优胜劣汰规律下,每一个产业都会存在亏损企业,但在退出壁垒不高的情况下,亏损企业占该产业企业总数的比率(即亏损企业率＝亏损企业数/企业总数)不会很高。如果旅游产业的亏损企业率较高,必然存在较高的退出壁垒。因此,我们可以用亏损企业率来度量旅游产业的退出壁垒,即该产业的亏损企业率越高,该产业的退出壁垒也就越高。

三、进入壁垒与退出壁垒的关系(The Relation Between Entry and Exit Barriers)

进入壁垒是对准备进入产业的潜在企业而言的,而退出壁垒则是对产业内准备退出产业的现有企业而言的。但从进入壁垒和退出壁垒的要素看,两者具有一定的联系,表现在两者具有一定程度的重复性和关联性。例如,在进入壁垒和退出壁垒中都有行政法规壁垒要素,一般地说,进入产业的行政法规壁垒越高,企业退出产业的行政法规壁垒也越高。又如,企业进入产业的规模经济壁垒越高,企业所需的必要资本量就越多,在资产专用性一定的情况下,企业退出产业时的沉淀成本壁垒也越高。可见,在一般情况下,进入壁垒较高的产业,退出壁垒也较高;而进入壁垒较低的产业,退出壁垒也较低,两者具有相当的关联性。从实证资料看,在旅游产业,进入与退出的现象会比另一些产业普遍。例如,在旅游市场上,新进入企业不计其数并且占有大量市场份额;而旅游产业的退出率也较高。显而易见,进入与退出高度相关:产业中那些促成进入的条件也促成了退出。当然,在旅游产业中也有进入壁垒较高而退出壁垒较低的情况。例如,虽然规模经济引起必要资本量壁垒,但如果旅游企业从租赁市场上取得设备从事生产和提供服务活动,虽然租赁设备时需要较大的资本量,但企业退出产业时,只要能归还设备,并不存在较大的沉淀成本,退出壁垒就不高。

第六节　我国旅游产业过度竞争的原因分析
(The Analysis of the Surplus Competition of National Tourism Industry)

一、我国旅游产业过度竞争状况的成因(The Reasons of the Surplus Competition of National Tourism Industry)

(1)根据产业组织理论,规模经济、绝对费用、产品差别化、政策和法规障碍等都会构成进入壁垒,抑制企业过度进入。但在我国由于存在许多特殊因素,导致部分进入壁垒失效。旅游业旺盛的市场需求诱发了各种利益主体的大量进入,而进入主体投资动机的多重性及预算约束等因素,使许多进入壁垒失效,导致了产业内过度进入状况的发生。我国实施改革开放政策以来,地方、部门以及企业的自主权不断扩大,成为经济运行中极其活跃的利益主体。随着我国宏观经济的增长和人民收入水平的提高,旅游业市场需求持续增长,国家也相继出台了促进旅游业发展的产业政策,因此,这些利益主体的投资冲动在旅游业发展中迅速得到释放并不断增强,导致旅游产业内企业的大量进入。首先,地方政府和部门在众多进入主体中起着十分重要的作用,由于它们进入产业的目标具有多重性,如扩大地方财源、城市建设、增加就业等,这使得一些行政法规壁垒失效。其次,对于企业来说,由于投融资体制不健全及其他原因,许多企业的预算约束是软的,企业容易筹措资金,使得潜在进入企业对进入产业的收益产生偏高的预期,而对进入成本产生偏低预期,导致与规模经济相关的必要资本量壁垒失效。

(2)旅游企业并购重组存在多种行政障碍,使得旅游产业集中度不能迅速提高到合适的水平,也是造成过度竞争的重要原因。生产要素的自由流动、企业并购重组是企业成长壮大的重要途径,也是提高产业集中度的重要手段。由于在我国旅游企业并购中存在多种行政障碍,导致大规模的饭店集团、旅行社集团很少出现,不能形成规模经济。

在我国旅游饭店业中差不多有一半的饭店和各级政府部门有直接隶属关系,因此地方所有与部门所有饭店存在事实上的分割与封闭,造成现阶段规范的饭店集团发展面临很大障碍,不仅需要克服部门管理权的矛盾,还要克服中央与地方、区域与区域之间的利益矛盾。企业通过产业组织调整行为合并、兼并、联合等扩大市场份额,提高产业集中度的方式不可能大规模出现。从旅行社业看,旅行社的经营依赖网络化,业务发展需要靠本地市场的门市和代理商输送客源,依靠外地市场的业务网络维持运作和确保质量,即通过地域扩大和网络化增强实力扩大业务。而现实条件下,企业在本地市场扩大受到审批的限制,在外地市场扩大受到各地旅游行政机关的抵制,因而难以实现企业规模上的突破,制约了旅行社的扩张和一体化进程。

(3)我国旅游业产品同质化程度高,旅游企业对新产品的开发程度不够,导致企业间在低层次上展开价格战成为最主要的竞争方式。我国旅游企业经营的产品同质化程度严重,替代性较强,企业不能根据市场需求不断开发有特色、有竞争力的旅游新产品。以我国旅行社行业为例,我国旅行社行业一直采取以市场分割为特征的水平分工体系,每家旅行社从产品开发到外联接待全方位出击,既无批发、零售的渠道差异,也无个性化的特色产品。产品差异化程度低,消费者对不同企业的产品没有形成突出的偏好,因此,消费者在选择时关心的主要问题是价格。从企业方面来讲,由于消费者对某一特定产品的忠诚度低,无法培育稳定的消费市场,在这种市场竞争格局下,企业只要稍微改变价格策略,就可以占有所有企业生产剩余,最大化实现自己的福利,从而使降低价格成为最有效的竞争手段,导致企业陷入以价格竞争为主的过度竞争的漩涡之中无法自拔。

(4) 资产专用性强、社会保障制度改革滞后等因素,导致旅游产业退出壁垒较高,致使过度竞争状况长期存在。退出壁垒是构成过度竞争的一个最主要因素,因为只要退出自由,过度进入和全行业低利润率或负利润率就只能是短期现象,过度竞争不会长期存在。在我国旅游企业中尤以饭店业退出市场障碍较高,主要表现在沉没成本上。饭店业资产通用性较差,很难转化为其他产品,而且目前我国生产要素市场尚不完善,企业退出过程需要克服较多困难。再加上我国社会保障制度(失业、医疗、养老)改革滞后,条块分割等因素的影响,产业退出壁垒极高。相反,为了社会安定,国家仍实行对亏损企业发放亏损补贴、减免税收等政策,限制市场对产业组织的整合过程,妨碍产业退出。

二、解决我国旅游产业过度竞争状况的对策

(1) 鼓励企业间通过并购重组等形式组建大型旅游企业集团,扩大企业规模,提高产业集中度,缓解过度竞争状况。

(2) 深化体制改革,消除产业过度进入。同时,旅游企业要开发特色旅游新产品,避免因产品雷同而导致的价格竞争。

(3) 降低企业退出壁垒,尤其是体制性退出壁垒,加速利用市场机制完成优胜劣汰,消除生产能力严重过剩。

复习思考题:

1. 什么叫市场结构?经济学把市场结构归为哪几类?每类市场结构有什么特征?
2. 如何理解市场集中度?从市场集中度的角度判断我国旅行社从80年代以来的市场结构类型的演变。
3. 试分析我国旅游企业产品差异情况。并结合实际谈谈我国旅游企业

品牌建设的重要性。
4. 在旅游产业存在哪些进入壁垒？重点分析旅游产业规模经济壁垒对旅游企业进入的限制。
5. 旅游企业存在哪些退出壁垒？进入和退出壁垒存在着什么关系？
6. 我国旅游产业为什么会存在过度竞争的状况？

第七章
旅游企业的价格行为
(The Price Behavior of Tourism Company)

在介绍了旅游产业的市场结构后,从本章开始,我们将重点介绍旅游企业的市场行为。针对旅游企业的特点,主要内容包括旅游企业的价格行为、旅游企业的竞争和合作行为、旅游企业的一体化行为等。在介绍旅游企业的这些行为之前,我们先简要介绍关于企业市场行为的一些概念。

第一节 市场行为概述
(The Outline of Market Behavior)

市场结构描述的是产业内部企业之间的竞争与协作的关系。在不同的市场结构中,企业为获取最大利润所采取的行为或策略是不同的。在所确定的市场结构框架内研究组织的行为是产业组织经济学的一个重要问题。对于市场行为要分类研究。

一、从对市场势力的运用和拓展看(View From Exploitation and Expansion of Market Power)

Conduct is behavior—what firms do with their prices, production levels, products, promotions, and other key operating variables. In one hand, market structure influence conduct, so the firms possessing market power may exploit that power by raising price above the competitive level to increase their profits. In the other hand, the firms' conduct in turn can influence the structure so they subdue rivals in order to augment or maintain their market power which be classified into the conduct to extend market power. In addition, there is still a conduct with a conjunction linking its reference to exploitation and extension. So there should be three possibilities for conduct: 1) conduct that exploits market power; 2) conduct that extends power; 3) combination conduct that may be both exploitative and expansionary at the same time.

1. 市场力量的运用(Exploitation of Market Power)

Exploitation of market power refers to that the firm in certain industry can exploit its power to gain the biggest profits according to the market structure. For example, in monopoly market, pure monopolists raise price and restrict output in order to maximize profit. The monopoly structure can yield monopolistic conduct. Through exploitation of market power, product costs can be reduced by reducing product quality, or by curbing customer service, to by cutting back on the investments in innovation so that the firms can make more profit. The exploitation of market power in short-run, however, in the long run those excess will shrink because new firms may enter the market to seek super-profit or some substitute products may appear to attract the customs.

2. 市场势力的延伸(Expansion of Market Power)

Compared with that exploitation market power will shrink profit in the long run, expansion of market power will extend or maintain the power in the long run. Although there may be some sacrifice of profits in the short run, profits eventually rise as market power is extended because that greater power can eventually be exploited. Conduct extending market power belongs to a larger class of conduct called strategic behavior. Strategic behavior is positioning oneself physically or psychologically so as to discourage or thwart actions or reactions by rivals and potential rivals that would, if taken, impair one's own goal attainment, broadly speaking, strategic behavior needs long-run planning and takes into account rivals' likely responses when evaluating alternative courses of action, and it uses tactics that depend on dynamic developments in the marketplace. Through strategic behavior dominant firms can use their relatively large size, first mover positions, low-cost raw material supplies, or some other advantages to injure weaker existing rivals or discourage the entry of potential rivals.

3. 利用和拓展市场势力结合(Combination Conduct, Exploitative and Expansionary)

It can be said that exploitation of market power is a short-run strategy and the expansion of market power is a long-run strategy. A dominant firm may employ strategic behaviors in both the short run and the long run, so the conduct is both exploitative and expansionary. Actually, there are so many similarities between expansionary conduct and combination conduct and sometimes it is difficult to distinguish them. However, it is still useful to separate them which we will discuss in detail in the following charter. For example, predatory pricing and entry-limit pricing typify expansionary conduct, however, exclusive dealing, tying, loyalty rebates, and exclusive cross-licensing of patents typify combination conduct.

二、从市场行为是否涉及价格看(View on Whether the Market Behavior Is Involved in Price)

In a general way, market conduct refers to the patterns of behavior which enterprises follow in adapting or adjusting to the markets in which they sell(or buy). If enterprises are referred to as sellers, market conduct encompasses two related sorts of behavior:

1. The "price policies" of enterprises(whether acting individually or collectively). These are effectively the principles, methods, and resultant actions, that they employ in establishing what prices to charge, what outputs to produce, what product designs to choose, what sales-promotion costs to incur, etc.

2. The process or mechanism of interaction, cross-adaptation, and coordination of the policies of competing sellers in any markets.

三、常见的市场行为类型(Regular Market Behavior Patterns)

1. The principle and the method employed by the firm or group of firms in calculating or determining price and output. For example,

when selling product, is a single price charged, or a set of discriminatory prices to different buyers?

2. The product policy of the firm or group of firms. For example, is product variation over time a part of the individual or collective market policy?

3. The sales promotion policy of the firm or group. Do advertising and other sales promotion play a significant role in the individual or collective market policy?

4. Means of coordination and cross-adaptation of price, product, and sales-promotion policies of competing sellers.

5. Presence or absence of, and extent of, predatory or exclusionary tactics directed against either established rivals or potential entrants.

第二节 旅游企业的成本加成定价
(Tourism Company's Cost-plus Pricing)

西方国家的大量调查表明,在现实世界中,绝大多数企业采用最普遍的定价方法是"成本加成定价"。在德国,70%以上的企业采用成本加成定价;在英国,这一比例接近60%;美国和其他欧美国家的情况较为类似。在我国,成本加成定价法也是占统治地位的企业定价法,在旅游企业中也被广泛采用。

一、成本加成定价的计算方法(Calculating Price Using the Cost-plus Method)

Cost-plus pricing is a pricing method commonly used by firms. It is used primarily because it is easy to calculate and requires little information. There are several varieties, but the common thread in all of them is you first calculate the cost of the product, then include an additional amount to represent profit.

There are several ways of determining cost, and the profit can be added as either a percentage markup or an absolute amount. One example is:

$$P = (AVC + FC\%) \cdot (1 + MK\%)$$

where:

- P = price
- AVC = average variable cost
- $FC\%$ = percentage allocation of fixed costs
- $MK\%$ = percentage markup

For example: If variable costs are 30 yuan, the allocation to cover fixed costs is 10 yuan, and you feel you need a 50% markup then you would charge a price of 60 yuan:

$$P = (30 + 10) \cdot (1 + 0.50)$$
$$P = 40 \cdot 1.5$$
$$P = 60$$

An alternative way of doing the same calculation is:

$$P = (AVC + FC\%) / (1 - MK\%)$$

To make things simpler, some firms, particularly retailers, ignore fixed costs and just use the purchase price paid to their suppliers as the cost term. They indirectly incorporate the fixed cost allocation into the markup percentage. To simplify things even further, sometimes a fixed amount is applied rather than a percentage. This fixed amount is usually determined by head-office to make it easy for franchisees and store managers. This is sometimes referred to as turnkey pricing.

Another variant of cost plus pricing is activity based pricing. This involves being more careful in determining costs. Instead of using arbitrary expense categories when allocating overhead, every activity is linked to the resources it uses.

Cost will need to be recalculated and the percentage markup will likely need to be adjusted as the product goes through its life cycle. This is sometimes referred to as product life cycle pricing, although it is seldom done deliberately or in a planned and organized manner. Price skimming and penetration pricing are also types of product life cycle pricing but they are demand based pricing methods rather cost based.

二、对成本加成定价法的评价(Comments on the Cost-plus Pricing Method)

企业在定价时,为什么很少根据利润最大化的要求按边际原则定价,而普遍采用成本加成定价呢？一般认为,原因有以下几个：(1)信息不充分。企业的财务资料与统计数据难以提供计算市场需求曲线以及边际收益和边际成本的数据,因此很难按边际原则定价。(2)企业目标多元化。不少企业并不把利润最大化作为经营目标,而可能以销售收入最大化、市场份额最大化、销售增长率最大化等作为目标；即使以利润最大化为目标的企业,在特定的时期,也可能以维持市场生存、反击价格挑战等作为定价目标。以利润最大化为目标的边际成本原则对这些企业并不适用。(3)成本加成定价法逻辑关系清楚,易为不同层次的企业经营者所接受,而且应用简便。(4)成本加成定价为企业变动价格提供了正当理由,想要提高价格的企业通常将提价的原因归结为成本的增加。

但是,成本加成定价法也受到了许多批评,其中最为有力的批评是：成本加成定价将价格视为平均成本的函数,完全颠倒了因果关系。因为,平均成本的高低由产量决定,而产量的大小取决于价格。如果我们将成本加成定价法的公式简写为：

$$P = AC(1+s) = FTC/Q + TVC/Q + \pi/Q$$

上式中,Q 是根据标准开工率计算出来的预计产量,如果市场需求不足,实际产量达不到预计产量,那么为了实现加成率 s,此时价格应该提高。但是,提价将使市场需求进一步减少,产量也进一步减少,很显然,在这一场合,成本加成定价导致了错误的结果。

另外,成本加成定价法也有以下不足之处：

- tends to ignore the role of consumers
- tends to ignore the role of competitors
- use of historical accounting costs rather than replacement value
- use of "normal" or "standard" output level to allocate fixed costs
- inclusion of sunk costs rather than just using incremental costs
- ignores opportunity costs

第三节　旅游企业的价格歧视
(The Price Discrimination of Tourism Company)

在旅游产业中,我们经常可以看到这样的价格行为:同一旅游企业对相同的旅游服务项目按照消费者的不同类型收取不同的价格,或对同一消费者的不同消费量收取不同的价格。例如,一些旅游景点对学生实行比较优惠的价格,而一些旅游社团针对同一旅游项目对个人与团体的收费标准也是不一样的。这些都属于旅游企业的价格歧视行为。本节探讨价格歧视的基本概念及主要内容。

一、价格歧视的概念及实现条件(Price Discrimination)

1. 价格歧视的概念(The Concept of Price Discrimination)

在完全竞争的市场中,厂商对产品的价格没有决策权,所有的厂商只能按照既定的价格销售产品。但现实中的厂商通常具有一定的市场势力,能够在一定程度上决定产品的价格,尤其是当厂商可以根据不同消费者的需求弹性区分消费者,对不同消费者销售同一商品时收取不同的价格,这时就发生了价格歧视。Price discrimination occurs whenever a seller sells the same commodity or service at more than one price. Moreover, even if the sale items are not exactly the same, but only related, price discrimination also occurs if the seller sells very similar products at different price-cost ratios. 也就是说,如果厂商向不同的消费者出售相同的产品时,收取不同的价格,这样的厂商就有价格歧视。从更广义的角度讲,即使所售商品不是完全相同,只是具有一定的相似性,如果厂商能够区分不同的消费者以不同的价格销售这些相似的商品,也可以说厂商实行了价格歧视。

2. 价格歧视实现的条件(The Conditions for Price Discrimination)

There are some conditions essential for price discrimination:

(1) The seller must have some market power. A firm in purely competitive market has no control over prices to engage in discrimination.

(2) The seller must confront buyers who have differing price elasticities of demand. The elasticity differences among buyers may be due to differences in income level, differences in needs, differences in

the availability of substitutes, differences in use of the product, and so on. 而对于这些具有不同需求弹性的消费者,厂商必须具有区分不同消费者的能力。

(3) 厂商必须能够阻止或限制转卖行为,即防止以低价购买的消费者再转售给另外的消费者。为了能够阻止转卖行为的发生,需求弹性不同的购买者必须被分开。Without separation, low-price customers could resell their purchases to the high-price customers. 如果在不同消费者之间的转卖行为可以发生,价格歧视的行为就不会发生。因此限制转卖行为是决定任何价格歧视成功的关键因素。

在不同消费者之间的价格差别越大,转卖行为就越容易发生,为了限制转卖,厂商必须采取一定的措施,或者在特定的情况下实行价格歧视,以有效阻止转卖的发生。如服务产品对于不同的消费者收取不同的价格,旅游产品属于服务产品,很可能发生价格歧视。又如厂商可以通过规定只对直接购买产品的消费者提供质量保证承诺,而对转卖的产品质量保证制度无效,从而增加转卖的难度。再如厂商可以通过改变产品成分,使成本基本一样而成分基本不同的产品适用不同的消费者,从而收取不同的价格。

二、价格歧视的种类(The Categories of Price Discrimination)

如果在消费者之间不发生转卖行为,厂商就可以实行价格歧视。从理论上讲,价格歧视可以分为三种:一级价格歧视(first-degree discrimination)、二级价格歧视(second-degree discrimination)、三级价格歧视(third-degree discrimination)。

1. 一级价格歧视(First-degree Discrimination)

First-degree discrimination can also be named perfect price discrimination(完全价格歧视). Each and every unit seller goes for the very highest price above cost it can fetch. Each and every buyer pays as much as he or she is willing to pay for the quantity he or she wants. In the purely competitive market, the price and quantity are determined in the point where marginal revenue equals to marginal cost. In the purely competitive market, consumer can maximize the consumer's surplus we have discussed in the charter 6. If the firm can implement the first-degree price discrimination, it can acquire the consumer's surplus as that of the firm in purely competitive market. 也就是说,实

行一级价格歧视的厂商可以将价格定在消费者剩余完全转移给厂商的水平上。假定厂商能够知道每个消费者愿意支付的最高价格,那么它就会对每个消费者收取不同的价格,从而获取全部的消费者剩余。其实,在完全价格歧视条件下,厂商所提供的产量与完全竞争市场的产量完全相同,也就是说,两者的效率是相同的。但在完全竞争市场上,消费者获取了最大的消费者剩余,而在完全价格歧视条件下,这部分消费者剩余却由厂商获得。也就是说,完全价格歧视并没有降低效率,只是影响了分配。

However, in the real world such perfect discrimination is extremely difficult and is never achieved in practice because most sellers cannot measure the depth of each buyer's desire and ability to pay.

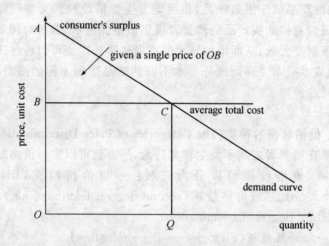

Figure 7-1　First-degree Discrimination

2. 二级价格歧视(Second-degree Discrimination)

Second-degree discrimination is like first-degree discrimination only less refined. We can express the second-degree discrimination as the following figure.

From figure 7-2, we can see the demand is partitioned into three blocks. Quantity OQ_1 is sold at price OG. Quantity Q_2Q_1 is sold at price OK. Quantity Q_3Q_2 is sold at price OJ. The consumer's surplus captured by sellers from consumer is less than that in first-degree

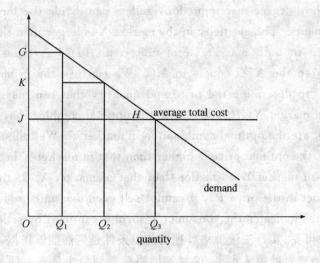

Figure 7-2 Second-degree Price Discrimination

discrimination. The shaded area is the consumer's surplus.

3. 三级价格歧视(Third-degree Discrimination)

(1) 三级价格歧视(Third-degree Discrimination)

在现实中,厂商通常难以准确判断每一位消费者愿意支付的价格,从而难以实行一级和二级价格歧视,但厂商却能够知道各个消费者是属于哪一类消费者集团,而且能知道各个消费者集团的总供给曲线,这样,厂商就可以对不同的消费者集团收取不同的价格。这就是三级价格歧视。我们可以用下图表示:

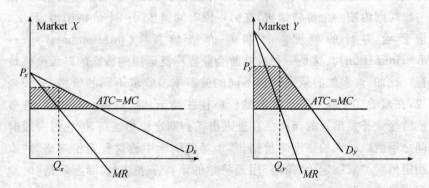

Figure 7-3 Third-degree Discrimination

In third-degree discrimination, sellers can divide the buyers into two segments. The elasticity in the market X is larger than that in the market Y. In both markets total unit cost (ATC) is the same and constant, so the ATC equals to MC. We can use the principle that $MR=MC$ to determine the price and quantity that can maximize the profit. In market X, P_x and Q_x are the optimal combination, whereas P_y and Q_y are the optimal combination in market Y. We can see that in market Y the optimal price is higher than that in market X because the elasticity of market Y is smaller than that of market X. If the sellers sell product in the price P_y, it cannot sell even one unit product. The shaded area indicates the consumer's surplus captured by sellers.

由此可见，实行三级价格歧视的前提条件是厂商能够根据一定的信息，比如消费者的收入水平、偏好等把消费者划分为具有不同消费弹性的群体。对于需求弹性较小的消费者可以收取较高的价格，而对于需求弹性较大的消费者团体则收取较低的价格，但在任何一个市场厂商都是以利润最大化的原则来确定生产数量和产品价格的。

现实中，三级价格歧视是经常被厂商使用的一种价格歧视，而一级和二级价格歧视则很少被使用，主要是因为厂商可以简单地划分消费者的类型，却不能准确确定每一个消费者或每一些消费者的愿意接受的价格。

（2）时期间价格歧视(Intertemporal Price Discrimination)

如果旅游企业将不同时间的消费者划分为需求曲线不同的市场，在一段时间内按一个价格销售，在另一段时间里按另一个价格销售，那么，该企业实行的就是"时期间价格歧视"（intertemporal price discrimination）。这是一种被旅游企业界广泛运用的特殊的三级价格歧视。比如，许多旅游景点会在不同的旅游季节收取不同的价格，一般来说，在旅游旺季或节假日收取的价格往往高于其他时期。再比如，许多旅游企业开发出来的新产品在进入市场初期定价相当高，但在过一段时间之后就以较大的幅度降价销售，市场营销学中称这种定价策略为"取脂定价"。"取脂定价"策略，用经济学的语言来表述，实际上就是"时期间价格歧视"。

为什么"取脂定价"能够成功？为什么消费者不等到降价后再购买？原因是第一批购买的消费者特别偏好这类商品，需求弹性很低，迫不及待地想拥有它;第二批购买的消费者通常有较高的需求弹性只有等到降价之后才会购买。

第一批购买者为了及时获得他们所偏爱的商品付出了代价,这个代价就是消费者剩余的损失,见图 7-4 中的阴影面积。这个消费者剩余,最终转移给企业,成为企业的超额利润。

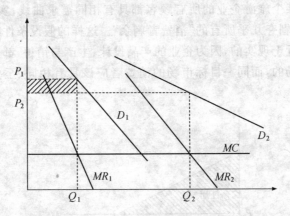

图 7-4 时期间价格歧视

在图中,企业对需求曲线为 D_1 的消费者,价格定在 P_1,销售量为 Q_1;降价为 P_2 后,需求曲线为 D_2 的消费者会购买 Q_2 的量。阴影面积表示企业从第 1 类顾客那里攫取的消费者剩余。

第四节 旅游企业的两部收费制
(Tourism Company's Two-part Tariff)

所谓"两部收费制"(two-part tariff),是指消费者购买某种产品或服务要支付两部分费用,一部分为"注册费",用于购买"消费权";另一部分为"使用费",用于直接购买产品或服务。"两部收费制"在旅游、娱乐、电信与零售等行业较为常见。譬如,大型游乐园除向游客收取门票外,每个娱乐项目又要单独计费。游乐场的所有者必须决定是收取高门票费而每个项目要低价,还是相反,免费让人们进场但每个项目都要高价。

企业为什么要实行"两部收费制"呢?"两部收费制"的目的是攫取消费者剩余,获取超额利润。"两部收费制"是企业攫取消费者剩余的定价策略。设厂商有一定的市场势力,它应该定一个高入门费和低使用费,还是相反？为了弄懂厂商怎样解决该问题,我们需要弄懂其中包含的基本原理。

一、有一类消费者的"两部收费制"(Two-part Tariff Including Only One Kind of Consumer)

假设某个旅游企业的所有顾客都具有相同需求曲线,实行"两部收费制"可以剥夺几乎所有的"消费者剩余"。这样的假设条件在不少场合是相当接近于现实的,因为企业的产品设计、生产与销售,都是针对特定的目标市场的,而同一目标市场的消费者应该具有相同、至少相近的需求曲线。

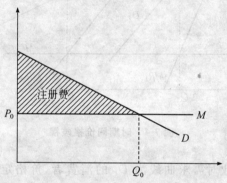

图 7-5　只有一类消费者的两部收费

图7-5说明了"两部收费制"是如何攫取全部消费者剩余的。厂商只要将价格定为等于边际成本,购买量就可以达到 Q_0。而将全部消费者剩余(三角形阴影面积)都定为注册费,从而可以最大限度地获取超额利润。

二、有二类消费者的"两部收费制"(Two-part Tariff Including Two Kinds of Consumers)

如果旅游企业的顾客数量众多,包含了若干种类需求特征不同的消费者,他们对同样的产品与服务有不同的需求曲线,那么,企业的"两部收费制"就不能完全攫取所有消费者剩余。我们将这类企业的所有消费者简化为两类:一类消费者的需求曲线为 D_1,另一类为 D_2。

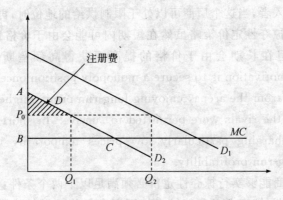

图 7-6 有两类消费者的两部收费

上图说明了有两类不同消费者时,企业如何设计"两部收费制"方案,才能获取更大的利润。假如把价格 P_0 定为等于 MC,那么,注册费只能等于第二类消费者的消费者剩余 $\triangle ABC$,企业获取的超额利润为所攫取的消费者剩余的两倍($2\triangle ABC$)。

但是,这不是企业的最优决策。如果将价格提高 $P_0 > MC$,同时,注册费定为第二类消费者减少了的消费者剩余($\triangle AP_0D$ 的面积),那么,企业所获取的超额利润将增加到 $2 \cdot \triangle AP_0D + (P_0 - MC) \times (Q_1 + Q_2)$。这个超额利润将大于原方案的超额利润 $2\triangle ABC$。

第五节 旅游企业之间的价格行为
(Pricing Behavior between Tourism Companies)

旅游企业价格行为一类是以攫取消费者剩余、增加超额利润为目的的价格行为,如价格歧视、两部收费制等;另一类是以排挤竞争对手、改变或维持市场结构,追求长期利润为目的价格行为。本节重点分析旅游企业的第二类价格行为,主要内容包括掠夺性定价与限制性定价。

一、掠夺性定价(Predatory Pricing)

Predatory pricing refers to temporary price cuts, not for purposes of enlarging demand but rather for purposes of eventually restricting supply. Once the predator is in a position to restrict supply (either by himself or with the cooperation of others), price is then increased. 掠夺性定价是指:一个厂商开始时降低价格将竞争对手驱逐出市场并吓

退潜在的进入者,当这个厂商可以处于限制供给的地位时,再提高价格。该厂商实行掠夺性定价策略虽然在短期内可能会由于价格低于成本而遭受损失,但在长期会由于价格的提高而获得高额垄断利润。The predator's motivation is to secure a monopoly position once rivals have been driven from the arena, enjoying long-run profits higher than they would be if the rivals were permitted to survive. In short, predatory pricing is charging particularly low prices temporarily in order to increase long-run profitability.

一个厂商能够实行掠夺性定价必须满足以下两个条件:(1)在实行低价格的时期,掠夺者必须能够承担因所定低价而引起的损失。(2)价格降低会引起消费者需求的增加,掠夺者为了驱逐竞争对手或阻止潜在的竞争对手进入,必须能够满足在低价位上的所有需求。

实行掠夺性定价厂商为达到目的,应该使竞争对手或潜在进入者形成惧怕而不敢进入的心态,应该确保被驱逐出市场的厂商永远被驱逐出该产业,或者破产或者被兼并。但如果该产业进入的沉淀成本为零①,而且企业对利润的反映是极其灵敏的,那么掠夺性定价就不太可能实行,因为,只要厂商把价格提高到边际成本之上,有一定的利润空间,就会吸引被驱逐的厂商或潜在进入者进入该产业。

John McGee对掠夺性定价策略提出了怀疑。他认为掠夺性定价是非理性的,因此存在的可能性很小。His arguments may be summarized as follows:

- Merger is a less costly means of doing away with rivals.
- Predatory pricing should not force exits once the intended victims recognize that the price cutting is temporary. The prospects of higher profits later should entice them to stay in and also entice investors and leaders to finance their persistence.
- He argued that even if victims do leave the market, they can easily reenter after the predator raises prices.

However, these arguments are seldom proven. First, merger is

---

① 根据鲍莫尔的可竞争市场理论,如果某产业的沉淀成本为零,企业进入产业是自由的。

not a good substitute for predatory pricing because it is illegal to lessen competition substantially by merger, and even if it were legal, predatory pricing can be a useful means of lowering the acquisition price paid by the predator.

Second, unless there is "symmetry" between the predator and prey in their knowledge, financial strengths, and motives, the second argument can not be true. In the real world of business, asymmetries are abound such as market share mismatches, first mover advantages, absolute product cost differences, and varying strengths of brand image under product differentiation.

The third argument that victims of predation may easily reenter the market once the predator is over can also be questioned. Some technical entry barriers like economies of scale may deter reentry, and at the same time predatory behavior may influence the entrants expectation of the profit and deter entry or reentry.

因此,掠夺性定价策略理论成立的前提条件是厂商之间存在着差异,各厂商由于信息不对称、先行者优势以及绝对成本优势等不对称性决定了所处地位是不对称的。实行掠夺性定价的厂商是为了通过在一个短时期内的低价驱逐竞争者或潜在竞争对手,同时给其他企业以警示并证明自己的能力,从而阻止潜在进入者的进入。但实行掠夺性定价的厂商也面临着一定的风险,即在实行低价策略时要负担很大的利润损失,驱逐策略成功之后所获收益极其微薄不足以弥补损失。因此,一个企业在实行掠夺性定价之前一定要确保提高所获收益能弥补低价损失,当然这个收益应该是从长期来衡量的。

二、限制性定价(Limit Pricing)

限制性定价行为是一种非合作性策略行为。The conduct of "limit pricing" refers to that sellers in concentrated markets will set prices high enough to make excess profits but not so high as to attract new entry. The theory bases on three assumptions:

- Established sellers and potential entrants seek maximum profits over the long run.
- Established sellers think potential entrants will expect them to

maintain their outputs in the event of new entry, letting price fall with the entrant's added output.
- Established sellers have no difficulty colluding to determine and set the entry-limiting price.

Both established sellers and entrants make decision to acquire maximum profits. Potential entrants calculate prospective profits from expected postentry demand and cost conditions which depend on the postentry behavior of established sellers. This can be expressed by the following figure:

From Chart 7-7, we can see that if the established firm produce Q_1, it will make price p_1 which will deter entrant to produce goods. If the established firm produce Q_2, it will make p_2 which will deter entrant to produce goods.

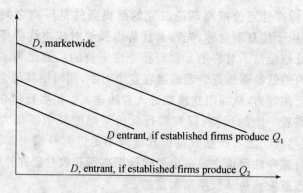

Chart 7-7 Limit Pricing

复习思考题：
1. 有哪几种市场行为？
2. 什么叫价格歧视？实行价格歧视的条件是什么？
3. 有哪几种价格歧视？每种价格歧视的内涵是什么？
4. 旅游企业如何通过时期间价格歧视在不同时期内进行定价？
5. 旅游企业如何实施两部类收费制？

第八章
博弈论与旅游企业的竞争行为
(Game Theory and Competition Among Travelling Forms)

现代旅游企业经营决策的成败之关键是策略运筹,在现代市场经济的激烈竞争中尤其如此。而博弈论的核心内容就是专门研究如何在真正的知己知彼条件下进行策略筹划。在这里的知己知彼,指的是不仅要全面了解自己所面临的各种情况,还特别强调要考虑到所有参与人(博弈方)的各种可行策略及变动时的相互影响(策略相互依赖)。因此,为了分析旅游企业的竞争行为,我们首先介绍博弈论的基本知识。

博弈论译自英文 Game Theory。其实 Game 的基本意义是游戏,因此 GameTheory 直译应该是"游戏理论"。说起游戏当然大家都非常熟悉,日常生活中的下棋、打牌、博彩和田径、球类等各种体育比赛等等都是不同种类、不同形式的游戏。人类创造的游戏种类丰富多彩,我们很难把它们一一列举出来,更不用说在一本书中对它们一一详细介绍和分析。不过,如果我们认真观察、思考一下就能发现,很多游戏都有这样一个共同的特点,即策略(或称计谋)在其中有着举足轻重的影响和作用。虽然在有些游戏中体力和其他固有条件的作用会更大,但一旦这些条件及其对结果的影响既定以后,策略选择的好坏就成了可以由游戏参加者掌握运用的能左右游戏结果的最关键的因素,而在各游戏参加者的初始条件完全平等的游戏中,策略选择就更成了游戏结果的唯一的决定因素。进一步观察还可以归纳出游戏的下列四个共同特征:第一,都有一定的规则。这些规则规定游戏的参加者(个人或队组)可以做什么,不可以做什么,按怎样的次序做,什么时候结束游戏和一旦参加者犯规将受怎样的处罚等等。第二,有一个结果。如一方赢一方输,平局或参加者各有所得等等,而且结果常能用正或负的数值表示,至少能按照一定的规则折算成数值。第三,策略至关重要。游戏者不同的策略选择常常对应不同的游戏结果。第四,策略有相互依存性。即每一个游戏者从游戏中所得结果的好坏不仅取决于自身的策略选择,同时也取决于其他参加者的策略选择。上述几点正是一般游戏的本质特征。但是,具有这样特征的却并不只有我们平常所理解的各种真正的游戏,许多我们平时并不以游戏相称的重要得多的活动同样具有这几个特征。如经济活动中的经营决策、市场竞争,政治、军事活动中的竞选、谈判、联合和战争等斗智斗勇的较量等等,如果抽象出它们的本质特征,也都是与一般游戏一样,在一定规则之下各参加方的决策较量。换句话说,从研究游戏规律得出的结论可用于指导经济、政治等重要活动中所遇到的决策问题。从旅游企业角度来看,在进行价格与产量决策时也必须选择正确的策略,以便在竞争中取得优势。本章对博弈理论中的一些基本知识作简要的介绍,并用博弈理论分析旅游企业的竞争行为。

第一节 博弈问题的基本概念及表述方式
(Basis and Forms of Game Theory)

一般认为,博弈理论开始于 1944 年由冯·诺依曼(von Neumann)和摩根斯坦恩(Morgenstern)合作的《博弈论和经济行为》(*The Theory of Games and Economic Behaviour*)一书的出版。但是现代博弈理论跟他们讲的东西关系不大,尽管有一些概念,特别是预期效用理论等,都是他们创立的。到 50 年代,合作博弈发展到鼎盛期,包括纳什(Nash, 1950)和夏普里(Shapley, 1953)的"讨价还价"模型,Gillies 和 Shapley(1953)关于合作博弈中的"核"(core)的概念,以及其他一些人的贡献。

50 年代可以说是博弈论的巨人出现的年代。合作博弈论在 50 年代达到顶峰,同时非合作博弈论也开始创立。纳什在 1950 年和 1951 年发表了两篇关于非合作博弈的重要文章,Tucker 于 1950 年定义了"囚徒困境"(Prisoners' dilemma)。他们两个人的著作基本上奠定了现代非合作博弈论的基石。到 60 年代后又出现了一些重要人物。泽尔腾(1965)将纳什均衡的概念引入了动态分析,提出了"精炼纳什均衡"概念;海萨尼(1967—1968)则把不完全信息引入博弈论的研究。然后到 80 年代出现了几个比较有影响的人物,包括克瑞普斯(Kreps)和威尔逊(Wilson),他们在 1982 年合作发表了关于动态不完全信息博弈的重要文章。本节从最简单的博弈问题开始,讲述博弈论中的一些基本概念及表述方式。

一、博弈论中的基本概念（Basis of Game Theory）

首先我们了解一下博弈论的基本含义以及博弈论中的基本问题。

As a mathematical tool for the decision-maker the strength of game theory is the methodology that provides for structuring and analyzing problems of strategic choice. The process of formally modeling a situation as a game requires the decision-maker to enumerate explicitly the players and their strategic options, and to consider their preferences and reactions. The discipline involved in constructing such a model already has the potential of providing the decision-maker with a clearer and broader view of the situation. In addition, game theory is a distinct and interdisciplinary approach to the study of human behavior. The disciplines most involved in game theory are mathematics, economics and the other social and behavioral sciences. Game theory (like computational theory and so many other contributions) was founded by the great mathematician John von Neumann. The first important book was *The Theory of Games and Economic Behavior*, which von Neumann wrote in collaboration with another great mathematical economist, Oskar Morgenstern. Certainly Morgenstern brought ideas from neoclassical economics（新古典经济学）into the partnership, but von Neumann, too, was well aware of them and had made other contributions to neoclassical economics.

Since the work of John von Neumann, "games" have been a scientific metaphor for a much wider range of human interactions in which the outcomes depend on the interactive strategies of two or more persons, who have opposed or at least mixed motives. Among the issues discussed in game theory are：

1) What does it mean to choose strategies "rationally" when outcomes depend on the strategies chosen by others and when information is incomplete?

2) In "games" that allow mutual gain (or mutual loss) is it "rational" to cooperate to realize the mutual gain (or avoid the mutual loss) or is it "rational" to act aggressively in seeking individual gain regardless of mutual gain or loss?

3) If the answers to 2) are "sometimes," in what circumstances is aggression rational and in what circumstances is cooperation rational?

4) In particular, do ongoing relationships differ from one-off encounters in this connection?

5) Can moral rules of cooperation emerge spontaneously from the interactions of rational egoists?

6) How does real human behavior correspond to "rational" behavior in these cases?

7) If it differs, in what direction? Are people more cooperative than would be "rational?" More aggressive? Both?

现在我们用博弈论中的一个非常有名的例子 The Prisoners' Dilemma(囚徒困境)来说明博弈论中的基本概念。

Recent developments in game theory, especially the award of the Nobel Memorial Prize in 1994 to three game theorists and the death of A. W. Tucker, in January, 1995, at 89, have renewed the memory of its beginnings. Although the history of game theory can be traced back earlier, the key period for the emergence of game theory was the decade of the 1940's. The publication of *The Theory of Games and Economic Behavior* was a particularly important step, of course. But in some ways, Tucker's invention of the Prisoners' Dilemma example was even more important. This example, which can be set out in one page, could be the most influential one page in the social sciences in the latter half of the twentieth century.

Tucker began with a little story, like this: two burglars, Bob and Al, are captured near the scene of a burglary and are given the "third degree" separately by the police. Each has to choose whether or not to confess and implicate the other. If neither man confesses, then both will serve one year on a charge of carrying a concealed weapon. If each confesses and implicates the other, both will go to prison for 10 years. However, if one burglar confesses and implicates the other, and the other burglar does not confess, the one who has collaborated with the police will go free, while the other burglar will go to prison for 20 years on the maximum charge.

The strategies in this case are: confess or don't confess. The payoffs (penalties, actually) are the sentences served. We can express all this compactly in a "payoff table" of a kind that has become pretty standard in game theory. Here is the payoff table for the Prisoners' Dilemma game:

Chart 8-1　Prisoners' Dilemma Game
(囚徒困境博弈)

		Al	
		confess	don't
Bob	confess	10,10	0,20
	don't	20,0	1,1

The table is read like this: Each prisoner chooses one of the two strategies. In effect, Al chooses a column and Bob chooses a row. The two numbers in each cell tell the outcomes for the two prisoners when the corresponding pair of strategies is chosen. The number to the left of the comma tells the payoff to the person who chooses the rows (Bob), while the number to the right of the column tells the payoff to the person who chooses the columns (Al). Thus (reading down the first column) if they both confess, each gets 10 years, but if Al confesses and Bob does not, Bob gets 20 and Al goes free.

So: how to solve this game? What strategies are "rational" if both men want to minimize the time they spend in jail? Al might reason as follows: "Two things can happen: Bob can confess or Bob can keep quiet. Suppose Bob confesses. Then I get 20 years if I don't confess, 10 years if I do, so in that case it's best to confess. On the other hand, if Bob doesn't confess, and I don't either, I get a year; but in that case, if I confess I can go free. Either way, it's best if I confess. Therefore, I'll confess."

But Bob can and presumably will reason in the same way—so that they both confess and go to prison for 10 years each. Yet, if they had acted "irrationally," and kept quiet, they each could have gotten off with one year each.

通过对以上囚徒困境博弈的描述，我们可以看出博弈论的基本概念包括参与人、行动、信息、战略、支付(效用)、结果和均衡，其中，参与人、战略和支付是描述一个博弈所需要的最少的要素,而行动和信息是其"积木"。参与人、行动和结果统称为"博弈规则"(the rules of the game)。博弈分析的目的是使用博弈规则预测均衡。我们现在给出这些概念的准确定义。

(1) 参与人(players):参与人指的是一个博弈中的决策主体。他的目的是通过选择行动(或战略)以最大化自己的支付(效用)水平。参与人可能是自然人,也可能是团体,如企业、国家,甚至若干个国家组成的集团(欧盟、北约等)。这里,重要的是,每个参与人必须有可供选择的行动和一个很好定义的偏好函数。那些不作决策的被动主体只能当作环境参数来处理。在囚徒困境博弈中我们知道有两个参与人,他们要做出坦白(confess)和抵赖(don't)的决策,目的是最大化自己的效用水平。

除一般意义上的参与人之外,为了分析的方便,在博弈论中,"自然"(nature)作为"虚拟参与人"(pseudo-player)来处理。这里,"自然"是指决定外生的随机变量的概率分布的机制。参与人决策的后果依赖于自然的选择。与一般参与人不同的是,自然作为虚拟的参与人没有自己的支付和目标函数(即所有结果对它都是无差异的)。在本章中,我们一般用 $i=1,\cdots,n$ 代表参与人,用 N 代表"自然"。

(2) 行动(actions or moves):行动是参与人在博弈的某个时点的决策变量。一般地,我们用 a_i 表示第 i 个参与人的一个特定行动。$A_i=(a_i)$ 表示可供 i 选择的所有行动的集合(action set)。在囚徒困境博弈中,每个参与人都只有两种行动可供选择,即(坦白,抵赖)。

(3) 信息(information):信息是参与人有关博弈的知识,特别是有关"自然"的选择、其他参与人的特征和行动的知识。信息集(information set)是博弈论中描述参与人信息特征的一个基本概念,在这里,我们可以将其理解为参与人在特定时刻有关变量的值的知识。一个参与人无法准确知道的变量的全体属于一个信息集。有关信息集的概念我们将在以后的章节中详细讨论。

(4) 战略(strategies):战略是参与人在给定信息集的情况下的行动规则,它规定参与人在什么时候选择什么行动。因为信息集包含了一个参与人有关其他参与人之前行动的知识,战略告诉该参与人如何对其他参与人的行动作出反应,因而战略是参与人的"相机行动方案"(contingent action plan)。在囚徒困境博弈中,每个参与人都有两个战略,即:坦白;抵赖。应该强调的是,战略与行动是两个不同的概念,战略是行动的规则而不是行动本身,战略要说明什么时候采取什么行动。

一个有助于理解二者区别的例子是,毛泽东讲的"人不犯我,我不犯人;人若犯我,我必犯人"是一种战略,这里的"犯"与"不犯"是两种行动,战略规定了什么时候选择"犯",什么时候选择"不犯"。当然,在静态博弈中,战略和行动是相同的,这是因为,作为参与人行动的规则,战略依赖于参与人获得的信息,在静态博弈中,所有参与人同时行动,没有任何人能获得他人行动的信息,从而,战略选择就变成简单的行动选择。

(5) 支付(payoff):在博弈论中,支付或者是指在一个特定的战略组合中参与人得到的确定效用水平,或者是指参与人得到的期望效用水平。支付是博弈参与人真正关心的东西。我们假定每一个参与人的偏好都可以由一个期望效用函数来代表,他的目标是选择自己的战略以最大化其期望效用函数。在囚徒困境博弈中,每个参与人的支付以效用的形式列于表格中。

(6) 结果(outcome):结果是博弈分析者所感兴趣的所有东西,如均衡战略组合、均衡行动组合、均衡支付组合等。由囚徒困境博弈,我们知道可能出现四个结果,即"坦白,坦白";"坦白,抵赖";"抵赖,坦白"和"抵赖、抵赖"。其中,引号中的第一个元素表示 Bob 的战略。

(7) 均衡(equilibrium):均衡是所有参与人的最优战略的组合。一般记为

$$s^* = (s_1^*, \cdots, s_i^*, \cdots, s_n^*)。$$

其中,s_i^* 是第 i 个参与人在均衡情况下的最优战略,它是 i 的所有可能的战略中使支付(效用)最大化的战略。在囚徒困境中,均衡为"坦白,坦白"。关于均衡的概念我们会在以后的章节中详细讨论。

应该指出的是,博弈论中的均衡概念与经济学的一般均衡理论中讨论的均衡概念是不同的。比如说,在一般均衡理论里,均衡指的是由个人最优化行为导致的一组价格;而在博弈论里,这样一组价格只是均衡的结果而不是均衡本身:均衡是指所有个人的买卖规则(战略)的组合,均衡价格是这种战略组合产生的结果。

二、博弈论的类型(The Types of Game Theory)

我们可以从不同的角度对经济中的博弈进行分类研究。从总体上讲,可以将博弈分为合作博弈(cooperative games)与非合作博弈(noncooperative games)。经济学诺贝尔奖得主纳什、泽尔腾和海萨尼的贡献主要是非合作博弈方面,而且现在经济学家谈到博弈论,一般指的是非合作博弈,很少指合作博弈。合作博弈与非合作博弈之间的区别

主要在于人们的行为相互作用时,当事人能否达成一个具有约束力的协议。如果有,就是合作博弈;反之,则是非合作博弈。例如,两个企业,如果它们之间达成一个协议,联合最大化垄断利润,并且各自按这个协议生产,就是合作博弈。它们面临的问题就是如何分享合作带来的剩余。但是如果这两个企业间的协议不具有约束力,就是说,没有哪方能够强制另一方遵守这个协议,每个企业都只选择自己的最优产量(或价格),则是非合作博弈。这就是这两个概念的区别。同时应该指出的是,合作博弈强调的是团体理性,就是 collective rationality,强调的是效率(efficiency)、公正(fairness)、公平(equity)。非合作博弈强调的是个人理性、个人最优决策,其结果可能是有效率的,也可能是无效率的。在本章中,除非特别说明外,我们讲的博弈都是指非合作博弈。

根据博弈中博弈者行动的先后顺序,可以把博弈分为静态博弈(static games)与动态博弈(dynamic games)。静态博弈指的是博弈中,参与人同时选择行动或虽非同时但后行动者并不知道前行动者采取了什么具体行动;动态博弈指的是参与人的行动有先后顺序,且后行动者能够观察到先行动者所选择的行动。

根据博弈者所掌握的信息的完全与完备程度,可以将博弈分为完全信息博弈(game with complete information)与不完全信息博弈(game with incomplete information)。信息是指参与人对有关其他参与人(对手)的特征、战略空间及支付函数的知识。完全信息指的是每一个参与人对所有其他参与人(对手)的特征、战略空间及支付函数有准确的知识;否则,就是不完全信息。

将上述两个角度的划分结合起来,我们就得到四种不同类型的博弈,这就是:完全信息静态博弈,完全信息动态博弈,不完全信息静态博弈,不完全信息动态博弈。与上述四类博弈相对应的是四个均衡概念,即:纳什均衡(Nash equilibrium)(纳什,1950,1951),子博弈精炼纳什均衡(subgame perfect Nash equilibrium)(泽尔腾,1965),贝叶斯纳什均衡(Bayesian Nash equilibrium)(海萨尼,1967—1968),及精炼贝叶斯纳什均衡(perfect Bayesian Nash equilibrium)。因为本章内容只是博弈论基础知识的讲解,而且不完全信息博弈的情况涉及到概率等知识,比较复杂,所以我们集中于完全信息静态博弈与完全信息动态博弈这两种情况,并根据这些基本原理来探讨旅游企业的博弈关系。

任何类型的博弈都可以用两种形式来表示,一种是标准形式的博弈(normal form games),另一种是扩展形式的博弈(extensive form games)。标准形式与扩展形式只是博弈表示的两种不同形式。任意一个博弈既可以用标准形式表示,又可以用扩展形式表示。在讨论具体问题时,视讨论的方便程度而采取其中一种形式。而且,由于标准形式与扩展形式只是博弈的不同表示形式,因此可以将其中的一种表示形式转化为另一种表示形式。但为了方便起见,一般来说,在讨论静态博弈时通常用标准形式,而在讨论动态博弈时用扩展形式。下面我们着重分析博弈的标准表示形式。

实际上,在以上讨论的囚徒困境博弈中我们就采用了标准形式。下面给出标准形式的准确定义。

The strategic form (also called normal form) is the basic type of game studied in noncooperative game theory. A game in strategic form lists each player's strategies, and the outcomes that result from each possible combination of choices. An outcome is represented by a separate payoff for each player, which is a number (also called utility) that measures how much the player likes the outcome. Let's first give the definition of a normal form game and then discuss what each of the various parts means.

Definition: A normal form game is a triple (N, S, u) where $N = \{1, 2, \ldots, n, \ldots, N\}$ is the set of players, $S = S_1 \times S_2 \times \cdots \times S_N$ is the set of profiles of pure strategies with S_n the finite set of pure strategies of player n, and $u = (u_1, u_2, \ldots, u_N)$ with $u_n : S \rightarrow R$ the utility or payoff function of player n. We call the pair (N, S) the game form. Thus a game is a game form together with a payoff function.

Thus we have specified a set of players and numbered them 1 through N. Somewhat abusively we have also denoted this set by N. (This is a fairly common practice in mathematics and usually creates no confusion). For each player we have specified a finite set of actions or strategies that the player could take, which we denote S_n. We have denoted the Cartesian product (笛卡尔乘积) of these sets by S. Thus a typical element of S is $s = (s_1, s_2, \ldots, s_N)$ where each s_n is a pure strategy of player n, that is, an element of S_n. We call such an s a pure strategy profile.

For each player n we have also specified a utility function: $S \rightarrow R$. We shall shortly define randomised or mixed strategies, so that each player will form a probabilistic assessment over what the other players will do. Thus when a player chooses one of his own strategies he is choosing a lottery over pure strategy profiles. So we are interpreting the utility function as a representation of the player's preferences over lotteries.

所以，博弈的标准形式由以下这样几个要素构成：第一，N 个博弈者 (player)；第二，每个博弈者 i 有一个行动集合 (action set) S；第三，每个博弈者有一个支付函数 (payoff function) u。以上这三种要素构成了标准形式博弈的完整描述。在囚徒困境博弈中我们用支付矩阵的形式刻画出了博弈的标准形式，可以看出这个标准形式博弈的三种构成要素。

扩展形式的博弈是博弈的另一种表示方式，在这里我们先简单描述一下这个概念，在讨论到动态博弈时再进行详细描述。

The extensive form, also called a game tree, is more detailed than the strategic form of a game. It is a complete description of how the game is played over time. This includes the order in which players take actions, the information that players have at the time they must take those actions, and the times at which any uncertainty in the situation is resolved. The process is modeled as a multi-player decision tree. (You might possibly have come across the use of decision trees to describe decision problems facing single decision makers.) We shall define such game trees or extensive form games in the next section. A game in extensive form may be analyzed directly, or can be converted into an equivalent strategic form.

第二节 完全信息静态博弈与纳什均衡
(Static Games with Complete Information and Nash Equilibrium)

本节讲述完全信息静态博弈以及与之相对应的纳什均衡概念。我们先从最简单的博弈开始，逐步探讨纳什均衡的概念。本节由浅入深地讲了纳什均衡四个方面的内容，即占优战略均衡、重复剔除的占优战略均衡、纳什均衡及混合战略纳什均衡。

一、占优战略均衡 (Dominant Strategy Equilibrium)

在第一节中所讲的囚徒困境的例子中，我们已经知道每个囚徒从自己的效用最大化出发,都选择了坦白这个战略,结果每个人都被判处十年。在这个博弈中,坦白是每个人的占优战略,"坦白,坦白"这个战略组合是这个博弈的一个均衡结果。下面我们给出占优战略及占优战略均衡的定义。

Dominant Strategy: Let an individual player in a game evaluate separately each of the strategy combinations he may face, and, for each combination, choose from his own strategies the one that gives the best payoff. If the same strategy is chosen for each of the different combinations of strategies the player might face, that strategy is called a "dominant strategy" for that player in that game.

Dominant Strategy Equilibrium: If, in a game, each player has a dominant strategy, and each player plays the dominant strategy, then that combination of (dominant) strategies and the corresponding payoffs are said to constitute the dominant strategy equilibrium for that game.

在博弈论里,每个参与人的最优战略选择依赖于所有其他参与人的战略选择,但在一些特殊的博弈中,一个参与人的最优战略可能并不依赖于其他参与人的战略选择。也就是说,不论其他参与人选择什么战略,他的最优战略是唯一的;这样的最优战略被称为占优战略。在囚徒困境,坦白是每个囚徒的占优战略。当每个参与人都有占优战略且都选择占优战略时,占优战略的组合就是占优战略均衡。"坦白,坦白"构成了囚徒困境博弈的占优战略均衡。In the Prisoners' Dilemma game, to confess is a dominant strategy, and when both prisoners confess, that is a dominant strategy equilibrium.

囚徒困境反映了一个很深刻的问题,这就是个人理性与集体理性之间的矛盾。如果两个人都抵赖,各判刑1年,显然比都坦白各判刑10年好,但是这个帕累托改进做不到,因为它不满足个人理性要求。

This remarkable result—that individually rational action results in both persons being made worse off in terms of their own self-interested purposes—is what has made the wide impact in modern social science. For there are many interactions in the modern world that seem very much like that, from arms races through road congestion and pollution to the depletion of fisheries and the overexploitation of some subsurface water resources. These are all quite different interactions in detail, but are interactions in which (we suppose) individually rational action leads to inferior results for each person, and the Prisoners' Dilemma suggests something of what is going on in each of them. That is the source of its power.

囚徒困境在经济学上有着广泛的应用。这里举几个它在实际中的应用的例子。考虑两个寡头企业选择产量的博弈。如果两企业联合起来形成卡特尔,选择垄断利润最大化的产量,每个企业都可以得到更多的利润。但卡持尔协定不是一个纳什均衡,因为给定对方遵守协议的情况下,每个企业都想增加生产,结果是,每个企业都只得到纳什均衡产量的利润,它严格小于卡特尔产量下的利润。这个例子也说明,在有些情况下,个人理性与集体理性的冲突对整个社会来说也许是一件好事,尽管它对该集体的成员而言是一件坏事。当然,这里的前提条件是集体成员的数量严格小于全体社会成员的数量。

公共产品的供给也是一个囚徒困境问题。如果大家都出钱兴办公用事业,所有人的福利都会增加。问题是,如果我出钱你不出钱,我得不偿失;而如果你出钱我不出钱,我就可以占你的便宜。所以,每个人的最优选择都是"不出钱"。这种纳什均衡使得所有人的福利都得不到提高。

还有军备竞赛。冷战期间,苏美两国都竞争增加各自的军费预算。如果不搞军备竞赛,各自把资源用于民用生产,不是很好吗?问题是,如果我把资源用于民用生产,你增加军费支出,我不是就受到威胁吗?这样对我不好。纳什均衡是两国都大量增加军费预算,两国的社会福利都变得更糟。

经济改革本身也可能是这样。在许多改革中,改革者要付出成本(包括风险),而改革的成果大家共享,结果是,尽管人人都认为改革好,却没有人真正去改革,大家只好在都不满意的体制下继续生活下去。

囚徒困境虽然揭示了博弈论的本质内容,但是囚徒困境毕竟是一个非常简单和抽象的例子,而现实世界是复杂和多变的。在实际应用中,在大多数情况下,我们必须对它做出修改,以使之更符合现实世界中的情况。下面就是对囚徒困境的几点可能拓展的地方。对于这些拓展中的一些,我们在下面的章节中也会讨论到。

We must also admit that the Prisoners' Dilemma is a very simplified and abstract—if you will, "unrealistic"—conception of many of these interactions. A number of critical issues can be raised with the Prisoners' Dilemma, and each of these issues has been the basis of a large scholarly literature:

- The Prisoners' Dilemma is a two-person game, but many of the applications of the idea are really many-person interactions.
- We have assumed that there is no communication between the two prisoners. If they could communicate and commit themselves to coordinated strategies, we would expect a quite different outcome.
- In the Prisoners' Dilemma, the two prisoners interact only once. Repetition of the interactions might lead to quite different results.
- Compelling as the reasoning that leads to the dominant strategy equilibrium may be, it is not the only way this problem might be reasoned out. Perhaps it is not really the most rational answer after all.

二、重复剔除的占优均衡(Iterated Dominance Equilibrium)

在每个参与人都有占优战略的情况下,占优战略均衡是一个非常合理的预测,但在绝大多数博弈中,占优战略均衡是不存在的。尽管如此,在有些博弈中,我们仍可以应用占优的逻辑找出均衡。

考虑"智猪博弈"(boxed pigs)的例子。这个例子讲的是,猪圈里圈着两头猪,一头大猪,一头小猪。猪圈的一头有一个猪食槽,另一头安装着一个按钮,控制着猪食的供应。按一下按钮,8个单位的猪食进槽,但需要付出2个单位的成本。若大猪先到,大猪吃到7个单位,小猪只能吃到1个单位;若小猪先到,大猪和小猪各吃到4个单位;若两猪同时到,大猪吃到5个单位,小猪吃到3个单位。这里,每头猪都有两种战略:按或等待。下表列出对应不同战略组合下的支付矩阵。如第一格表示两头猪同时按按钮,因而同时走到猪食槽,大猪吃到5个单位,小猪吃到3个单位,扣除2个单位的成本,支付水平分别为3个单位和1个单位。

表8-2 智猪博弈(Boxed Pigs)

		小猪	
		按	等待
大猪	按	3, 1	2, 4
	等待	7, -1	0, 0

显然,这个博弈没有占优战略均衡,因为尽管"等待"是小猪的占优战略,但大猪没有占优战略。大猪的最优战略依赖于小猪的战略:如果小猪选择"等待",大猪的最优战略是"按";反之,如果小猪选择"按",大猪的最优战略是"等待"。因此,我们不能应用占优战略找出均衡。

那么,什么是这个博弈的可能的均衡解呢?假定小猪是理性的,小猪肯定不会选择"按"的战略。因为,不论大猪选择什么战略,对小猪来说,"等待"严格优于"按",因而理性的小猪会选择"等待"。再假定大猪知道小猪是理性的,那么,大猪会正确地预测到小猪会选择"等待";给定这个预测,大猪的最优选择只能是"按"。这样,"按、等待"是这个博弈的唯一的均衡,即大猪选择"按",小猪选择"等待",支付水平分别为2和4个单位。这是一个"多劳不多得,少劳不少得"的均衡。

在找出智猪博弈的均衡解时,我们实际上是应用了"重复剔除严格劣战略"(iterated elimination of strictly dominated strategies)的思路。这个思路是这样的:首先找出某个参与人的劣战略(dominated strategies),把这个劣战略剔除掉,重新构造一个不包含已剔除战略的新的博弈;然后再剔除这个新的博弈中的某个参与人的劣战略;继续这个过程,一直到只剩下一个唯一的战略组合为至。这个唯一剩下的战略组合就是这个博弈的均衡解,称为"重复剔除的占优均衡"(iterated dominance equilibrium)。在上例中,我们首先剔除掉小猪的劣战略"按",在剔除掉这个战略后的新的博弈中,小猪只有一个战略"等待",大猪仍有两个战略。但此时,"等待"已成为大猪的劣战略,剔除这个战略,剩下的唯一战略组合是(按,等待)。

下面我们给出重复剔除的占优均衡的定义。战略组合 $s^* = (s_1^*, \cdots, s_i^*, \cdots, s_n^*)$ 称为重复剔除的占优均衡,如果它是重复剔除劣战略后剩下的唯一的战略组合。如果这种唯一的战略组合是存在的,我们说博弈是重复剔除占优可解的(dominance solvable)。

智猪博弈在实际中也有许多应用的例子。例如,市场中大企业与小企业之间的关系。进行研究开发,为新产品做广告,对大企业是值得的,对小企业则得不偿失。所以,一种可能的情况是,小企业把精力花在模仿上,或等待大企业用广告打开市场后出售廉价产品。

类似的情况在公共产品的提供上也可能出现。比如说,村里住两户人家,一户富,一户穷,有一条路年久失修。这时候,富户一般会承担起修路的责任,穷户则很少这样干。因为富户家常常是高朋满座,坐车坐轿的都来,而穷户家只是自己穿着破鞋走路,路修好了他走起来舒服,路修不好他也无所谓。

再如，我们也可以用智猪博弈模型来解释OPEC（石油输出国组织）的分配方案。OPEC的成功之处可能相当程度上归属于它的最大成员国——沙特阿拉伯的愿望。沙特阿拉伯希望所有的成员国都能节制石油产量以使油价保持在较高水平之上。当某些小石油输出国"偷偷"增加自己的产量时，沙特阿拉伯"大度地"削减自己的产量以保持总产量的稳定。因为沙特阿拉伯与那些小石油输出国都明白此时除非沙特阿拉伯限制自己的产量，否则OPEC可能面临崩溃；小成员国依赖于沙特阿拉伯对OPEC的努力而从中渔利。事实上，沙特阿拉伯为了自己赢得高价利润的足够享受，理性地愿意忍受维持OPEC的不匀称摊派。

为了加深对重复剔除的占优均衡的理解，我们再看一个两个企业关于价格竞争的例子。

Here is a very simplified model of price competition. We will think of two companies that sell mineral water. Each company has a fixed cost of $5000 per period, regardless whether they sell anything or not. We will call the companies A and B, just to take two names at random.

The two companies are competing for the same market and each firm must choose a high price ($2 per bottle) or a low price ($1 per bottle). Here are the rules of the game:

1) At a price of $2, 5000 bottles can be sold for a total revenue of $10000.

2) At a price of $1, 10000 bottles can be sold for a total revenue of $10000.

3) If both companies charge the same price, they split the sales evenly between them.

4) If one company charges a higher price, the company with the lower price sells the whole amount and the company with the higher price sells nothing.

5) Payoffs are profits—revenue minus the $5000 fixed cost.

Here is the payoff table for these two companies.

Table 8-3　Iterated Dominance Equilibrium

（重复剔除劣战略均衡）

		B	
		Price= $1	Price= $2
A	Price= $1	0,0	5000,-5000
	Price= $2	-5000,5000	0,0

In this example, if we add up the wins and losses in this game, treating losses as negatives, we find that the sum is zero for each set of strategies chosen, then we call the game a "zero-sum game." In less formal terms, a zero-sum game is a game in which one player's winnings equal the other player's losses. Do notice that the definition requires a zero sum for every set of strategies. If there is even one strategy set for which the sum differs from zero, then the game is not zero sum.

这是一个零和博弈(zero-sum game)，因为如果我们把每一个战略组合的支付相加，我们会发现其和等于零。在这个价格竞争的零和博弈中，我们可以看到，选择价格为 2 是 A 公司的劣战略，同时，价格为 2 也是 B 公司的劣战略。经过剔除劣战略后，我们求出这个博弈的唯一纳什均衡，即两个公司都索要的价格为 1，每个公司获得零利润。

三、纳什均衡(Nash Equilibrium)

对于相当多的博弈，我们无法使用重复剔除劣战略的办法找出均衡解。这时，对任何一个参与人来说，没有任何一种战略优于另一种战略，每一个参与人的最优战略都依赖于另一个人的战略。为了找出这个博弈的均衡解，我们需要引入纳什均衡的概念。纳什均衡是完全信息静态博弈解的一般概念，构成纳什均衡的战略一定是重复剔除严格劣战略过程中不能被剔除的战略，也就是说，没有任何一个战略严格优于纳什均衡战略。很多不存在占优战略均衡或重复剔除的占优均衡的博弈，却存在纳什均衡，而且很可能还存在多个纳什均衡。下面我们以几个具体的例子来介绍纳什均衡的概念。

1. 价格竞争博弈(Price Competition Game)

Following a long tradition in economics, we will think of two companies selling "widgets" at a price of one, two, or three dollars per widget. The payoffs are profits—after allowing for costs of all kinds—and are shown in Table 8-4. The general idea behind the example is that the company that charges a lower price will get more customers and thus, within limits, more profits than the high-price competitor.

Table 8-4 Price Competition Game(价格竞争博弈)

		Acme Widgets		
		$p=1$	$p=2$	$p=3$
Widgeon Widgets	$p=1$	0,0	50,-10	40,-20
	$p=2$	-10,50	20,20	90,10
	$p=3$	-20,40	10,90	50,50

We can see that the profits depend on the strategies that the two competitors choose. We can also see fairly easily that there is no dominant strategy equilibrium. Widgeon company can reason as follows: if Acme were to choose a price of 3, then Widgeon's best price is 2, but otherwise Widgeon's best price is 1—neither is dominant.

We will need another, broader concept of equilibrium if we are to do anything with this game. The concept we need is called the Nash Equilibrium, after Nobel Laureate (in economics) and mathematician John Nash. Nash, a student of Tucker's, contributed several key concepts to game theory around 1950. The Nash Equilibrium conception was one of these, and is probably the most widely used "solution concept" in game theory.

Nash Equilibrium: If there is a set of strategies with the property that no player can benefit by changing her strategy while the other players keep their strategies unchanged, then that set of strategies and the corresponding payoffs constitute the Nash Equilibrium.

Let's apply that definition to the widget-selling game. First, for example, we can see that the strategy pair $p=3$ for each player (bottom right) is not a Nash-equilibrium. From that pair, each competitor can benefit by cutting price, if the other player keeps her strategy unchanged. Or consider the bottom middle—Widgeon charges $3 but Acme charges $2. From that pair, Widgeon benefits by cutting to $1. In this way, we can eliminate any strategy pair except the upper left, at which both competitors charge $1.

We see that the Nash Equilibrium in the widget-selling game is a low-price, zero-profit equilibrium. Many economists believe that result is descriptive of real, highly competitive markets—although there is, of course, a great deal about this example that is still "unrealistic."

Let's go back and take a look at that iterated dominance equilibrium in Table 8-3. We will see that it, too, is a Nash-Equilibrium. (Check it out). Also, look again at the dominant-strategy equilibrium in the Prisoners' Dilemma. It, too, is a Nash-Equilibrium. In fact, any dominant strategy equilibrium is also a Nash Equilibrium. The Nash equilibrium is an extension of the concepts of dominant strategy equilibrium。

在上述的价格竞争博弈中，不存在占优战略均衡，也不存在重复剔除的占优战略均衡，但是我们也得到了一个均衡结果，两个公司都选择价格为1，都到了零利润。而且我们看出，两个公司都没有积极性偏离这个均衡：给定任何一个公司的价格选择，如果另一个公司偏离这个均衡，那么它将得到更少的利润。我们把这个均衡叫做纳什均衡。纳什均衡是占优战略均衡概念的扩展。可以验证，我们前面所讲的占优均衡及重复剔除的占优均衡都符合纳什均衡的概念，它们都是纳什均衡的特例。然而，博弈论的一个主要问题是可能存在多个纳什均衡。当一个博弈有多个纳什均衡时，要所有参与人预测同一个纳什均衡会出现是困难的。在这种情况下，尽管所有参与人都预测纳什均衡会出现，但如果不同参与人预测的不是同一个纳什均衡，实际出现的就不是纳什均衡，而是非纳什均衡。下面我们以例子来说明多重纳什均衡的情况。

2. 多重纳什均衡(Multiple Nash Equilibria)

Game theory provides a promising approach to understanding strategic problems of all sorts, and the simplicity and power of the Prisoners' Dilemma and similar examples make them a natural starting point. But there will often be complications we must consider in a more complex and realistic application. Let's see how we might move from a simpler to a more realistic game model in a real-world example of strategic thinking: choosing an information system.

For this example, the players will be a company considering the choice of a new internal e-mail or intranet system, and a supplier who is considering producing it. The two choices are to install a technically advanced or a more proven system with less functionality. We'll assume that the more advanced system really does supply a lot more functionality, so that the payoffs to the two players, net of the user's payment to the supplier, are as shown in Table 8-5.

Table 8-5　Multiple Nash Equilibria(多重纳什均衡)

		User	
		Advanced	Proven
Supplier	Advanced	20,20	0,0
	Proven	0,0	5,5

We see that both players can be better off, on net, if an advanced system is installed. (We are not claiming that that's always the case! We're just assuming it is in this particular decision.) But the worst that can happen is for one player to commit to an advance system while the other player stays with the proven one. In that case there is no deal, and no payoffs for anyone. The problem is that the supplier and the user must have a compatible standard, in order to work together, and since the choice of a standard is a strategic choice, their strategies have to mesh.

Although it looks a lot like the Prisoners' Dilemma at first glance, this is a more complicated game. Looking at it carefully, we see that this game has no dominated strategies. The best strategy for each participant depends on the strategy chosen by the other participant. Thus, we need a new concept of game-equilibrium that will allow for that complication. When there are no dominant strategies, we often use an equilibrium conception called the Nash Equilibrium, named after Nobel Memorial Laureate John Nash. The Nash Equilibrium is a pretty simple idea: We have a Nash Equilibrium if each participant chooses the best strategy, given the strategy chosen by the other participant. In the example, if the user opts for the advanced system, then it is best for the supplier to do that too. So "Advanced, Advanced" is a Nash-equilibrium. But, hold on here! If the user chooses the proven system, it's best for the supplier to do that too. There are two Nash Equilibria! Which one will be chosen? It may seem easy enough to opt for the advanced system which is better all around, but if each participant believes that the other will stick with the proven system—being a bit of a stick in the mud, perhaps—then it will be best for each player to choose the proven system—and each will be right in assuming that the other one is a stick in the mud!

从以上这个例子中我们看出，这个博弈存在两个纳什均衡，"advanced,advanced"和"proven,proven"。这两个纳什均衡都有可能出现。"advanced,advanced"这个均衡的结果是两个公司分别得到20单位的支付，"proven,proven"这个均衡的结果是两个公司分别只得到5单位的支付。显然，"advanced,advanced"比"proven,proven"有更好的纳什均衡结果。仅仅从数学的角度来看，哪个均衡更可能出现很可能是不确定的。但是实际生活中，参与人可能使用某些被博弈模型抽象掉的信息来达到一个"聚点"均衡(focal point)或协调均衡(coordination equilibrium)。这些信息可能与社会文化习惯、参与人过去博弈的历史等有关。保证一个纳什均衡出现的另一种方法是参与人在博弈开始之前进行不花什么成本的"廉价磋商"(cheap talk)，事前磋商可以使某些纳什均衡实际上出现。就拿上面的例子来说，如果两个公司在事前进行了磋商，那么"advanced,advanced"是更有可能出现的纳什均衡。

下面给出了一个协调博弈的例子，这个例子说明了从社会学的角度来讲，纳什均衡的多重性可能并不是一个问题。

Here is another example to try the Nash Equilibrium approach on. Two radio stations (WIRD and KOOL) have to choose formats for their broadcasts. There are three possible formats: Country-Western (CW), Industrial Music (IM) or All News (AN). The audiences for the three formats are 50%, 30%, and 20%, respectively. If they choose the same formats they will split the audience for that format equally, while if they choose different formats, each will get the total audience for that format. Audience shares are proportionate to payoffs. The payoffs (audience shares) are in Table 8-6.

Table 8-6 Coordination Game(协调博弈)

		KOOL		
		CW	IM	AN
WIRD	CW	25,25	50,30	50,20
	IM	30,50	15,15	30,20
	AN	20,50	20,30	10,10

You should be able to verify that there are no dominant strategy equilibria. If we find the Nash Equilibria by elimination, we find that there are two of them—the upper middle cell and the middle-left one, in both of which one station chooses CW and gets a 50 market share and the other chooses IM and gets 30. But it doesn't matter which station chooses which format.

There are multiple Nash Equilibria in which neither of these things is so, as we will see in some later examples. But even when they are both true, the multiplication of equilibria creates a danger. The danger is that both stations will choose the more profitable CW format—and split the market, getting only 25 each! Actually, there is an even worse danger that each station might assume that the other station will choose CW, and each choose IM, splitting that market and leaving each with a market share of just 15.

More generally, the problem for the players is to figure out which equilibrium will in fact occur. In still other words, a game of this kind raises a "coordination problem": How can the two stations coordinate their choices of strategies and avoid the danger of a mutually inferior outcome such as splitting the market? Games that present coordination problems are sometimes called coordination games.

From a mathematical point of view, this multiplicity of equilibria is a problem. For a "solution" to a "problem," we want one answer, not a family of answers. And many economists would also regard it as a problem that has to be solved by some restriction of the assumptions that would rule out the multiple equilibria. But, from a social scientific point of view, there is another interpretation. Many social scientists believe that coordination problems are quite real and important aspects of human social life. From this point of view, we might say that multiple Nash Equilibria provide us with a possible "explanation" of coordination problems. That would be an important positive finding, not a problem!

我们再给出实际生活中的一个例子。这个例子说明人们可以利用社会习惯来解决多重纳什均衡的问题，从而在实际生活中，实际出现的纳什均衡是唯一的。

Another source of a hint that could solve a coordination game is social convention. Here is a game in which social convention could be quite important. That game has a long name: "Which Side of the Road to Drive On?" In Britain, we know, people Drive on the left side of the road; in the US they drive on the right. In abstract, how do we choose which side to drive on? There are two strategies: Drive on the left side and drive on the right side. There are two possible outcomes: The two cars pass one another without incident or they crash. We arbitrarily assign a value of 1 each to passing without problems and of 10 each to a crash. Here is the payoff table:

Table 8-7 Coordination Game(协调博弈)

		Mercedes	
		L	R
Buick	L	1,1	-10,-10
	R	-10,-10	1,1

Verify that LL and RR are both Nash Equilibria. But, if we do not know which side to choose, there is some danger that we will choose LR or RL at random and crash. How can we know which side to choose? The answer is, of course, that for this coordination game we rely on social convention. Conversely, we know that in this game, social convention is very powerful and persistent, and no less so in the country where the solution is LL than in the country where it is RR.

四、混合战略纳什均衡(Mixed Strategy Nash Equilibrium)

在上面的分析中,我们将纳什均衡定义为一组满足所有参与人的效用最大化要求的战略组合。根据这一定义,有些博弈并不存在纳什均衡。考虑下列两个例子。

例一,猜谜游戏(Matching Pennies)

这个故事讲的是,两个儿童手里各拿着一枚硬币,决定要显示正面向上还是反面向上。如果两枚硬币同时正面向上或同时反面向上,儿童 A 付给儿童 B 一分钱;如果两枚硬币只有一枚正面向上,儿童 B 付给儿童 A 一分钱。下表给出了这个博弈的支付矩阵。

Table 8-8 猜谜游戏(Matching Pennies)

		B	
		正面	反面
A	正面	-1,1	1,-1
	反面	1,-1	-1,1

这个博弈事实上是一个零和博弈,一方所得即另一方所失,也没有纳什均衡。比如说,"正面,正面"不是纳什均衡,因为给定 B 选择正面,A 的最优选择是反面;"反面,正面"也不是纳什均衡,因为如果 A 选择反面,B 也将选择反面。类似地,"正面,反面"和"反面,反面"都不是纳什均衡。

例二,监督博弈(Inspection Game)

Suppose a consumer purchases a license for a software package, agreeing to certain restrictions on its use. The consumer has an incentive to violate these rules. The vendor would like to verify that the consumer is abiding by the agreement, but doing so requires inspections which are costly. If the vendor does inspect and catches the consumer cheating, the vendor can demand a large penalty payment for the noncompliance.

Table 8-9 Inspection Game(监督博弈)

		consumer	
		comply	cheat
vendor	Don't inspect	0,0	-10,10
	inspect	-1,0	-6,-90

Table 8-9 shows possible payoffs for such an inspection game. The standard outcome, defining the reference payoff zero to both vendor (player I) and consumer (player II), is that the vendor chooses "Don't inspect" and the consumer chooses to "comply". Without inspection, the consumer prefers to cheat since that gives him payoff 10, with resulting negative payoff -10 to the vendor. The vendor may also decide to inspect. If the consumer complies, inspection leaves him payoff 0 unchanged, while the vendor incurs a cost resulting in a negative payoff -1. If the consumer cheats, however, inspection will result in a heavy penalty (payoff -90 for player II) and still create a certain amount of hassle for player I (payoff -6).

In all cases, player I would strongly prefer if player II complied, but this is outside of player I's control. However, the vendor prefers to inspect if the consumer cheats (since -6 is better than -10), indicated by the downward arrow on the right in table 8-9. If the vendor always preferred "Don't inspect", then this would be a dominating strategy and be part of a (unique) equilibrium where the consumer cheats.

The circular arrow structure in table 8-9 shows that this game has no equilibrium in pure strategies. If any of the players settles on a deterministic choice (like "Don't inspect" by player I), the best response of the other player would be unique (here cheat by player II), to which the original choice would not be a best response (player I prefers Inspect when the other player chooses cheat, against which player II in turn prefers to comply). The strategies in a Nash Equilibrium must be best responses to each other, so in this game this fails to hold for any pure strategy combination.

上述两个博弈的显著特征是,每一个参与人都想猜透对方的战略,而每一个参与人又都不能让对方猜透自己的战略。这样的问题在诸如扑克比赛、橄榄球赛、战争等情况中都会出现。在所有这类博弈中,都不存在纳什均衡。

尽管上述两个博弈不存在前面所定义的纳什均衡,却存在下面将要定义的混合战略纳什均衡。这里,混合战略指的是参与人以一定的概念选择某种战略。比如说,参与人以各以0.5的概率选择两种战略。如果一个参与人采取混合战略,他的对手就不能准确地猜出他实际上会选择的战略。为了区别这种情况,我们将前面所定义的纳什均衡称为"纯"战略纳什均衡(pure strategy Nash Equilibrium),而将上述两个博弈中的存在的纳什均衡称为"混合"战略纳什均衡(mixed strategy Nash Equilibrium)。我们要在纯战略与混合战略之间做出区分。如果一个战略规定参与人在每一个给定的信息情况下只选择一种特定的行动,我们称该战略为纯战略。相反,如果一个战略规定参与人在给定信息情况下以某种概率分布随机地选择不同的行动,我们称该战略为混合战略。If a player in a game chooses among two or more strategies at random according to specific probabilities, this choice is called a "mixed strategy."在静态博弈里,纯战略等价于特定的行动,混合战略是不同行动之间的随机选择(randomization)。下面我们以监督博弈为例来说明如何求解混合战略纳什均衡。

What should the players do in the game of table 8-9? A mixed strategy of player I in this game is to Inspect only with a certain probability. In the context of inspections, randomizing is also a practical approach that reduces costs. Even if an inspection is not certain, a sufficiently high chance of being caught should deter from cheating, at least to some extent.

The following considerations show how to find the probability of inspection that will lead to an equilibrium. If the probability of inspection is very low, for example one percent, then player II receives (irrespective of that probability) payoff 0 for comply, and payoff $0.99 \times 10 + 0.01 \times (-90) = 9$, which is bigger than zero, for cheat. Hence, player II will still cheat, just as in the absence of inspection.

If the probability of inspection is much higher, for example 0.2, then the expected payoff for cheat is $0.8 \times 10 + 0.2 \times (-90) = -10$, which is less than zero, so that player II prefers to comply. If the inspection probability is either too low or too high, then player II has a unique best response. As shown above, such a pure strategy cannot be part of an equilibrium.

Hence, the only case where player II himself could possibly randomize between his strategies is if both strategies give him the same payoff, that is, if he is indifferent. It is never optimal for a player to assign a positive probability to playing a strategy that is inferior, given what the other players are doing. It is not hard to see that player II is indifferent if and only if player I inspects with probability 0.1, since then the expected payoff for cheat is $0.9 \times 10 + 0.1 \times (-90) = 0$, which is then the same as the payoff for comply.

With this mixed strategy of player I (Don't inspect with probability 0.9 and Inspect with probability 0.1), player II is indifferent between his strategies. Hence, he can mix them (that is, play them randomly) without losing payoff. The only case where, in turn, the original mixed strategy of player I is a best response is if player I is indifferent. According to the payoffs in table 8-9, this requires player II to choose comply with probability 0.8 and cheat with probability 0.2. The expected payoffs to player I are then for Don't inspect $0.8 \times 0 + 0.2 \times (-10) = -2$, and for Inspect $0.8 \times (-1) + 0.2 \times (-6) = -2$, so that player I is indeed indifferent, and his mixed strategy is a best response to the mixed strategy of player II.

This defines the only Nash Equilibrium of the game. It uses mixed strategies and is therefore called a mixed equilibrium. The resulting expected payoffs are -2 for player I and 0 for player II.

在混合战略纳什均衡中，尽管每个参与人在所有构成均衡的纯战略之间是无差异的，均衡却要求每个参与人以特定的概率选择纯战略。进一步，一个参与人选择不同纯战略的概率分布不是由他自己的支付决定的，而是由他的对手的支付决定的。由于这个原因，许多人认为混合战略纳什均衡是一个难以令人满意的概念。难道在现实世界人们真的是使用类似掷硬币的方法来决定选择什么行动的吗？既然参与人在构成混合战略的不同纯战略之间是无差异的，他为什么不选择一个特定的纯战略而要以特定的概率随机地选择不同的纯战略呢？对此可以做出的一个解释是，一个参与人选择混合战略的目的是给其他参与人造成不确定性，这样尽管其他参与人知道他选择某个特定纯战略的概率是多少，但他们并不能猜透他实际上会选择哪个纯战略。事实上，正是因为他在几个纯战略之间是无差异的，他的行为才难以预测，混合战略均衡才会存在。如果他严格偏好于某个特定的战略，他的行为就会被其他参与人准确地猜透，就不会有混合战略均衡出现。

尽管混合战略不像纯战略那样直观,但它确实是一些博弈中参与人的合理行为方式。扑克比赛、垒球比赛、划拳就是这样的例子。在这类博弈中,参赛者总是随机地行动以使自己的行为不被对手所预测。另外还应该注意的是,我们前面所讨论的是不存在纯战略纳什均衡却存在混合战略纳什均衡的博弈,有些博弈既存在纯战略均衡,也存在混合战略均衡。所谓的"性别战"就是这样一个博弈。性别战说的是一男一女约会,或者去看足球比赛,或者看芭蕾舞演出。男的偏好足球赛,女的偏好芭蕾舞,但他们都宁愿在一起而不愿分开。表8-10给出支付矩阵。

表8-10　性别战(Battles of the Sexes)

		女	
		足球	芭蕾
男	足球	2,1	0,0
	芭蕾	0,0	1,2

这个博弈有两个纯战略纳什均衡:"足球,足球","芭蕾,芭蕾"。事实上,这个博弈还有一个混合战略纳什均衡,这就是:男的以2/3的概率选择足球赛,1/3的概率选择芭蕾舞;女的以1/3的概率选择足球赛,2/3的概率选择芭蕾舞。类似性别战这种存在两个纯战略纳什均衡和一个混合战略纳什均衡的博弈的例子还有斗鸡博弈、商场消耗战博弈等。

至目前为止,我们相继引入了占优战略均衡(DSE)、重复剔除的占优均衡(IEDE)、纯战略纳什均衡(PNE)和混合战略纳什均衡(MNE)四个均衡概念。每个均衡概念依次是前一个均衡概念的扩展,或者说,前一个均衡概念是后一个均衡概念的特例;纯战略纳什均衡是混合战略纳什均衡的特例,重复剔除的占优均衡是纯战略纳什均衡的特例,占优战略均衡是重复剔除的占优均衡的特例。如果我们将存在某个适当定义的均衡的所有博弈定义为一个集合,那么,存在前一个均衡的集合依次为存在后一个均衡的集合的子集:占优战略均衡的集合是重复剔除的占优均衡的集合的子集,重复剔除的占优均衡的集合是纯战略纳什均衡的集合的子集,纯战略纳什均衡的集合是混合战略纳什均衡的集合的子集,如图所示。

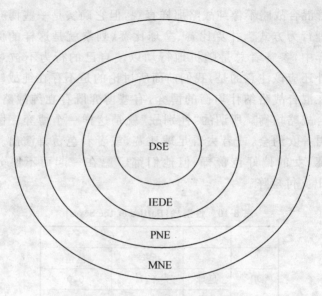

图 8-1 不同均衡概念之间的关系
(Relationship Between Different Equilibrium Concepts)

第三节 完全信息动态博弈
(Dynamic Games with Complete Information)

前面我们介绍了纳什均衡的概念。但纳什均衡有三个问题。第一，如前所述一个博弈可能有不止一个纳什均衡。事实上，有些博弈可能有无数个纳什均衡，究竟哪个纳什均衡实际上会发生？在前面我们讲到，社会文化习惯、参与人过去博弈的历史以及谈判磋商等可能减少纳什均衡的数量，但在大多数情况下，人们无法准确预测到底哪个纳什均衡会实际发生。第二，在纳什均衡中，参与人在选择自己的战略时，把其他参与人的战略当作给定的，不考虑自己的选择如何影响对手的战略。这个假设在研究静态博弈时是成立的，因为在静态博弈下，所有参与人同时行动，无暇反应。但对动态博弈而言，这个假设就有问题了。当一个人行动在先，另一个人行动在后时，后者自然会根据前者的选择而调整自己的选择。前者自然会理性地预期到这一点，所以不可能不考虑自己的选择对其对手的选择的影响。第三，与第二个问题相联系，由于不考虑自己的选择对别人选择的影响，纳什均衡允许了不可置信威胁的存在。泽尔腾(1965)通过对动态博弈的分析完善了纳什均衡的概念，定义了"子博弈精炼纳什均衡(subgame perfect Nash Equilibrium)"。这个概念的中心意思是将纳什均衡中包含的不可置信的威胁战略剔除出去。就是说，使均衡战略不再包含不可置信的威胁。它要求参与人的决策在任何时点上都是最优的，决策者要"随机应变"、"向前看"，而不是固守旧略。由于剔除了不可置信的威胁战略，在许多情况下，精炼纳什均衡也缩小了纳什均衡的个数。这一点对预测是非常有意义的。本节就介绍动态博弈以及与之相应的子博弈精练纳什均衡的概念，包括三部分的内容：博弈的扩展式表述，扩展式表述的纳什均衡及子博弈精练纳什均衡。

一、博弈的扩展式表述(Extensive Form)

在静态博弈中，所有参与人同时行动(或行动虽有先后，但没有人在自己行动之前观测到别人的行动)。Games in strategic form (normal form) have no temporal component. In a game in strategic form, the players choose their strategies simultaneously, without knowing the choices of the other players. 在动态博弈中，参与人的行动有先后顺序，且后行动者在自己行动之前能观测到先行动者的行动。正如博弈论专家习惯于用战略式(标准式)表述描述和分析静态博弈一样，他们也习惯于用扩展式(extensive form)表述来描述和分析动态博弈。回顾一下，博弈的战略式表述包括三个要素：(1)参与人集合；(2)每个参与人的战略集合；(3)由战略组合决定的每个参与人的支付。博弈的扩展式表述所"扩展"的主要是参与人的战略空间。战略式表述简单地给出参与人有些什么战略可以选择，而扩展式表述要给出每个战略的动态描述：谁在什么时候行动，每次行动时有些什么具体行动可供选择，以及知道些什么。A game in extensive form, formalizes interactions where the players can over time be informed about the actions of others. In an extensive game with perfect information, every player is at any point aware of the previous choices of all other players. Furthermore, only one player moves at a time, so that there are no simultaneous moves. 简单地说，在扩展式表述中，战略对应于参与人的相机行动规则(contingent action play)，即什么情况下选择什么行动，而不是简单的、与环境无关的行动选择。

具体来说，博弈的扩展形式包含下述信息与内容：

(1) 参与人的集合(player set)。记为 $i=1,2,\cdots,n$。这与静态情

况完全一样，参与人当然地构成博弈的最基本要素。我们将用 N（nature）表示虚拟参与人"自然"。

（2）行动的次序（the order of moves），即谁在什么时候行动。

（3）当一个参与人行动时他的选择是什么，实际上就是轮到他行动时，他从该时刻的行动空间（action set）中选取了什么策略。

（4）当参与人做出他的行动决策时，他所观察到或他所了解的东西，这就是他在此时获得的信息集合（information set）。

（5）参与人的支付（payoff）或效用（utility），它们是已采取行动的函数。像静态时一样，支付函数构成博弈的基本要素。

（6）外生事件（即自然的选择）上的概率分布（probability distribution）。例如，动态博弈在天是否下雨的条件下以不同方式展开，这里天是否下雨是博弈的外生事件，关于晴天或者下雨的概率分别被认为是"自然"采取的行动。因为我们只讨论完全信息的情况，所以在以后的章节中，在博弈的扩展式表述中，我们没有引入"自然"的概念。

正因为行动具有次序，可以依次序将一步又一步的行动展开成图形。我们称该图形为博弈树（game tree），它有效地向人们展示了参与人的行动、选择这些行动的次序以及做出决策时参与人所拥有的信息集。

下面我们给出博弈树的构成要素及博弈树的规则。

Game tree: Time structure of possible moves describing an extensive form game. A game tree is a set of nodes some which are linked by branches. A tree is a connected graph with no cycles. The first move of the game is identified with a distinguished node that is called the root of the tree. A play of the game consists of a connected chain of branches starting at the root of the tree and ending, if the game is finite, at a terminal node. The nodes in the tree represent the possible moves in the game. The branches leading away from a node represent the choices or actions available at that move. Each node other than the terminal node is assigned a player's name so that it is known who makes the choice at that move. Each terminal node must be labeled with the consequences for each player if the game ends in the outcome corresponding to that terminal node.

博弈树是由结（nodes）与枝（branches）组成的图。博弈树中的每一个结表示某参与人的决策点，并称此点属于在该点行动的参与人。常在该点上方(或旁侧)标上行动参与人的代号。枝则表示参与人可能的行动,每一个枝连接两个结并且具有从一个结到另一个结的方向,常用箭头来表示。如果枝是从属于参与人 i 的结 N_i 到属于参与人 j 的结 N_j,那么动态博弈中参与人 i 行动在参与人 j 之前,并称结 N_i 直接位于结 N_j 之前。在所有的结中,有两种特殊的结:初始结(initial node)与终点结(terminal nodes)。初始结即在它之前没有任何其他的结,它表示由某个参与人(例如参与人1)开始的行动。这是整个动态博弈的出发结。终点结则是没有任何后续结(即位于它后面的结)的结,它实际上表示博弈的结束,因此在该结点没有任何参与人行动,在它的上方或旁侧就没有标上任何参与人代号。各参与人通过博弈到达终点结时各有所获,于是在终点结那儿会出现支付(或效用)向量,分别表示各参与人的获益。

博弈树上的所有决策结分割成不同的信息集。每一个信息集是决策结集合的一个子集,该子集包括所有满足下列条件的决策结:(1)每一个决策结都是同一参与人的决策结;(2)该参与人知道博弈进入该集合的某个决策结,但不知道自己究竟处于哪一个决策结。引入信息集的目的是描述下列情况:当一个参与人要做出决策时他可能并不知道"之前"发生的所有事情。一个信息集可能包含多个决策结,也可能只包含一个决策结。只包含一个决策结的信息集称为单结信息集。如果博弈树的所有信息集都是单结的,该博弈称为完美信息博弈(game with perfect information)。完美信息博弈意味着博弈中没有任何两个参与人同时行动,并且所有后行动者能确切地知道先行动者选择了什么行动。我们在本节讨论的完全信息动态主要是指完美信息博弈的情况。

下面以一个具体例子来说明动态博弈是如何用博弈树来表示的。

Example: Quality choice with commitment

Figure 8-2 shows the quality choice game. This is a game tree with perfect information. Every branching point, or node, is associated with a player who makes a move by choosing the next node. The connecting lines are labeled with the player's choices. The game starts at the initial node, the root of the tree, and ends at a terminal node, which establishes the outcome and determines the players' payoffs. In Figure 8-2, the tree grows from left to right; game trees may also be drawn top-down or bottom-up.

The service provider, player I, makes the first move, choosing High or Low quality of service. Then the customer, player II, is informed about that choice. Player II can then decide separately between buy and don't buy in each case. The resulting payoffs are in the figure 8-2. The players now move in sequence rather than simultaneously.

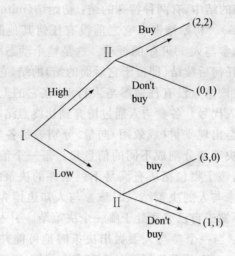

Figure 8-2　Game Tree(博弈树)

从以上的例子,我们也可以看出构造博弈树的几条规则。

博弈树规则一:每一个结至多有一个其他结直接位于它的前面。我们希望博弈树中排除多个其他结的情况是因为考虑在模型中,博弈树的每一个结意指在它之前发生的所有事件的全部描述。当规则一被满足时,谈论一个决策结跟在另一个结的后面才有意义。

博弈树规则二:在博弈树中没有一条路径可以使决策结与其自身相连。这事实上避免了具有循环图的决策树。

博弈树规则三:每个结是唯一的初始结的后续者。也就是说,博弈树必须有初始结。我们研究的动态博弈是从最初时刻开始逐步展开的,因此总是要求博弈树具有初始结。

博弈树规则四:每个博弈树正好"只"有一个初始结。规则四并不意味着所有的博弈树不会发生多于一个初始结的情况。但是在一般情况下,倘若发生了两个及两个以上的初始结,我们常常可以将它们分解为若干博弈树,或者利用"自然"构成一个限于这几个初始结的"原始初始结"。因此在扩展式博弈中我们总是假设初始结是唯一的。

根据上述博弈树的规则,对于博弈树中的每一个终点结,我们可以完全确定从初始结到该终点结的一条路径,同时也展示了到达该结局的动态博弈过程。

二、扩展式表述博弈的战略形式(Strategic Form of the Extensive Game)

在引入博弈的扩展式表述后,我们就要讨论扩展式表述博弈的纳什均衡。但为了使用上一节定义的纳什均衡概念,我们的第一步工作是将博弈的扩展式表述和战略式表述联系起来。战略式表述与扩展式表述的不同之处在于,在扩展式表述博弈中,参与人是相机行事,即"等待"博弈到达自己的信息集(包含一个或多个决策结)后再决定如何行动;在战略式表述博弈中,参与人似乎是在博弈开始之前就制定出了一个完全的相机行动计划,即"如果……发生,我将选择……"。

为了说明如何从扩展式表述构造战略式表述,让我们考虑前面提到的质量选择的例子。这是一个完美信息博弈(每个人的信息集都是单结的)。为了构造出这个博弈的战略式表述,首先要注意到,卖主只有一个信息集,两个可选择的行动,因而它的行动空间也即战略空间为"高质量,低质量"。但消费者有两个信息集,每个信息集上有两个可选择的行动,因而他有四个战略,分别为:(1)不论产品是高质量的还是低质量的,他都会购买;(2)如果是高质量的,他购买,如果是低质量的,他不购买;(3)高质量的他不购买,低质量的他购买;(4)不论是高质量的还是低质量的,他都不购买。这样,消费者的上述四个纯战略可以简写为"H:buy, L:buy"、"H:buy, L:don't"、"H:don't,L:buy"和"H:don't,L:don't"。因此,根据上述卖主和消费者的战略,我们可以写出这个博弈的标准形式如下:

Table 8-11　Quality Choice Game(质量选择博弈)

		Consumer			
		H:buy L:buy	H:buy L:don't	H:don't L:buy	H:don't L:don't
Provider	High	2,2	2,2	0,1	0,1
	Low	3,0	1,1	3,0	1,1

We can obtain the strategic form of the extensive game. As in the strategic form games shown before, this tabulates all strategies of the players. In the game tree, any strategy combination results into an outcome of the game, which can be determined by tracing out the path of play arising from the players adopting the strategy combination. The payoffs to the players are then entered into the corresponding cell in the strategic form. Table 8-11 shows the strategic form for our example. The second column is player II's strategy, where "buy if offered high-quality service, don't buy if offered low-quality service" is abbreviated as "H: buy, L: don't". A game tree can therefore be analyzed in terms of the strategic form.

显然,用博弈树的形式表示动态博弈要比用标准形式简洁得多。我们看到的是,博弈树只有四个结果,而用标准式表述表示则有八个结果。

A game that evolves over time is better represented by a game tree than using the strategic form. The tree reflects the temporal aspect. The strategic form typically contains redundancies. Table 8-11, for example, has eight cells, but the game tree in Figure 8-2 has only four outcomes. Every outcome appears twice, which happens when two strategies of player II differ only in the move that is not reached after the move of player I. All move combinations of player II must be distinguished as strategies since any two of them may lead to different outcomes, depending on the action of player I.

三、子博弈精炼纳什均衡(Subgame Perfect Nash Equilibrium)

现在,我们已经看到,战略式表述可以用来表述扩展式博弈,从而,纳什均衡的概念适用于动态博弈,而不仅仅是参与人同时行动的静态博弈。但是,如果博弈分析的目的是预测博弈中参与人的行为,纳什均衡给出的可能并不是一个非常合理的预测。我们在上一节已经指出,一个博弈可能有多个(甚至无穷多个)纳什均衡,究竟哪一个均衡更为合理,博弈论没有一般的结论。但是,均衡的多重性并不是纳什均衡存在的最严重的问题。最严重的问题是,纳什均衡假定每一个参与人在选择自己的最优战略时假定所有其他参与人的战略选择是给定的,就是说,参与人并不考虑自己的选择对其他人选择的影响。由于这个原因,纳什均衡很难说是动态博弈的一个合理解,因为在动态博弈中,参与人的行动有先有后,后行动者的选择空间依赖于前行动者的选择。前行动者在选择自己的战略时不可能不考虑自己的选择对后行动者选择的影响。纳什均衡的这个缺陷促使博弈论专家从60年代开始就不断寻求改进(perfecting)和精炼(refining)纳什均衡概念,以得到更为合理的博弈解。下面将要讨论的"子博弈精炼纳什均衡"(subgame perfect Nash Equilibrium)是纳什均衡概念的第一个最重要的改进,它的目的是把动态博弈中的"合理纳什均衡"与"不合理纳什均衡"分开。这里,所谓的子博弈是指原博弈的一部分,它本身可以作为一个独立的博弈进行分析(我们也把原博弈视为一个子博弈)。需要注意的是,子博弈必须从一个单结信息集开始。正如纳什均衡是完全信息静态博弈解的基本概念一样,子博弈精炼纳什均衡是完全信息动态博弈解的基本概念。子博弈精炼纳什均衡要求均衡战略的行为规则在每一个信息集上都是最优的。它必须满足两个条件:(1)它是原博弈的纳什均衡;(2)它在每一个子博弈上给出纳什均衡。我们从下面的例子中可以清楚地看到这些要求。

现在,我们来看看质量选择博弈的纳什均衡。在这个博弈的标准式表述中,应用前面我们所讲到的求解纳什均衡的方法,我们发现这个博弈有两个纯战略纳什均衡,分别为"High;H:buy,L:don't"和"Low;H:don't,L:don't"。在每一个均衡,给定对方的战略,自己的战略是最优的。"High;H:buy,L:don't"这个战略的均衡结果是卖主提供高质量的产品,消费者购买。"Low;H:don't,L:don't"这个战略的均衡结果是卖主提供低质量的产品,消费者不购买。注意,这里,均衡与均衡结果是不同的(不同均衡可能对应相同的均衡结果)。

接下来的问题是,这两个纳什均衡哪一个是更合理的呢?在实际中是不是它们都会出现呢?也就是说,我们如何把动态博弈中的"合理纳什均衡"与"不合理纳什均衡"分开呢?对于有限完美信息博弈,后向归纳法(backward induction)是剔除不合理纳什均衡求解子博弈精炼纳什均衡的最简便方法。所谓后向归纳法是指从博弈的最后阶段开始推理直到博弈的起始阶段。下面给出用后向归纳法求解子博弈精炼纳什均衡的步骤。

1. 给定博弈到达最后一个决策结,该决策结上行动的参与人有一个最优选择,这个最优选择就是该决策结开始的子博弈的纳什均衡(如果该决策结上的最优行动多于一个,那么我们允许参与人选择其中的任何一个;如果最后一个决策者有多个决策结,那么每一个决策结开始的子博弈都有一个纳什均衡)。

2. 然后,我们倒回倒数第二个决策结(最后决策结的直接前列结),找出倒数第二个决策者的最优选择(假定最后一个决策者的选择是最优的),这个最优选择与我们在第一步找出的最后决策者的最优选择构成从倒数第二个决策结开始的子博弈的一个纳什均衡。

3. 如此不断直到初始结,每一步都得到对应子博弈的一个纳什均衡。并且,根据定义,这个纳什均衡也一定是所有子博弈的纳什均衡。在这个过程的最后一步得到的整个博弈的纳什均衡也就是这个博弈的子博弈精炼纳什均衡。

我们以上述的质量博弈为例来说明如何求解子博弈精炼纳什均衡以及不合理的纳什均衡是怎样被剔除的。

Extensive games with perfect information can be analyzed by backward induction. This technique solves the game by first considering the last possible choices in the game. Here, player II moves last. Since he knows the play will end after his move, he can safely select the action which is best for him. If player I has chosen to provide high-quality service, then the customer prefers to buy, since his resulting payoff of 2 is larger than 1 when not buying. If the provider has chosen Low, then the customer prefers not to purchase. These choices by player II are indicated by arrows in Figure 8-2.

Once the last moves have been decided, backward induction proceeds to the players making the next-to-last moves (and then continues in this manner). In Figure 8-2, player I makes the next-to-last move, which in this case is the first move in the game. Being rational, he anticipates the subsequent choices by the customer. He therefore realizes that his decision between High and Low is effectively between the outcomes with payoffs (2, 2) or (1, 1) for the two players, respectively. Clearly, he prefers High, which results in a payoff of 2 for him, to Low, which leads to an outcome with payoff 1. So the unique solution to the game, as determined by backward induction, is that player I offers high-quality service, and player II responds by buying the service.

The backward induction solution specifies the way the game will be played. Starting from the root of the tree, play proceeds along a path to an outcome. Note that the analysis yields more than the choices along the path. Because backward induction looks at every node in the tree, it specifies for every player a complete plan of what to do at every point in the game where the player can make a move, even though that point may never arise in the course of play. Such a plan is called a strategy of the player. For example, a strategy of player II in Figure 8-2 is "buy if offered high-quality service, don't buy if offered low-quality service". This is player II's strategy obtained by backward induction. Only the first choice in this strategy comes into effect when the game is played according to the backward-induction solution.

Not all Nash Equilibria in an extensive game arise by backward induction. In table 8-11, the rightmost bottom cell (Low; H: don't, L: don't) is also an equilibrium. Here the customer never buys, and correspondingly Low is the best response of the service provider to this anticipated behavior of player II. Although "H: don't" is not an optimal choice (so it disagrees with backward induction), player II never has to make that move, and is therefore not better off by changing his strategy. Hence, this is indeed an equilibrium. It prescribes a suboptimal move in the subgame where player II has learned that player I has chosen High. Because a Nash Equilibrium obtained by backward induction does not have such a deficiency, it is also called subgame perfect.

由此看出,我们通过后向归纳法求解出的子博弈精炼纳什均衡是"High; H: buy, L: don't",其均衡结果是卖主提供高质量的产品,消费者购买。在这里,我们剔除了"Low; H:don't, L:don't"这个纳什均衡,因为从动态的角度来看,它不符合子博弈精炼纳什均衡的要求。后向归纳法剔除了不合理的结果,使纳什均衡的概念得到精炼。

为了对博弈的扩展形式表述及对后向归纳法求解子博弈精炼纳什均衡的方法加深了解,我们再举出一个比较复杂一点的例子。

In order to deepen our understanding of extensive-form games, we need an example with more interesting structure than the quality choice with commitment. Consider the game described by this tree:

This game is not intended to fit any preconceived situation; it is simply a mathematical object in search of an application. (L and R here just denote 'left' and 'right' respectively.)

Now consider the strategic form of this game:

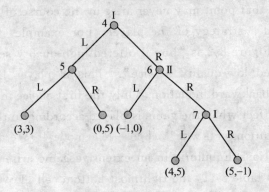

Figure 8-3 Game Tree(博弈树)

Table 8-12 Strategic Form of the Game(博弈的战略形式)

		II			
		LL	LR	RL	RR
I	LL	3,3	3,3	0,5	0,5
	LR	3,3	3,3	0,5	0,5
	RL	−1,0	4,5	−1,0	4,5
	RR	−1,0	5,−1	−1,0	5,−1

(If you are confused by this, remember that a strategy must tell a player what to do at every information set where that player has an action. Since each player chooses between two actions at each of two information sets here, each player has four strategies in total. The first letter in each strategy designation tells each player what to do if he or she reaches their first information set, the second what to do if their second information set is reached. I. e., LR for Player II tells II to play L if information set 5 is reached and R if information set 6 is reached.) If you examine this matrix, you will discover that (LL, RL) is among the NE*. This is a bit puzzling, since if Player I reaches his second information set (7) in the extensive-form game, I would hardly wish to play L there; he earns a higher payoff by playing R at node 7. Mere NE analysis doesn't notice this because NE is insensitive to what happens off the path of play. Player I, in choosing L at node 4,

---

* 即 Nash Equilibrium

ensures that node 7 will not be reached; this is what is meant by saying that it is "off the path of play". In analyzing extensive-form games, however, we *should* care what happens off the path of play, because consideration of this is crucial to what happens on the path. For example, it is the fact that Player I would play R if node 7 were reached that would cause Player II to play L if node 6 were reached, and this is why Player I won't choose R at node 4. We are throwing away information relevant to game solutions if we ignore off-path outcomes, as mere NE analysis does. Notice that this reason for doubting that NE is a wholly satisfactory equilibrium concept in itself has nothing to do with intuitions about rationality, as in the case of the refinement concepts discussed before.

Now apply backward induction to the extensive form of our current example. Begin, again, with the last subgame, that descending from node 7. This is Player I's move, and he would choose R because he prefers his payoff of 5 to the payoff of 4 he gets by playing L. Therefore, we assign the payoff $(5, -1)$ to node 7. Thus at node 6 II faces a choice between $(-1, 0)$ and $(5, -1)$. He chooses L. At node 5 II chooses R. At node 4 I is thus choosing between $(0, 5)$ and $(-1, 0)$, and so plays L. Note that, as in the PD, an outcome appears at a terminal node—$(4, 5)$ from node 7—that is Pareto superior to the NE. Again, however, the dynamics of the game prevent it from being reached.

The fact that backward induction picks out the strategy vector (LR, RL) as the unique solution to the game shows that it's yielding something other than just an NE. In fact, it is generating the game's subgame perfect equilibrium (SPE). It gives an outcome that yields a NE not just in the whole game but in every subgame as well. This is an extremely persuasive solution concept because, it does not demand "more" rationality of agents, but less. The agents, at every node, simply choose the path that brings them the highest payoff in the subgame emanating from that node; and, then, in solving the game, they foresee that they will all do that. Agents who proceed in this way are said to be modular rational, that is, short-run rational at each step. They do not imagine themselves, by some fancy processes of hyper-rationality, acting against their local preferences for the sake of some wider goal. Note that, this can lead to outcomes which might be regretted from the social point of view. In our current example, Player I would be better off, and Player II no worse off, at the left-hand node emanating from node 7 than at the SPE outcome. But Player I's very modular rationality, and Player II's awareness of this, blocks the socially efficient outcome. If our players wish to bring about the more equitable outcome (4,5) here, they must do so by redesigning their institutions so as to change the structures of the games they play. Merely wishing that they could be hyper-rational in some way does not seem altogether coherent as an approach.

第四节 旅游企业的价格竞争战略
(Price Competition Strategy of Travelling Firms)

现代旅游企业市场竞争的特点更趋明确化、直接化、激烈化、集中化以及高层次化,而现代博弈理论是研究经营决策问题的有力的武器和有效的工具之一。由于博弈论是从利益主体的行为特征入手,以及该理论本身的完整性和精确性,并且同现代科学技术的发展有着密切的内在联系和同步性,因而当企业行为在不同的社会经济环境和发展阶段中发生变化时,博弈论就能随之对其新的行为特征加以概括,进而研究在此基础上的经营战略新方法。所以,博弈论为深入确切地研究旅游企业的竞争战略提供了方法和工具。本节运用博弈论分析了旅游企业的价格竞争模式,主要包括三个方面的内容:经营同一旅游业务的企业的价格竞争、经营差异旅游业务的企业之间的价格竞争以及旅游企业的价格领导模型。

一、经营同一旅游业务的企业的价格竞争(Price Competition with Product Similarity)

为简化分析,我们设两个旅游企业,它们经营同一项目的旅游业务。例如,两家旅行社经营同一条旅游线路或两家旅游车船公司为同一个旅游景点服务。在这里,我们说,这两家旅游企业经营的产品是同质的,在消费者效用函数中是完全的替代品。消费者自然购买要价更低的产品。但如果两个旅游企业对同一经营项目要价相同,那么必须假定消费者在两个企业间的分配,这里假设消费者均匀分配。这意味着各个企业的剩余需求为市场需求的一半。

我们还假设模型的其他条件如下：

1) The two firms is indistinguishable to consumers and market demand is $q=D(p)$. Suppose now that their per unit cost is c and there is no constraint on capacity—how much they can produce.

2) Firms compete over price just once and they make their pricing decision simultaneously. Firms produce to meet demand.

3) There is no entry by other producers.

这样一来,如果需求函数是 $q=D(p)$,而不变的边际成本为 c。企业 i 的利润函数为 $\pi^i(p_i,p_j)=(p_i-c)D(p_i,p_j)$,对符号的说明是：把 i 放在上面,是为了和后面要表示偏导的方式区分,i,j 不要表示为 1 和 2,因为这个表示可以同时表示两个企业的利润函数,也可以有效地反映出两个企业的对称性。(对称性假设包括了两个内容,一是需求的均匀分配,另一个是相同的成本)。1 和 2 的表示则带有了次序内容。

企业 的需求可以表示为下面的分段函数：

$D_i(p_i,p_j)=D(p_i)$,如果 $p_i<p_j$；

$D_i(p_i,p_j)=\frac{1}{2}D(p_i)$,如果 $p_i=p_j$；

$D_i(p_i,p_j)=0$,如果 $p_i>p_j$。

不论市场结构如何,即无论一个企业还是两个企业共同供应市场,总利润是一样的。并且可以表示为 $\pi^i+\pi^j=\max_{F_i}(p_i-c)D(p_i)$,用 $\pi^m=\max_{F}(p-c)D(p)$ 表示单个企业在相同需求和成本条件下的垄断利润,那么下面的约束是自然的：$0\leqslant\pi^i+\pi^j\leqslant\pi^m$。

如前面的假定,博弈的规则是两个企业同时也非合作地选择价格,博弈的时期只有一次。

对这个假设条件的理解很重要,理解之后我们可以简化处理并理解均衡。同时选择价格的含义是每个企业都无法在决定价格时获得其他企业的定价信息,这在博弈论当中属于静态博弈。但是从理解企业的行为来说,这意味着一个企业必须推测其他企业的价格(引入动态的含义就是还要推测其他企业对自己定价的反应,这属于动态博弈的内容),从而纳什均衡的一个必要条件是推测必须是正确的。

这样的博弈规则限定了企业竞争的范围,纳什均衡是一对价格

(p_1^*, p_2^*),它满足 $\pi^i(p_1^*, p_2^*) \geqslant \pi^i(p_i, p_2^*)$,$\forall p_i$,$\forall i=1,2$。

这个价格就是纳什均衡,而根据我们的前面的假设,这个均衡价格等于竞争性的价格,即 $p_1^* = p_2^* = c$。

下面我们来证明这个均衡。因为需求函数是分段的,所以利润函数是非连续的,因此无法运用求导的方法解一阶条件。因此我们运用否证的方法来排除不可能的情况。这样我们需要设想不同于这个均衡的其他价格结果,然后逐一排除。下面是证明的过程。

第一种情况,$p_1^* > p_2^* > c$。显然,在这种情况下,企业 1 的利润为零,重要的是这不是纳什均衡,因为企业 1 可以通过索取 $p_1 = p_2^* - \varepsilon$,获得全部市场需求,并得到正的利润边际。This is not an equilibrium, at these prices firm 1's sales and profits are both zero. Firm 1 could profitably deviate by setting $p_1 = p_2^* - \varepsilon$, where ε is very small, so firm 1's profit would increase to $\pi_1 = D(p_2^* - \varepsilon)(p_2^* - \varepsilon - c) > 0$ for small ε.

第二种情况,$p_1^* > p_2^*$。不盈利的企业 2 可以通过略微提高价格($p_2 = p_1^* - \varepsilon$)获得正的利润。This is not an equilibrium. Firm 2 captures the entire market, but its profit are zero. Firm 2 could profitably deviate by setting $p_2 = p_1^* - \varepsilon$, where ε is very small. Firm 2's profit would increase to $\pi_2 = D(p_1^* - \varepsilon)(p_1^* - \varepsilon - c) > 0$ for small ε.

第三种情况,$p_1^* = p_2^* > c$。这样,企业 1 或 2 略微降低价格就可以增大利润。This is not an equilibrium since either firm (say, firm 1) could profitably deviate by setting $p_1 = p_1^* - \varepsilon$, then, instead of sharing the market equally with firm 2 and earning profit of $\pi_1 = \frac{1}{2}D(p_1^*)(p_1^* - c)$, firm 1 would capture the entire market, with profits of $\pi_1 = D(p_1^* - \varepsilon)(p_1^* - \varepsilon - c)$. For small ε this almost doubles firm 1's sales and profits.

第四种情况,$p_1^* = p_1^* = c$。There are the Nash Equilibrium strategies. Neither firm can profitably deviate and earn greater profits even though in equilibrium, profits are zero. If a firm raises its price, its sales fall to zero and its profits remain at zero. Charging a lower price increases sales and ensure a market share of 100%, but it also reduce profits since price falls below unit cost,从而实际上均衡结果就只有 $p_1^* = p_2^* = c$。

The Nash Equilibrium to this game has two significant features:

1) Two firms are enough to eliminate market power.

2) Competition between two firms results in complete dissipation of profits.

其经济学含义是：企业按边际成本定价，企业没有利润。我们知道，在完全竞争的市场下，企业的价格等于边际成本。而在这里，我们仅设定了两个旅游企业，我们也得出了两个企业的定价都等于边际成本这一结论。这一结论告诉我们，垄断可能需要非常严格的条件。如果在一个旅游行业中只有几个旅游企业，它们都经营相同的旅游项目，且它们的经营成本是相同的话，那么任何一个旅游企业都不能成功地操纵市场价格，旅游企业的行为就变成了竞争性的行为。

显然上面的分析对两个旅游企业作了较为严格的假定。如果放松这些假设，我们就会得到旅游企业不同的价格策略。例如，假如放松两个旅游企业经营成本相同的假定，设存在 $c_1 < c_2$，那么竞争结果将是 $p_1^* = p_2^* = c_2$，企业 2 获得零利润，而企业 1 获得超额利润。

上述两个旅游企业经营同一旅游业务的价格竞争模式虽然具有内在的逻辑一致性，但是这个价格竞争模式的理论结论与现实经验观察并不具有一致性。我们在平时也都观察到，即使两个旅游企业经营的是同一旅游业务，它们对这个项目的要价也是千差万别的。借助于模型，人们将复杂的现实抽象为一系列的假设，然后又依靠严格可靠的逻辑推理出具体的结论。如果理论和现实相去甚远，则说明我们对现实的假设有问题。通过对假设的一步步放松，经济模型也就将一步步逼近现实情况。

我们可以通过放宽这一模型的基本假定来使模型中的旅游企业的价格竞争行为更接近于现实情况。

第一种情况是，任何一个旅游企业的满足消费者需求的能力都是有限的，它不可能供给整个旅游市场。由于现实生活中旅游企业的市场供给能力是有限制的，旅游企业不能满足它没有能力供给的旅游项目，所以，只要一个旅游企业的全部能力可供量不能全部满足社会需求，则另一个企业对于剩余消费者需求就可以收取超过边际成本的价格。举例说来，如市场上只有两家旅游企业，旅游企业 1 与旅游企业 2，生产的边际成本都为 c。设旅游企业 1 的全部可供量为价格等于 c 时的需求量 $D(c)$。在这种条件下，$(p_1^*, p_2^*) = (c, c)$ 就不是一个均衡的价格体系。因为，即使旅游企业 1 按 $p_1 = c$ 出售商品，消费者的需求都会转到它提供的旅游项目上来，但仍有一部分消费者需求无法得到满足，他们就会购买旅游企业2提供的旅游项目。如果旅游企业2收取的价格$p_2>c$,消费者仍需支付p_2。当然,谁以$p_1=c$的价格购买企业1的旅游服务,谁以$p_2>c$的价格购买企业2的服务,这是一个排队或者配额的方式问题,但肯定有人得以$p_2>c$去购买,企业2肯定可以获得超额利润。这种解释叫做生产能力约束解。显然,这种模型的核心内容需要设定两个条件,一是旅游企业旅游服务项目供给能力的边界,一是配给的方式,这都会影响到对旅游企业2的需求。

第二种情况是,如果考虑到博弈的时序性,两家旅游企业价格竞争行为也可能会改变。上述的提供同一旅游业务的两家企业的价格竞争均衡的证明是依赖于两家企业的竞争降价来追求消费者对于降价的反应这一逻辑为基础的。然而,如果上述的模型只是一个同时的价格博弈,则不应包括一家企业降价造成的消费反应这样一个带时序性的博弈过程。如果真要分析价格博弈中的时序性,即分析两家企业竞相降价的序列后果,则马上会遇上一个问题:当一家企业看到自己降价之后会引起另一家企业更低的定价的竞争,这家企业还敢降价吗?每一家企业都得比较降价在短期中带来的好处与在长期中由于价格战而带来的损失。如果作这样的时序分析,现实生活与两家旅游企业导致竞争性的均衡价格之间的不一致就可以得到解释:因为企业怕降价引发长期的价格战,所以两家企业很可能在$p_1^*=p_2^*>c$的某一点达成协议,它们不再降价了。这就是所谓的串谋(collusion)。我们下面还要谈到这一模型。

第三种情况是两家旅游企业提供的旅游服务是有差异的。竞争性均衡价格是假定企业间提供的旅游服务是同一的,是完全可以相互替代的,这会引发企业间的价格战,使价格往边际成本靠拢。但旅游服务的差别削弱了这种价格竞争的动力。由于企业提供的旅游是有差别的,它们之间不是可以完全替代的,因而每个旅游企业都对旅游服务有了一定的价格控制力,这就改变了上述的竞争性均衡价格的情况。我们接下来就重点分析在旅游服务差异的情况下两家旅游企业是如何竞争的。

第四种情况是引入信息问题,尤其是价格分布的搜寻成本。上述竞争性均衡价格模型的一个假设是如果一个企业的价格略低于另一个企业,就可以获得全部市场需求,这要求消费者拥有价格分布的完全信息,一旦引入搜寻成本,价格离散就会出现。

但不管怎样,上述的竞争性均衡价格模型代表了少数厂商尖锐竞争的想法。它的另一个极端是垄断的形式,例如卡特尔。因此,这样的模型显然构成了一种重要的参照系,因为现实当中的寡头市场不外乎在这两个极端之间,理论研究需要说明的就是哪些因素导致这个市场具有更强的竞争性或垄断性。

二、经营差异旅游业务的企业的价格竞争(Price Competition with Product Differentiation)

前面我们已经说明,如果两家旅游企业提供的旅游服务是有差异的,那么就会改变竞争性均衡价格这个结果。现在我们就具体分析在这种情况下旅游企业之间是如何竞争的。我们主要讨论两种情况,一是两家旅游企业提供的旅游服务本身就是有差异的,另一种情况是即使它们提供的旅游服务本身没有差别,一些外生因素也导致了旅游服务的差别。

我们先来看第一种情况,两家企业提供的旅游服务本身就是有差别的。如果两家旅游企业实行差异化战略,比如,它们经营不同的旅游线路,显然,这两家企业的市场空间是不同的,它们提供的旅游服务不具有完全的替代性。即使两家旅游企业向同一个消费群体提供服务,比如说它们经营的是同一条旅游线路,但由于不同旅游企业的实力、声誉的不同,消费者偏好的不同等因素,我们也认为这两家旅游企业提供的服务是不同的。以上两种情况,虽然提供的旅游服务是不同的,但是在它们之间还是有一定替代性的:一家企业的市场扩大意味着另一家企业市场需求的缩小。也就是说,整个市场需求要受到这两家旅游企业制定的价格的影响。因此,我们设需求函数是两家企业制定的价格的函数。

In many markets products that compete with each other are not perfect substitutes. Some individuals will prefer the product of firm 1 over the product of firm 2 even if the price of firm 1's product is higher than that of firm 2. We would expect, however, that as firm 1 raises the price of its good, its demand will fall as more and more consumers substitute away from it to firm 2. What are the implications of introducing product differentiation into the game?

Suppose two traveling firms provide goods that are imperfect substitutes. The demand function for firm 1 will depend on not only its price, but also on the price firm 2 charges. Recognizing this interdependence in demand, we see that the demand function for firm 1 and firm 2 are $q_1(p_1, p_2)$ and $q_2(p_1, p_2)$. Increases in p_i decrease demand for product i, but because the two goods are substitutes, increases in p_j increase demand for good i. We assume that both firms have unit costs of production equal to c.

What are the Nash Equilibrium prices? To find the equilibrium prices requires that we first derive the price best-response func ion(最优反应函数). The Nash Equilibrium prices will simultaneously satisfy the two price best-response functions.

The profits of firm 1 are defined as
$$\pi_1(p_1,p_2)=p_1q_1(p_1,p_2)-cq_1(p_1,p_2)$$
Firm 1's optimal price will depend on the price firm 2 charges. Suppose that firm 1 expects firm 2 to charge price p_2. Given this belief, firm 1 must consider how changes in its price will affect its profit.

Similarly, the profits of firm 2 are
$$\pi_2(p_1,p_2)=p_2q_2(p_1,p_2)-cq_2(p_1,p_2)$$
The first-order conditions for the profit maximization problem of firm 1 and firm 2 are
$$q_1(p_1^*,p_2^*)+(p_1^*-c)\frac{dq_1(p_1^*,p_2^*)}{dp_1}=0$$
$$q_2(p_1^*,p_2^*)+(p_2^*-c)\frac{dq_2(p_1^*,p_2^*)}{dp_2}=0$$
where, p_1^*, p_2^* are the optimal prices of profit maximization. From the first-order conditions we can get the best-response functions of the two firms. Now, we define the best-response functions as $R_1(p_2)$ that is for firm 1 and $R_2(p_1)$ that is for firm 2.

At the Nash Equilibrium, both firms are on their best-response functions. Because demand curves slope downward and sales will be positive ($q_1>0$, $q_2>0$), from the first-order conditions we can get $p_1^*>c$, $p_2^*>0$. When goods are differentiated, traveling firms realize that they cannot undercut their rival and capture the entire market. As a result, the severity of price competition is reduced and both firms exercise market power in equilibrium. Figure 8-4 describes the Nash Equilibrium with product differentiation, the competitive outcome, where prices equal marginal costs, is point C in figure 8-4.

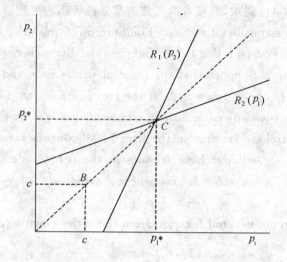

Figure 8-4　Nash Equilibrium with Product Differentiation
（产品差异下的纳什均衡）

　　以上的分析表明，如果两个旅游企业提供的旅游服务是有差异的，那么我们就会得到与前面的竞争性均衡价格不同的结果。这时，两个旅游企业相互博弈，每一个企业在制定价格时都要考虑另一个企业的价格对其的影响。通过解两个企业的价格最优反应函数，我们得到了两个企业的最优价格。博弈的结果表明，两个旅游企业制定的价格不再等于边际成本，而是大于边际成本。

　　现在我们看另一种情况，即使两家旅游企业提供的服务是相同的，但由于很多外生因素的影响，也会导致它们的旅游服务是有差异的。我们现在考虑一种特殊的差异，即空间上的差异（spacial differentiation）。假设旅游企业提供的旅游服务是相同的，但两家旅游企业处于不同的空间位置上。因为不同位置上的消费者要支付不同的运输成本，他们关心的是价格与运输之本之和，而不仅仅是旅游服务的单价。假定有一个长度为 1 的线性城市，消费者均匀地分布在 $[0,1]$ 区间里，分布密度为 1。假定有两个旅游企业，分别位于城市的两端，旅游企业 1 在 $x=0$，旅游企业 2 在 $x=1$，它们都提供相同的旅游服务。每个企业旅游服务的成本为 c，消费者购买服务的旅行成本与离企业的距离成比例，单位距离的成本为 t。这样，住在 x 的消费者如果在企业 1 购买服务，要花费 tx 的旅行成本；如果在企业 2 购买服务，要花费 $t(1-x)$ 的旅行成本。假定消费者具有单位需求,即或者购买旅游服务或者不购买旅游服务。

Now we consider the Nash Equilibrium of the price competition between the two traveling firms. Suppose two firms choose the price at the same time. Suppose that the price of firm i is p_i and its demand function is $D_i(p_1,p_2)$, $i=1,2$. If the two firms are no differentiation to consumers who dwell in x, then all consumers who dwell in the left of x will purchase services in the firm 1, all consumers who dwell in the right of x will purchase services in the firm 2, demand for the services are $D_1=x$, $D_2=1-x$, where x satisfies

$$p_1+tx=p_2+t(1-x).$$

We can get demand function from the above equation, that are

$$D_1(p_1,p_2)=x=\frac{p_2-p_1+t}{2t}$$

$$D_2(p_1,p_2)=1-x=\frac{p_1-p_2+t}{2t}$$

so, profit functions are

$$\pi_1(p_1,p_2)=(p_1-c)D_1(p_1,p_2)=\frac{1}{2t}(p_1-c)(p_2-p_1+t)$$

$$\pi_2(p_1,p_2)=(p_2-c)D_2(p_1,p_2)=\frac{1}{2t}(p_2-c)(p_1-p_2+t)$$

Given p_j, firm i choose p_i to maximize profits. The two first-order conditions are

$$\frac{\partial \pi_1}{\partial p_1}=p_2+c+t-2p_1=0$$

$$\frac{\partial \pi_2}{\partial p_2}=p_1+c+t-2p_2=0$$

From the above first-order conditions, we can get the optimal solutions:

$$p_1^*=p_2^*=c+t$$

Profits of the two firms are:

$$\pi_1=\pi_2=\frac{t}{2}$$

如前所述,我们将两个旅游企业提供的旅游服务的差异解释为消费者购买服务的旅行成本。旅行成本越高,旅游服务的差异就越大,均衡价格从而均衡利润也就越高。原因在于,随着旅行成本的上升,不同企业出售的旅游服务之间的替代性下降,每个企业对附近的消费者的垄断力加强,企业之间的竞争越来越弱,消费者对价格的敏感度下降,从而每个旅游企业的最优价格更接近于垄断价格。另一方面,当旅行成本为零时,不同企业的旅游服务项目之间具有完全的替代性,没有任何一个商店可以把价格定得高于成本,这样我们就会得到竞争性均衡价格结果。

在以上的分析中,我们假定两个旅游企业分别位于城市的两个极端。事实上,均衡结果对于企业的位置是很敏感的。考虑另一个极端的情况,假定两个旅游企业位于同一个位置 x。此时,它们提供的旅游服务是同质的,消费者关心的只是价格,那么这时竞争性均衡价格是唯一的均衡:

$$p_1 = p_2 = c, \ \pi_1 = \pi_2 = 0$$

更为一般地,我们可以讨论两个企业位于任何位置的情况。假定企业 1 位于 $a \geqslant 0$,企业 2 位于 $1-b$(这里 $b \geqslant 0$)。为不失一般性,假定 $1-a-b \geqslant 0$(即企业 1 位于企业 2 的左边)。如果旅行成本为二次式,即旅行成本为 td^2,这里 d 是消费者到旅游企业的距离,那么,需求函数分别为:

$$D_1(p_1, p_2) = x = a + \frac{1-a-b}{2} + \frac{p_2 - p_1}{2t(1-a-b)}$$

$$D_2(p_1, p_2) = 1 - x = b + \frac{1-a-b}{2} + \frac{p_1 - p_2}{2t(1-a-b)}$$

需求函数的第一项是旅游企业自己的地盘(a 是住在企业 1 左边的消费者,b 是住在企业 2 右边的消费者),第二项是位于两企业之间的消费者中靠近自己的一半,第三项代表需求对价格差异的敏感度。

纳什均衡为:

$$p_1^*(a, b) = c + t(1-a-b)\left(1 + \frac{a-b}{3}\right)$$

$$p_2^*(a, b) = c + t(1-a-b)\left(1 + \frac{b-a}{3}\right)$$

当 $a = b = 0$ 时,企业 1 位于 0,企业 2 位于 1,我们回到前面讨论的第一种情况:

$$p_1^*(0, 1) = p_2^*(0, 1) = c + t$$

当 $a = 1-b$ 时,两个旅游企业位于同一个位置,我们走到另一个极端:

$$p_1^*(a, 1-a) = p_2^*(a, 1-a) = c$$

总之,如果两个旅游企业提供的旅游服务项目是有差别的,每个旅游企业都对自己的服务项目具有了一定程度的市场垄断力,每个企业的定价不再等于边际成本,这时,两个旅游企业价格竞争的结果不再是竞争性均衡价格。显然,通过假定旅游服务的差异性,我们得出了更符合实际情况的结论,这在一定程度上解释了旅游企业千差万别的定价模式。

三、旅游企业的价格领导模型(The Price Leadership Model in Travelling Firms)

当一个旅游企业制定价格,而另外的旅游企业视其为给定时,就出现了价格领先。这种价格竞争模式是由某个旅游企业充当价格领袖首先变动价格,其他的旅游企业充当价格随从,按照价格领袖确定的价格变动价格。因此,在这种价格竞争模式下,旅游企业并不互相竞相压价。充当制定价格领袖的旅游企业究竟制定多高的价格要看该企业是否是本产业的主导企业(dominant firm)。如果这个旅游企业是本产业的主导企业,它可以按照追求自己利润最大化的原则确定价格,而不必考虑其他企业的反应。如果充当价格领袖的旅游企业不是本产业的主导企业,那么它在制定价格时就必须考虑其他企业的反应。我们以主导企业充当价格领袖为例分析价格领先模型中的旅游企业的定价行为。在这里,我们要用前面讲到的动态博弈的知识及后向归纳法。

Price leadership occurs when one traveling firm sets the price which the other firm then takes as given. The price leadership model can be solved by dynamic game: First we derive the behavior of the follower, and then derive the behavior of the leader.

Let $x_i(p_1,p_2)$ be the consumer demand for the service of firm i. The follower chooses p_2 taking p_1 as given, that is, the follower maximizes

$$\max_{p_2} p_2 x_2(p_1,p_2) - c_2(x_2(p_1,p_2))$$

We let $p_2 = g_2(p_1)$ be the reaction function that gives the optimal choice of p_2 as a function of p_1.

Then the leader solves

$$\max_{p_1} p_1 x_1(p_1,g_2(p_1)) - c_1(x_1(p_1,g_2(p_1)))$$

An interesting special case occurs when the firms are selling identical traveling service. In this case, if firm 2 sells a positive amount of output, it must sell it at $p_2 = p_1$. For each price p_1, the follower will choose to provide the amount of service $S_2(p_1)$ that maximizes its profits, taking p_1 as given. Hence, the reaction function in this case is simply the competitive supply curve.

If firm 1 charges price p_1, firm 1 will sell $r(p_1) = x_1(p_1) - S_2(p_1)$ units of service. The function $r(p_1)$ is known as the residual demand curve(剩余需求曲线) facing firm 1. Firm 1 wants to choose p_1 so as to maximize

$$\max_{p_1} p_1 r(p_1) - c_1(r(p_1))$$

This is just the problem of a monopolist facing the residual demand curve $r(p_1)$.

The solution is depicted graphically in figure 8-5. We subtract the supply curve of firm 2 from the market demand curve to get the residual demand curve. Then we use the standard $MR = MC$ condition to solve for the leader's service.

下面我们用图形来更形象地描述旅游企业的价格领导模型。

在下图中,市场需求曲线为 D,S_F 是除主导旅游企业之外该产业其他旅游企业所提供的旅游服务的数量。D_L 为市场对主导企业旅游服务的需求曲线。D_L 等于市场需求 D 与该产业其余企业供给数量的差额。在价格等于或高于 P_1 时,对主导企业服务的需求为 0,所以除主导企业以外该产业其余企业的供给等于市场供给。当价格等于或低于 P_2 时,除主导企业以外该产业其余企业的供给等于 0,所以主导企业所面临的需求曲线就是市场需求曲线。在 P_1、P_2 两种价格之间,主导企业所面临的需求曲线为 D_L。与 D_L 相对应的边际收益曲线为 MR_L。MC_L 为主导企业的边际成本曲线。

显然,主导企业要想充当制定价格的领袖,根据边际收益等于边际成本的利润最大化原则,则它的最佳定价策略是把价格定为 P_L,提供 Q_L 数量的服务。就像在完全竞争市场中的情况一样,其他价格跟随企业是价格的接受者,它们视 P_L 为给定的价格,并按照价格等于边际成本的原则来获取最大利润。由图中可见,价格跟随企业所提供的服务数量为 Q_F。价格领导企业与价格跟随企业的供给数量等于市场需求数量,即 $Q_F + Q_L = Q_T$,Q_T 为 P_L 价格下的市场需求量。

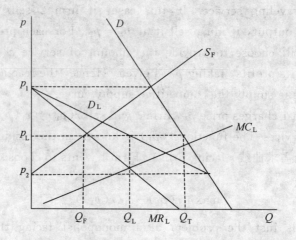

图 8-5　价格领导模型(Price Leadership Model)

第五节　旅游企业的竞争与合作选择
(Competition and Cooperation in Travelling Firms)

一、竞争还是合作？(Competition or Cooperation?)

在上节中我们所讲的模型都是一种非合作的均衡(noncooperative equilibrium)，即在给定竞争对手行为的条件下，每个企业都做出使自己利润最大化的决策。实际上，企业在非合作的情况下获得的利润要低于合作情况下所获得的利润。那么，企业是否可以通过合作达到共谋均衡，以便获得更高的利润呢？在没有反垄断法的情况下，企业之间的串谋(collusion)行为不会导致诉讼的麻烦。如果存在着反垄断法，企业间明目张胆的串谋行为是违法的。但是企业之间实行一种默契的配合是可以的。企业间密切配合，共同制定高价而达到的均衡是一种合作的均衡(cooperative equilibrium)。如果两个企业间真的能够默契配合，对于每一个企业当然是一件幸事。但是如果两者配合的不够默契，情况将会如何？如果企业对自己的产品制定较高的价格，并且设想其竞争对手会与之配合也制定较高的价格，而竞争对手却制定较低的价格或保持原价格不变，结果会如何？我们以一个具体的例子分析这种情况。

设两个旅游企业1和2进行价格竞争。为简单起见，设它们都有两种价格可供选择，产品定价或者为4或者为6，它们会通过不同的定价策略而获得不同的利润。设其支付矩阵如下。

表 8-13　定价博弈(Price Making Game)

		企业 2	
		定价为 4	定价为 6
企业 1	定价为 4	24，24	40，8
	定价为 6	8，40	32，32

　　在上述的支付矩阵中，前一个数字代表在一定的价格策略组合下企业 1 的利润。相应地，后一个数字代表企业 2 的利润。若两个企业都制定低价为 4，则每个企业可获得 24 单位的利润。若两个企业都制定高价为 6，则每个企业可获得 32 单位的利润。若一个企业定高价，另一个企业定低价，则定低价的企业可获得 40 单位的利润，而定高价的企业只能获得 8 单位的利润。

　　支付矩阵表明，若两个企业能密切配合，制定高价，二者都能获得较高的利润。但是如果两个企业不能密切配合，我们可以得到这个博弈的纳什均衡为两个企业都制定低价。因为一旦一方制定高价，另一方制定低价，制定高价的一方将损失较多的利润，而使制定低价的一方受益。两个企业都制定高价所得到的解称为合作的解，两者都制定低价所获的解称为竞争的解。

　　实际上，我们看到，上述的企业价格竞争行为类似于前面所讲的囚徒困境。在囚徒困境中，两个囚徒如果合作(都选择抵赖)，他们可以少判刑，但博弈的结果是每个囚徒都从自身利益出发而选择了不合作(都选择坦白)，结果每个囚徒的状况都没得到改善。那么，囚徒的不合作策略是否意味着企业间也总是采取不合作的策略呢？答案是不确定的。在某些条件下，企业将采取竞争的策略；在另一些条件下，企业可能会采取合作的策略。在前面的几节中，我们已经利用博弈论讨论过企业在不同条件下的不同策略。这里，我们将利用在经济中观察到的实际情况说明企业所采取的策略有可能不同于囚徒困境中囚徒的策略，即企业的策略可能是合作的，而不是竞争的。

二、价格刚性(Price Inelasticity)

　　一些经济学家通过对寡头市场的观察发现，某些带有寡头特征的产业产品的价格相当稳定，而不是采取竞相压价的策略争夺市场。这些寡头的行为不同于囚徒的困境中囚徒的行为。寡头的产品表现出价格刚性。在旅游市场上，我们也看到，旅游企业制定的价格也具有一定的稳定性,特别是如果某个特定的旅游细分市场被几个大企业所垄断的时候。那么如何解释旅游企业的这种价格行为呢?斯威齐模型(Sweezy model)为这种价格刚性行为提供了一种解释。斯威齐模型是以经济学家斯威齐的名字命名的。模型假定,一旦某个寡头降低价格,试图夺取其竞争对手的市场份额,其竞争对手将如法炮制,降低自己产品的价格,因而这个企业降价后不会增加多少销售量。如果该寡头提高其产品的价格,它的竞争对手则维持原价格不变,以便夺取其市场份额,因而该寡头的销售量会大幅度下降。这就造成了折弯的需求曲线(kinked demand curve)。下面具体描述这个模型。

Joan Robinson hypothesized in 1936 that demand curves might be other than the traditional downward sloping curves that we have encountered so far. Specifically she thought there might be a demand curve with a "kink" in it. Theories to explain these "imaginary curves" were developed in a rare instance of simultaneous discovery by Paul Sweezy at Harvard and by R. L. Hall and C. J. Hitch in Oxford in 1939. Both publications produced versions of a kinked demand curve。

Suppose that the current price is determined by cost-plus pricing. Above this price, an individual firm is afraid of putting up prices. A price increase would, he assumes, not be matched by his competitors, hence the demand curve above P^* (See Figure 8-6) is elastic. It will be remembered that if demand is elastic and price rises—revenue falls.

Similarly a price fall has the same effect on revenue. This time the firm imagines that dropping its own price leads to others dropping theirs. Overall, quantity demand increases as the demand curve slopes down, but the increase is less than proportionate. That is the demand curve below price P^* is inelastic. The implication here is that the prices in oligopoly tend to be more stable than in the other theories of the firm. Further insight can be gained by examining the marginal revenue curve. The marginal revenue recall, falls at twice the rate of the average revenue (demand) curve. The kinked demand curve can be thought of as two demand curves. The marginal revenue curve MR_1 is related to demand curve D_1 and MR_2 is related to demand curve D_2. (see Figure 8-7)

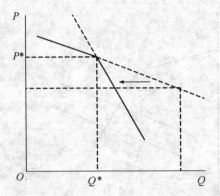

Figure 8-6　Kinked Demand Curve(折弯的需求曲线)

The dotted sections of D_1 and D_2 are irrelevant as consumers are always going to choose any given quantity at the lower price, so the relevant sections of the marginal revenue curves are as in figure 8-6.

The two parts of the marginal revenue curve are joined with a vertical section to help show where the MC and MR curves intersect. In this diagram when costs rise, from an increase in sales taxes for example, the marginal cost curve MC_1 moves upward to MC_2. The profit maximizing oligopolist still equates MC with MR in order to determine the level of output. But because the MC curves cut MR where it is dis-continuous and vertical the output remains at Q^*, and hence the price P^* remains constant too. The firm can keep their price stable by reducing the overall level of profit earned, and if they can sustain this stability in the long run it implies that a measure of abnormal profit was being earned before the cost increases.

For prices to change, costs would need to rise above that part of the MR curve which is dis-continuous.

If demand increased, this too might not lead to an increase in price unless the demand curve moved far enough to the right to make the MC curve cut MR above the discontinuity of MR.

The main problem with the kinked demand curve model is that it fails to explain oligopolists' behavior consistently. It does help to explain price rigidity and why entrepreneurs are wary of price cutting as a business tactic.

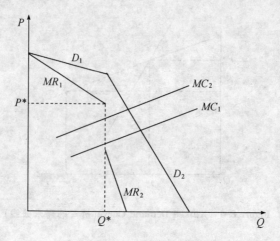

图 8-7 斯威齐模型(Sweezy Model)

斯威齐模型解释了寡头市场下的价格刚性现象。我们可以认为这种价格刚性的出现也是企业之间博弈的结果。在寡头市场下,每个企业都害怕因降低或提高价格而失去市场份额,这种互相之间的担心导致了企业之间的默契,从而维持价格在一定范围内的稳定性。这也为旅游市场上旅游服务价格的稳定性提供了有力的解释。

三、旅游企业的卡特尔(Cartel in Travelling Firms)

1. 卡特尔的内涵(The Concept of Cartel)

Broadly defined, a cartel is an explicit arrangement among, or on behalf of, enterprises in the same line of business that is designed to limit competition among them. Cartel includes price fixing, explicit collusion, and conspiracy. There are buyer cartels and seller cartels. They may be open or secret, governmental or private, legal or illegal, local or international. In short, the typical purpose and effect of cartelization is to set prices higher than would prevail under competition, to reduce them as seldom as possible, and to raise them further whenever the opportunity permits.

旅游企业成立卡特尔的目的就在于削弱卖方市场的竞争程度,限制市场供应量,提高旅游产品价格,以获取更多的利润。卡特尔在提高价格的同时一定要限制各旅游企业的产量,因为作为卡特尔而存在的这个垄断厂商面临着一条向下倾斜的需求曲线。但对于每一个旅游企业来说,当价格提高时都想提供更多的产量以获得更大的利润。所以作为卡特尔而要求每个企业减少产量和每个企业在价格提高时都想提高产量之间就产生了矛盾。这个矛盾是许多卡特尔寿命较短或根本无法建立的一个根本原因。

2. 卡特尔的形成机制(The Forming System of Cartel)

在竞争性市场结构中,旅游产业的均衡由市场供给和需求曲线的交点决定,此时消费者剩余和生产者剩余之和达到最大。生产者和消费者都是利润最大化的理性经济人,都是按照利润最大化的原则来决策的。也就是说,在竞争性市场中,生产者已经获得了最大化的利润。而当旅游产业内部的所有企业都形成卡特尔时,整个产业中其实就只有一个垄断者厂商。为什么在竞争市场中已获得最大化利润的企业却有形成卡特尔的倾向。卡特尔与竞争市场中企业的利益分配机制有什么不同呢?

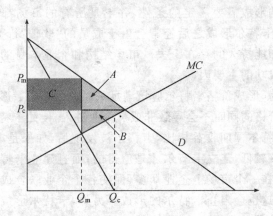

图 8-8 卡特尔的形成机制(Forming Mechanism of Cartel)

在图 8-8 中,MC 是市场总供给曲线,它是由每个企业的供给曲线在水平线上的加总。在竞争性市场上需求曲线为 D,供给和需求曲线的交点决定了竞争市场上所有企业的供给总量。而当所有企业结合成一个卡特尔企业后,卡特尔企业利润最大化的原则是 $MR=MC$,根据此原则所确定的数量要比竞争性市场中的 Q_c 要小,而价格要比竞争性市场中的均衡价格 P_c 要高。因此,卡特尔的形成提高了产品价格并限制了产品的数量,同时卡特尔还导致了社会福利的损失和收入的重新分配。一部分消费者剩余由消费者转移给供货商,同时社会总福利减少了 $A+B$ 的面积。另外,由于产量的减少,企业的剩余也减少了 B 的面积,但只要从消费者处所获得的剩余 C 比损失的 B 大,那么就可以形成卡特尔。

可以看出,在卡特尔中每个成员所生产的产量并没有达到利润最大化点。虽然卡特尔中每个企业都签订了遵守一定的价格和产量协议,但受利润最大化的驱使,每个企业都想要扩大自己的产量,并隐藏自己的这种行为,以使其他企业遵守协议维持较少的产量。每个企业都有扩大自己产量的动机。因此,一般来说,卡特尔难以形成并长久维持,主要是从这个意义上来说的。但以后我们会讲到只要有合适的市场结构,卡特尔还是可以长久维持的,但这需要一定的条件。

3. 卡特尔的形成条件和影响因素(The Forming Conditions and Impacting Factors of Cartel)

(1) 卡特尔的形成条件(The Forming Conditions of Cartel)

卡特尔的形成需要一定的条件,并不是所有的市场都能形成卡特尔,而且有的卡特尔形成之后经常会由于成员的"欺骗"行为而破产,而有的卡特尔却能持久的存在下去。市场结构和企业本身的特性是决定卡特尔能否成功的主要因素。

一般认为,形成价格卡特尔应该满足一系列的条件:形成卡特尔的企业在提高价格的同时不会导致非成员企业进入,侵蚀卡特尔成员的市场份额;与卡特尔预期收益相比,卡特尔被发现后,如果是非法的,所受到的惩罚应该较低,建立卡特尔才是值得的;而且建立卡特尔的成本应该较低,如果在一个市场上企业众多,促使各个企业联合成卡特尔的成本必定很高,这也会阻止卡特尔的形成。另外,卡特尔形成之后还要应该符合一定的条件才能维持,如比较容易发现欺骗行为,而且发现欺骗行为之后,其他卡特尔成员应该能够实行比较有力的惩罚措施。另外,应该从企业本身所具有的特性来认识,即企业由于其边际成本曲线比较陡峭,或企业的固定成本较低,或企业的客户较多,没有欺骗的动机,那么卡特尔也就比较容易形成并维持。

(2) 卡特尔的决定因素(The Impacting Factors of Cartel)

如果不能满足以上条件,卡特尔成员总会秘密地降低价格(或增加产量),破坏协议。虽然很多卡特尔都因为这些条件无法满足而破裂了,但有些卡特尔却可以长久的维持。The feasibility, incidence, and endurance of collusion are all largely determined by structural and technological conditions.

We know now that the purpose of all collusion is to maximize joint profits, for only when firms act together can they price and produce like a monopolist. Cartelization occurs only when it is both feasible and necessary to achieving the objective of the joint-profit maximization. If cartelization is not feasible, it would not occur. If it is not necessary to achieving the objective, it would not occur either, especially if it is illegal and heavily penalized.

There is a concept of tacit collusion that is different from cartel. Tacit collusion refers to oligopolistic uniformity of behavior without overt communication or agreement, but solely through a rational calculation by each seller of what the consequences of his price decision would be, taking into account the probable or virtually certain reactions of his competitors. Cartel needs some contracts or agreement to maintain relations among firms in the cartel.

The following factors are important for the forming of cartel.

- The number of firms. If there are hundreds of small firms selling a standardized product, it is necessary but impossible to set up cartel to achieve joint maximization of profit because of the cost for cartelization among so many firms. If there are only two firms in a market, the firms are interdependent so closely that they will make tacit collusion. There are no incentives for price cutting. Only are there neither too many firms nor too few firms that cartelization is necessary and impossible.
- Concentration. There is obvious relation between the number of firms and the concentration. A research by George Hay and Dan Kelley also proves that the preponderance of conspiracies lasting ten or more years were in markets with high degrees of concentration.
- Type of product and technological change.
- Type of sale and opportunity for secret dealing.
- Rate of growth and elasticity of demand. If the rate of growth in industry is high, the firm in collusion may feel the gains acquired from collusion and cartel less attractive to potential

participants. Elasticity of demand also can influence the forming of cartel. As Hay and Kelley put it, "The more inelastic is industry demand, the greater are the potential rewards to the price fixers. Concomitantly the smaller will be the sacrifice in terms of capacity utilization."

- Production costs. Widely divergent costs across firms would breed divergent opinions concerning what price should prevail, threatening the success of negotiations.

(3) 各个因素的重要性(The Importance of Different Factors)

对于上述所列的各个因素的重要性很难依靠经验数据检验。一方面，衡量这些因素本身就很困难，而且这些因素也不像我们在表格中所列的这样清晰直接。各种因素之间又会相互影响。比如快速技术进步可能会增强旅游企业之间的竞争而阻碍卡特尔的形成，但如果其他因素有利于卡特尔的形成，则很难判断技术进步对卡特尔的影响。对于两个结构相同的两个产业，一个产业可能很容易形成卡特尔，而另一个产业则不能形成卡特尔。各种因素之间的相互作用不利于对单个因素影响的经验研究。

复习思考题：

1. 理解博弈论的基本概念。
2. 根据不同的分类标准，博弈可以分为哪些类型？
3. 什么叫纳什均衡和混合战略纳什均衡？什么叫子博弈精炼纳什均衡？
4. 用博弈论分析经营同一旅游业务和差异旅游业务的企业的价格竞争。
5. 什么叫价格卡特尔？旅游企业能否形成价格卡特尔？

第九章
旅游企业的一体化与纵向控制
(The Integration and Vertical Control of the Tourism Corporations)

第一节 旅游企业的一体化战略
(The Integration Strategy of Tourism Corporations)

一体化行为可分为三类：横向一体化(horizontal integration)、纵向一体化(vertical integration)和混合一体化(conglomerate integration)。The union of two or more direct competitors is called a horizontal integration. 例如两个生产汽车轮胎的企业合并就是横向一体化。A vertical integration links companies that operate at different stages of the production-distribution process. 属于同一个产业上下游企业的合并就属于纵向一体化。Besides the horizontal integration and vertical integration, all the other integrations are the conglomerate integration. This definition is relatively broad, so we can subdivide it into three kinds: (1) product extension, involving producers of two different but related products, such as bleach and detergent; (2) market extension, involving firms producing the same product but occupying different geographic markets; (3) pure conglomerate, involving firms with nothing at all in common.

实施一体化战略是扩大企业规模、构建大企业的有效途径。旅游企业可采取水平一体化(horizontal integration)、垂直一体化(vertical integration)和混合一体化(conglomerate integration)这三种战略以形成大型企业，提高市场竞争力。

一、水平一体化战略(Horizontal Integration Strategy)

水平一体化(horizontal integration),是指旅游企业在原有生产经营范围内,通过兼并、联合同类企业或投资兴建新的经营单位,形成多工厂企业,以扩大企业规模。The acquisition of additional business activities at the same level of the value chain is referred to as horizontal integration. Horizontal growth can be achieved by internal expansion or by external expansion through mergers and acquisitions of firms offering similar products and services. A firm may diversify by growing horizontally into unrelated businesses.

水平一体化所带来的经济效率主要来自"多工厂经济性"(multiplant economies),因为多工厂企业有条件充分利用多工厂运作的各种经济。主要表现在:企业能够把相对稳定的固定成本(如管理成本)分摊到各经营单位所提供的旅游服务项目中,从而获得多工厂规模经济;相对于产品价值而言,旅游企业可以通过在不同地理位置上设立企业,就近供应目标市场,以减少经营成本;多工厂企业有能力剔除过剩的生产能力,它可以关闭那些老化的、低效的经营单位,以调整产品结构,使企业的生产能力与市场需求相适应。The following are some benefits sought by firms horizontally integrated.

- Economies of scale—achieved by selling more of the same product, for example, by geographic expansion.
- Economies of scope—achieved by sharing common resources to different products. Commonly referred to as "synergies".
- Increased market power (over suppliers and downstream channel members)
- Reduction in the cost of international trade by operating factories in foreign markets.

Sometimes benefits can be gained through customer perceptions of linkages between products. For example, in some cases synergy can be achieved by using the same brand name to promote multiple products.

水平一体化战略的最大优势是操作简单,它可以通过横向并购或横向联合实现。横向并购是指两个或两个以上生产或销售相同、相似产品的企业间的并购,其目的在于消除竞争、扩大市场份额、增加并购企业的垄断实力或形成规模效应。例如提供同类旅游服务的企业间或在同一市场领域出售相互竞争商品的分销商之间的并购。横向并购的结果是资本在同一生产、销售领域或部门的集中,优势企业吞并劣势企业组成横向托拉斯,扩大生产规模以达到新技术条件下的最佳经济规模。横向联合则是由两个或两个以上的生产相同或相近产品的企业,为了总体市场的预期目标而采取的一种长期性联合与合作的经营行为。

采取水平一体化战略也有其自身的劣势:水平一体化实现的规模扩大,有可能会在市场上形成垄断势力。由于一体化使企业在一种产品或一个产品链上进入较深,因而可能会产生退出障碍。Horizontal integration by acquisition of a competitor will increase a firm's market share. However, if the industry concentration increases significantly, anti-trust issues may arise accordingly. Aside from legal issues, another concern is whether the anticipated economic gains will be materialized. Before expanding the scope of the firm through horizontal integration, managers should be sure that the imagined benefits are real. Many blunders have been made by firms that broadened their horizontal scope to achieve synergies that did not exist, for example, computer hardware manufacturers who entered the software business on the premise that there were synergies between hardware and software. However, a connection between two products does not necessarily imply realizable economies of scope. Finally, even when the potential benefits of horizontal integration exist, they can't be materialized spontaneously. There must be an explicit horizontal strategy in place. Such strategies generally do not arise from the bottom-up, but rather, must be formulated by corporate management.

就中国目前的旅游企业来看,由于中国的旅游市场容量相对较大,而现有旅游企业规模普遍较小,因此,即使是通过水平一体化进行联合或合并,也不可能在短期内形成垄断局面。其次,从退出障碍来看,由于中国是发展中国家,目前的消费行为仍是建立在中低收入基础上的,消费者的消费习惯变化相对较慢。因此,一般性旅游项目,特别是已经被消费者普遍接受的旅游项目能维持较长的寿命期。即使是出现了某个旅游行业的衰退迹象,较长的衰退和消失过程也能为企业调整资源、采取退出战略提供所需要的时间。另外,由于中国旅游市场表现出较强的地区性和地区发展不平衡性,如东西部地区的经济发展和消费水平差距较大,因而可以在国内不同地区间实现旅游业务转移。通过业务的地区转移可以大大延长产品的寿命期。

值得注意的是,虽然水平一体化对单个企业来说,不失为迅速扩大企业规模和市场份额的有效方式,但它并不会直接导致企业规模和市场份额的叠加。这是因为企业在兼并另一个处于同一生产阶段的企业之前,这两个企业就已经存在了。它们本身已经具有各自的企业规模和市场份额。并购或联合的结果只是原本属于两个企业名下的规模和市场份额,经过一体化行动后只属于一个企业而已。只有当其中一个企业虽然具有一定的规模,但由于各种原因企业自身已经丧失了继续有效利用现有规模的能力,而相应于这一规模的市场需要仍然存在的情况时,水平一体化才会显示出对社会总体而言的规模和市场的扩大。另外,如果在水平一体化过程中经过合理化调整,剔除原有两个企业在独立情况下重复的活动,或是原本存在的不合理的流程和活动组织,水平一体化才会产生协同效益。

二、垂直一体化战略(Vertical Integration Strategy)

垂直一体化(vertical integration),即企业在供、产、销方面实行纵向渗透和扩张。企业可进入当前业务的供应阶段或使用阶段,实现在同一产品链上的延长。例如,一家旅游服务企业可以控制一个旅游景区或者控制建立旅游项目的分销系统,以实现垂直一体化战略。The degree to which a firm owns its upstream suppliers and its downstream buyers is referred to as vertical integration. Because it can have a significant impact on a business unit's position in its industry with respect to cost, differentiation, and other strategic issues, the vertical scope of the firm is an important consideration in corporate strategy. Vertically integrated companies are united through a hierarchy and share a common owner. Usually each member of the heirarchy produces a different product, and the products combine to satisfy a common need.

There are three varieties of this vertical integration: backward vertical integration, forward vertical integration, and balanced vertical integration. In backward vertical integration, the company sets up subsidiaries that produce some of the inputs used in the production of it's products. For example, an automobile company may own a tire company, a glass company, and a metal company. Control of these three subsidiaries is intended to create a stable supply of inputs and ensure a consistent quality in their final product. In forward vertical integration, the company sets up subsidiaries that distribute or market products to customers or use the products themselves. An example of this is a movie studio that also owns a chain of theaters. In balanced vertical integration, the company sets up subsidiaries that both supply them with inputs and distribute their outputs.

Two issues that should be considered when deciding whether to vertically integrate is cost and control. The cost aspect depends on the cost of market transactions between firms versus the cost of administering the same activities internally within a single firm. The second issue is the impact of asset control, which can impact barriers to entry and which can assure cooperation of key value-adding players.

Vertical integration potentially offers the following advantages:

- Reduce transportation costs if common ownership results in closer geographic proximity.
- Improve supply chain coordination.
- Provide more opportunities for differentiation by means of increased control over inputs.
- Capture upstream or downstream profit margins.
- Increase entry barriers to potential competitors, for example, if the firm can gain sole access to a scarce resource.
- Gain access to downstream distribution channels that otherwise would be inaccessible.
- Facilitate investment in highly specialized assets in which upstream or downstream players may be reluctant to invest.

总体上来看，实行垂直一体化的主要动因是：节省交易成本，实现规模经济效益。如果市场交易的成本很低，企业就应该到公开市场（open market）上去购买投入品，并通过批发向下游企业营销其产品。但在实际运作中，从原材料供应、产品生产到产品销售的各垂直层次企业在相互交易过程中，都会产生大量的交易成本。而垂直一体化的实质就是把原来由不同企业承担的供、产、销职能不断集中于单个企业的过程,也就是把供、产、销活动由原来的市场协调转化为企业内部管理协调的过程。垂直一体化的经济合理性就在于它能减少交易成本。垂直一体化战略的潜在利益在于通过向上游或下游业务的扩展,能够在一定程度上避免投入品的价格、供应量(或需求量)的波动对企业成本及业务水平的影响,从而降低经营风险。从近年的旅游行业情况来看,一方面,旅游行业投入品的价格出现持续的上升趋势;而另一方面,许多旅游产品价格和服务项目却由于竞争加剧、消费水平稳定和各地区发展不平衡等特点,呈现稳定、甚至下降的趋势。这就使处于旅游产业链中游的企业降低成本的压力加大。在这种情况下,企业实施后向一体化战略,进入上游业务,对于控制投入品的价格波动无疑是有效的;而目前我国企业间协作关系尚不尽人意,或是由于地区利益本位意识的影响使跨地区的协作网络难以建立的情况下,企业直接进入下游业务,实施前向一体化,也不失为绕过地区障碍的可行途径。同时,实施垂直一体化战略虽然要求企业进入不同于原有业务特点的活动领域,但由于新增加的业务与原有业务具有相同的周期特性,以及在技术上和管理上的一致性,因此具备了统一战略规划、统一资源调配、统一管理的可能,可以使管理效益大大提高、并能保持企业组织的稳定。可见,垂直一体化战略是提高现有旅游企业经营效率的有效途径,也是以较低的资本支出,实现我国旅游产业结构优化、产业内组织结构优化的有效途径。

但是,垂直一体化战略的实施也可能产生以下负面效应。While some of the benefits of vertical integration can be quite attractive to the firm, the drawbacks may negate any potential gains. Vertical integration potentially has the following disadvantages:

- Capacity balancing issues. For example, the firm may need to build excess upstream capacity to ensure that its downstream operations have sufficient supply under all demand conditions.
- Potentially higher costs due to low efficiencies resulting from lack of supplier competition.
- Decreased flexibility due to previous upstream or downstream investments. (Note however, that flexibility to coordinate vertically-related activities may increase.)
- Decreased ability to increase product variety if significant in-

house development is required.
- Developing new core competencies may compromise existing competencies.
- Increased bureaucratic costs.

我们可以把垂直一体化战略的负面效应归结为这样几点：(1)垂直一体化可能会减少改变交易对象的灵活性。垂直一体化意味着加强了产业链中各经营单位的相互依赖性，但一体化企业内部之间可能因技术上的变化、产品设计的变化或管理上的问题等产生不协调。如，旅游企业投入品的成本上升、原材料的质量下降，而旅游营销部门的市场开拓不力等现象。此时，企业要改换供应部门或营销部门，其成本要比调换独立的供应商和客户的成本大得多。因此，从这个意义上来说．垂直一体化减少了灵活性。(2)垂直一体化提高了退出障碍。有时，垂直一体化后，提高了资产的专用性，加上各营业单位之间的感情较深，因此，垂直一体化可能会提高总的退出障碍。(3)垂直一体化会增加成本。首先，垂直一体化可能减少企业分配投入资金的灵活性。因为整个纵向链的业绩取决于各个环节，因此企业可能必须投资于那些入仅敷出或入不敷出的环节上，以保证整个实体的运作，而不能向其他方面投资。这样就可能会造成企业缺乏其他方向成长的资金。其次，为维持纵向生产力的平衡需要更多的费用。纵向产业链中的生产过剩(或需求过量)阶段必须在公开市场上出售某些过剩产品(或购买某些不足的投入品)，在这种情况下维持平衡就变得很困难。因为这种纵向关系往往迫使企业与其竞争对手交易，而竞争对手则由于担心在交易中处于劣势地位可能不愿意交易。此外，生产能力的增加可能在上下两个阶段是不平衡的，这些不平衡会导致各阶段生产平衡的难度加大、费用增加。再次，由于纵向链各环节的管理上存在差异，因此，不能将相同的管理方式和方法运用于纵向链中的不同环节，这样一方面会增加管理协调的难度，另一方面也会增大管理成本和风险。(4)弱化激励。由于垂直一体化将交易内部化，可能不如市场机制更有刺激的动力。强刺激动力指的是与市场体制相伴随的利润刺激动力，而弱的刺激力则与科层组织相联系。有时人为地保护内部市场会助长企业内部的惰性，削弱市场的竞争性，不利于提高企业的创新能力。

下面我们分析一下旅游企业实行垂直一体化的有利因素与不利因素。

The following situational factors tend to favor vertical integration:

- Taxes and regulations on market transactions.
- Obstacles to the formulation and monitoring of contracts.
- Strategic similarity between the vertically-related activities.
- Sufficiently large production quantities so that the firm can benefit from economies of scale.
- Reluctance of other firms to make specific investments to the transaction.

The following situational factors tend to make vertical integration less attractive:

- The quantity required by a supplier is much less than the minimum efficient scale for producing the product.
- The product is a widely available commodity and its production cost decreases significantly as cumulative quantity increases.
- The core competencies between the activities are very different.
- The vertically adjacent activities are in very different types of industries. For example, manufacturing is very different from retailing.
- The addition of the new activity places the firm in competition with another player with which it needs to cooperate. The firm then may be viewed as a competitor rather than a partner.

三、企业的混合一体化战略(Conglomerate Integration Strategy)

混合一体化(conglomerate integration),是指企业通过一定的方式控制多个产业中的若干生产经营单位,实行跨产业经营。Conglomerate integration involves a company spreading its risks by buying a range of other business interests with no real relationship with each other. In this way the business will be operating in several major markets at the same time. However, in the modern world businesses will only integrate if there is a real logic to do so based on businesses with something in common.

企业选择混合一体化的刺激首先来自"分散风险"(risk spreading)。

The main purpose of conglomerate integration is to allow the firm to diversify against risk. Having operations in different sectors of the economy protects the firm from a downturn in one of them. 因为旅游产业市场具有波动性，季节性较强，一些月份景气，另一些月份比较萧条，企业对之无能为力，从而使只在单一市场上经营的企业的销售额和利润额在很大程度上取决于市场状况，其稳定性较差。如果旅游企业同时在多个相关的产业控制一批旅游项目的经营单位，就能烫平企业收入的波动性。稳定收入是企业追求的一个重要目标，混合一体化能使企业避免破产倒闭的威胁，保证企业持续发展。其次，通过混合一体化，企业将其闲余的资源要素进行广泛运用，在不增加成本的基础上，可通过增加产品品种，获得范围经济效应。最后，实行混合一体化还可避免与反垄断法规的冲突。因为一些国家通常是以某一市场集中率来界定垄断企业的，当企业在待定产业中的市场集中度达到一定比率时就成为反垄断法的制裁对象。显然，水平一体化和垂直一体化都会明显提高企业的市场集中度，而混合一体化是对不同产业市场业务的集中控制，它对在特定产业中的市场集中度没有直接影响。

但是，混合一体化所降低的风险有时是以管理效率为代价的。从事多元化经营的企业，其管理人员至少需要了解两个以上业务的基本特点，能制定并实施有利于每项业务正常发展的战略和对各项业务活动的业绩进行恰当的评价。如果从混合一体化使企业同时进入了陌生的业务和陌生的市场这一角度看，混合一体化本身就是风险。20世纪60年代、70年代是西方国家的企业实施多元化战略的高潮时期。但是到了80年代，这些企业逐渐认识到多元化投资引起的管理权利过于分散、管理部门重叠、高层管理部门脱离经营现场等结果给企业带来的伤害，远远大于可能降低的风险给企业带来的好处。整个经济的不景气也使那些投资过于分散的企业无法再继续为处于不同产业的企业提供发展、甚至是维持的资金。因此，西方国家的企业开始出售或剥离那些与企业主要业务完全无关的业务部分，重新回到集中战略或一业为主的战略，掀起了"返回核心"的热潮。因此，我国的旅游企业在决定是否采取混合一体化战略时应该慎重，至少需要考虑的问题有：

首先，企业是否具有进入新业务的技术和管理经验。尽管混合一体化能使企业进入比原有业务更有市场发展潜力的产业，从而扩大企业的销售量和利润量，提高企业的发展速度。但是在这些新行业中，企业可能缺乏经验和应付困难局面的技能。

其次，公司是否具有协调各项不同业务的能力。由于通过混合一体化组成的企业内各项业务之间缺乏战略上的一致性和协调性，使得企业总体经营效果并不一定会比各个业务经营效果之和要好。更有甚者，公司的集中管理政策会妨碍各项业务潜力的最大发挥，从而压抑了各项业务的发展。例如，为了支持某项业务的发展，要求其他业务提供资金和资源，而一旦该项业务不能实现公司要求的发展目标时，无疑就影响了整个公司。

最后，混合一体化所产生的效应能否足以弥补由业务多样化带来的管理成本的增加。从理论上讲，混合一体化由于进入不同的业务领域，从而能使企业获得最大的业务平衡性，分散经营风险。但事实上通过混合一体化平衡业务周期的目的很难实现，而由此引起的管理困难和混乱的风险并不一定就比投资单一的风险要小。20世纪80年代后期出现的大企业病不能不说是混合一体化的结果。由此出现了许多大企业再度集中、回归原主要业务的浪潮，即从混合一体化到归核化。

因此，我国的旅游企业在实行混合一体化时要充分考虑各种因素，在综合平衡的基础上做出决策，切不可盲目冒进，从而影响旅游企业的长远和持续发展。

四、企业一体化战略的新动向(New Trends in Corporate Integration)

随着科学技术的发展，企业的发展环境发生了重大的变化，企业的发展战略也将面临新的挑战。一些新的企业经营发展战略和模式不断出现，将给企业的传统发展战略带来巨大的冲击，企业的一体化战略将会因环境的变化而出现新的发展形式。

1. 供应链管理与一体化战略(Supply Chain Management and Integration Strategy)

进入90年代以来，供应链管理(Supply Chain Management，简称SCM)已为企业界所关注。世界权威的《财富》杂志就将供应链管理能力作为企业一种重要的战略竞争资源。在全球经济一体化和信息技术迅猛发展的今天，企业间的合作正日益加强，它们之间跨地区乃至跨国合作经营的趋势日益明显。企业往往从供应链的角度来考虑企业的整个生产经营活动，从而形成核心竞争能力。

Since its inception in the early 1990's, the field of supply chain management has become tremendously important to companies in an increasingly competitive global marketplace. The term supply chain refers to the entire network of companies that work together to design, produce, deliver, and service products. A supply chain essentially has three main parts, the supply, manufacturing and distribution. The supply side concentrates on how, where from and when raw materials are procured and supplied to manufacturing. Manufacturing converts these raw materials to finished products and distribution ensures that these finished products reach the final customers through a network of distributors, warehouses and retailers. In the past, companies focused primarily on manufacturing and quality improvements within their four walls; now their efforts extend beyond those walls to encompass the entire supply chain.

Supply chain management flows can be divided into three main flows: (1) the product flow, (2) the information flow (3) the finances flow. The product flow includes the movement of goods from a supplier to a customer, as well as any customer returns or service needs. The information flow involves transmitting orders and updating the status of delivery. The financial flow consists of credit terms, payment schedules, and consignment and title ownership arrangements.

There are two main types of SCM: planning applications and execution applications. Planning applications use advanced algorithms to determine the best way to fill an order. Execution applications track the physical status of goods, the management of materials, and financial information involving all parties.

Some SCM applications are based on open data models that support the sharing of data both inside and outside the enterprise (this is called the extended enterprise, and includes key suppliers, manufacturers, and end customers of a specific company). This shared data may reside in diverse database systems, or data warehouses, at several different sites and companies. By sharing this data "upstream" (with a company's suppliers) and "downstream" (with a company's clients), SCM applications have the potential to improve the time-to-market of products, reduce costs, and allow all parties in the supply chain to better manage current resources and plan for future needs.

Increasing numbers of companies are turning to Web sites and Web-based applications as part of the SCM solution. A number of major Web sites offer e-procurement marketplaces where manufacturers can trade and even make auction bids with suppliers.

供应链管理是对整个供应链中各参与者之间的物流、信息流、资金流进行计划、协调和控制。其目的是通过优化提高所有相关过程的速度和确定性，最大化所有相关过程的净增加值，提高组织的运作效率和效益。随着供应链管理的重视和加强，传统的一体化战略，尤其是垂直一体化战略将受到很大冲击。因为传统的垂直一体化战略是通过对企业原材料供应或产成品销售行业的并购或投资来实现的，这需要投入大量的资本，实现紧密联合，风险较大。而供应链中的各个组织的关系较为松散，供应链管理是通过对业务链中的各个参与者进行信息和技术控制来达到的，投资少、风险小，比传统的垂直一体化战略具有更大的优势。对于我国的旅游企业来说，通过旅游企业之间的联合实行旅游服务项目的供应链管理是提高旅游企业竞争力的有效途径。

2. 虚拟经营与一体化战略(Virtual Management and Integration Strategy)

虚拟经营是近几年来迅速发展的一种新型的企业经营管理模式。它是指在有限的资源条件下，为了取得竞争中的最大优势，仅保留企业中最关键的功能，而将其他的功能虚拟化，即通过各种方式借助外力进行整合弥补。其目的是在竞争中最大效率地发挥企业有限的资源。

The virtual organization had its beginnings 15-20 years ago as people began to see the possibility of using technology for work at home. What began as a vision of futurists has become a possibility for business theorists and an economic necessity for corporate executives. All of this occurred in little more than a decade, underscoring an inevitability of this new business model as well as hinting at the sped-up sense of time that characterizes it. The virtual organization carries the concept of flexible specialization a step further than the dynamic network organization, because it is not limited by physical locations or by complex contractual arrangements. Corporations are evolving into virtual enterprises using integrated computer and communications technologies to link hundreds, thousands, even tens of thousands of people together. These collaborative networks are not defined by concrete walls or physical space, but make it possible to draw upon vital resources as needed, regardless of where they are physically located and regardless of who owns them. This does not mean that these organizations have no physical space that they occupy, merely that the physical location need not be a fixed site. Solid, traditionally defined, and sharply delineated companies are evolving into virtual organizations with structures and systems that are loose and fuzzy, so they can assume whatever form is needed to respond to a rapidly changing marketplace.

Virtual organizations are the result of a competitive push to deliver these virtual products. For an entity or object to be virtual used to mean that it possessed powers or capabilities of another entity or object. Now the term means that previously well-defined structures begin to lose their edges, seemingly permanent things start to change continuously, and products and services adapt to match our desires. Virtual products, whether goods or services, mostly exist even before they are produced. They can be made available at any time, in any place, and in any variety; but they can only be offered because of the latest innovations in information processing, organizational dynamics, and manufacturing systems. Virtual products delivered instant customer gratification in a cost-effective way, can be produced in diverse locations and offered in a great number of models or formats, and ideally are produced instantaneously, customized to the customer's request. A new kind of company is necessary to produce and distribute this new kind of product, one that can control ever more sophisticated types of information and master new organizational and production skills.

Virtual organizations are likely to be reliant on cyberspace (the medium in which electronic communications flow and software operates); can be enabled by new computing and communications developments; and can initially exist only across conventional organizational structures. Four different versions of the virtual organization have been identified:

- **Telecommuting.** With telecommuting, or homeworking, employees use a remote terminal to access their office system.
- **Hot-desk environment.** In a hot desk environment, individual desks are abandonded. Employees arriving at work are allocated a desk for the day from which they can access their electronic mails and computer network files.
- **Hotelling.** Hotelling acknowledges the fact that many workers have no need of a permanent desk at their parent company. Instead, they spend much of their working lives with clients, using client facilities much like a hotel.
- **Virtual teams.** By working in virtual teams, people collaborate closely but may be physically located in a variety of locations.

Along with these changes to organizational structure, Information System must also make adjustments to bring crucial information instantly to the right decision maker and then transmit the decision back through the network just as quickly.

虚拟经营的基本特点是:(1)虚拟公司的成员之间,可以借助合作关系降低部分人事、机器设备、研究开发和管理方面的成本。由于企业机构的简化,从而进一步提升了企业的经营效率。(2)虚拟公司的相关企业间是独立的运营关系,每个企业拥有相当大的弹性。例如在旅游市场景气时,企业不必投入大规模的固定资本,即可迅速扩大服务范围;而在旅游市场不景气时,各个企业能够配合本身的条件,迅速调整经营范围,实现资源重组,从而避免大量的固定资产及人员的闲置,减轻与缓和经营方面的风险。(3)由于企业与企业之间的长期合作而建立的了解和信赖,较容易取得关键资源。(4)企业用虚拟公司将其内部的劣势功能外部化,本身只从事最专业的活动,能使自己比竞争对手为顾客创造更多、更新的价值,以满足不同层次的不同顾客的多样化需求。

虚拟经营的发展使传统的一体化战略可能向虚拟一体化发展,将供应和销售链上各个环节的企业通过信息技术实现资源共享,使得企业与企业之间传统的界限变得模糊。从更为宏观的角度看,这些若干联系起来的企业组成了一个更大的虚拟企业。实现虚拟的一体化经营,是在信息技术基础上形成的一类由多个独立的企业通过股份以外的手段构成相对稳定的产品和服务分工协作体系,因而是无形的一体化。虚拟一体化的实质是最大限度地保留产品协作关系中的有利因素,同时又充分利用信息技术有效地降低利用市场的协调成本和交易成本。

第二节　旅游企业一体化战略的实现途径(1):并购
(Way of Fulfilling Tourism Corporation Strategy:(1) Merger & Acquisition)

一、并购(merger & acquisition)是旅游企业实现一体化战略的有效途径(Merger & Acquisition is an Effective Way to Realize Integration Strategy for Tourism Corporation)

企业成长的途径主要有两种:一种是内部成长,企业主要利用内部资源,靠自己积累的资源或筹集的资金投资建厂、成立新的经济单位获得发展;另一种是外部成长,企业主要通过兼并、收购或合并其他企业而获得成长。

内部成长与外部成长都能实现企业一体化战略目标。但从企业内部发展新业务、进入新产业,从而实现规模扩张这一方式需要经过周密的调查、建立和形成新的生产能力、寻找生产投入品的供应商、建立配销渠道和用户信誉等一系列耗时、耗资、耗力的过程。因此,在决定是否采取内部成长方式时,企业需要考虑以下一些因素:一是企业是否有足够的财力形成最基本的有效生产规模,有效生产规模是否能实现经济效益的最低生产规模;二是企业是否有能力克服进入新产业的障碍;三是企业是否有能力抵御产业内其他企业的排斥行动,例如,现有旅游企业是否会共同采取削价政策等;四是新业务能提供的利润及现金流量。只有当新产业经营的利润量高于平均利润水平,现有企业的排斥行动力量较弱,进入新产业的成本较低,进入新产业后能提高企业的竞争力和市场地位,同时新产业尚处于发展阶段时,企业才会愿意经过长时间的努力,依靠企业内部的发展形成新的生产能力。可见,通过内部成长方式发展成大企业比较困难。在这里,我们主要讨论企业如何通过外部成长方式特别是并购方式扩大规模,形成一体化经营大企业的。

并购是企业进入新业务领域的最方便、最直接、需要时间最短的途径,是在经济增长速度缓慢时期提高生产率、降低成本的好办法。并购也是最简单的扩大事业的手段。通过并购,企业不但在生产技术方面,而且在流通渠道上也可以全盘接收对自己有用的部分。并购对于被出售的企业也可以是有益的,因为按较为有利的价格出售本企业的股票,可以使原股东的利益得到更好的保护。在成熟的产业里,为了职工和股东的切身利益,需要采用多角化经营来实现企业自身的发展,这同样要求企业进行并购。并购已成为成熟经济的代表性经营方式。

二、并购的经济效应分析(Economic Effect Analysis of Merger & Acquisition)

A corporate merger is the combination of the assets and liabilities of two firms to form a single business entity. In ordinary life, the term "acquisition" tends to be used when a larger firm absorbs a smaller firm, and "merger" tends to be used when the combination is between equals. In a merger of firms which are approximate equals, there is often an exchange of stock in which one firm issues new shares to the shareholders of the other firm at a certain ratio. For the sake of this discussion, the firm whose shares continue to exist (possibly under a different company name) will be referred to as the acquiring firm and the firm whose shares are being replaced by the acquiring firm will be referred to as the target firm.

Excluding any synergies which result from the merger, the total post-merger value of the two firms is equal to the pre-merger value. However, the post-merger value of each individual firm will likely be different from the pre-merger value, because the exchange ratio of the shares probably will not reflect the firms' values exactly with respect to one another. The exchange ratio is skewed because the target firm's shareholders are paid a premium for their shares.

Synergy takes the form of revenue enhancement and cost savings. When two companies are in the same industry merge, the revenue will decline to the extent that the businesses overlap. There should be cost saving opportunities to offset the revenue decline.

For the merger make sense of the acquiring firm's shareholders, the synergies resulting from the merger must be more than the initial lost value. The minimum required synergies are found to solve the synergies in the following equation:

$$\frac{\text{(pre-merger value of both firms + synergies)}}{\frac{\text{stock price}}{\text{post-merger number of shares}}} = \text{pre-merger stock price}$$

where the pre-merger stock price refers to the price of the acquiring firm.

The success of a merger is measured by whether the value of the acquiring firm is enhanced by it. The practical aspects of mergers often prevent the forecasted benefits from being fully realized and the expected synergy may fall short expectations.

具体来说,并购对企业的有利影响主要有:

1. 通过企业并购活动,有利于实现企业一体化经营的协同效应。所谓协同效应(synergy)是公司兼并与收购过程中追求的目标,合并后的企业实现总体绩效超过原来分散企业的绩效之和,即 $1+1>2$。它可以给企业规模带来以下好处:(1)企业可以通过并购对工厂的资产进行补充和调整,达到最佳经济规模的要求,使工厂保持尽可能低的生产成本。(2)并购还能够使企业在保持整体产品结构情况下,在各个分厂中实现产品单一化生产,避免由于产品品种的转换带来的生产时间的浪费,可以集中在一个企业中大量进行单一品种生产,从而达到专业化生产的要求。(3)在某些场合中,企业并购又能够解决由于专业化带来的一系列问题。由于科学技术发展,在很多领域中要求连续化生产。在这些部门,各生产流程之间的密切配合有着极其重要的意义。企业通过并购,特别是纵向兼并,可以有效地解决由于专业化引起的各生产流程分离。将它们纳入同一企业中,可以减少生产过程中的环节间隔,降低操作成本、运输成本,充分利用生产能力。同时,通过并购将许多工厂置于同一企业领导之下,可以实现企业规模经济。主要表现为:(1)节省管理费用。由于中、高层管理费用将在更大量的产品中分摊,单位产品的管理费用可大大降低。(2)多厂企业可以对不同需要的顾客进行专门化生产,更好地满足不同顾客的不同需要。而这些不同的产品和服务可以利用同一销售渠道来推销,利用相同的技术扩散来生产,达到节约营销费用的效果。(3)可以集中足够的经费用于 R&D,改进生产工艺,迅速推出新产品,采用新技术。(4)企业规模的相对扩大,使企业的直接筹资和借贷都比较容易。它们有充足的财务能力采用各种新发明、新设备、新技术,适应环境变化的要求。

2. 并购往往比通过内部投资新建方式能够更有效地扩大生产能力。这是因为:(1)并购有效地降低了进入新行业的壁垒。并购可以减少企业进入新行业的成本劣势,以及在产品差异、建立销售渠道等方面的不利因素。(2)并购可大幅度降低企业发展的风险和成本。通过投资新建的方法增加企业的生产能力,往往需要花费大量的人力和物力去寻找原材料和销售渠道,涉及更多的不确定性,相应的投入和风险均较大。但在并购的情况下,企业可以利用被并购企业的原料来源、销售渠道和已占有的市场,可以大幅度减少发展过程中的不确定性,降低风险和成本。(3)运用并购发展的另一巨大优势就是取得经验——成本曲线效应。因为当企业进入一个新行业时,由于对生产作业的方法、专用设备和技术的应用、市场规律的把握等缺少经验,成本和风险都较大。而当企业通过并购发展时,不但获得了原有企业的生产能力和各种资产,还获得了原有企业的经验,从而大大降低生产经营成本。经验—成本曲线效应尤其对混合并购有着特别重要的作用。因为混合并购往往需要进入一些新的经营领域。在这些领域中,经验往往是一种有效的进入壁垒。而通过混合并购,混合一体化企业的各部分可以实现经验分享,形成一种有力的竞争优势。

3. 通过并购,企业的份额可得以扩大,可以使企业获得某种形式的垄断,它可给企业带来垄断利益和竞争优势。就通过并购增强对市场的控制能力的效果来看,横向兼并的效果最为明显。纵向兼并次之。混合兼并的作用是间接的。具体来说:

(1)横向兼并对于行业结构的影响表现为:①减少竞争数量,改善行业结构。并购可使行业集中度提高,当行业相对集中于一家或少数几家企业时,能有效地降低竞争的激烈程度,使行业内所有企业均能保持较高的利润率。②解决了行业整体生产能力扩大速度和市场扩大速度不一致的矛盾。在规模经济支配下,企业不得不大量增加生产能力才能提高生产效率,但企业扩大生产能力往往是与需求的增加不一致的,从而破坏供求平衡关系,使行业面临生产能力过剩的问题。实行企业并购,使行业内部企业相对集中,既能实现规模经济的要求,又能避免生产能力的盲目增加。③横向兼并降低了行业的退出壁垒。由于某些行业的资产具有高度的专业性,并且固定资产占较大比重,从而这些行业中的企业很难退出该领域,有时只能顽强地维持下去,致使行业内过剩的生产能力无法减少,整个行业的平均利润保持在较低水平。通过兼并和被兼并,行业可调整其内部结构,将低效和陈旧的生产设备淘汰,解决了退出壁垒成本过高的问题,达到稳定供求关系、稳定价格的目的。

(2)纵向兼并是将企业关键性的投入—产出关系纳入控制范围,以行政手段而非市场手段处理一些业务,达到提高企业对市场控制能力的一种方法。它主要通过对原料和销售渠道及用户的控制来实现目的。

纵向兼并使企业明显提高了与供应商和买主之间讨价还价的能力。这种讨价还价的能力主要是由买卖双方的行业结构，以及它们之间的相对重要程度决定的。企业通过纵向合并，降低了供应商和买主的重要性，特别是当纵向兼并与行业集中趋势相结合时，能极大地提高企业的讨价还价能力。当然，纵向兼并往往会导致"连锁"反应。一个控制了大量关键原料或销售渠道的企业，可以通过对原料和销售渠道的控制，有力地控制竞争对手的活动。因此，即使是垂直一体化不存在明显的经济效益，为防止被竞争对手控制，当一家企业率先实行纵向兼并时，其余企业出于防卫的目的，也必须考虑实行垂直一体化，这是经济学上的"寡占"反应。

(3) 混合兼并的市场优势往往是隐性的。在多数情况下，企业通过混合兼并，往往进入与原有产品相关的经营领域。在这些领域，它们使用与主要产品一致的原料、技术、管理规律或销售渠道。这方面规模的扩大，使企业对原有供应商和销售渠道的控制加强了，从而提高了企业对主要产品市场的控制。另一方面，企业通过混合兼并增加了绝对规模，使企业拥有相对充足的财力，可与原市场或新市场上的竞争者进行价格战，采用低于成本的定价方法迫使竞争者退出某一领域，从而达到独占或垄断的目的。

The benefits and rewards of a successful merger or acquisition can be very lucrative. Economies of scale, increased efficiencies, entrance into new markets, new core competencies, and greater reach into existing markets are just the tip of the iceberg when companies successfully merge. But in today's economic situation, corporations need to take their blinders off and take a close look at the risks involved before, during, and after a merger.

In our increasingly competitive world, mergers and acquisitions are often the answer to getting ahead. But the downside is that it's not easy integrating two or more organizations, much less gaining top efficiency and productivity. That's why half of all mergers and acquisitions fail to produce the returns expected. One of the biggest and potentially most destructive risks of M&A activity is not knowing enough about the other company. Cultural issues, process issues, and data issues can all be compounded exponentially if an M&A is done with an incompatible firm. All of these issues will be present, even in the most successful mergers, but the key to success is preparing for the problems you will be facing and to what extent these problems will cause.

Many mergers and acquisitions never reap the promised benefits and expectations that are promised. Experts in M&A activity, have identified six aspects of M&A on which to concentrate.

- **M&A Strategy**—A firm must align its M&A strategy and overall corporate strategy with clearly defined objectives.
- **Strategic Alliances**—A firm must always be evaluating alternatives to M&A.
- **Pricing**—A firm must evaluate business needs and financial objectives in determining the target company's value.
- **Strategic Due Diligence**—A firm must always dig deeper than just the numbers.
- **Post-Merger Integration**—A firm must have a strategy in place to deal with cultural, financial, process, organizational, and data issues.
- **Measuring Success**—A firm must establish relevant criteria upfront in order to truly measure success.

三、中国旅游企业如何通过并购方式实现一体化(How China Tourism Companies Achieve Incorporation through Acquisition)

当前,我国旅游企业在实施并购战略时,必须围绕使资本、技术、人才和市场份额不断地、快速地向优势企业集中,缩短优势企业的大型化过程这一目标。当前我国旅游企业在并购活动中要注意:(1)要围绕着企业的发展战略进行并购。企业的并购必须明确主业,围绕主业进行并购和资产重组活动。过分强调并购活动,把企业做大,把资产规模、销售额搞上去,为并购而并购,为享受政策优惠而并购是不足取的。(2)要立足优势互补。旅游企业寻找并购对象的标准首先是符合企业的发展战略,与并购企业达到优势互补。(3)要全面计算并购成本。整个并购成本不仅包括前期的谈判、合同签订和执行成本,还包括并购后的技术改造、网络建设、组织结构的整合和人事调整、资源再配置等资产重组成本。(4)要重视并购后的整合。购并成功与否不在于把企业并过来,而在于能否将所有成员企业加以整合,使之相互协调,互相补充,形成合力。

总之,企业并购重组仅仅是一种手段,并购的目的在于实现旅游企业的一体化经营,从而,使社会资源向优势企业集中,并塑造更具活力和具有国际市场竞争力的大企业。因此,目前我国旅游企业并购的取向是:

1. 在并购行为上,采取大力鼓励和扶持横向并购为主,适当扶持部分大企业纵向并购为辅,限制混合并购。大力鼓励横向并购行为主要是因为:(1)从西方的企业并购史来看,横向并购具有操作简单、并购风险小、并购双方生产要素的融合快等优势,有利于迅速降低企业生产经营成本,促进企业管理效率的提高,对增强我国旅游企业的实力有重要意义。(2)横向并购可以减少竞争者数量,实现规模经济,提高行业集中度,而这正是解决目前我国旅游企业规模不经济、能力利用不充分,由盲目投资、重复建设所造成的地区产业结构严重趋同化的有效方法。而采取适当扶持部分大企业纵向并购,是因为大企业的国际竞争力是一个国家综合经济实力的体现。在全球经济一体化和国际贸易自由化进程加快的情况下,通过适当扶持部分大企业的纵向并购行为,可以使这些企业实现供、产、销一体化,尽快积累特定领域的技术、专业人才和经营技能,扩大企业及其产品的影响范围,强化市场应变能力,为参与和提高我国旅游企业的国际竞争能力创造条件。采取限制混合并购行为,主要是由于:(1)正在席卷西方各国的第五次并购浪潮表明,混合的行业并购行为虽然能扩大企业的绝对规模,但对提高企业存量资产使用效率、优化企业结构、增强企业的国际竞争力作用不大。(2)混合的行业并购行为增加了企业的并购成本,主要表现为:造成机制重叠,增加管理成本;扩大不相关业务范围,增加运营成本;造成市场分散,增加销售成本;造成企业各部分互补性减弱,增加合作成本等。(3)混合并购行为很难把企业部分整合为一体,容易造成各部门之间的磨合困难,不利于企业协调发展。

2. 在并购模式上,可采取强强并购为主、强弱并购和弱弱并购为辅的取向。从提高我国旅游企业国际竞争力和在我国产业整合中的作用来看,中小企业间的弱弱并购模式虽然从长期看能够扩大企业规模,增强企业实力,逐步提高企业的国际竞争力,但在整合我国产业中的作用有限。中小型企业并购大中型企业的弱弱并购模式,一般都具有投机性。从世界各国的企业并购史看,这种并购模式在提高国际竞争力和产业整合中的作用更为有限。因此,弱弱并购模式和弱强并购模式都不应是我国旅游企业并购的主导模式。而大中型企业兼并或收购中小企业的强弱并购模式能在较短时期内扩大企业规模、增强企业实力,直接整合我国的旅游产业,因此是我国可以考虑采用的并购模式。但由于这种模式下的并购规模相对较小,在短期内很难起到提高我国旅游企业竞争力和整合产业的作用。因此,大中型企业间的强强并购,不仅能在短期内增强企业实力,而且还能对优化我国旅游产业结构起重要作用。

3. 在并购主体上,放手国有企业的并购行为,积极鼓励股份制企业和民营企业的并购行为。目前国有企业客观上在我国经济中处于主导地位,其行业结构的调整要依靠政府的支持,但当前政府要在明晰产权、明确定位、转变角色、转变职能的基础上,放松对国有企业的非市场控制,让企业根据自身的发展,更多地通过市场的力量,以一体化为目标进行并购活动。同时,对股份制企业和民营企业的并购活动给予积极的支持和鼓励。一是因为近年来我国民营企业发展迅速、股份制企业也有了较好的发展,它们在我国经济中将占据越来越重要的地位;二是因为这些企业的产权关系相对较清楚,有利于并购的正常进行。

4. 在兼并地域上,采取地域内的企业先并购,然后地域间企业并购的取向。这里所指的地域是以大中城市为核心形成的经济圈。如华东地区以上海、南京为中心形成长江三角洲经济圈,华北地区则是以北京、天津为中心形成京津经济圈。从旅游产业整合的角度看,我国地域性强强并购、强弱并购和弱弱并购应首先在经济圈内进行。通过经济圈内的企业并购,不仅可以消除经济圈内各地区产业结构同化问题,更重要的是能够把各经济圈内的企业通过并购机制联合成一个整体,首先实现各经济圈内的产业整合。目前,围绕经济圈展开的旅游企业间的强强并购在我国部分地区已初露端倪。在经济圈内的企业通过兼并联合成为一个整体后,如果条件具备,还可以进一步进行跨经济圈的旅游企业间的强强并购,并最终在我国旅游行业形成几家具有国际竞争力的世界级的大企业。

第三节 旅游企业一体化战略的实现途径(2)：联合(Realization Approach of Tourism Companies Incorporation Strategy：(2) Union)

一、联合与并购的区别(Difference Between Union and Acquisition)

联合是指两个或两个以上企业为了抵御风险或实现互利的目的而共同投资开发某个项目或分享信息及其他资源所结成的合作关系。联合是一种与并购相比较更为松散的实现一体化战略的有效途径。企业兼并和收购是指一个企业购买其他企业的产权，使其他企业失去法人资格或改变法人实体的一种行为。可见，兼并和收购涉及产权的变化，而两个或两个以上企业的联合一般不改变产权关系。通过兼并和收购，一个企业吞并另一个企业，被并购企业不复存在。而两个企业进行联合后，仍是两个企业。因此，联合相对于并购来说，有以下优点：(1)对企业的资本要求较低。由于企业之间的联合不是通过购买其他企业的产权实现，因此对企业的资本要求较低。(2)关系松散，弹性大。(3)企业的退出壁垒小。(4)操作的障碍较小。(5)在技术和信息日益发展的今天，联合有着更广泛的发展前景。如虚拟联合。当然，相对于并购来说，联合也存在合作各方的关系松散，协同效应不明显等不足。

二、旅游企业一体化的主要途径：组建企业集团(Chief Approach of Tourism Companies Incorporation：Building Corporate Group)

企业联合可分为组建企业集团和建立企业间分工协作关系两种基本形式。从当前来看，组建企业集团是形成大型旅游企业的重要途径。

企业集团是一种以资产和业务为联结纽带，带有多层次结构的高水平的企业联合体。在发达国家，企业集团是主要的企业组织形式，在经济中占有重要的地位。在国际竞争中领先的企业几乎无一不是以企业集团形式出现的。目前培育企业集团对抑制我国旅游业中普遍存在的过度竞争，实现规模经济具有重要的现实意义。首先，企业集团是通过现有企业之间的合并与联合来扩大组织规模从而实现规模经济的，这种规模经济是一种内涵扩大再生产的规模经济。因为处于低水平过度竞争状态的企业不仅达不到经济规模要求，而且存在大量闲置的生产资源。因此，无论是提供同类产品的若干企业加入企业集团，还是有着不同经营方式的若干企业加入企业集团,都会实现生产经营规模的扩张,通过减少企业过度竞争所造成的磨擦而形成协作,在不追加新投资的条件下,提高原有资源的使用效率,实现规模经济。其次,培育企业集团是冲破条块分割,消除地方与部门行政垄断的主要手段。企业集团可以由不同地区和部门的企业联合而成,能以其经济实力打破各地区、各部门的自我封锁、相互分割的垄断状况。同时,通过扩大市场范围而实现规模经济。再次,当一个产业存在的企业大多加入到某些集团后,集团组织本身构成了一个产业进入壁垒,集团组织的协调使集团内各个企业形成的规模经济又形成一个进入产业规模经济壁垒。总之,企业集团的建立和发展对于旅游市场结构和市场效率将产生重大影响。

三、旅游企业一体化的有效形式:战略联盟(Effective Formation of Tourism Companies Incorporation: Strategic Alliance)

Corporations have increasingly seen alliances as attractive vehicles through which they can grow and expand their scope, and the rate at which interfirm alliances have been formed in the last two decades has been unprecedented. A notable characteristic of this growth has been the increasing diversity of interfirm alliances. The nationalities of partners, their motives and goals in entering alliances, and the formal structures used to organize the partnerships have all become increasingly varied. The variety of organizing structures implies that firms face numerous choices in structuring their alliances.

旅游企业通过联合实现一体化的另一种有效形式是战略联盟(strategic alliance)。战略联盟是指两个以上的企业出于对总体市场的预期目标和企业自身总体经营目标的意愿,采取一种长期性联合与合作的经营行为。它是一种专业化分工协作关系的联合,相对于组建企业集团而言,其程度较为松散。战略联盟的主要特征是:联合是出于自发的、非强制性的;联盟各方仍保持着本公司经营管理的独立性和自主经营权,彼此依靠相互间达成的协议联结成松散型的整体。战略性联盟的主要形式有:战略性的合资企业;相互持股投资;功能性协议等。

An alliance is commonly defined as any voluntarily initiated cooperative agreement between firms that involves exchange, sharing, or co-development, and it can include contributions by partners of capital, technology, or firm-specific assets. The governance structure of the alliance is the formal contractual structure participants used to formalize it. Researchers has distinguished from such formal structures in terms of the degree of hierarchical elements they embodied and the extent to which they replicate the control and coordination features associated with organizations, which are considered to be at the hierarchical end of the spectrum. On one side are joint ventures, which involve partners creating a new entity in which they share equity and that most closely replicate the hierarchical control features of organizations, on the other side are alliances with no sharing of equity that have few hierarchical controls built into them.

战略联盟的优势在于：(1)以最快的速度和最低的成本进入市场。(2)合作企业之间优势互补,利益均沾。(3)有助于联盟各方涉足新的业务领域,实行集团多用化经营。(4)获得关键性技术。从目前的情况来看,近几年的企业间的战略联盟的主要特点有：(1) While alliance use is appearing across many industries, the spread of alliances seems especially prevalent in the high-technology industries, where both the number of alliances and the average value per alliance have been increased steadily. (2) These alliances tend to focus on the transfer of knowledge and technology in industries characterized by rapid change in both structure and competitive dynamics. Indeed, an emerging management view is that firms can no longer develop, manufacture, and market products on their own, and alliances are a means to gain access to complementary resources and capabilities they lack. (3) technology complementarity, innovation time-span reduction, market access, and market structure influence are the most mentioned motives behind technology alliances. Other motives behind alliance formation in volatile, high-tech industries include: the immense costs of developing the technology, uncertainty in terms of emerging technologies, the convergence of several industry segments, and a "follow the herd" mentality. Although it seems to be an increase in the number of alliances formed, at the same time, there is also evidence that strategic alliances are underperforming.

Alliance partners can be suppliers, customers, complementors, competitors, or others (i.e., a partner outside the industry).

Researchers use the term of competition to describe the multiple roles of a partner, and how a partner may simultaneously be both a competitor and complementor to a firm. In fact, this seems to be occurring with respect to alliance formations in practice: over 50 percent of organizations surveyed today admit that they are partnering with competitors. If we extend the notion of partner role to alliance formations, we can investigate why firms form alliances with their competitors, complementors, suppliers, and customers.

The issue of value creation through alliance structures has received significant attention over the years. One perspective that addresses this value question is called the relational view of the firm. The relational view of the firm argues that a firm's critical resources may extend to its boundaries, and the firms that combine resources in unique ways with alliance partners may realize a competitive advantage over competing firms. The firm's network of alliance partners is the important unit of analysis, and network positioning is the key performance issue. A strong network position provides the firm with competitive advantage. The relational view differs from the more traditional perspectives of the firm, such as the resource-based view of the firm and capabilities view of the firm, which describe competitive advantage as an outcome of resources and capabilities residing within the firm.

战略联盟要求共担责任,相互协调,要求精心设计各类活动的时间衔接,因而模糊了公司的界限,使联盟后的企业组织为着一个共同的目标采取一致的行动。但有一点,联盟伙伴之间既是合作关系又是竞争关系。虽然联盟伙伴在部分领域中进行合作,但在协议之外的领域以及在公司活动整体态势上仍保持着经营管理的独立自主,相互间仍是竞争对手。

四、我国旅游企业间联合的发展趋向(Developing Trend of China Tourism Companies' Union)

通过企业联合,实现旅游企业一体化经营,从而使企业竞争从无序走向有序、从分散走向集中、从过度竞争变为适度竞争,实现规模经济效应,要求旅游企业间的联合向以下方向发展:

1. 从行政性联合到经济性联合。我国目前许多旅游企业联合体(包括企业集团)主要是用行政手段捏合的,缺乏凝聚力。有不少旅游企业集团是行政公司的翻牌,在组织形式上维持着政企合一,在管理上也明显带有隶属色彩。因此,我国旅游企业的联合要真正达到优化产业结构、培育大企业的目标,必须打破行政束缚、条块分割的局面,按照经济发展的规律、市场运行规则和企业自身利益的发展需要,自发地建立企业之间的联合。政府要为旅游企业的联合创造良好的环境,应通过政策引导规范企业的联合。

2. 从弱弱联合到强强联合。当前,要提高我国旅游企业的国际竞争力,仅靠弱弱联合是不够的。当今世界强强联合的趋势十分明显,我国旅游企业的规模本来就很小,在这基础上进行的弱弱联合,虽然可以起到联小为大,缓和过度竞争的局面,但离培育具有国际竞争力的大企业目标还很遥远。因此,目前应着重引导和推动大企业之间的联合。

3. 从联合走向兼并,实现从经营联合到资产联合、从资产联合到资本联合。目前,我国许多旅游企业联合没有实行资本联合,未利用股份制形式组建联合体,这样的联合关系非常脆弱,有相当一部分企业联合体成立不久即告解体。究其原因主要是靠比较松散的协作关系作为联结的纽带。如有的联合体是通过行政权力作为纽带,当行政权力减弱或丧失时,联合体就会随之解体;有的联合体将经济合同或技术协作作为联结的纽带,当市场供求发生变化时,就会产生"劳燕分飞"的现象。目前我国大多数旅游企业联合仍停留在经营联合上;没有足以使成员凝聚在一起的资本联结纽带。因此,旅游企业要真正实现联合,要从经营联合走向资产联合。可能的话,要在联合的基础上进一步走向兼并,实现资产重组,从资产联合走向资本联合。

4. 从本地区的联合到跨地区乃至跨国联合,建立具有中国特色的旅游企业集团。开展国际间的经济联合,建立跨国企业集团是社会分工从国内分工发展到国际分工的内在要求。尤其当前在全球经济一体化的进程中,我国旅游企业更要抓住机遇,通过开展一体化国际经营,将经营体系向国际市场延伸,这对于提高我国旅游企业的国际竞争力具有重要的战略意义。

总之,无论旅游企业间是采取并购还是联合的形式,其目的都在于通过实施一体化战略,提高产业的集中度,培育具有国际竞争力的大规模企业。

第四节 旅游企业的纵向控制行为
(Vertical Control of Tourism Corporations)

旅游企业除了一体化之外,在企业与企业之间还存在着技术上的纵向关系,并且可以按照投入的方向分为上游企业和下游企业,下游企业把上游企业的产品作为投入。但下游企业的行为会影响到上游企业的利润。为了克服这里的外部性,上游企业有控制下游企业决策的动机。控制的程度是可以不同的,当然存在着部分的控制,但如果上游企业控制了其所在的纵向结构中所作出的全部决策,我们就说该企业是纵向一体的(vertically integrated)。但是需要注意的是在考察纵向控制问题时,需要和纵向一体化概念相区分。原因在于纵向一体化是从所有权角度来说的。但是我们需要知道的是,在一种特定的所有权结构下,由于信息不对称仍然会出现激励性的授权,这意味着并没有实现全部的控制,而在信息重复的条件下,没有所有权的安排同样可以通过契约实现全部控制,如果这些决策参数不仅可以观测而且可以证实。在这部分的分析中,我们最需要注意的是为了比较纵向控制和分散决策的差异,我们要构造纵向一体化的解,这个解被称为纵向一体解(vertically integrated solution),这是比较分析的最重要的基准(benchmark)。

一、基本概念与框架(Basic Concept and Frame)

首先需要理解的是,上下游本身构成的是一对交易关系,而交易关系的最简单的情况是线性定价,即买者的支付与购买数量成比例。而纵向关系常常包含更为复杂的合约内容,这些合约安排通常可以称为纵向约束(vertical restraints)。是从非线性的收费方式到限制品牌内竞争和品牌间竞争的手段。

设一个旅游企业具有垄断地位,以不变的单位成本 c 生产一种中间产品,一个下游企业拥有一种技术可以把一个单位的中间产品转化为一个单位的最终产品。以 p_w 表示中间价格,p 表示消费者价格或者说最终价格。以 q 表示下游企业所购买的数量,并假设全部销售给最终的消费者。消费者的需求函数表示为 $q=D(p)$。

上游企业和下游企业之间的常见的契约关系有以下几种。

第一种,线性价格契约 $T(q)=p_w q$,产量由下游企业选择,而价格由上游企业选择。

第二种，二部定价，$T(q)=A+p_w q$，A 为特许费。例如销售特许费。

第三种，转卖价格持平 RPM（resale-price maintenance），在契约中就下游企业最终价格的选择作出限定的一种规定，并且有最高限价和最低限价两种。

第四种，数量定额（quantity fixing）。规定下游企业购买的数量，同样可以分为数量强销（quantity forcing）和数量配给（quantity rationing）两种。显然这两种方法具有等价关系，数量强销等价于价格上限，数量配给等价于价格下限。

显然，上游企业在实践中可以推行的纵向约束取决于相关的信息环境，例如价格维持就取决于上游企业能否观察并证实下游企业的隐性折扣行为，而数量定额则会被套利活动所限制。

我们引入进一步的约束考察纵向约束的其他方面。如果存在几个竞争性的下游企业，那么上游企业可以使用排他性经营区域（exclusive territories），即在下游企业之间划分最终市场。经营区域可以在空间的意义上理解，也可以在市场细分的意义上理解，例如区分为公共市场和私人市场，或者说区分为公司客户和居民客户。这样的纵向约束限制了品牌内的竞争。

如果下游企业在销售上游企业供给的产品的同时，也销售其相近的替代品。上游企业可以通过排他性经营（exclusive dealing）约束以限制品牌间的竞争。

二、纵向控制的一个思想模型：消除外部性（An Ideal Model of Vertical Control: Dispelling Externality）

这里的外部性有两种，可以分为纵向的外部性和横向的外部性，后者针对的是存在竞争性的下游企业的情况。

如果中间产品采取线性定价方法，且这个中间价格为 p_w，那么上游企业利用垄断力量制定的价格 $p_w>c$，这个价格成为下游企业的边际成本。纵向外部性指的是下游企业所作出的任何使其对中间产品的需求增加一单位的决策，都为上游企业带来一个利润增量 p_w-c，但是下游企业的决策仅仅考虑自身的利润最大化，并不考虑上游企业的利润增量，因而倾向于做出使中间产品的消费水平太低的决策。可以简单地来理解这里的问题，由于中间产品对下游企业的边际成本为 p_w，而对整个纵向结构则为 c，因此，分散的结构下的总利润小于纵向一体利润。解决的办法是通过纵向控制来消除外部性。下面我们将分别介绍三个著名的假说。

1. 双重加价模型(Double Marginalization)

假定零售价格是下游企业要做的唯一的决策,从而也是纵向控制的唯一的目标。纵向控制的目标 p^m,满足 $q^m = D(p^M)$,而且能够使 $(p-c)D(p)$ 最大。确定了这个目标之后,我们来看在分散的结构下的价格和产量决策。这时,上游企业选择中间价格、并简化为线性;下游企业选择消费价格,并假定下游企业也是一个垄断者。这样就会出现双重加价。因为上游企业制定的中间价格高于边际成本 c,而下游企业把这个中间价格作为边际成本再次加成,结果导致最终的消费价格 $p > p^m$。显然这个更高的价格降低了上游企业和下游企业的总的利润水平,这种情况就产生决策的外部性。可以举一个简单的例子来说明这一点。给出一个简单的需求函数 $D(p) = 1-p$,且 $c<1$。分别用 π_m, π_r 表示上游企业和下游企业的利润。首先来求解非一体化的价格和利润。第一步,通过下游企业的利润最大化得到最终价格与中间价格的关系。由最大化 $(p-p_w)D(p)$ 可以得到 $p = \frac{1+p_w}{2}$,对最终产品,从而也是对中间产品的需求为 $q = \frac{1-p_w}{2}$,下游企业的利润为 $\pi_r = \left(\frac{1-p_w}{2}\right)^2$。根据这里的结果,上游企业求解 $\max\limits_{p_w}\left[(p_w-c)\left(\frac{1-p_w}{2}\right)\right]$,由此可得,$p_w = \frac{1+c}{2}$。由此可以得到分散结构下的解。最终价格 $p = \frac{3+c}{4}$,利润等于 $\pi_m + \pi_r = \frac{3}{16}(1-c)^2$。

现在考虑一体化的解。整个一体化组织求解 $\max\limits_{p}[(p-c)(1-p)]$,由此可得,$p = \frac{1+c}{2}$,利润为 $\pi = \frac{(1-c)^2}{4} > \pi_m + \pi_r$。比较价格最容易理解这里的扭曲,在分散的情况下,中间产品的价格就已经加价了,但下游企业的垄断力量还要进一步加价。从消费者的角度来看,纵向一体化可以降低消费者的负担,而纵向一体的利润也可以增加,当然实施控制的方法是消除下游企业的利润,限制它的垄断力量发挥作用,显然这种控制具有福利改善性质。

下面我们考察解决这种双重加价的方法。

特许费。纵向一体化的好处是因为线性定价过于简单导致的。实际上,上游企业可以采取二部收费制度。分散决策的问题在于下游企业的边际成本不等于生产的边际成本。为消除这种扭曲,上游企业需要选择中间价格为边际成本,并把特许费制定在下游企业的利润水平上。它意味着上游企业把纵向结构以一个特许费的水平卖给了下游企业,下游企业由此成了剩余索取者。

特许费制度也存在一些局限,主要表现在:上游企业需要获得充分的信息,否则就需要通过下游企业的自我选择来实现筛选;下游企业如果是风险规避性的,这样的制度也存在问题;如果销售商存在竞争,这样的制度也存在问题。

转卖价格持平。即上游企业规定下游企业的最高售价为中间价格,这样的规定自然消除了双重加价的条件,外部性也就消除了。最高限价和数量强购的效果是一样的。

2. 下游道德风险:推销努力及其外部性(Moral Risk of Downstream Enterprises: Market Efforts and Externality)

下游企业经常提供一些可以增大最终需求的推销努力。我们可以把这些归入推销服务或服务的概念之下。由于这些活动可以增大最终的需求,从而对上游企业有利,这是正的外部性问题,显然上游企业希望通过一定的契约形式规定这些活动,但如果这些活动努力本身不可观测或证实,就存在着下游企业的道德风险问题。

我们以一个简单的模型来说明这里的外部性问题。设 s 表示服务水平,其成本为 $\phi(s)$,总的服务成本为 $q\phi(s)$,服务可以增加需求,需求函数可以表示为 $q=D(p,s)$。我们首先确定参照系,纵向一体化的利润函数为 $\pi=(p-c-\phi(s))D(p,s)$。边际条件为 $p^m+\dfrac{D(p^m,s^m)}{D'(p^m,s^m)}=c+\phi(s^m)$,这就是边际收益和边际成本相等的条件;$D'(p^m,s^m)[p^m-c-\phi(s^m)]=D(p^m,s^m)\phi'(s^m)$,这表示的是增加一个单位的服务水平的边际成本与边际收益相等。

但是在一个分散的结构中,下游企业的决策是最大化 $[p-p_w-\phi(s)]D(p,s)$,显然分析的结果表明不仅存在我们在前面已经考察过的双重加价问题,而且也导致了服务供给的扭曲,下游企业并不考虑因服务增加给上游企业带来的利润增加 $(p_w-c)(\partial D/\partial s)$。简单地说,这是因为上游企业对成本的加价,使得下游企业的利润边际低于纵向一体化的利润边际,由此导致服务供给不足。当然这是典型的正的外部性的结论。

这个结论可以扩展到下游企业处于竞争性市场的情况。在那里,不考虑竞争对价格的纠偏作用,唯一的不同是下游企业选择的价格和服务试图最大化的是消费者的剩余而不是利润。这显然消除了双重加价问题,服务水平的选择就仅仅因为这里的外部性,而这种外部性显然因为上游垄断者加价造成。

3. 投入替代与技术选择(Input Substitution and Technology Option)

现在假定下游单位是一个以数种投入生产一种最终产品的企业。为简单,假设下游单位使用两种投入:上游企业的产品和另一种中间产品。成本和售价均为 c',用 x 表示上游垄断企业的投入,竞争性的中间投入为 x',产出为 $q=f(x,x')$,假设次生产函数为一阶齐次的,但是重要的是两种投入再生产是可替代的。纵向一体的利润为 $\pi^m = p(f(x,x'))f(x,x')-cx-c'x'$。纵向结构的两种投入满足 $\frac{\partial q/\partial x}{\partial q/\partial x'} = \frac{c}{c'}$,但在分散结构下,由于垄断上游企业制造了价格加成,因此下游生产者的选择变成 $\frac{\partial q/\partial x}{\partial q/\partial x'} = \frac{p_w}{p'_w} > \frac{c}{c'}$。这意味着下游单位进行了替代选择导致过少的消费垄断上游企业的中间产品。

解决这一问题的方法包括,纵向一体化下游单位,或者采取一些纵向约束的方法。显然这与双重加价类似,从而方法也类似。它包括特许费制度,搭配销售加上转卖价格持平。实际上,所有这些约束的目的就是为了使下游单位的要素投入选择面对正确的价格。

三、品牌内竞争与横向外部性(Competition Inside Brand and Horizontal Externality)

这里的分析主要说明这样的问题:下游单位的竞争如何改变了推销服务的提供。我们可以集中考虑这样的一个例子,一个下游企业向消费者提供售前信息,例如广告,而这些消费者最终却向别的下游企业购买。下游企业之间的竞争可能会损害这类信息的提供。与其他没有提供信息的下游企业相比,一个因提供信息而增加了成本的下游企业必须收取更高的价格。消费者因而就有动因到第一个下游企业那里取得信息,再到第二个下游企业那里购买产品。

为清楚地解说这种现象,我们考虑一个极端情形。在其中,下游企业提供的服务不能为自己所用。假设需求为 $q=D(p,\bar{s})$,其中 $\bar{s}$ 为各下游企业提供的服务的最高水平,p 是各下游企业收取的价格的最低水平,$\phi(s)$ 现在是提供给那些只看不买的消费者的服务的单位成本。假定 $\phi(0)=0$,提供服务 $\bar{s}$ 的下游企业必须在销售中有足够的收入,以抵消所增加的成本。同时,它的零售价格必须不高于批发价格。因为如果这样,另一个下游企业就可以略微降低其价格,不提供任何服务,而获得全部需求。换句话说,对于一个给定的 $\bar{s}$,竞争性价格为 $p=p_w$。但是因为 $p-p_w-\phi(\bar{s})\leqslant 0$,所以,$\bar{s}=0$,没有任何服务被提供。

更一般地说,横向外部性造成了一个公共物品问题。下游企业相互搭便车。公共物品——提供给消费者的信息——因此而供给不足。为鼓励下游企业提供充足的服务,竞争必须减少或消除。上游企业必须保护下游企业免受不公平竞争之害,从而使它们对它们所提供的服务拥有产权。减少竞争型纵向约束如 RPM 和排他性经营区域可以达到这一目的。RPM 鼓励消费者在提供服务的地方购买(因为他们在别的地方也不会发现更好的价格)。排他性经营区域也足以达到同样的目的。例如,上游企业可以给予一个下游企业以垄断地位。竞争的消失排除了任何横向外部性存在的可能性。这类约束一般是福利增进型的,因为它们使下游企业可以向消费者提供有价值的信息。

复习思考题:
1. 旅游企业一体化有哪几种类型?每种类型具有什么特征?在中国旅游企业实行一体化战略有什么战略意义?
2. 什么叫并购?并购具有哪些经济效应?
3. 旅游企业如何通过并购实现旅游企业一体化?
4. 我国旅游企业实现战略联盟的发展方向是什么?
5. 纵向控制具有什么意义?旅游企业如何实施纵向控制?

第十章
旅游产业的市场绩效
(Market Performance)

第一节 市场绩效的内涵和评价
(The Concept and Assessment of Market Performance)

市场绩效是指在一定的市场结构下,由一定的市场行为所形成的价格、产量、成本、利润、产品质量和品种以及在技术进步等方面的最终经济成果。市场绩效受市场结构和市场行为的共同制约,是市场关系或资源配置是否合理的最终成果标志,它反映市场运行的效率。The main topic covered by market performance are: 1) allocation efficiency; 2) income distribution; 3) technical efficiency; 4) technological progress. In the traditional SCP theory, structure and conduct vitally influence performance. For the most part there is substantial positive correlation between structure and performance, so good structure leads to good conduct and good performance. However, there is also some exception in the relation. In traditional economics, complete competition was regarded the best market structure, but in natural monopoly market, workably competitive structures do not always provide good performance. It is important to research the relation between structure and performance in certain market structure.

对市场绩效的评价,即判断一个产业或整个经济的绩效是"好"是"坏",是"高"是"低",取决于所设立的评价准则,这种评价准则就是规范目标。

How to measure the market performance? The principal aspects or dimensions of market performance include prominently:

(1) The height of price relative to the average cost of production, and thus the size of profits.

(2) The relative efficiency of production so far as this is influenced by the scale or size of plants and firms(relative to the most efficient), and by the extent, if any, of excess capacity.

(3) The size of sales-promotion costs relative to the costs of production.

(4) The character of the product, including choice of design, quality, and variety of products within any market.

(5) The progressive rate of the firm and industry in developing both products and techniques of production, relative to evidently attainable rates and relative to the costs of progress.

第二节 旅游产业市场绩效的衡量指标
(The Indexes for Measuring Market Performance of Tourism Industry)

当 SCP 传统的产业组织经验研究方法为爱德华 S. 梅森（Edward S. Mason,1939,1949）及他在哈佛的同事们所采用时，它成为一个革命性的变化。最早的工作大部分涉及的是单个行业的案例研究（如华莱士[Wallace,1937]的研究）。SCP 理论最初的经验运用是由梅森的同事和学生们如乔 S. 贝恩进行的。与案例研究相反，这些研究进行跨行业的比较。由于缺乏可得性，特殊厂商的数据很少被使用。

SCP 模型第一次使用了由微观经济分析得出的推断来讨论产业组织。在 SCP 示例中，产业的业绩取决于卖方和买方的行为，而卖方和买方的行为取决于市场结构。结构反过来又取决于基本状况，如技术和产品需求。但确切的联系没有被合理详细地阐明。

典型的 SCP 研究分两阶段：第一，通过直接衡量而非估计来获得业绩的衡量结果；第二，结构衡量被用来解释跨行业市场业绩的差异。本节我们主要讨论市场业绩的衡量指标，主要有三种直接或间接反映利润或价格与成本间关系的不同衡量方法。

- 收益率，以每元投资所赚得的利润为基础。

- 价格—成本加成,以价格和边际成本间的差异为基础。尽管在实际中,研究者常用某种形式的平均成本来替代边际成本。
- 托宾(Tobin)的 q,是一厂商的市场价值与以其资产重置成本为基础的价值之比率。

一、收益率(Profit Rate)

收益率是一种衡量每元投资赢利多少的方法。以下将解释经济利润与收益率之间的关系。收益率的正确计算可能很难,有时候还必须作出使最终结果发生偏差的折衷。还将讨论衡量收益率的几种不同方法。

收益率是利润的一种衡量方法。我们首先要区分经济利润与会计利润。经济利润,是用收入减去机会成本,会计利润由会计使用标准会计原则来衡量。在计算收益率时,应该在计算任何收益率前调整会计利润以反映经济利润。

经济利润与会计利润间存在着几个重要的区别。主要的区分是关于长期资本资产,如工厂与设备。经济利润等于收入减去劳动力、原材料和正确衡量的资本成本。收入、劳动力成本和原材料成本的衡量一般来说是容易的。问题是衡量年资本成本。若所有的资本资产是租赁得来的,年资本成本等于年租赁费用。总租赁费用等于每单位租金率乘以资本单位数,即,恰当的资本成本衡量方法是流量(每一时段租赁资本的价格)而不是存量(持续许多时段的资本(如机器)的成本)衡量方法。如果存在发展良好的租赁市场——譬如说,二手设备的租赁市场——计算资本的相关租金率和经济利润就较容易。当租金率不是现成可得时,经济学家必须在计算经济利润前明确算出租金率。

在计算用以决定长期经济利润的内含资本租金率的过程中,资本资产应以重置成本估价。重置成本是购买可比质量资产的长期成本。若资本以重置成本估计。那么低收益率便是不应有新的资本进入产业的一个信号。这并不意味着厂商应停产或厂商在过去的投资决策中犯了错误。举例说,一家在机器便宜时购买机器的厂商根据重置成本可能获得一个低收益率,但它就其最初购买而言仍享有大额利润。一个高的收益率是新资本应进入产业的一个信号。

研究者经常用经济利润去除以厂商的资本价值,以获得资本的一个赚得的收益率。这一收益率是控制厂商间资本差异的赢利能力的衡量。经济利润、资本的赚得等收益率和资本租金率间存在着密切的关系。展开这一关系需要了解资本的租金率到底是什么:在设备提取折旧后,租金率必须能向资本所有者提供某一特定的收益率。

折旧是在资本使用期间经济价值的降低。举个例子,如果你以每年1000美元出租你的房屋,而房屋的损耗是每年300美元,那么折旧就是300美元,而考虑到折旧后你的净年租费为700美元。如果房屋最初值10000美元,那么你的收益率为7%,折旧率为3%。对投资者关系重要的是减去折旧率后的收益率。因此,租金率可表示为赚得的收益r加上折旧率δ。

下面讨论收益率的计算方法。利润为:

$$\pi = R - 劳动力成本 - 原材料成本 - 资本成本$$

这里,R是收入,资本成本是资本的租金率乘以资本价值。资本价值是$P_K K$,其中P_K是资本价格而K是资本量。如果租金率为$(r+\delta)$,那么利润为:

$$\pi = R - 劳动力成本 - 原材料成本 - (r+\delta)P_K K$$

赚得的收益率是使经济利润为零的那个r。令$\pi=0$并解上式中的r,得,

$$r = \frac{R - 劳动力成本 - 原材料成本 - \delta P_K K}{P_K K} \tag{9.1}$$

因此,赚得的收益率是净收入除以资产价值,这里净收入等于收入减去劳动力成本减去原材料成本减去折旧。

二、价格—成本加成(Price-Cost Add-on)

为了避免有关收益率计算的问题,许多经济学家使用一种不同的方法来衡量厂商业绩,这就是勒纳指数,即价格—成本加成$(P-MC)/p$。价格—成本加成是将价格P和边际成本MC的差额作为P的分子而得到的。由于会计收益率与价格—成本加成间的相关程度可能相对较低(Liebowitz,1982),这两种业绩衡量方法的使用存在着差异。

经济学原理告诉我们,利润最大化厂商的价格—成本加成等于厂商面临的需求弹性ε的负倒数

$$(P-MC)/P = -1/\varepsilon \tag{9.2}$$

竞争性厂商的定价为$P=MC$,这是因为它的剩余需求的价格弹性为负无穷。

不幸的是,由于边际成本的数据很难获得,因此许多研究人员运用价格—平均可变成本加成而不运用合宜的价格—边际成本加成。其对价格—平均成本加成的近似方法一般是用销售收入减去工资,再减去以

销售额平均的原料成本。也就是说,倾向于忽略资本、研究和开发及广告成本。

这种方法可能导致严重偏差。假设边际成本固定不变且给定为

$$MC=v+(r+\delta)\ P_KK/Q \tag{9.3}$$

式中 r 是竞争性收益率,δ 是折旧率,而生产1单位产出 Q 所需的劳动力和原材料成本是 v。方程描述了一项需要 K/Q 单位的资本(每单位资本的成本为 P_K)来生产1单位的产出的技术。但是,使用 v 来替代边际成本将导致严重偏差,这可通过将方程9.3中的 MC 代入方程9.2看出:

$$(P-v)/P=-1/\varepsilon+(r+\delta)\ P_KK/(PQ) \tag{9.4}$$

因此,$(P-v)/P$ 与正确的衡量 $(P-MC)/P=-1/\varepsilon$ 相差方程9.4中的最后一项 $(r+\delta)\ P_KK/(PQ)$,这一项是资本的租金价值除以产出的价值。

三、托宾 q(Tobin q)

另一种业绩衡量方法——托宾 q,是一家厂商资产的市场价值(通过其已公开发行并售出的股票和债务来衡量)与这家厂商资产的重置成本的比率(Tobin,1969)。这一业绩衡量方法既没有收益率也没有价格—成本加成用得多。若一厂商比以重建成本为基础的价值所值更多,那么它赚得超额利润。这些利润远远超出了使厂商留在产业中所必需的利润水平。

使用托宾 q 的优点是避免了估计收益率或边际成本的困难。另一方面,为了使 q 具有意义,厂商资产的市场价值和厂商资产的重置成本都需要精确的衡量。

为了获得一家厂商资产市场价值的精确估计,通常可能的方法是加总厂商已发行的证券(如股票和债券)的价值。获得厂商资产重置成本的估计要困难得多,除非存在二手设备市场。而且,广告及研究和开发的费用产生了难以估价的无形资产。构造托宾 q 的研究者们通常在他们的计算中都忽略了这些无形资产的重置成本。由于这一原因,q 通常大于1。相应地,使用 q 来衡量市场力量而不作进一步的调整将是误导性的。

如果能够正确计算托宾 q,就可以确定垄断厂商超额索价的程度。为了做到这一点,必须计算要使 q 等于1要降低多少收益(除去资本收

益)。例如,令 e_m 为一垄断厂商固定不变的年收益,e_c 为竞争厂商固定不变的年收益。资产市场价值与其重置成本的比 q 等于 e_m 与 e_c 的比。例如,若 q 等于 2,在厂商索取竞争价前其收益必须降低一半。

第三节 旅游产业竞争力分析——以旅游目的地为例
(The Analysis of Tourism Industry Competitiveness——An Example of Tourism Destination)

一、旅游目的地的竞争力(Tourism Destination Competitiveness)

1. 旅游目的地①(Tourism Destination)

旅游目的地是拥有特定性质旅游资源、具备一定旅游吸引力、能够吸引一定规模数量的旅游者进行旅游活动的特定区域。深刻认识旅游目的地的内涵和外延是评价旅游目的地竞争力的前提和基础。

一个特定的地区要成为旅游目的地,必须具备三个条件:一是要拥有一定数量的旅游资源,同时,这种资源可以满足旅游者某些旅游活动的需要;二是要拥有各种与旅游资源性质相适应的地面旅游设施和交通条件,如旅游饭店、度假村和通往各地的航空港、火车站和公路交通网,旅游者可以借助这些设施从不同的地区顺利地到达旅游地并利用这些设施在该地停留;三是该地区具有一定的旅游需求流量。可见,旅游目的地是一种集资源、旅游活动项目、旅游地面设施和市场需求为一体的空间复合体。这三个条件是特定地区要成为旅游目的地的必备条件,因此评价一个旅游目的地是否具有竞争力以及竞争力有多强时也必须以这些条件为基础。

旅游目的地是一个具有某种功能与性质的旅游胜地,按空间范围大小来划分,可以分为国家性旅游目的地、区域性旅游目的地、城市旅游地和旅游景区四种类型。由于在此我们以中国旅游目的地竞争力为评价对象,而我国区域性旅游目的地又没有形成,所以关于旅游目的地竞争力的评价只包括城市性和景区性两种情况。

2. 旅游目的地竞争力(Tourism Destination Competitiveness)

(1) 竞争力(Competitiveness)

20世纪90年代以来,竞争力成为一个非常热门的话题,人们从各

---

① 关于旅游目的地的认识请参见《旅游经济论》,张辉著。

个层面和各个角度来论述竞争力的问题。但是关于什么是竞争力以及如何来评价竞争力等理论和实证问题却没有统一的认识。Newall(1992a:94)将竞争力定义为"竞争力是产出更多、更好的优质产品与服务,在国内或国际市场上成功地向消费者销售。它引致了服务于公众的有优厚报酬的就业岗位和充分有效的资源利用,同时避免对于公众的消极影响"。

金碚(2003)将竞争力定义为"在市场经济中,竞争力最直观地表现为一个企业能够比其他企业更有效地向消费者(或者市场)提供产品或者服务,并且能够获得自身发展的能力或者综合素质"。[①] 而所谓"更有效地"是指,以更低的价格或者消费者更满意的质量持续地生产和销售;所谓"获得自身发展"是指,企业能够实现经济上长期的良性循环,具有持续的良好业绩,从而成为长久生存和不断壮大的强势企业。因此金碚关于竞争力的评价一方面从企业的经营业绩入手,另一方面从公众对企业产品的印象入手。

(2) 旅游目的地竞争力(Tourism Destination Competitiveness)

关于旅游竞争力的理解有多个层次,即首先是以国家、区域或地方为研究对象的区域旅游竞争力;其次是以产业或行业为对象的旅游产业竞争力;最后是以特定市场上的企业为对象的旅游企业竞争力。研究旅游目的地的竞争力问题,显然更接近第一种理解(曹宁、郭舒、隋鑫,2003.11)。

从旅游目的地竞争力研究的价值来说,其目的就是要解释"为什么有些旅游目的地发展的竞争力强,有些竞争力弱"或者"什么样的旅游目的地能够具有长久的竞争力,什么样的旅游目的地一定不会有竞争力"。

Richardson(1987:61)认为:在某种意义上,旅游属于国际贸易的一种形式,在完全自由竞争市场条件下,任何国家的旅游供给都能够在国际市场上展开竞争。由于旅游者流向目的地的主要需求是获得包括目的地服务在内的真实经历,因此,(构成经历的)条件因素就成为决定目的地吸引力的重要因素。由此,持有比较优势理论的学者认为与旅游产品相联系的要素禀赋在特定区域上的空间分布情况,解释了这个作为旅游目的地的特定区域的竞争力大小的原因。当比较优势所依赖的资源的可得性,对于彼此竞争的目的地来说差异很小时,

---

① 金碚关于竞争力的定义是从企业的角度出发的,可以用于旅游景区的竞争力研究。

按照长期的眼光对可得资源进行高效率利用的能力便成为影响目的地竞争力大小的关键,竞争优势的重要性便凸现出来。竞争优势理论认为一个资源禀赋充裕的旅游目的地可能不如一个资源禀赋存量少的目的地的竞争力更强,因为也许资源禀赋少的区域能够更加充分、高效地利用较少的资源。

国内学者在目的地旅游竞争力研究中广泛借鉴了地学、经济学、传播学等学科的相关理论,主要观点有:用生命周期理论结解释旅游目的地的竞争表现,认为旅游资源的垄断性特征是目的地竞争力差异的主要原因;依据旅游空间供求理论解释不同区域旅游竞争力的差异化表现;综合考虑旅游资源、社会经济、环境和科学技术等因素对区域旅游持续发展潜力的作用;从目的地形象策划角度考察旅游地竞争力问题。

如果把旅游目的地更进一步划分为旅游城市和旅游景区,那么从目前关于旅游目的地竞争力研究来看,主要集中在旅游城市的竞争力研究上。在国外,关于城市旅游的研究最早的是斯坦费尔德(Stanstield,1964)的对城市旅游业重要性的论述。威廉姆斯和绍(Shaw & Williams,1984)从表意、组织上(时间序列)和感知上分析了城市旅游吸引力的三个层次。沃波(K. Wober)等在20世纪80年代末,通过旅游需求、过夜旅游增长率、游客季节分布及旅游地承载力等几项指标对当时欧洲39个首都城市进行比较研究,勾画出1975年以来各个城市的旅游综合竞争力空间分布图。20世纪末21世纪初,知识、技术、人才成为决定城市旅游竞争力大小的重要因素。库得纳(C. Coeldner)提出旅游产品竞争的信息指向概念,孚敦斯与斯彻特尔(Dfodness, W. Schertler)认为旅游竞争地可以通过信息结构、信息可达性、信息质量以及传播速度体现竞争力。国内直接针对旅游城市的竞争力研究较少,主要有屈海林、邱汉琴(1996)对香港,郭阳旭(2000)对重庆,万绪才等(2001)对江苏省各地市城市旅游竞争力的研究,其中万绪才等的研究从旅游资源与产品条件、社会经济条件和其他条件三个方面建立了城市国际旅游竞争力评价研究的指标体系。

3. 旅游目的地竞争力的影响因素(Factors Influencing the Tourism Destination Competitiveness)

关于旅游目的地竞争力的理论研究已经取得了一定的进展,但真正地评价旅游目的地竞争力的大小却需要设计一整套指标体系,通过对指标的测定来反映旅游目的地竞争力的大小。现有对旅游目的地竞争力等级的衡量,仍然以考察旅游收入、旅游人次、游客满意度等颇具经济意义的特征为主。但很多学者都认为,竞争力是衡量旅游目的地综合发展能力的指标,不可能只用几个指标就可以完全表现的,也不能仅仅用具有经济意义的指标来反映。曹宁、郭舒、隋鑫(2003.11)认为:关于旅游目的地竞争力研究的一个基本认识就是把旅游者的需要与当地居民的需要同时加以考虑。一个能够带来区域经济繁荣,并且有利于环境经营,同时又能够为居民提供高质量生活保障的旅游目的地,才是真正"有竞争力的旅游目的地"。

可以说,影响旅游目的地竞争力的因素的确是非常复杂,但认识问题应该抓住问题的主要方面和主要矛盾,通过指标反映这些主要矛盾就能大致反映目的地的竞争力,而研究旅游目的地竞争力影响因素是设定竞争力评价指标体系的基础。

(1) 核心吸引物(Core Attraction)

旅游目的地的吸引物主要包括自然景观、文化和历史、客源地与目的地之间的先天联系(如寻根)、参与性活动、特殊事件(路径依赖)、旅游设施等。

(2) 基础性因素(Fun Damental Elements)

基础性因素主要是目的地与旅游活动密切相关的资源禀赋。

(3) 支持性因素(Supportive Elements)

支持性因素主要包括:基础设施、相关企业和可进入性。旅游目的地的基础设施并非完全是为了旅游产业的发展而存在,但却影响着旅游目的地的竞争力。旅游相关企业的效率、品牌则也影响着目的地的竞争力。而可进入性则是指航空的班次、往来的护照与签证、定期的联运、交通枢纽等政治经济开放程度方面,也表现在机场容量、景区的道路、公园的容量与目的地物理承载力相关的方面。

(4) 发展性因素(Developmental Elements)

发展性因素主要是指目的地对各类资源加以利用的能力。

(5) 资格性因素(Qualificatory Elements)

资格性因素包括:目的地的区位、目的地的安全感、目的地的成本(货币兑换率、旅游产品和服务的成本等)。资格因素不受目的地旅游产业的影响和控制,相反它却会增强或弱化目的地的竞争优势。

二、旅游目的地竞争力的评价方法和指标体系(Assessing Methods and Indexes System of Tourism Destination Competitiveness)

1. 评价旅游目的地的基本方法(Basic Means in Assessing Tourism Destination)

为了对竞争力进行评价,国内外的学者和研究者采用了多种多样的方法,各种方法各有利弊。最常用的方法大致有三种:

(1) 因素分析法(Factor Analyzing Method)

因素分析法是从最表面容易感知的属性入手,逐步深入更为内在的属性和因素。一般来说,越是内在的因素对竞争力的影响越深刻,越长久,但其产生作用的逻辑因果关系可能非常复杂;而越是表面的因素对企业竞争力的影响越直接,越短暂,但其产生作用的逻辑因果关系也较简单。因素分析法的基本要求是尽可能地将决定和影响企业竞争力的各种内在因素分解和揭示出来。这种研究方法主要涉及以下几个环节:第一是选取指标;第二,构造各指标之间的因果关系;第三,确定各指标所占的权重;第四,计算出各种因素共同发生作用所导致的竞争力的计量值,即对决定和影响竞争力的各种分解出的数值进行综合;第五,对统计结果进行合理性判断和解释。

(2) 对比差距法(标杆法)(Benchmarking Method)

对竞争力的评价可以采取直接比较的方式:假定同类对象中最优秀主体(也被称作标杆)一系列显性特征对竞争力的影响,通过被评价对象与标杆的一系列显示性指标的比较对被评估对象的竞争力进行评价。

对比差距法的环节主要包括:第一,选取对比指标;第二,比较被评估对象与标杆的各指标的差距;第三,进行综合汇总,评价被评估对象与标杆企业的差距。对比分析法与因素分析法的共同之处在于都是要进行详细的因素分析和统计数值的计算。不同之处是后一种方法是一对一的比较,可以进行多指标的比较,而不必进行数值的加总比较,因此可以避免确定各因素的权重过程中的主观因素。但对比分析法在如何确定标杆方面存在一定困难,而且当被评估对象很多时,不能对众多评估对象进行综合排名。

(3) 内涵解析法(Connotation Interpreting Method)

这种方法的特点是将定性分析和定量分析相结合,重点研究影响竞争力的内在决定性因素,对于一些难以直接量化的因素可以采取专家意见或者问卷调查的方式进行分析判断。与前两种方法主要分析竞争力的外延指标不同,这种方法重点分析竞争力的内涵性分析因素。这种方法要达到的目的是揭示被评估对象的核心竞争力,并对其作用进行评价。

这种研究方法的环节是:第一,确定决定和影响竞争力的主要因素,并分析其因果关系;第二,通过统计分析、专家意见、问卷调查等方式,分析竞争力的实际情况;第三,深入剖析核心竞争力,发现核心理念及其渗透性,以判断竞争力的强弱。这种分析方法的优点是可以深入到核心能力的分析,具有深刻性。缺点是难以全面量化,可能含有较大程度的主观性。而且,有些因素在性质上是难以进行直接比较的。

综上所述,我们在对旅游目的地竞争力进行评价时,最好选择因素分析法。

2. 选择竞争力指标的原则(Principles on Choosing Index)

对旅游目的地竞争力进行测度,必须建立一套严格而科学的指标体系。而要达到这个目标,则首先要明确建立这个体系的原则并恰当地选择评价指标。

(1) 评价指标的对应性(Corresponding of Assessing Index)

旅游目的地竞争力的评价指标应该有两类,即显示性指标和分析性指标。显示性指标反映的是竞争的结果或者竞争的最终表现,分析性指标用于反映竞争力的原因或其决定因素。显示性指标应该简单明了,像足球赛一样,谁进球多谁就赢了,可以直接说明你具有较强的竞争力,尽可能使用较少的指标就可以基本上反映竞争力的结果。而分析性指标则需要通过构建多角度、多层次的指标体系来解释为什么有的旅游目的地拥有旅游竞争力,而有的就缺乏竞争力。所选择的指标要十分明显地同竞争力有很密切的关系,能够通过对所选指标的测定反映旅游目的地的竞争力。

(2) 评价指标的系统性(Systematic of Assessing Index)

必须按照系统论的观点、以强化"旅游性质"为系统目标构建旅游目的地竞争力的指标体系。这要求测度指标涉及旅游目的地竞争力的各个方面,能较为详细地反映出目的地的各个子系统和要素对旅游目的地竞争力的贡献。系统性的另一层含意是指指标体系内部要有层次划分,可以分为一级指标、二级指标、三级指标等。这样可以反映出指标体系的内在关联性以及每个指标对城市竞争力的贡献程度,并利于对旅游目的地开展综合评价和排名。

(3) 评价指标的可获得性(Attainable of Assessing Index)

对一个旅游目的地竞争力进行评价除了采用定性的方法,更重要的是采用定量的方法,而定量方法则要求所设定的指标体系可以获得。为了保证指标的可获得性,应该选择那些根据现行的旅游统计体系便于采集并可用于比较的指标。有的指标的意义很重要,但无法采集也无法在不同旅游目的地之间比较,就应避免选入旅游目的地竞争的指标体系中。另外,对于现行的统计体系或有关学科体系中尚未有明确定义的指标,如需选入指标体系,应按照指标的含义科学地加以定义和计算。对于不可量化但又十分重要的指标"旅游城市或旅游景区的人气"和"旅游目的地管理效率"等问题就通过对特殊人群的问卷调查来解决。一般来说,分析性指标更需要对那些难以计量的非经济性因素给予关注。

三、旅游目的地竞争力评价指标体系(Index System for Assessing Tourism Destination Competitiveness)

1. 旅游城市竞争力指标评价体系(Index System for Assessing Tourism City Competitiveness)

苏伟忠、杨英宝、顾朝林在《城市旅游竞争力评价初探》一文中建立了旅游城市竞争力评价指标体系,该指标体系包括以下三个方面:(1)城市旅游竞争业绩评价。城市旅游竞争业绩评价虽然只反映某城市旅游业过去和现在竞争行为的结果,但能以此反映城市旅游业未来的竞争态势。对旅游竞争业绩的评价主要通过现在的旅游收入、旅游接待量和旅游企业的经济效益来进行评价。(2)旅游竞争潜力。旅游竞争潜力主要测度竞争力的后续能力,它是旅游竞争力的主要源泉。可从旅游资源条件、旅游资金来源和旅游技术人才三个方面来评价。(3)城市整体环境。城市整体环境好坏对旅游业发展影响非常重要。因为除具备丰富的传统旅游资源的城市外,大部分城市依靠的是其整体环境,尤其是经济环境来发展旅游业。因此,对于大部分城市而言,经济环境是旅游业发展的关键因素,社会环境、生态环境和政策环境起保障作用。城市旅游业综合竞争力的评价主要是测度旅游业整体竞争能力,即对城市旅游竞争业绩、竞争潜力和城市旅游环境支持力进行综合评价。

表10-1 指标体系及权重

一级指标	权重	二级指标	权重	三级指标	权重
B1:竞争业绩		C1:旅游外汇收入 C2:旅游接待量 C3:客房出租率 C4:旅游饭店营业收入 C5:旅游业总收入			

续表

一级指标	权重	二级指标	权重	三级指标	权重
B2：竞争潜力		C6：资源条件		D1：资源品位度 D2：资源垄断度 D3：资源丰度	
		C7：经济来源		D4：人均GDP D5：城市化水平 D6：第三产业主导性 D7：对外经济联系	
		C8：技术人才		D8：每万人拥有高等学校在校学生数 D9：第三产业从业人员构成 D10：国际旅游从业人员数	
B3：竞争环境支持力		C9：自然环境		D11：每平方公里二氧化硫排放量 D12：环境噪声达标面积 D13：城市建成区绿化覆盖率 D14：人均绿化面积 D15：工业废水达标率	
		C10：经济社会环境		D16：区位条件 D17：年客运总量 D18：人均铺装道路面积 D19：人均拥有邮电业务总量 D20：百人拥有影剧院数 D21：公交车普及度 D22：旅游住宿接待能力	
		C11：其他环境		D23：居民对游客的态度 D24：竞争环境 D25：政策环境	

可以说，以上指标是一个相对完整的指标体系，从竞争业绩、竞争潜力和竞争环境支持力三个方面考察城市竞争力。

2. 旅游景区竞争力评价指标体系（Index System for Assessing Tourism Spot Competitiveness）

为了使竞争力评价指标具有可获得性，对旅游景区竞争力的评价可以通过对旅游景区管理公司竞争力的评价间接获得。对旅游景区管理公司竞争力的评价体系可参照中国经营报企业竞争力监测体系（CBCI），通过对旅游景区上市公司的财务指标赋予一定权重,并通过加权平均计算出基础指数,另外再通过调查问卷获得被调查人群对于旅游景区的人气指数,通过把基础指数和人气指数加权平均得出旅游景区上市公司的综合指数,并根据综合指数的大小对旅游景区竞争力进行排名。

根据竞争力监测指标体系(CBCI),结合旅游景区的特点,可选取以下指标作为旅游景区竞争力评价指标体系。

表10-2 竞争力监测指标体系构成

目标	因素	子因素	指标
竞争力	基础数据	规模子因素	营业收入 近三年营业收入增长 净资产
		效益子因素	净利润 近三年净利润的平均增长 净资产利润率 总资产贡献率
	问卷		知晓程度 综合印象 发展信心

四、2003年旅游景区上市公司竞争力简单评价(The Simple Evaluation of the Competitiveness Listed Traveling Companies in Scenic Spots in 2003)

1. 旅游景区主营业务收入大幅度下跌(Substantial Decrease of Prime Operating Income of the Tourism Scenic Spots)

表10-3 2003年旅游景区主营业务收入(单位:人民币元)

证券代码	证券简称	2003年	2002年	增减幅度(%)
000690	华侨城	496,603,240	593,623,837	-16.34
000802	京西旅游	345,281,282	373,342,728	-7.52
600054	黄山旅游	295,235,175	456,801,571	-35.37
000888	峨眉山	160,135,974	172,437,993	-7.13
000978	桂林旅游	147,081,157	225,402,765	-34.75
000430	张家界	82,250,657	76,401,897	7.66

从表中可以看出,深圳华侨城主营业务收入在景区上市公司中名列第一位。2003年旅游景区上市公司的主营业务收入除张家界外增长了7.66%外,其余全部下降,而且其中的黄山旅游、桂林旅游和深圳华侨城的下降幅度还比较大,分别下降了35.37%、34.75%和16.34%。

旅游景区上市公司在2003年主营业务收入整体上大幅度下降的最主要原因时2003年上半年我国遭受非典疫情,国内外游客锐减,使得旅游景区公司的主营业务收入大幅度下降。但张家界能在非典疫情的严峻考验下,实现了主营业务收入的上升,这主要是由于张家界能够积极开辟旅游项目,拓宽收入来源取得的。公司2003年上半年受非典影响旅游业收入同比下降达到31%,导致公司最终未能完成年初制定的主营业务收入增长20%的经营目标(实际增长7.66%),但由于市场转暖和措施得力,公司2003年下半年的经营情况已经全面复苏,所有分子公司接待游客人次和营业收入都创造了同时期历史最好成绩,在一定程度上弥补了上半年非典疫情给公司带来的损失,使得全年经营业绩与2002年相比仍有小幅提升,这表明公司经过2001年的资产重组和2002年的整合培育,企业核心竞争能力正在逐步形成,整体实力和抗风险能力都得到了极大的增强。

2. 净利润出现了大幅度下跌(Substantial Decrease of the Net Profit)

表10-4 2003年旅游景区净利润(单位:人民币元)

证券代码	证券简称	2003年	2002年	增减幅度(%)
000690	华侨城	229,695,248	270,241,171	−15.00
000802	京西旅游	−76,188,567	−67,640,361	−12.64
600054	黄山旅游	−61,208,189	25,507,902	−339.96
000888	峨眉山	32,398,510	29,537,489	9.69
000978	桂林旅游	9,981,239	46,348,035	−78.46
000430	张家界	17,242,208	15,368,352	12.19

从上表可以看出,除了峨眉山和张家界,其余旅游景区上市公司的净利润都出现了下跌,其中黄山旅游和桂林旅游下降的幅度很大,分别下降了339.96%和78.46%。京西旅游下降的幅度虽然不大,只下降了12.64%,但京西旅游从2002年以来一直处于亏损状态。总体来看,京西旅游和黄山旅游在2003年陷入了亏损的境地。

张家界在2003年是旅游景区上市公司中唯一实现主营业务收入上升的公司,而且其净利润上升的幅度比主营业务收入上升的幅度还大。

这主要得力于面对突如其来的非典疫情,公司下属经营机构一方面积极配合各级地方政府进行非典防治,把广大游客的身体健康放在第一位,采取严格的检测和消毒措施阻止疫情传播到景区;另一方面,公司严格控制各项费用支出,压缩经营成本,维持公司日常正常运转,利用空闲时间组织员工进行培训,并对部分景区接待设施进行了修缮,保持最佳状态等待旅游行业的复苏。

而2003年峨眉山在主营业务收入下降7.13%的情况下,却实现了净利润上升9.69个百分点的业绩。公司借助于峨眉山风景区打造"中国第一山",全面推行诚信服务,提升峨眉山在国内国外的知名度、美誉度,改变了以往营销模式,主动出击,积极开拓新的消费能力强的游客市场,公司新的营销模式以直接与终端有旅游需求的客源互动为基础,重点开拓消费水平高的新市场,同时巩固现有的"川渝"市场。为此,公司在全国绝大多数省市共建立了48家峨眉山专卖店。公司利用专卖店更加直接有效地与终端客户接触。公司与国内数十家百强旅行社建立了战略联盟,由旅行社、公司营销部直接与终端旅游需求者联系,使公司下半年经营业绩大幅提升。公司将峨眉山景区的旅游服务拓展至景区以外,作为拓展服务的第一步,公司在成都建设旅游中转基地(成都长业大厦),以保证省外游客能更方便、更舒适地到峨眉山景区游览,形成对海外和省外游客的一条龙服务。公司围绕旅游六要素,进一步加快资源优势向产业优势的转化,公司组建了峨眉山灵秀文化有限公司以开发旅游产品,充分利用资源、挖掘内涵,形成旅游、商贸、文化一体化发展的新格局。在收入增加的同时,公司加大内部改革力度,推行以成本控制为核心的内部管理制度,向管理要效益。采取各种措施控制可变费用的增加。尤其是下半年,公司实现主营业务收入11656万元,比计划增加2244万元,比去年同期增加1501万元,实现利润3689万元,比计划增加1503万元,比去年同期增加1023万元,使公司超额完成今年的盈利预测。

3. 净资产收益率出现了大幅度的下降趋势(Substantial Decline of the Return on Asset Net)

表10-5 2003年旅游景区净资产收益率

证券代码	证券简称	2003年(%)	2002年(%)
000690	华侨城	16.17	22.74
000802	京西旅游	−32.94	−22.04
600054	黄山旅游	−8.9	3.4

续表

证券代码	证券简称	2003年(%)	2002年(%)
000888	峨眉山	7.56	7.45
000978	桂林旅游	2.62	12.49
000430	张家界	7.26	6.98

从旅游景区的净资产收益率也可以看出，除了峨眉山和张家界有少许提升，其余景区的净资产收益率都呈下降趋势，而且下降的幅度都很大，表现出了和净利润相同的变化趋势。净资产收益率的下降主要是由于各景区净利润的大幅度下降造成的。

由以上分析可以看出，2003年除张家界和峨眉山之外，其他各旅游景区上市公司的营业收入、净利润和净资产收益率都出现了大幅下降。营业收入、净资产和净资产收益率都是测量旅游景区竞争力的重要指标，它们的下降使2003年旅游景区竞争力大幅度下降。但2003年旅游景区重要财务指标的下降主要是因为非典对旅游产业具有致命性的打击，因此2004年在旅游业整体复苏的形势下，旅游景区的竞争力有望大幅度提升。

复习思考题：
1. 什么叫市场绩效？其评价标准有哪些？
2. 衡量旅游企业市场绩效的指标有哪些？如何计算？
3. 试评价我国饭店业的市场绩效？

第十一章
旅游产业政策
(Tourism Industrial Policy)

第一节 产业政策概述(Outline of Industrial Policy)

产业政策是对以产业组织理论、产业结构理论、产业布局理论和产业发展理论为基本内容的产业经济学基本理论的应用。因此,产业政策研究成为产业经济学的重要组成部分。

一、产业政策概念(Concepts of Industrial Policy)

尽管产业政策的概念是20世纪70年代以后开始出现,并被广泛关注,但是产业政策的实践随着农牧业的出现和政府的诞生就已经存在了。现代产业政策是随着现代大工业的发展而形成的。产业政策一词最早出现在1970年日本通产省代表在OECD(经济合作与发展组织)大会上所作的题为《日本的产业政策》的演讲。

目前国际上还没有关于什么是产业政策的统一的定义,归纳起来有以下六种比较典型的解释。

1. 产业政策是政府有关产业的一切政策的总和(The Sum of Governmental Policies related to Industry)

日本经济学家下河边淳和菅家茂主编的《现代日本经济事典》中解释说:"产业政策是国家或政府为了实现某种经济和社会目的,以全产业为直接对象,通过对全产业的保护、扶植、调整和完善,积极或消极参与某个产业或企业的生产、营业、交易活动,以及直接或间接干预商业、服务、金融等的市场形成和市场机制的政策的总称。"

2. 产业政策就是计划,是政府对未来产业结构变动方向的干预(A Plan Which Intervene in the Development Direction of Industrial Structure Used by Government)

例如美国社会学家阿密塔伊·艾特伊奥利说:"产业政策就是计划,无非是采用了一个温和的、更加悦目的名词。"又如,美国的玛格里特·迪瓦尔说:"部门政策——鼓励向一些行业或部门投资和不鼓励向其他行业或部门投资——仍然是产业政策讨论中心。"

3. 产业政策主要是为了弥补市场机制所可能造成的失误,而由政府采取的一些补救政策(Aiming at Making up Failures Caused by Market Mechanism)

日本经济学家小宫隆太郎认为:"产业政策的中心课题,就是针对在资源分配方面出现的市场失败而进行干预。"

4. 产业政策是后发国家在努力赶超发达国家时所采取的政策总称(The Policy for Developing Countries to Catch with Developed Countries)

日本经济学家并木信义指出,产业政策就是当一国的产业处于比其他国家落后的状态,或者有可能落后于其他国家时,为了加强本国产业所采取的各种政策。

5. 产业政策是为了加强本国产品的国际竞争力的政策(A Policy Improving Product International Competitiveness)

美国学者查默斯·约翰逊认为,"产业政策是政府为了取得在全球的竞争能力打算在国内发展或限制各种产业的有关活动的总的概括。作为一个政策体系,产业政策是经济政策三角形的第三边,它是对货币政策和财政政策的补充。"

6. 产业政策是指国家(政府)系统设计的有关产业发展,特别是产业结构演变的政策目标和政策措施的总和(The industry policy refers to the combination of policy's objections and measures which focus on the related industry's development designed systematically by government, especially on the evolution of industry's structure.)

我国经济学家周叔莲等在其主编的《中国产业政策研究》中认为,"产业政策是国家干预或参与经济的一种高级形式,它是从整个国家产业发展的全局着眼而系统设计的较完整的政策体系,而不仅仅只是关于某两个产业的局部性政策。"

综上所述,我们认为,产业政策是指一个国家的政府根据产业发展规律的客观要求,综合运用经济手段、法律手段以及必要的行政手段,调整产业组织结构、产业结构和产业分布结构,以及实现社会资源的最优配置,推动整个产业持续、稳定、健康发展的政策体系。

二、产业政策的内容与类型(Contents and Types of Industrial Policy)

(一)产业政策的主要内容(Main Contents of Industrial Policy)

由产业政策的概念可知,产业政策是关于产业发展的政策,它主要包括产业组织政策、产业结构政策、产业分布政策等。在不同时期,不同的国家侧重不同,相互联系较差。

1. 产业组织政策(Industrial Organizational Policy)

The aim of industrial organizational policy is to realize the resource allocation between corporations in the industry. In essence, the government solves the conflict between free market competition and economy of scale to maintain the proper market order and promote effective competition.

产业组织政策是指为实现产业内部企业之间资源配置而制定的政策的总称。其实质是政府通过协调自由竞争与规模经济的矛盾,以维持正常的市场秩序,促进有效竞争的形成。防止大规模企业凭借其垄断地位,通过不正当手段来获取高额利润、抑制竞争。

产业组织政策从政策取向来分有两大类:鼓励竞争、限制垄断的竞争促进政策与鼓励专业化和规模经济的产业合理化政策。从政策对象来分,产业组织政策可分为市场结构控制政策和市场行为控制政策两大类。

产业组织政策的内容,大致包括反垄断和反不正当竞争政策、产业合理化政策和直接规制政策。反垄断和反不正当竞争政策是发达国家产业组织政策的重点,这里所说的垄断主要指人为垄断,而不是自然垄断。该政策表现在三个方面:禁止私人垄断和卡特尔协议;禁止市场过度集中;禁止滥用市场势力。产业合理化政策是为了促进规模经济形成、改善产业组织结构、建立大批量生产方式和增加产业利润、实现产业振兴的基本政策。该政策主要表现为产业组织的合理化和高效化,其基础是流通过程的改组,产品的规格化、标准化、定型化,以及加工的专业化。直接规制政策主要是针对自然垄断产业,目的是防止因重复投资与过度竞争所带来的资源低效配置,并确保产品的稳定供给、收入的公正分配、物价的稳定,以及产业的健康发展。该政策包括进入规制、数量规制、质量规制、设备规制、价格规制和退出规制等。由于直接规制政策在一定程度上制约了企业的经营自主权,极易偏离公众利益最大化的目标。所以,政府应该尽量缩小直接规制的对象范围。

2. 产业结构政策(Industrial Structural Policy)

Industrial structural policy aims to better the industrial structure through the technological advancement. It needs to define the relationship and order for an industry development. It reflects the economy strategy.

产业结构政策是指政府根据产业结构变动规律的客观要求,通过确定产业的构成比例、相互关系和产业发展序列,为实现产业结构合理化和高度化而实施的政策。产业结构政策的目的是以技术进步来不断促进产业结构的优化,既是现代经济增长的内在要求,又是各国经济发展战略的体现。

产业结构政策大致可以分为以产业结构合理化为目标的产业调整政策和以产业结构高度化为目标的产业援助政策两种基本类型。产业结构合理化是产业结构高度化的基础,而产业结构高度化又是产业结构合理化的高级表现形式。

具体来说,产业结构政策一般包括:幼小产业保护政策、主导产业选择政策、战略产业扶植政策和衰退产业调整政策。战略产业(strategic industry)是指能够在未来成为主导产业(leading industry)或支柱产业(supporting industry)的新兴产业。战略产业的扶植政策是产业结构政策中的主导方面和关键部分。该政策以非均衡发展和争取动态比较优势(comparative advantage)的战略思路为指导,着眼于未来的产业优势,直接服务于产业结构的高度化。通过政府有力地介入,来加强对战略产业的生产要素投入,再通过战略产业的超常规发展来带动整个产业结构的高度化。衰退产业是指经历了幼小期(infant period)、成长期(growth period)、成熟期(mature period)之后,进入了产业生命周期的最后一个阶段,此时企业创新能力衰退,产品滞销,新兴产业的替代品销售大幅上升。衰退产业调整政策关系到经济与社会的稳定,因此是产业结构高度化过程中至关重要的一步。其出发点是帮助衰退产业实行有秩序的收缩、撤让,并引导其资本存量向高增长率产业部门有效转移。衰退产业调整政策主要包括:加速设备折旧;市场保护、援助;促进转产;技术与经营支持和转岗培训。

3. 产业分布政策(Industrial Location Policy)

Industrial location policy is about how to locate industry and how to harmonize economy among different areas. In essence, the proper industry location means to establish proper relationships of work attribution.

产业分布政策是指政府根据产业区位理论以及国民经济与区域经济发展的要求,制定和实施的有关产业空间分布、区际经济协调发展的政策总和。产业分布合理化过程的本质是建立合理的地区分工关系的过程。产业布局政策既是产业政策体系中必要的组成部分,又是区域政策体系中很重要的内容。

制定产业分布政策要考虑:自然因素、运输因素、人力资源因素、市场因素、集聚因素和社会因素。产业分布政策从促进经济增长和社会福利的提高出发,通过政府制定规划干预产业空间分布,来获得集聚效益。该政策包括区域发展重点的选择和产业集中发展战略的制订两方面。区域发展重点的选择主要是通过国家产业布局战略的制定,规定战略期内重点支持发展的区域。产业集中发展战略是通过政府直接规划,建立有关产业开发区等产业布局手段来实现。

4. 产业技术政策(Industrial Technology Policy)

Industrial technology policy is about government to advise, make choice, promote and control the industrial technology development. It aims at industrial technology directly.

产业技术政策是指国家对产业技术发展实施指导、选择、促进与控制的政策的总和。它以产业技术为直接的政策对象,是保障产业技术适度和有效发展的重要手段。技术的进步不仅能够导致相关资本和劳动力等资源的节约,而且还能在一定程度上影响产业结构,加速某些产业的发展,从而推动经济增长。

产业技术政策涉及两方面的内容:确定产业技术的发展目标和具体计划;技术进步促进政策。前者如制定技术标准、技术发展规划等,后者包括技术引进政策、技术扩散政策、技术开发扶植政策。

(二)产业政策的基本类型(Types of Industrial Policy)

一个国家在不同的经济发展阶段,或者同处于一个经济发展阶段的不同国家,可能会制定不同的产业政策。因为他们所面临的国情和国际环境会有所不同。

1. 赶超型产业政策(Catch-up Industrial Policy)

赶超型产业政策的出发点是动态比较利益,扶植本国的劣势或空白产业,以达到甚至赶超国际先进水平。后进国家的产业整体素质不高,竞争力较弱,国内市场受发达国家的产品冲击,这时后进国家利用产业政策,在那些技术成熟的先进国家有较强国际竞争力的基础上,建立或提高本国在这些产业上的生产能力,然后择机在国际市场上与发达国家的同类产品竞争,来达到占领国际市场的目的。一般来说,后进国家有两种途径可以选择。首先,后进国家交叉运用进口替代和出口导向两种战略,以达到产业素质螺旋式提高和产业升级。其次,政府对特定行业实行直接资助和间接资助。直接资助是对支柱产业的生产和产品出口给予财政补贴,使其以较低的价格进入国际市场。间接资助是提供支柱产业以更多的税收、信贷等方面的优惠。

2. 调整型产业政策(Adjusting Industrial Policy)

调整性产业政策的出发点是调整产业发展序列,防止或撤让衰退产业而采取的政策。一般来说,可以通过三个途径来实现:一是为传统产业设定一个保护期,在保护期内通过产业现代化来实现其生产规模的扩张;二是收缩衰退产业的生产能力,保留还有国际竞争力的部分生产能力,而把明显丧失国际竞争力的企业向国内非衰退产业或向国外转移;三是用新技术改造传统产业,使其提高竞争力,重新获得国际市场占有率。

3. 先导型产业政策(Leading Industrial Policy)

先导型产业政策的出发点是政府为了支持鼓励高新技术产业的发展,促进产业升级和产业结构高度化。开发高新技术产业,一方面可以在国内市场和国际市场获得比较经济利益,另一方面又可以提高和改造传统产业的技术水平,推动产业结构高度化发展。

三、产业政策的特点与功能(Characteristics and Function of Industrial Policy)

(一)产业政策的特点(Characteristics of Industrial Policy)

1. 目标的多重性(Multiple Aims)

产业政策不仅包括经济目标,也包括社会目标。所以产业政策既能弥补资源配置的市场缺陷,获得较高的经济增长速度,创造经济效益,又能保证社会稳定,充分就业和经济的公平。

2. 产业政策体系的复杂性(Complexity of Industrial Policy System)

产业政策是一个复杂的政策体系,涉及到多层次的内容。在宏观层次上,产业政策主要是改善一般的产业环境,为产业的发展提供良好的环境,包括基础设施的建设、科技的进步等等方面。在中观层次上,产业政策主要是调整产业结构,对新兴产业、战略产业和衰退产业出台不同的产业政策引导,使其合理化。在微观层次上,产业政策主要是通过调整产业内的组织关系,维护市场秩序,保证有效竞争。

3. 产业政策作用范围的广泛性(Wide Rang of Industrial Policy)

产业政策要研究和解决产业组织的合理化,产业结构的高度化,产业分布的协调性和经济增长的效益性。产业政策不一定以产业为直接对象,但产业政策直接或间接地与产业有关。

4. 产业政策的实施手段的多样性(Multiple Means of Industrial Policy)

产业政策实施手段多种多样主要表现在非指令性的经济计划、经济措施、经济立法,也不排除必要的行政指导。产业政策是诱导性政策,尽可能避免国家直接介入资源的分配。

(二)产业政策的功能(Function of Industrial Policy)

1. 弥补市场失灵,增强资源配置的有效性(Make up the Market Failure and Improve the Effectiveness of Resource Distribution)

The existence of market failure because of economy of scale, public product, externality and so on will lead to improper attribution of resource like monopoly, improper competition, lack of infrastructure, environmental pollution and so on. The government needs to carry out certain industrial policy to make up the market failure and improve the effectiveness of resource attribution. 同时,由于市场配置资源存在时滞性和波动性,当市场配置成本高于政府采取产业政策来引导资源配置的成本时,实施产业政策能降低资源配置的成本,提供资源配置的效率。

2. 有助于实现超常规发展,增强国家经济实力(Facilitating Over-conventional Development and Improve National Economy Strength)

经济后进国家在其发展的初期,都会遇到基础设施和基础工业薄弱的瓶颈制约,而这些产业往往外部性较强,所以通过适当的产业倾斜政策,保证在短期内达到经济起飞的要求,较快地接近国际先进水平,缩短赶超时间。Through implementation of industrial policy, some common problems such as the weakness of infrastructure can be well solved. Less-developing countries can catch the opportunity to take off in economy development.

3. 增强产业的国际竞争力（Improving Industry International Competitiveness）

International competitiveness in one country is based on the international comparative advantage, productivity of key corporations, technological innovation and exploit of international market and so on. Industrial policy will help improve international competitiveness.

4. 在全球化过程中保证经济稳定健康发展（Maintaining the Development of Stable and Healthy Economy Globalization）

产业政策是20世纪70年代后为人们所重视，被广泛采纳的。在当今全球经济一体化，区域合作不断加强的时代，经济结构出现剧烈动荡，在急剧扩张期后，往往伴随出现生产能力过剩、退出壁垒，需要政府制定产业政策来有效调节经济。

四、产业政策的理论依据（Theoretical Basis of Industrial Policy）
（一）市场失灵与产业政策（Market Failure and Industrial Policy）

当市场机制无法有效地配置社会资源时，就出现了市场失灵。

1. 垄断（Monopoly）

The market cannot impose a price on a monopolist as it imposes a price on the price-taking competitive firm. But the monopolist cannot select both price and the quantity it sells. In accord with the demand curve, the higher the price it sets, the less it can sell.

Compared with the perfectly competitive ideal, the monopolist restricts output and charges a higher price. We must note that under monopoly, the firm and the industry are exactly the same entity. But under perfect competition, any firm is just a small portion of the industry. Monopoly output is determined by the profit-maximization requirement, the $MC = MR$. But long-run competitive equilibrium occurs when price and average cost are equal and economic profit is zero.

By comparing the equilibrium point in long-run competition with the monopolist's equilibrium, we see that the monopolist produces fewer units of output than that of a competitive industry with the same demand and cost conditions.

We conclude, then, that a monopoly will charge a higher price and produce a smaller output than will a competitive industry with the same demand and cost conditions. A competitive industry devotes "just the right amount" of society's scarce resources to the production of its particular commodity. Therefore, a monopolist produces too little. Adam Smith's invisible hand is sending out the wrong signals. Consumers are willing to pay an amount for an additional unit of the good that exceeds what it costs to produce that unit, but the monopoly refuses to increase production, for if it raise output by one unit, the revenue it will collect will be less than the price the consumer will pay for the additional unit. The monopolist does not increase production, and resources are allocated inefficiently.

作为一种产品的唯一生产者，垄断者拥有价格的控制权，价格远超过边际成本，并且产量低于有效产出水平。根据利润最大化的原则和边际收益等于边际成本而确定的垄断厂商的要素投入远没有达到合理的阶段。因此，垄断厂商的资源配置效率很低，引发资源浪费、不充分就业等问题。20世纪中叶，西方发达国家的政府通过控制企业的价格和利润来抑制垄断势力，如公用事业的控制，禁止合谋定价和禁止价格歧视，颁布反托拉斯法等等。

非竞争行为造成的市场失败，靠市场自身是没法解决的，必须通过政府制定和推行产业政策的外部力量才能得到有效缓解。实行以经济计划和经济措施为主要手段的产业政策的主要目的，在于完善市场机制，强化产业结构的转换能力，有效地发挥产业结构自我调整、自我演进的功能。

2. 外部性（Externalities）

Externalities is one of the least obvious, yet one of the most consequential of the imperfection of the price system. Many economic activities provide incidental benefits to others for whom they are not specifically intended. For example, homeowners who plant beautiful gardens in front of their homes incidentally and unintentionally provide pleasure to their neighbors and to those who pass by—people from whom they receive no payment. We say then that their activity generates a beneficial externality. An activity is said to generate a beneficial or detrimental externality if that activity causes incidental benefits or damages to others, and no corresponding compensation is provided to or paid by those who generate the externality. Similarly, there are activities that indiscriminately impose costs on others. For example, the operators of a motorcycle repair shop, from which all sorts of noise besieges the neighborhood and for which they pay no compensation to others, are said to produce a detrimental externality. 所谓外部性是指某个经济主体生产和消费物品及服务的行为不以市场为媒介,面对其他的经济主体产生的附加效应的现象。也就是说,外部性是市场价格没有完全反映交易的额外成本或收益。

外部性可以分为积极的和消极的两种:当某种经济的社会成本(经济中所有个人所承担的边际成本)小于私人边际成本(单个生产者所承担的边际成本)时,将产生积极的外部性;反之,就存在消极的外部性。In discussing externalities, it is crucial to distinguish between social and private marginal cost. The marginal social cost of an activity is the sum of its marginal private cost plus the incidental cost (positives or negative) which is borne by others.

Where the firm's activity causes detrimental externalities, free markets will leave us in a situation where marginal benefits are less than marginal social costs. Smaller outputs than those that maximize profits will be socially desirable.

Where the firm's activity generates beneficial externalities, free markets will produce too little output. Society would be better off with larger output levels.

An industry that generates detrimental externalities will have a marginal social cost higher than its marginal private cost. If the price is equal to its own marginal private cost, it will therefore be below the true marginal cost to society. The market mechanism thereby tends to encourage inefficiently large outputs of products that cause detrimental externalities. The opposite is true of products that cause beneficial externalities—private industry will provide inefficiently small quantities of these products.

由于外部性的存在,使个人或者企业的边际成本与社会边际成本形成一定的差额。同时,个人或者企业的边际成本与社会边际成本也会形成一定的差额,这两个差额便是外部成本和外部效益。当产生外部成本时,便是外部不经济;当产生外部效益时,便是外部经济。无论是外部经济还是外部不经济,个人或企业在达到他们各自效用最大化的时候,社会资源不能实现优化配置,经济活动出现不公平,基础设施投资不足,生态破坏,环境污染等问题大量出现。此时,必须依靠政府有力的产业政策来干预经济,纠正外部性导致的市场的无效率。

3. 公共物品(Public Goods)

所谓公共物品是指一个人对某些物品或劳务的消费并未减少其他人同样消费或享受的物品。Public goods are commodities that are valuable socially but whose provision, for reasons we will now explain, cannot be financed by private enterprise, or at least not at socially desirable prices. Thus, government must pay for public goods if they are to be provided at all. Standard examples range from national defense to coastal lighthouses.

公共物品具有消费的非排他性和消费的非竞争性两大特性。It is easy to explain the nature of public goods by contrasting them with the sort of commodities, called private goods. Private goods are characterized by two important attributes. One can be called depletability. If you eat a steak or use a gallon of gasoline, there is much less beef or fuel in the world available for other people, either temporarily of permanently.

But pure public goods are like the legendary widow's jars of oil, which always remain full no matter how many people use them. For example, once the snow is removed from a street, the improved driving conditions are available to all the drivers who use that street, to 10 or 1000 cars which pass that way. 公共物品的这一特点被称为非竞争性。非竞争性意味着某个人对一种物品的消费并不妨碍别的任何人对该物品的享受。由于个人或企业能受益于这种物品,无需花费代价就可以得到该物品,因此,市场无法制定出公共物品的最适宜消费水平。

The other property that characterizes private goods but not public goods is excludability, meaning that anyone who does not pay for the goods can be excluded from enjoying its benefits. If you do not buy a ticket, you are excluded from the basketball game. If you do not pay for an electric guitar, the storekeeper will not give it to you.

But some goods or services, once provided to anyone, automatically become available to many other persons, to whom it is difficult, if not impossible, to exclude from the benefits. If a street is cleared of snow, everyone who uses the street benefits, regardless of who paid for the snowplow. 非排他性,是指对一种物品未付费的各个人不可能被阻止享受该物品的好处。在这种情况下,个人或企业将不负担某一物品的费用,而能免费获得该物品。

Public goods are defined as goods that lack depletability. Very often, it also lacks excludability. Since nonpaying users usually cannot be excluded from enjoying public goods, suppliers of such goods will find it difficult or impossible to collect fees for the benefits they provide. This is the so-called "free rider" problem. Services such as transportation system and public health, which are depletable and where excludability is simply impossible, cannot be provided by private enterprises because people will not pay for what they can get free. Since private firms are not in the business of giving services away, the supply of public goods must be left to government authorities and nonprofit institutions.

由于外部性的存在,市场将过少地生产具有外部正效应的公共物品,而过多地生产具有外部负效应的公共物品,外部性带来的帕累托无效率问题大量存在。

4. 信息的不对称导致逆向选择和道德风险(Asymmetry of Information Leads to Adverse selection and Moral Hazard)

完全竞争的均衡会产生帕累托效率,因为一个完全竞争的市场的前提是买卖双方拥有完全对称的信息。但是,在现实生活中,买卖双方处在一个信息不完全对称的环境中,不仅所拥有的信息的数量不一致,而且信息的真实性还要靠买卖双方自己去作判断。如果在错误信息的基础上,那么就会做出错误的推断。由于信息不完善,企业事前的分散决策,很难避免事后的重复生产和无效率,从而导致生产资源配置的无效率。

To make informed choices among goods and services available in the market, households must have full information on product quality, availability, and price. To make sound judgments about what inputs to use, firms must have full information on input availability, quality, and price.

The absence of full information can cause households and firms to make mistakes. A voluntary exchange is almost always evidence that both parties benefit. Thus most voluntary exchanges are efficient. However, in the presence of imperfect information, not all exchanges are efficient. An obvious example is fraud.

Firms as well as consumers can be the victims of incomplete or inaccurate information. Recall that a profit-maximizing competitive firm will hire workers as long as the marginal revenue product of labor is greater than the wage rate. How can a firm judge the productivity of a potential hire? Also, suppose that a worker steal from the firm. The cost of employing that worker is greater than just the wage of that employee.

The problem of adverse selection can occur when a buyer or seller enters an exchange with another party who has more information. Suppose there are only two types of workers: lazy workers and hard workers. Workers know which type they are, but employers cannot tell. If there is only one wage rate, lazy workers will be overpaid relative to their productivity and hard workers will be underpaid. Recall that workers weigh the value of leisure and nonmarket production against the wage in deciding whether to enter the labor force. Because hard workers will end up underpaid relative to their productivity, fewer hard workers will be attracted into the labor force. Similarly, because lazy workers are overpaid relative to their productivity, more of them will be attracted into the labor force. Hence, the market has selected among workers adversely.

Adverse selection is also a problem in insurance markets. Insurance companies insure people against risks like health problems or accidents. Individuals know more about their own health than anyone else, even with required medical exams. If medical insurance rates are set at the same level for everyone, then medical insurance is a better deal for those who are unhealthy. This forces insurance companies to raise premiums.

假定在一个旧货市场上,有高质量的车和低质量的车。在实际生活中,旧车的卖主对车的质量比买主要知道的多得多。那么,如果卖主知道车的质量而买主不知道,那么买主在购买时会把所有的车都看作是

"中等"质量的。这样,市场价格太低而不能使高质量车进入市场出售。消费者在购买以前不能容易地确定一辆旧车的质量,因此旧车的价格下跌。由于信息的不对称,低质量商品把高质量商品逐出市场。当不同质量的产品以单一价格出售时,逆向选择就出现了。结果,市场上就有太多的低质量产品和太少的高质量产品。

　　保险市场上,即是保险公司坚持要做医疗检查,购买保险的人对他们总的健康情况也要比任何保险公司所希望知道的清楚的多。结果就像旧车那样,也出现了逆向选择。

　　Another information problem that arises in insurance markets is moral hazard. Often, people enter into contracts in which the result of the contract, at least in part, depends on one of the parties' future behavior. A moral hazard problem arises when one party of a contract passes the cost of its behavior on to the other party of the contract. For example, accident insurance policies are contracts that agree to pay for repairs of your car if it is damaged in an accident. Whether you have an accident or not in part depends on whether you drive cautiously. Similarly, apartment leases may specify that the landlord perform routine maintenance around the apartment. If you punch the wall every time you get angry, your landlord ultimately pays the repair bill.

　　Such contracts can lead to inefficient behavior. The problem is like the externality problem in which firms and households have no incentive to consider the full costs of their behavior. If my car is fully insured against theft, why should I lock it? If visits to the dentist are free under my dental insurance plan, why not get my teeth cleaned six times a year?

　　Like adverse selection, the moral hazard problem is an information problem. Contracting parties cannot always determine the future behavior of the person with whom they are contracting. If all future behavior could be predicted, contracts could be written to try to eliminate undesirable behavior. Sometimes this is possible. Life insurance companies do not pay off in the case of suicide. Fire insurance companies will not write a policy unless you have smoke detectors. If you cause unreasonable damage to an apartment, your landlord can retain your security deposit.

（二）政府失败与产业政策（Government Failure and Industrial Policy）

当市场遇到自身无法解决的问题，出现市场失灵时，政府会制定和推行产业政策来进行干预。但是，我们应该看到，市场做不好的事情，政府不一定能完全满意地解决。政府调节机制中存在的内在缺陷，我们称为政府失败。政府失败主要表现在以下几个方面：

1. 有限信息（Imperfect Information）

市场的信息不足是造成市场失败的一个因素。对于私人难以掌握的信息，政府也未必能完全掌握。政府作出有效决策的前提是掌握充分的信息。由于不完全信息的存在，政府要做出正确的分析判断是比较困难的。在一个不成熟的市场和正处在发育过程中的社会主义市场经济中，政府也有一个学习和了解的过程。在这个过程中由于信息不完善，知识不具备，政府政策可能会出现失误。

2. 官僚主义（Bureaucracy）

政府在做决策时，追求风险的最小化。因此，通常采用集体决策。但是这种集体反复讨论后做出的决策要经过几个时滞，难免有官僚主义之嫌做这是政府本身不可避免的自身缺陷。

第一个是认识时滞（recognition lag），是指从问题产生到被发现并纳入政府讨论日程的这段时间。

第二个是决策时滞（decision lag），是指从政府认识问题到政府最后得出解决方案的这段时间。

第三个是执行与生效时滞（execution and effecting lag），是指从政府公布某项决策到付诸实施的这段时间。

由于有以上三个时滞的存在，所以当旧问题开始着手解决时，可能解决问题的最佳时机已经过去，新问题成为更大的问题。

Recent work in economics has focused not just on the government as an extension of individual preferences but also on government officials as people with their own agendas and objectives. That is, government officials are assumed to maximize their own utility, not the social good. To understand the way government functions, we need to look less at the preferences of individual members of society and more at the incentive structures that exist around public officials.

Officials we seem to worry about are the people who run

government agencies—the Social Security Administration, the Department of Housing and Urban Development, and state registries of motor vehicles, for example.

In the private sector, where firms compete for profits, only efficient firms producing goods that consumers will buy survive. If a firm is inefficient—if it is producing at a higher-than-necessary cost—the market will drive it out of business. This is not necessarily so in the public sector. If a government bureau is producing a necessary service, or one mandated by law, it does not need to worry about customers. No matter how bad the service is at the registry of motor vehicles, everyone with a car must buy its product.

The efficiency of a government agency's internal structure depends on the way incentives facing workers and agency heads are structured. If the budget allocation of an agency is based on the last period's spending alone, for example, agency heads have a clear incentive to spend more money, however inefficiently. This point is not lost on government officials, who have experimented with many ways of rewarding agency heads and employees for cost-saving suggestions.

However, critics say such efforts to reward productivity and punish inefficiency are rarely successful. It is difficult to punish, let alone dismiss, a government employee. Elected officials are subject to recall, but it usually takes gross negligence to rouse voters into instituting such a measure. Also, elected officials are rarely associated with problems of bureaucratic mismanagement, which they decry daily.

3. 企业的寻租行为使政府对私人市场反应的控制有限(Rent-seeking Behavior Limiting the Control by Government on the Private Market Reaction)

寻租一般用于描述个人或厂商投入精力以获得租金,或者从政府那里获得其他好处的行为。如政府可以通过创造、提高和保护一个利益集团甚至某个企业在市场上的垄断地位,或者给予一些企业特殊权利,从而使偏爱的市场主体获得一定的垄断租金和优惠权利。

由于政府掌握着干预经济的权利,政府官员控制资源的分配权这种稀缺的珍贵资源。在追求这种分配权的角逐中,官员们从最大化自身效用处罚往往会倾向于"政治设租",人为制造稀缺,使经济不能实现有效的资源分配;而对于企业来说,为了实现利益最大化,也更倾向于寻租活动,而不是寻利。通过各种方式来游说政府制定一些有利于自己企业的政策、制度和规则来获得租金,便成为这些企业主要的经济行为。在这种情况下,政府对经济的干预将失灵。

Another problem with public choice is that special-interest groups can and do spend resources to influence the legislative process. As we said before, individual voters have little incentive to become well informed and to participate fully in the legislative process. Favor-seeking special-interest groups have a great deal of incentive to participate in political decision making. We saw that a monopolist would be willing to pay to prevent competition from eroding its economic profits. Many—if not all—industries lobby for favorable treatment, softer regulation, or antitrust exemption. This, as you recall, is rent-seeking.

Rent-seeking extends far beyond those industries that lobby for government help in preserving monopoly powers.

This theory may suggest that unregulated markets fail to produce an efficient allocation of resources. This should not lead you to the conclusion that government involvement necessarily leads to efficiency. There are reasons to believe that government attempts to produce the right goods and services in the right quantities efficiently may fail.

由以上可以看出,政府失败主要是国家对经济的过度干预,即国家干预的范围和力度,超过了弥补市场失效和维护市场机制正常运作的合理需要。正确的产业政策正确确定市场机制和政府干预的各自作用的合理边界,应有效地发挥二者的组合功效。

五、实施产业政策的原则和手段(Principles and Methods of Industrial Policy Implementation)

(一)产业政策的原则(Principles of Industrial Policy)

产业政策的实施必须遵循科学的原则,才能有效发挥产业政策的作用,引导产业之间和产业内部的协调发展。

1. 遵循市场经济规律,注重发挥市场机制的基础作用(Comply with the Market Law and Bring the Market Mechanism into Play)

实施产业政策的基础是建立竞争有序的市场机制,优化资源配置,促进产业结构的协调。虽然市场在调节社会资源的配置方面存在不足和缺陷,但从整体上看,它是最有效的资源配置手段。市场能解决的问题,政府就不应该再去干预了;市场无法解决的问题,政府就应该有所为。产业政策应注重发挥市场的作用,维护市场功能,离开市场的产业机制是低效的。

2. 发挥市场机制与政府作用的组合功效,使成本最小化(Exert the Combined Function of Market Mechanism and Government Regulation to Minimize the Lost)

政府和市场是社会资源配置的两种形式或手段,不能相互替代,而是战略互补。因此,政府在实施产业政策的时候,首先要确定哪些是市场本身能做好的,哪些是存在市场缺陷需要产业政策引导的。政府管住管好力所能及的事情,市场能做好的尽可以由市场去调解。其次,选择由产业政策和市场作用组合的成本最小的战略互补型结构。

3. 科学制定产业发展序列(Establish the Sequence of Industrial Development Scientifically)

产业政策的制定,关系到宏观经济的中长期发展,涉及各方面的经济利益,是一项复杂的系统工程。

同一时期的不同国家产业政策不同,一个国家在不同时期的产业政策也会不同。一个国家的产业政策的重要目标包括优化资源配置,优化产业结构,增强产品的国际竞争力,合理分布生产力,实现地区产业的协调发展。

科学制定产业发展序列首先要全面分析产业发展的历史和现状,研究其面临的主要问题,使产业政策有针对性,有轻重缓急。其次,加强研究产业发展前景的预测研究,准确把握不同产业的发展趋势。第三,加强科学论证和民主审议,组织有关部门、产业界、学术界和消费者群体进行论证和审议,由国家批准才能实施。同时,在产业政策实施的过程中,加强监督、检查和分析,提出改进建议。

4. 坚持系统原则和整体原则,使产业政策成为相互配套的政策体系(Making the Industry Policy Become a Coordinative Policy System by Insisting on Systematic and Unitary Principles)

产业政策具有目标的多重性,作用范围的广泛性等特点,涉及到宏观、中观、微观多层面,结构政策、组织政策、布局政策、技术政策多方面的内容。因此,在制定产业政策的时候,必须从整体观念出发,研究产业之间和产业内部的关系,避免相互脱节。

(二) 实施产业政策的手段(Methods of Industrial Policy)

1. 直接干预(Direct Intervention)

是运用政府的行政权力来调整产业经济活动的硬性手段。包括政府以配额制、许可证制、审批制、政府直接投资经营等方式,直接干预某产业的资源分配与运行态势,及时纠正产业活动中与产业政策相抵触的各种违规行为,以保证预定产业政策目标的实现。

2. 间接诱导(Indirect Inducement)

主要是指通过提供行政指导、信息服务、税收减免、融资支持、财政补贴、关税保护等方式,诱导企业自觉服从政府的产业政策目标。

3. 法律规制(Law's Regulation)

法律规制是依靠国家法权的力量,通过经济立法、司法和手法来调整产业中的经济关系,维护市场秩序,保障和促进各产业的协调发展。

首先要建立一套比较完备的符合国情、符合产业发展趋势的法律法规,保证有法可依。其次,必须健全司法,监督、检查产业政策的落实情况,提出改进的建议。

第二节 旅游产业政策(Tourism Industrial Policy)

一、旅游产业政策的目标和特征(Objectives and Characteristics of Tourism Industrial Policy)

旅游产业政策是政府根据一定时期内旅游发展的目标以及旅游发展所存在的问题而制定的。

(一) 旅游产业政策的目标(Objectives of Tourism Industrial Policy)

1. 社会目标(Social Objective)

随着生活质量的提高,人们外出旅游,有助于消除紧张和疲劳,得到身心的放松和愉悦。心理学研究表明,一个身心放松的人更容易接受他人的意见,更容易同他人友好相处。许多政府通过制定资助低收入者出游(social tour)和保护旅游消费者权益(consumer protect)等政策来促进旅游需求的增长。同时,政府还要考虑到当地居民的利益,使他们能够享受到旅游发展带来的好处。

2. 经济目标(Economic Objective)

旅游政策的经济目标应该有利于优化旅游资源配置,鼓励旅游投资,推动经济结构调整,壮大旅游产业,提高旅游经济效益。政府还应注意到太依赖于季节性强的旅游活动,会导致社会和经济的不稳定。即使在那些旅游经济在国民经济中所占份额高的地区,也要鼓励发展多种经济形态。旅游是综合性产业,比较敏感,对经济环境等要求较高。因此,旅游产业政策要建立灵活的预警机制,减少由于环境的不稳定带来的旅游产业的波动。

3. 环境目标(Environmental Objective)

旅游是一种高度依赖环境的活动。一项不适当的旅游政策会因为过多影响了环境质量而不可避免地带来损失。旅游政策的环境目标就是要在发展旅游与保护环境之间寻求一种平衡,并且两者能够互相促进。要使各种建筑物、旅游设施与周围环境相协调,防止对环境产生不利影响;还要制定综合性的土地使用政策,防止土地被过度开发。旅游发展可持续进行是环境目标的重要内容。

(二)旅游产业政策的特征(Characteristics of Tourism Industrial Policy)

由于旅游产业政策与旅游经济的发展程度直接相关,不同的国家旅游产业政策的内容和作用是不同,但在本质上,旅游产业政策一般都具有以下特征:

1. 诱导性和间接性(Inducement and Indirection)

旅游产业政策形成以后,相应地,财政、货币等政策的制定、实施都要在产业政策指导下或约束下发挥作用。诱导性是指政策制定的逻辑出发点是促进社会生产力的提高,全面提升产业素质,提高社会经济效益,促进技术进步的发展等,具有一定的意义和作用。旅游产业政策的制定主要是为了维护旅游市场秩序、促进有序竞争,优化资源配置,但不是直接干预企业的经营活动,而是以间接的引导作用来实现产业政策。

2. 序列性和动态性(Sequence and Mobility)

旅游产业政策包括了旅游产业组织政策、旅游产业结构政策、旅游产业分布政策等。在经济水平发展的不同阶段,旅游产业政策的侧重点也会发生变化。另外,随着收入水平的不断提高,旅游需求层次会发生变化,从观光旅游到休闲度假,产业政策处于动态的变化中。

3. 稳定性和连续性(Stability and Continuity)

稳定性和上面的动态性不是相矛盾的,因为每一项产业政策从制定到实施不可避免地会遇到时滞性问题。为了保证产业政策在一个较长时期能促进旅游产业的健康发展,在一个较长时期内必须要有稳定性,同时每一阶段的产业政策之间必须要有连续性,以保证产业政策的连贯,不脱节,符合旅游产业的发展趋势。

4. 开放性(Internationalism)

在经济全球一体化的今天,旅游产业同样也要参与国际交流合作。每个国家的旅游经济发展模式均包括入境旅游、出境旅游和国内旅游,因此,必然会受到其他国家旅游经济发展的影响。旅游在本质上是一项经济性很强的文化产业,旅游产业从某种意义上是各种文化、资源的相互交汇,因此,一国的旅游产业政策必然具有国际性。

二、我国旅游产业政策的发展(China's Tourism Industrial Policy Development)

1978年,为了获取外汇、吸引外商,我国实行以入境观光旅游为先导的非常规发展的旅游战略。从理论上讲,这是对旅游认识的萌芽阶段,旅游被认为是"无烟工业","投资少,收益大,就业多,见效快"。在这种被盲目夸大的认识下,同年,提出"大力发展旅游业"。1981年,国务院做出了关于加强旅游工作的八项决定,提出要逐步走出一条适合国情的旅游道路,"积极发展、量力而行、稳步前进"。1984年,中共中央办公厅、国务院办公厅转发国家旅游局《关于开创旅游工作新局面几个问题的报告》,又提出加快旅游基础设施的建设要采取国家、地方、部门、集体和个人一起上,自力更生和利用外资一起上的方针,即"五个一起上"的方针。同年,国务院又批转了国家旅游局关于旅游体制改革的报告,进一步明确了上述方针,并提出了加强国内旅游的管理,发挥各个方面的积极性,引导和鼓励各方面进行国内旅游设施的建设,以满足广大人民群众日益增长的需要。1985年,国务院又召集会议研究发展我国旅游事业。1986年,国务院召开全国旅游工作会议,确定旅游业正式纳入国民经济和社会发展计划。1987年,提出"大力发展旅游业"。1988年,国务院办公厅转发国家旅游局关于加强旅游工作的十条意见,原则上明确了旅游的行业范围。以上的方针政策对旅游产业化形成和供给市场化起到了一定的作用。

进入20世纪90年代后,我国旅游业的发展有了理性的指导,并出现了两种旅游业的发展模式。1990年,国务院发展研究中心、国家旅游局、中国社科院财贸所在第五次旅游经济理论研讨会上,集中讨论了国际重点科研项目:《中国旅游经济发展战略研究报告(纲要)》。研讨会上出现了两种战略思想,旅游发展应当是与社会经济发展相适应,还是应当超前于社会经济发展。两种模式的出现,说明在中国这样一个发展中国家,幅员辽阔,各地的资源类型、特点差异性很大,经济发展不平衡,各地发展旅游的侧重点不同,因此没有必要,也不可能按一种模式发展,任何模式都必须因地制宜,适合当地经济发展的总体要求。

三、我国旅游产业政策的内容(The Content of Our Tourism Industry Policy)

1. 旅游产业结构政策(Tourism Industrial Structure Policy)

由于旅游产业的综合性和依赖性都很强,旅游产业的结构问题包括:

第一,产业定位问题,即旅游产业在国民经济产业体系中的位置。近年来,各地非常重视旅游产业的发展,对旅游产业有明确的定位,如国民经济的支柱产业、先导产业、龙头产业、经济的新增长点等。第二,产业宏观问题,即国际旅游、国内旅游以及出境旅游三种不同层次的旅游形式之间的相互协调、和谐发展问题。我国的旅游经济是从发展入境旅游开始的。随着我国经济的发展,目前我国外汇储备充足,外汇创收作为改革开放初期旅游业承担的重大角色已不再重要。而且伴随着人民收入水平和国民旅游需求层次的提高,国内旅游红红火火,出境旅游的需求也日益增长。所以,要根据新情况来安排入境、出境和国内旅游三种不同层次的发展格局。再如,在旅游业的起步阶段,为了给外商提供良好的住宿环境,酒店业最早引入外资,建了一批由国外酒店管理集团经营的涉外星级宾馆,因此造成目前星级酒店较多,而经济性饭店较少的局面,成为制约国内旅游发展的瓶颈。因此,饭店业的结构也需要调整。第三,产业配套问题,即旅游产业内各单项结构的合理化。旅游产业是包括"食"、"住"、"行"、"游"、"购"、"娱"六大因素的综合产业。在这六大因素中,"食"、"住"、"行"也是日常生活的组成部分,"游"、"购"、"娱"才是旅游者真正要追求的。但是旅游产业整体的健康稳定运行离不开各个环节的配套,离不开基础部门的配合与支持。因此,要制定相关政策,防止各环节的脱节。20世纪90年代以来,我国的基础产业逐渐引入了竞争机制,广泛吸引社会投资,从而使我国基础产业有了较快发展,基础产业的瓶颈制约有了相当程度的缓解。

2. 旅游产业组织政策（Tourism Industrial Organizational Policy）

旅游产业组织政策和旅游产业结构政策等政策是相互配套的，既配合了产业结构的调整，调整了产业组织关系，又维持了市场机制的基本功能。旅游产业的组织政策是为了协调竞争和规模经济的关系，既要防止垄断对旅游经济运行造成的破坏，又要形成一定的规模经济，从而提高资源的有效配置，公平分配，增加经济效益。产业组织政策涉及旅游企业的准入制度、经济规模等，包括市场结构控制政策、旅游市场行为调整政策和优化资源配置政策。旅游产业组织政策包括两个方面：一是鼓励竞争、限制垄断的市场秩序政策，如组建跨地区、跨行业、跨所有制的旅游企业集团，打破地区垄断和部门垄断；二是鼓励规模经济、防止过度竞争，如企业通过兼并、收购、相互持股等方式，进行资助联合改组和资产运营。国家应鼓励大中型企业实现现代企业制度、小型企业网络化、推动旅游产业分工体系的建成。

3. 旅游产业分布政策（Tourism Industrial Distributive Policy）

由于旅游业是人的流动，旅游经济是人流带来的经济，而不像工业是产品的流动，因此旅游目的地的资源状况、交通条件等因素在旅游发展中起了很大的作用。旅游产业与农业、工业等其他产业的差别在于，既有产业分布的区域性问题，也有产业分布的点线结合、点面结合问题。各地的资源禀赋不一样，客观上造成了不同的比较优势。在制订旅游产业政策时，应根据旅游吸引物分布的特殊性，强调形成旅游区域的专业化分工，比如海南的海滨度假，黑龙江、吉林的冰雪旅游，云南、西藏的生态旅游等等。另外，还要根据各地的区位优势，如沿海、沿边、沿江等，形成有相对优势的旅游产品分布。根据资源的互补性、产品的相关性和交通的便利状况等条件，加强旅游产品的点线、点面之间的联系，开发出有较强竞争力的独特的产品。

随着市场结构的改变和交通运输的发展，我国旅游产业的空间布局正在发生深刻变化。首先，在大的空间尺度上，旅游产业的增长表现出多中心性。在过去的20多年里，旅游产业的增长主要依靠北京、深圳、上海、杭州、南京、西安、桂林等著名旅游城市的发展。90年代以来，中国东部沿海新兴旅游城市和西南、西北边远省区旅游产业的增长势头表现得更为强劲。东部沿海得益于改革开放，经济发达、人民收入水平高，旅游产业增长是必然的。中国西南、西北边远省区的优势则主要体现在旅游资源禀赋方面，地质地貌景观独特、历史资源悠久、民风淳朴，符合当前回归自然的生态旅游。但西南、西北边远省区旅游产业发展的主要制约因素是交通条件。随着西部开发,西南、西北会成为中国旅游产业最有潜力的地区。由于社会经济水平的不同,我国西南、西北的旅游发展与东部沿海的旅游发展道路也有差异,表现在:前者处于发展的初级阶段,强化基础设施,扩大数量规模是其发展的主要方向。后者则更多地凭借系统经济的优势,通过深度开发、综合利用、多种经营来谋求旅游产业的持续发展。为了配合国家开发西部的战略,在继续发展好东部地区旅游业的同时,对西部的旅游发展给予一定的政策优惠措施。

4. 旅游产业市场开发政策(The Opening Policy of Tourism Industrial Market)

由于旅游行业是个开放性的行业,国际竞争激烈,从供求关系上分析,呈现出买方市场的特点。因此,旅游产业市场开发政策成为旅游产业政策的重要组成部分。旅游产业市场开发政策是为提升旅游目的地国家的形象,刺激旅游企业进行市场开拓的积极性而制定的,因为旅游企业才是旅游产业中真正的主体。

旅游产业市场开发政策是对旅游市场中出现的问题进行引导,鼓励或限制某些方面,促进整体的协调发展。例如,SARS之后为了重新启动旅游市场,国家通过对旅游企业的减税、补贴等政策来支持旅游企业。

5. 旅游产业技术政策(The Technological Policy of Tourism Industry)

尽管旅游产业属于劳动密集型产业,但是随着高新技术的发展,先进技术与旅游业的联系越来越紧密。如电脑预订网络、饭店的电子监控设备、通讯技术等。这些技术渗透到旅游业中,大大提高了旅游产业的生产效率,使人们的出行更加舒适、便捷、安全。旅游产业的技术政策包括旅游产业技术进步的指导性政策、旅游产业技术进步的组织政策、旅游产业技术进步的激励性政策等。政府在制定和实施产业技术政策时,要考虑到技术的实用性,鼓励产学研结合,加快技术的转化,推进标准化工作进程,完善管理信息系统的开发,推广新技术,淘汰落后技术。

6. 旅游产业保障政策(The Maintaining Policy of Tourism Industry)

旅游业综合性的特点决定了旅游业的发展与交通运输部门、经贸部门等的政策有强的相关性。一项产业政策制定完成之后,要有相应的旅游产业保障政策来保证各项政策能够落实到位,监督各项产业政策的实施,对实际工作中出现的问题及时反馈,以修正相关政策。

产业保障政策是依据产业政策目标和调整取向,由宏观调控部门协调相关部门作出的配合、支持政策及手段措施。旅游业是整个经济系统中的一个子系统,其政策保障体系是国家宏观产业政策的组成部分。经过二十多年的发展,我国旅游产业的政策是大力发展入境旅游、积极发展国内旅游、适度发展出境旅游。随着我国加入世贸组织,欧盟等旅游目的地向中国的开放,出境旅游在未来几年会有较大的发展。

第三节 世界各国旅游产业政策
(Tourism Policy Around the World)

旅游产业发达国家大多为混合型经济国家,即市场和计划两种资源配置手段在该国经济发展特别是旅游产业经济发展中形成互补,共同作用产生合力。在这些国家中,公共部门和私人部门共同存在,并且共同促进旅游产业的发展。在旅游经济发展的不同阶段,两者仅在干涉的程度上发生变化。如对自由企业体系和联邦宪法充满自信的美国,授权各州和私人组织资助促销旅游产品,中央政府的干预就限于采取措施保护公民的健康和安全。由于各国旅游产业在国民经济体系中占据的地位不同,所以各国旅游产业政策的作用机理等不尽一致,同时一国对产业的指导与控制长度也不同,即旅游产业政策存在着横向和纵向的差异。如经济高度依赖旅游产业的西班牙、肯尼亚和英国,各自设立了专门的旅游产业管理机构,并由其制定和组织实施具体的产业政策。这些机构分别是:旅游、运输和通讯部,旅游和野生动物保护部,文化传媒和体育部。三国旅游资源的差异形成了迥然不同的旅游产品特色,因而对旅游经济活动的计划管理也形成了各自鲜明的特点。

针对旅游贸易中出现的大量赤字,从20世纪50年代起,美国就开始了国家旅游政策的研究,并以《国家旅游政策研究的概念基础》、《国家旅游政策确定阶段》和《国家旅游政策研究最后报告》等三个连续性的报告为其研究成果。1981年通过立法程序的国家旅游政策由总统签发颁布。国家旅游政策法案的主要目标是发展美国入境旅游,刺激经济和美国旅游业的稳定增长,减少国家旅游赤字,增进美国人民与其他国家人民的相互理解和友谊。国家旅游政策法案的实施,促进了美国国际旅游的发展,旅游业在美国商务部的地位迅速上升。

一、北美自由贸易协定和北美旅游发展政策(NAFTA and Tourism Development Policy in North America)

The North American Free Trade Agreement(NAFTA), involving the USA, Mexico and Canada, is one of the most recent trading blocs to emerge as part of the global trend towards closer economic ties between neighbouring countries. Created in January 1994, NAFTA is the largest free trade area in the world, with a $6.5 trillion market and 370 million people, as compared to the European Community which has a GDP of $3 trillion and a population of 357 million.

The NAFTA agreement, a document of over 2000 pages long, represents US, Mexican and Canadian commitment to the free flow of trade in goods and services. Its primary objective is to eliminate barriers to trade in products and services. While the provisions of the USA-Canada Free Trade Agreement (FTA) identified specifically targeted sectors, the strength of the NAFTA is that all services were covered by the agreement unless specifically excluded. Aviation, for example, was excluded from coverage under the NAFTA and operates under bilateral arrangements, which must be negotiated separately. Tourism does not have a special chapter or article in the NAFTA agreement but is covered more generally in sections dealing with trade in services (cross-border transactions), financial and telecommunications investments, and temporary entry.

Regional trading blocks such as NAFTA are expected to have positive tourism implications to the extent that closer economic relations between countries facilitate investment in infrastructure, stimulate intra-regional tourism flows and increase international competitiveness among member countries. Here we will provide a preliminary assessment of the tourism impacts of NAFTA. This task is compounded by the fact that many of these impacts will be long term and therefore not immediately apparent. Also, isolating NAFTA's impacts from those of other factors is difficult, especially when NAFTA-related changes coincide with other events such as the Mexican economic crisis precipitated by the devaluation of the peso. Not withstanding these difficulties, however, it is possible to provide a qualified assessment of NAFTA's tourism implications by summarizing the impacts that were anticipated prior to its inception and reviewing the debate that has occurred regarding its impacts since 1994. In particular, data on tourists movements between the three countries indicate mixed results to date.

1. 北美自由贸易协定对旅游业的影响(NAFTA's Anticipated Effects on the Tourism Industry)

Before its implementation, NAFTA was heralded by its supporters as an agreement that would benefits the three countries' tourism industries. Specifically, benefits were anticipated in the following areas: globalization of North American tourism services(北美旅游业的全球化); increase in business and pleasure travel(商务旅游的增长); facilitation of travel credit finance(旅游信用的便利发展); increased tourism investments in Mexico(墨西哥的旅游投资的增长); increased concern for the environment(对环境关注的加强).

(1) 北美旅游业的全球化(Globalization of North American Tourism Services)

By linking the United States to its first and third trading partners, Canada and Mexico, NAFTA, said its supporters, would allow US, Canadian and Mexican companies the same competitive edge that trade ties have given European and Japanese business concerns. The larger market would help the tourism industry be more competitive in global markets, with Europe, Asia and the rest of the world.

(2) 商务旅游的增长(Increase in Business and Pleasure Travel)

Travel between the three countries was expected to increase as a result of NAFTA. As more goods and services crossed the border, more travelers of all types would follow, promoting increased use of credit cards, airlines, hotels, restaurants, rental cars, tour buses, cruise lines and other travel-related products and services. Tourism is dependent on economic growth and therefore any NAFTA-generated improvement in the economies of the three countries would automatically result in an increase in discretionary and business-related travel. In addition, since international tourism is classified as an export, and raising exports is one of the single most effective ways to create jobs and stimulate economic growth, any increase in tourism that resulted from the NAFTA agreement would be of significant benefit to the USA, Mexico and Canada. Travel credit in the form of credit card usage was to be facilitated by the NAFTA, which provides national treatment for US banks in Mexico. The transaction volume for US bank and non-bank credit cards—such as Visa, Mastercard, American Express, etc.—was anticipated to increase, along with all the accompanying linkages to frequent traveler programmes and airline, hotel and car rental computerized reservations systems.

(3) 墨西哥旅游投资的增长(Increased Tourism Investments in Mexico)

NAFTA was expected to broaden tourism investment opportunities in Mexico. Not only was the Mexican tourism industry supposed to expand through the influx of American investments in its hotel and foodservice industry, but it was also anticipated to become more attractive to German, French and other country's tourists who may stay, for example, in Canadian and US-owned properties in Mexico and then continue on northward to visit the other two countries.

It is in the hotel sector that specific language on tourism appears in the NAFTA document under entry procedures and documentation. Hotel managers, accredited through certain educational qualifications, who seek entry to Mexico now, may do so more easily under NAFTA through certain visa processes which speed up entry procedures.

(4) 对环境关注的加强(Increased Concern for the Environment)

The tourism industry was anticipated to benefit from NAFTA's historic orientation towards environmental issues. Concepts crucial to tourism planning, management, trade and promotion were to be promoted by the NAFTA and its supplemental agreements. This in turn was anticipated to help facilitate understanding of the common ground between developmental and environmental priorities, and create a better balance between economic development and the preservation of natural and multicultural resources.

To oversee implementation of the environmental supplemental agreement, the three countries agreed to create the North American Commission on the Environment (NAAEC) with a council and secretariat. In addition, there is a joint advisory committee of non-governmental organizations to advise the council on its deliberations. The scope of the Commission is extremely broad. The Commission, through its work programme, may address any environmental or natural resource problem subject to consultations among the parties. This ensures an ongoing, trilateral dialogue focused on improving environmental cooperation throughout North America. Mutual cooperation and transparency of the process, coupled with strong dispute settlement measures, were envisioned to promote improved enforcement of environmental laws.

(5) 总结(Summary)

Prior to the NAFTA, there were few major barriers with respect to tourism between the United States, Mexico, and Canada. In essence, the three countries have had close to a NAFTA-like agreement from a tourism perspective. The NAFTA applied finishing touches to tourism relations that were basically positive and already open by guaranteeing market openness between the three countries into perpetuity. With tourism barriers reduced, it was expected that travel organizations would feel the pressure to develop higher quality products, price more competitively, generating tourism industry growth beneficial to both workers and consumers.

二、欧盟旅游政策(The Tourism Policy of the EU)

从 80 年代中期起,欧盟就采取了一系列措施来提升旅游业在欧盟中的地位。1991年欧盟发表的旨在促进旅游发展的"共同行动纲领",为建立欧盟内部大市场的旅游政策奠定了基础。而一些其他领域内的政策,如:"消费者保护政策"、"开放边界、实行人员自由流动政策"、"环境政策"、"金融政策"等,因对旅游发展具有一定的影响,也成为欧盟旅游政策的基础。欧盟旅游政策的目标主要反映在(1)将旅游业作为繁荣成员国内部一些相对落后地区经济的重要途径,推动较不发达地区的经济结构调整;(2)把旅游业作为欧盟强势国向弱势国转移资金的特殊渠道,促进欧盟国家经济发展;(3)鼓励和提倡各成员国居民,尤其是青年参加旅游,加强和增强各成员国人民之间的交往和了解;(4)采取市场多元化策略,分散客源,改善季节和地区分布不均衡状况。

1. 欧盟内部的旅游政策(Tourism Policy within the EC)

The commission does not give a treaty base for community involvement in tourism field, but cites a 1984 judgment by the

European court instead, which confirmed that community nationals going abroad within the community for the purpose of tourism are regarded as "recipients of services". Tourism has only recently attracted the attention of the EC institutions, as awareness has grown concerning tourism's ability to promote closer relations between EC and its member states, its importance as an economic activity within the community, and a large number of community policies which, directly or indirectly, have an impact on this industry. These policies range from the free movement of persons, through passenger transportation and regional development, to the numerous measures preparing for the internal market.

Since 1988, the community's ministers for tourism and the commission have held regular meetings to exchange informations on tourism policy in each member state and discuss the approach to community action in their field. At the meeting in November 1990 in Brussels, the ministers asked the commission to put forward guidelines for a community action program on tourism. Consequently, in April 1991, the commission presented its community action plan to assist tourism. The strategy contained in the commission's action plan has determined community policy and involvement in tourism over the following years.

2. 欧盟在旅游方面采取的行动(Action on Tourism Already Undertaken by the EC)

Many measures aimed directly at tourism have been adopted by the European parliament or are currently in the process of passing into European law. These measures may be divided into: (1) General measures connected with the completion of the internal market; and (2) Indirect actions resulting from the application of community policies.

In July 1987, the single European act came into force, to prepare for the creation of single, internal market throughout the EC. The key benefits of the internal market, as identified by the commission, are: improved competitiveness via lower costs; trade creation; and closer coordination of monetary and economic policies.

The target date for the completion of the single, internal market is December 31,1992, by which date, most of the remaining barriers to trade within the EC—physical, technical and fiscal—should have been removed.

The act included 300 proposals to remove these barriers to trade within the community. Many of these proposals have a direct bearing on the tourism industry as a whole. The principal measures affecting tourism are: frontier controls(边界控制); sales of duty-free goods(免税品的销售); harmonization of VAT rates(VAT 比率的协调); deregulation of air travel(航空业的放松管制); and deregulation of coach travel(海运业的放松管制); Environmental policy(环境政策).

(1)边界控制(Frontier Controls)

The commission aims to abolish all intra-community frontier controls. However, a general declaration attached by member governments to the act states that the provisions of the act will not affect the rights of its member states to take such measures as they consider necessary for the purpose of controlling the problems of drug trafficking, terrorism, crime and illegal immigration. Already, member states have chosen to exercise their rights under this declaration in quite contrasting ways. France, Germany, the Netherlands, Belgium and Luxembourg, known as the scheme group, are committed to the complete removal of frontier controls. Thus, since 1985, EC nationals displaying a green "nothing to declare" disk on their car windscreens have been able to cross the borders between these countries, subject only to spot checks carried out in special bays so as not to obstruct traffic flows.

The British government, on the other hand, remains adamant that customs and immigration check must continue, to combat the problems of terrorism, etc, and looks set to exercise its right to impose these controls as defined in the declaration. Thus, while all other member states allow customs and immigration checks to be carried out on trains, the British government is insistent that customs checks will be imposed at points of arrival for those traveling to Britain on channel tunnel trains. With the possible result of increased delays and inconveniences for tourists entering Britain, the British tourism industry may suffer if controls are much more stringent than those adopted by other member states.

(2) 免税品的销售(Sales of Duty-free Goods)

The proposed ending of duty-free sales for intra-EC travelers at ports and airports is one of the most controversial moves envisaged by the commission. Commission officials argue that after 1992, the logic for duty-free sales will disappear with the removal of internal community customs barriers. This step has yet to be approved by EC governments, many of whom are voicing rising concern over the issue.

Duty-free sales represent an important source of revenue for ports, ferry companies, airports, and airlines. A report for the international civil airports associate by consultants Coopers & Lybrand estimates that duty-free goods worth 1.6 billion ECU were sold by EC airlines and airports alone, in 1988, 1 billion ECU of them, to intra-EC passengers. Airports, which normally receive a share of the turnover of duty-free shops, would be particularly vulnerable to the abolition of intra-EC sales. For example, these currently account for around 15 per cent of income at Amsterdam's Schiphol airport, while baa, formerly the British airports authority, earns about a fifth of its annual profits from duty-free sales. The baa estimates that ending intra-EC sales would halve these profits, and that such losses would lead to a rise in airport handling charges, with the consumer ultimately paying more for air travel-between 1.1 and 2.3 per cent extra on intra-EC scheduled services, according to Coopers and Lybrand.

In 1988, charter operators on intra-EC routes sold 230 million ECU worth of duty-free goods on flights. Many only made a profit because of these sales, and these operators would be particularly hard hit if they were to lose revenue from in-flight duty-free sales. For the traveler, the cost of package tours would inevitably rise as a result, by between 1.5 and 2.3 per cent.

The ending of duty-free sales for intra-EC passengers would also create costs for airports towards the refurbishing of their facilities, since intra-EC travelers would have to be separated from those traveling to or from mom-EC destinations. Airports claim that this would necessitate extensive alterations to terminal buildings.

(3) VAT 比率协调(Harmonization of VAT Rates)

In 1989, the commission put forward a package of measures designed to harmonize indirect taxation between member states. In essence, these recommended an alignment within three community VAT rate bands, for all member states: a minimum standard rate, a reduced rate of four to nine per cent and a limited zero rate. However, this proved to be a controversial proposal, with member states remaining divided on this issue. Disagreement continues over what the standard rate of VAT should be, and even over whether VAT alignment is a pre-requisite of the single market. The commission's original proposals stated passenger transport, along with other basic and energy for heating and lighting. If this is accepted, it would lead directly to an increase in fares for airlines, trains, ferries, etc, since passenger transport is currently zero-rated for VAT in some Member States. Similarly, acceptance of the proposal to introduce VAT at the reduced rate on publications would lead to increased costs for tourism promotional and sales literature in countries where no VAT is currently payable on such products.

The European tourism industry is showing considerable concern at the prospects of VAT being introduced on passenger transport and publications, since this would inevitably lead to price increases for their products. As with the case of duty-free sales, travel to destinations outside the EC would be unaffected, since this does not incur VAT charges. It is feared that this could distort travel movements to the detriment of intra-EC tourism.

(4) 航空业的放松管制(Deregulation of Air Travel)

Traditional rules for air transport traffic sharing within the EC do not meet the needs of the Single Market Europe of 1992. Through a long-established system of privileges and uncompetitive practices, large European airlines operating scheduled services have been able to retain control of almost all high intensity, high profitability routes, creating huge obstacles to real competition in Europe. The small, independent airlines have faced unfair competition from the big national flag carriers, most of which, including Lufthansa, Air France and Alitalia, are state-owned and heavily subsidized by their governments. As a result, for example, Lufthansa has an 80 per cent grasp on former West Germany capacity, and British Airways, a 68 per cent grip on British airline traffic.

The tourism industry as a whole would benefit from a system which created lower air fares for the public, and, therefore, increased incentive to travel. The capacity of these agreements to bring down air fares in the short term will certainly be limited by the pressures to raise air fares due to changes in VAT and duty-free regulations. However, they do provide for a potentially more open and market-orientated environment within which Europe's airlines will learn to operate and, therefore, the long-term effects are likely to be beneficial to the consumer, and all sectors of Europe's tourism industry.

(5) 海运业的放松管制(Deregulation of Coach Travel)

Coach operators in the EC can already take passengers to other countries and travel freely through these countries. The commission's proposal for coach travel means that in the future coach operators will be able to provide "cabotage" services in other EC countries, i. e. operate regular services outside the country in which they are based. The ability of coach operators to benefit from this new right will be limited by several factors, however: in certain Member States, the viable coach/bus network is already highly developed, offering little room for newcomers. Some Member States have invested heavily in rail infrastructure, and their governments are fundamentally opposed to encouraging a transfer of traffic to roads. Driver/Operator regulations differ considerably from country to country, with those of certain Member States. Operators may also be deterred from expanding into other countries by costs of having to establish offices abroad to service customers' needs and vehicle servicing facilities, etc.

Consequently, practical difficulties may mean that instead of a completely deregulated market, a system of bilateral agreements between Member States, for coach/bus services may evolve. This system of partners looks attractive as it will minimize operators' costs as contract boundaries will be formally agreed, and companies will be able to make us of each others' marketing outlets, vehicle servicing facilities, etc.

(6) 环境政策(Environmental Policy)

The increasingly vocal concern that tourism should develop in harmony with the environment is reflected in various EC policy statements, including a Resolution on mass tourism adopted by the European Parliament in July 1990.

The commission, in formulating the rules governing the use of the EC's Structural Funds, has made efforts to ensure that Member States take account of the environmental impact of the investment projects they propose for Community financing. According to these rules, Community funds must be used to support investments and projects which are in accordance with Community policy on the environment.

Otherwise, a number of environmental measures which the Community has adopted or planned to adopt will have an impact on tourism, included in these measures are community legislation on impact assessment of environmental projects, the quality of bathing water, waste management and the control of industrial or other emissions. The Commission's Green Paper on the urban environment underlines the need to develop a planning strategy for urban tourism.

Community policy for tourism during the 1990s was shaped by a detailed Action Plan drawn up in 1991 by the commission. In the document containing details of their Community Action Plan to Assist Tourism, the Commission made the following statement: in response to the needs of the tourism industry resulting from changes in the business environment and shifts in demand, the community would implement a coherent plan to supplement initiatives already undertaken under common policies of specific programmes. The plan covered all aspects of tourism and would aim to: achieve an all-round improvement in the quality and competitiveness of tourism facilities and services on offer in the community; facilitate awareness of the demand for tourism; and satisfy that demand.

三、印度的旅游政策(Tourism Policy of India)

The 1980s witnessed the era of liberalization initiated by the Congress Government at the Centre. The process of liberating the Indian economy from the shibboleths of "license-permit Raj" culminated in the initiation of the structural adjustment programme in 1992.

Tourism Policy, as a statement of intent by the Government, would form the reference point for action and criticism. Any initiative of Government in Tourism by way of legislation or direct investment is envisaged within the framework of Tourism Policy. The debates in Parliament had taken recourse to the received policy of the Union Government while making references to particular cases. The backdrop of a policy always serves as a guideline for further executive and legislative initiatives. It would be cynical to regard these policy statements as mere exercises in eloquence and additions to the already existing volumes of wishful thinking.

Furthermore, Policy statements by Government should be viewed in their evolutionary stance. It would be a negation of the democratic content of political system to view a Policy statement as a static and rigid formulation, at a point in time, applicable for years to come. Thus, since 1982, various initiatives undertaken by the Government need to be perceived as additions or modifications to the received policy.

The first ever Tourism Policy was announced by the Government of India in November 1982. It took ten long years for the Government to feel the need to come up with a possible improvement over this. Thus the National Action Plan for Tourism was announced in May 1992. Between these two policy statements, various legislative and executive measures were brought about. In particular, the report of the National Committee on Tourism, submitted in 1988 needs special mention. In addition, two five-year plans—the Seventh and the Eighth—provided the basic perspective framework for operational initiatives.

1. 七五计划(The Seventh Five-year Plan)

The Seventh Five-year Plan advocated a two-pronged thrust in the area of development of tourism, viz., to vigorously promote domestic tourism and to diversify overseas tourism in India. While laying stress on creation of beach resorts, conducting of conventions, conferences, winter sports and trekking, the overall intention was to diversify options available for foreign tourists.

The Tourism Policy 1982 was more an aggressive statement in marketing than a perspective plan for development. Its main thrust was aimed at presenting India to the foreigners as the ultimate holiday resort. With a view to reach this destination, the following measures were suggested by the Policy:

(1) to take full advantage of the national heritage in arriving at a popular campaign for attracting tourists;

(2) to promote tourist resorts and make India a destination of holiday resorts;

(3) to grant the status of an export industry to tourism;

(4) to adopt a selective approach to develop few tourist circuits;

(5) to invite private sector participation into the sector.

The Planning Commission recognized tourism as an industry by June 1982. However, it took ten years to make most of the States to fall in line and accord the same status within their legislative framework. At the beginning of the Eighth Plan (1992-1997), 15 States and 3 Union Territories had declared tourism as an industry. Four States had declared hotels as an industry.

The National Committee on Tourism was set up in July 1986 by the Planning Commission to prepare a perspective plan for the sector. Within the broad framework of the Seventh Plan, the Committee had to evolve a perspective plan for the coming years.

The Committee in its Report recommended that the existing Department of Tourism be replaced by a National Tourism Board. It suggested that there be a separate cadre of Indian Tourism Service to look after the functioning of the Board. It also submitted proposals for partial privatization of the two airlines owned by the Union

Government.

By September, 1987, the Central Government declared more concessions for the sector: these included tax exemption on foreign exchange earnings from tourism (a 50% reduction on rupee earnings and a 100% reduction on earnings in dollars), a drastic reduction in tariff on import of capital goods, and confessional finance at the rate of 1% to 5% per annum.

The National Action Plan for Tourism, published in May 1992, and tabled in the Lok Sabha on 5 May 1992, charts 7 objectives as central concerns of the Ministry:

- socio-economic development of areas;
- increasing employment opportunities;
- developing domestic tourism for the budget category;
- preserving national heritage and environment;
- development of international tourism;
- diversification of the tourism product;
- increasing in India's share in world tourism (from the present 0.4% to 1% during next 5 years)

As per the Action Plan, foreign exchange earnings are estimated to increase from Rs. 10,000 crores in 1992 to Rs. 24,000 crores by 2000 AD. Simultaneously, the Plan aims at increasing employment in tourism to 28 million from the present 14 million. Hotel accommodation is to be increased from 44,400 rooms to 120,000 by 3 years. Other provisions in the Action Plan include a discontinuance of subsidies to star hotels, encouraging foreign investment in tourism and the setting up of a convention city for developing convention tourism.

The Action Plan envisages the development of Special Tourism Areas on lines of export processing zones. Special central assistance is to be provided for the States to improve the infrastructural facilities at pilgrimage places. It proposes to set up a National Culinary Institute, and projects a liberalised framework for recognition of travel agents and tour operators.

2. 八五计划(The Eighth Five-year Plan)

The Eighth Plan document makes a special mention that the future expansion of tourism should be achieved mainly by private sector participation. The thrust areas as enumerated in the Plan include development of selected tourist places, diversification from cultural related tourism to holiday and leisure tourism, development of trekking, winter sports, wildlife and beach resort tourism, exploring new source markets, restoration of national heritage projects, launching of national image building, providing inexpensive accommodation in different tourist centers, improving service efficiency in public sector corporations and streamlining of facilitation procedures at airports.

The Eighth Plan aims at luring the high spending tourists from Europe and USA. It also envisages a "master plan" to integrate area plans with development of tourism. This is envisaged to ensure employment opportunities for the local population.

In April 1993, the Government announced further measures aimed at export promotion. The existing Export Promotion of Capital Goods Scheme (EPCG) was extended to tourism and related services. Against the existing 35%, the tourism sector would now pay an excise duty of 15% only on capital goods import, subject to an export obligation of 4 times the cargo, insurance and freight (CIF) value of imports. With an obligation period of five years, this came as a boon to the hotel industry. The cost of construction had also come down by 20%.

The Eighth Plan document stipulates that the strategy in such designated special areas is to devise suitable location-specific solutions, so as to reverse the process of degradation of natural resources and ensure sustainable development. The Department of Tourism (under the Ministry of Civil Aviation and Tourism at the Centre) undertakes certain promotional and developmental activities with a view to enhance the sectoral potential. The Department has certain regulatory functions to perform involving the hotel industry, travel agencies and tourist operators. Over the years, there has been considerable erosion of powers so far as State Governments are concerned. The sustained campaign for privatisation in all the policy documents has left limited space of operation for the States. The public sector is increasingly being perceived as an agent of inertia than of change and hence the pressure for a hands-off policy. The Economic Survey 1991-1992 aptly summarizes the ultimate aim of such incentives for private sector participation: "The Government has tried to expand the economic space in which the people can exercise their initiative and ingenuity. It hopes to do more to expand their opportunities, to enhance their potential."

复习思考题:
1. 产业政策包括哪些内容? 具有哪些功能?
2. 为什么要实行产业政策?
3. 旅游产业政策的目标和特征是什么?
4. 如何通过制定旅游产业政策促进我国旅游产业的发展?

第十二章
旅游产业发展模式的特征和类型
(The Features and Types of Pattern of Tourism Industry Development)

第一节 旅游产业发展模式的特征和类型
(The Features and Types of Pattern of Tourism Industry Development)

　　旅游产业发展模式是一国旅游产业政策在产业发展战略上的体现。在一个国家旅游产业发展过程中,如何选择适合本国国情的旅游产业发展模式是一个至关重要的问题。所谓旅游产业发展模式(Pattern of Tourism Industry Development),一般是指在特定的时期内,一个国家和地区旅游产业发展的总体方式,它包括旅游产业的发育和演进两层内容。旅游产业的发育是指旅游产业的形成方式,也就是在一定的经济条件下,旅游产业以何种方式形成、发育的问题;而旅游产业的演进模式是指在旅游产业发展到一定的时期,以什么样的方式促进旅游产业向高度化和现代化方向发展。

　　一、旅游产业发展模式的特征(The Features of Pattern of Tourism Industry Development)
　　总的来说,旅游产业的发展模式主要有以下几个主要特征:
　　1. 概括性(Generality)
　　作为旅游产业发展的总体方式,旅游产业的发展模式是建立在对旅游产业发展战略高度凝炼的基础之上,旅游产业发展模式可以全面概括一定时期旅游产业发展的总体思想和战略特征,充分体现旅游产业发展战略的内在要求和发展方向。

2. 阶段性(Stage)

旅游产业发展模式不仅指出了旅游产业发展的总体方式,也规定了在一定的时期内旅游产业的发展方式,勾画出旅游产业在某一时期内的发展方向和发展重点。

3. 相对稳定性(Reletive Stability)

一个特定时期的旅游产业发展模式一旦确立,旅游产业运行的基本性质和发展方向就得以明确,并在特定的历史阶段具有相对稳定性,只有当旅游经济环境内部和外部发生了质的变化,而原有的发展模式成为旅游产业发展的桎梏时,才会出现新的发展模式代替旧的发展模式的客观要求。

4. 特指性(Particularity)

旅游产业的发展模式总是根据特定的社会经济条件、历史发展进程和自然环境状况加以规定的,因此在不同的国家和地区,旅游产业的发展模式是不尽相同的。

二、旅游产业发展模式的类型(The Types of Pattern of Tourism Industry Development)

从不同的角度分析旅游产业的发展模式,可以形成不同的类型。纵观世界旅游的发展过程,根据不同的划分标准,可以将旅游产业的发展模式分为以下几种:

1. 超前型和滞后型旅游产业发展模式(Pattern of Preceding and Following Development of Tourism Industry)

从旅游产业成长和国民经济的总体关系划分,旅游产业发展模式可以分为超前型和滞后型两种不同的形式。超前型旅游产业发展模式(Pattern of Preceding Development of Tourism Industry)是指旅游产业的发展超越国民经济的总体发展水平,通过发展旅游产业来带动相关产业和地区经济进步的一种发展模式。选择这一模式必须具备三个条件:首先,具有丰富的旅游资源;其次,有强大的外部需求;再次,有外部投资的注入。一般来说,这种旅游产业发展模式主要适用于国民经济基础较好的旅游城市和沿海地区。滞后型旅游产业发展模式(Pattern of Following Development of Tourism Industry)是指旅游产业的成长滞后于国民经济的总体发展水平,即国民经济发展一定的阶段后,带动旅游产业成长的一种模式。这种旅游产业发展的模式的主要特点是旅游产业的成长是由适应本国居民对旅游劳务消费增长的需要而逐步推动的。滞后型旅游产业发展模式是一种常规型的发展模式,反映了旅游活动是社会经济发展的必然产物的客观规律的要求。

2. 市场主导型发展模式和政府主导型发展模式(Market-Dominating Pattern and Government-dominating Pattern of Tourism Industry Development)

按照旅游成长的协调机制来划分,旅游产业的发展模式可以分为市场型和政府主导型两种。市场型旅游产业发展模式(Market-Dominating Pattern of Tourism Industry Development)是以市场竞争作为主要动力来推动旅游产业成长与演变的一种模式。政府在一定时期内不对旅游业的成长施加任何影响,而完全由市场这只"看不见的手"自动调节旅游产业的资源配置的过程,调节旅游产业的成长过程和变动趋势。按照这一模式发展的旅游产业具有以下三种特点:第一,旅游产业的成长侧重于产业内部的自主均衡、自动调节的过程;第二,外部政策的作用是间接的,是通过一定的市场参数进行的;第三,产业政策对旅游产业的成长主要侧重于市场需求方面。相对于市场型旅游产业的发展模式,政府主导型发展模式(Government-dominating Pattern of Tourism Industry Development)是以政府规划或者通过政府制定产业政策来干预旅游产业成长和演进的一种模式。这一旅游发展模式具有两个重要的实施前提:一是有国家干预和控制经济的历史传统;二是短时期内具有快速推进旅游产业成长的战略目标。

3. 延伸型旅游发展模式和推进型旅游发展模式(Extending and Propelling Pattern of Tourism Industry Development)

按照旅游产业的演进模式来划分,旅游产业的发展模式可以分为延伸性(extending)旅游发展模式和推进型(propelling)旅游发展模式。前者是一种先以国内旅游为产业成长基础,通过国内旅游产业的发展、国际旅游产业的成长,最终实现两个产业融合的发展模式。推进型旅游产业发展模式与之相反,是先以国际旅游产业为成长基础,通过国际旅游接待产业的发展来推动国内旅游产业的成长,最终形成完整的旅游产业体系。

以上对旅游产业发展模式的分类,实际上是在不同经济水平下各个国家旅游产业的成长模式的分类。经济学认为,选择不同的产业发展模式,是由一定时期的经济发展和文化传统等因素共同决定的。从旅游经济和国民经济之间的关系分析,推进型和延伸型旅游产业发展模式是不同经济水平条件下世界各国在旅游发展道路上的两种不同选择,具有一定的客观必然性。两种旅游产业的发展模式运行环境以及表现出来的经济特点具有明显的差异。推进型发展模式是建立在国民经济发展水平较低的情况下的,因而,这种发展模式追求的不是旅游产业的内存的

表 12-1　世界主要国家旅游发展模式分析*

国家类型			旅游产业发展的主要特点	旅游产业发展模式的选择
经济非常发达,旅游业也非常发达的国家	代表	美国法国英国日本德国	国内旅游和国际旅游都比较发达; 发展旅游业以扩大就业、稳定经济为目标; 旅游管理体制以半官方旅游机构为主,而管理职能主要是协调和推销; 旅游经营体制以大公司为主,小企业为基础	国民经济发展到一定阶段后带动旅游产业发展的滞后型旅游发展模式; 以市场导向为主的旅游产业发展模式; 由国内旅游为成长基础,由国内旅游产业发展带动国际旅游产业发展的延伸型发展模式
经济比较发达,旅游业非常发达的国家		西班牙墨西哥瑞士以及东南亚的一些国家	旅游产业是国民经济的支柱产业; 旅游产业的发展速度很快; 旅游管理体制以官方旅游机制和半官方旅游协会共同协调; 主要以大众旅游为市场定位	先是由国民经济带动旅游产业的发展,而后由旅游产业带动国民经济发展的旅游产业发展模式; 政府主导型旅游产业发展模式; 由国际旅游接待业带动国内旅游产业成长推进型的发展模式
发展中国家	国家	印度、中国及拉美、非洲的一些发展中国家	旅游产业的发展经历了一个复杂的过程; 具有丰富的旅游资源,旅游产业的发展受到相对落后的经济的制约; 旅游产业发展的主要目标是以增加创汇、改善落后的经济状况为目标; 跨国公司、国有企业控制着旅游产业的发展; 非常规的旅游产业发展模式,存在一定的社会问题	由旅游产业带动国民经济发展的超前型发展模式; 政府主导型旅游产业发展模式; 由国际旅游接待业带动国内旅游产业推进的推进型发展模式

* 根据张辉(2002)和唐留雄(2001)有关论述整理而成。

经济效益,而是旅游经济的波及效益(张辉,2002),即,利用旅游产业是一个以旅游为中心的配置产业这一基本性质,通过对以国际旅游为主体的旅游产业高强度的经济投入,来全面带动国民经济相关产业的发展。在这种旅游产业发展模式下,旅游产业的作用不仅仅是为经济建设获取外汇和回笼货币,而且还是新的经济增长点,是带动整个国民经济发展的发动机。另外,由于这种旅游发展模式是建立在高投入基础之上的,因而在发展的初期和中期,旅游产业不具备"投资少,见效快,收益大"的经济发展特性。相反,延伸型旅游发展模式是建立在国民经济发展较高的基础之上,旅游产业的发展不是为了经济建设的发展的需要,而是内部人民消费的要求,因此这种模式追求的是旅游产业的内存效益,只要以较少的投入就能够换来丰厚的经济回报,具有"投资少,见效快,收益大"的经济性质。因此,在旅游产业国际扩张的过程中,"延伸型"产业发展模式更具有产业扩张的比较优势(张辉、厉新建,2002)。

第二节 我国政府主导型旅游发展模式的制定和实施
(Framing and Executing of the Government Dominating Pattern of Tourism Industry Development)

一、模式的提出(The Proposal of the Pattern)

1995年,国家旅游局下达了创建中国优秀旅游城市的通知,在此基础上,逐步明确了政府主导型的发展战略。从1997年开始,正式明确提出了政府主导型的旅游发展模式。政府主导不同于政府干预,在以市场为基础配置资源的前提下,全面实行政府主导型旅游发展模式,以全面发动社会力量,进一步加大旅游发展的力度,加快旅游发展的速度,使旅游业为经济、社会、文化发展做出更大的贡献。

二、旅游产品的特性决定了政府主导模式的可行性(The Feasibility of the Government-dominating Pattern Decided By the Feature of Tourism Product)

旅游资源有自然旅游资源、人文旅游资源和社会旅游资源。旅游资源是旅游吸引力所在。针对市场需求,开发旅游资源,并配以一定的基础设施,把资源优势转化成产品优势,再针对特定市场组织宣传促销,最终形成市场优势。旅游产品体现在旅游线路上,但是旅游线路不同于一般的工业产品,旅游线路是把各种旅游资源进行组合形成的一条线路,本身具有开放性,很难对它进行专利的保护。这样,一项旅游产品经过前期的调研、实地考察到后期的营销、监控,被完整地开发出来以后,很容易被很快模仿,开发旅游新产品的企业的利益受损,边际收益小于边际成本。因此,旅游企业都不愿意去创新,都等着"搭便车"。由于创新能力的减弱,旅游企业的竞争力下降,长期下去,对我国旅游产业的发展不利。因此,需要政府主导的模式来鼓励旅游企业的创新。

旅游产品在消费的时候,具有非竞争性,即同一产品可以被很多人同时消费,其中某个人的消费并不影响其他人对该物品的消费。同时旅游产品还具有消费的非排他性,即任何人都无法剥夺或削弱其他人对公共物品消费的资格。由于旅游产品具有非竞争性和非排他性,因此,很多景区,往往游客数量超过了合理的景区承载量,破坏了景区的生态环境。各景区由于短期利益也不能很好地监控每日的接待量,也缺乏有效的市场监督。

旅游资源属于国家所有,所以第一位的利用主体是国家,第一位的操作主体也是国家。对旅游资源应该兼有开发和保护,进行可持续的发展需要政府主导。

旅游产品具有综合性的特点,旅游产业是由食、住、行、游、购、娱六大因素组合而成的综合性产业。在旅游产品中,很难区分开各个组成部分,因此需要政府统一进行管理。

三、政府主导型旅游发展模式的实践(The Practice of the Government-dominating Pattern)

政府主导型发展战略是各个国家尤其是发展中国家旅游发展过程中的共同经验。之所以会形成这一战略,一是因为旅游发展必须以基础建设为先;二是旅游产品具有公共性产品的特点;三是旅游市场的开发首先是形象宣传,然后才是产品促销。

从政府主导模式在我国实行的经验来看,有如下几个阶段:

1. 中央重视阶段(Central Government's Recognition Period)

邓小平同志于1978年10月到1979年7月这10个月中,连续讲了5次旅游发展的问题。文献研究室和国家旅游局共同出版了《邓小平论旅游》,国家旅游局也明确了"邓小平旅游经济思想"这一提法。中央领导人到各地考察工作,都会提到旅游发展的问题,充分体现了中央领导的重视。在80年代,从1979年到1986年以国务院的名义召开了四次全国旅游工作会议,那时候中央重视的力度非常大,一系列的政策也是那时候出台的,包括确定每年给旅游5亿元的投资。2000年,国务院组建了假日旅游部际协调机构,作为国务院的非常设机构运转,使假日旅游市场秩序法制化。2002年,首次发行了42亿旅游国债。2003年旅游国债在全国国债总量中的比例进一步加大。历年的政府报告中,一般会从扩大内需、经济结构调整、促进产业发展和扩大开放等角度涉及到旅游,说明旅游对经济发展的作用被决策者认识到了。说明中央非常重视旅游的发展。

2. 地方重视阶段(Local Government's Recognition Period)

到了80年代下半期90年代上半期,进入到第二个阶段,即地方重视。这是在经济社会发展过程之中,旅游的优势不断发挥的结果,也是各地在经济发展战略的制定过程中进行比较和选择的结果。所以地方重视旅游的积极性大为高涨,普遍重视。

3. 共同重视阶段(Common Recognition Period)

即现在这个阶段。中央和地方共同重视,而且力度也非常高,各个部门对旅游的支持和以前已经截然不同了。中央明确了旅游作为新的经济增长点的产业地位,明确了在产业结构调整里要大力发展第三产业等一系列宏观政策,在经济发展的过程中大家普遍感觉到旅游优势的发挥和发展的前景,应该重视旅游。

政府主导型旅游发展模式表现在如下几个方面:

1. 政策的制定(Policy Framing)

政策研究、论证与制定,是各国政府主导发展本国经济的一个基本手段。在我国,实行政府主导型旅游发展模式的过程中,大政方针的研究与制定是政府主导的主要职能。为使假日更为集中,我国采取了调休制度。从1999年国庆开始,每年都有春节、五一和国庆三个黄金周,集中休假7天,为中长线旅游提供了时间。此外,我国还在积极探讨带薪休假制度。在不久的将来,带薪休假将成为推动我国经济发展的新的动力。

2. 周期调控(Period Regulating)

周期性是任何经济系统都具有的内在特性,为了使经济稳定持续发展,各国政府都会干预经济领域,减少周期性带来的损失。旅游业是一个综合性的产业,受食、住、行、游、购、娱六大因素的影响,其中任何一个因素的不良运行都会导致旅游业出现波动,而且资源尤其是自然旅游资源具有季节性,但是住宿业等旅游的硬件基础设施具有刚性,因此旅游经济也会出现季节的波动。如黄金周期间住宿、交通运力吃紧,而到了旅游淡季饭店入住率较低。国际国内政治、宏观经济的影响都会使旅游出现波动。如1989年的政治风波使旅游也几乎停滞。

3. 设施建设(Establishment Constructing)

旅游基础设施属于公共产品或准公共产品,政府要投资于旅游基础设施的建设来弥补市场缺陷。在我国旅游发展过程中,星级旅游厕所的建设是政府主导的一个典型表现。长期以来,旅游景区景点的厕所脏、乱、差,国外游客对此意见很大,严重影响了我国的旅游形象。近年来,国家推出评比全国卫生城市、中国优秀旅游城市等活动,国家旅游局联合有关部门专门下发了文件,推动建设全国范围内的"旅游厕所工程",许多城市加大了对厕所建设的投入,消灭了厕所的脏、乱、差问题,并且积极创新,在修建厕所的同时考虑到环保,修建了生态厕所、绿色厕所,完善厕所内相关设施,极大地方便了游客。

4. 投资引导(Investment Leading)

引导和保护投资行为,是通过政府的力量来扩大旅游生产力规模。我国旅游业利用外来、私营资本时间较早。改革开放初期,外资就进入了旅游业,1984年,"五个一起上"政策明确了个人可以投资旅游。再后来的16个省、自治区、直辖市颁发的《旅游业管理条例》中,9个省、自治区和直辖市明确提出个人开发旅游资源,私营资本投资旅游业主要在景区景点,并且经济效益普遍较好。随着投资领域国退民进政策的深入,私营资本投资旅游业的热情高涨,投资领域从景区景点向上游的旅行社渗透。

5. 市场推广(Market Extending)

政府主导旅游目的地的营销,有利于整体旅游形象的策划、设计与推广,因为旅游产品的促销首先是旅游目的地形象的促销,其次是旅游产品的促销。与其他国家旅游促销费用相比,我国用于旅游促销的费用还很少。目前,中国平均每个过夜海外旅游者的宣传促销投入仅为2元到3元人民币,而国际上的平均水平为5美元。中国还没达到国际水平的1/10。这和我国接待入境过夜旅游者人次世界排名第5位的情况极不相称。

6. 环境营造(Environment Creating)

旅游业是个敏感的行业,国际政治、宏观经济、社会文化等方面的变化都可能影响其发展。安全是旅游者的基本需要,没有安全的环境就不可能吸引旅游者前来旅游。我国SARS期间,世界卫生组织向其他国家发出了安全警告。旅游是以人的流动为根本。因此,海外旅行社纷纷要求退团。旅行社、酒店没有客源。因此,对于类似事件,国家要建立预警机制来应对危机事件。

四、政府主导模式的终极模式：市场主导、政府调控(The Terminal Pattern of the Government-dominating Pattern: Market-dominating as well as Government Regulating)

任何一种经济发展模式都具有阶段性,随着条件的成熟,经济发展模式也要有所调整。政府主导型战略本质上是一个对市场经济条件下的政府行为进行合理界定的问题。随着我国社会主义市场经济的不断发育完整,政府与市场的关系也必将随之发生变化。根据中国旅游业目前状况和发展趋势判断,21世纪的前15年到前20年,我国仍将继续完善与巩固政府主导型战略。2020年前后,我国旅游业将进入一个新的发展时期。我国将建设成为世界旅游强国,最大的旅游目的国。市场经济各个领域也比较成熟,市场主导型的战略模式将作为政府主导型战略模式的继承,有利于旅游产业规模的扩大,旅游企业素质的提高和旅游企业的集团化。此时,政府发挥调控作用,加强法制建设、国家形象的促销和基础设施建设,政府主要扮演行业管理的角色。

第三节 我国旅游产业发展中的市场和政府
(The Market and Government in the Development of China's Tourism Industry)

一、我国旅游产业发展过程中政府与市场职能的演变(The Evolution of the Function of the Government and Market in the Development of China's Tourism Industry)

我国的旅游产业是在由计划经济体制向市场经济体制过渡的大背景下发展起来的。在原有计划经济时期依靠政策法规等强制性行动来推动产业经济发展可能是最优选择,但随着社会主义市场经济体制的建立与健全,僵化的旅游管理体制日益显示出其弊端。在特定的历史条件下,市场机制在产业发展的初期尚难以带动产业迅速形成规模经济,市场体制无法自发地生长,必须要有政府的干预。在我国的经济体制转轨时期,政府在旅游产业起步中不是扮演市场的替代者,而是扮演了市场制度的导入者和市场体系的完善者的角色。从我国旅游产业的发展过程来看,我国旅游产业管理体制的演进是一个不断与市场化改革相适应的过程,形成了一种明显的"权力下放、企业激活、市场强化"的制度演变与旅游产业成长的模式。在这个演变过程中,市场机制在旅游产业中作为资源配置的基础性作用逐步得到了重视和强化,相关政府部门的职能也得到了相应的转变或职能范围发生了变化。因此,我国旅游产业的市场化进程在很大程度上可以视作政府主导下的旅游管理体制演变史,是一种政府主导下的强制性制度变迁行为。

我们可以从不同历史时期我国旅游业管理体制的演变与产业成长情况来看出我国旅游业发展过程中政府与市场作用的演变历史。改革开放初期,我国建立了国家旅游管理总局,各省市区成立旅游局;政治工作归地方党委领导,业务上归旅游总局指导,成立由计委、建委、外贸等部门的负责同志组成的旅游工作领导小组。"六五"期间,发展旅游业正式纳入国民经济和社会发展计划,集中统一的管理体制不能适应各地旅游业的快速成长,这时旅游管理体制由领导与经营集中统一的一体化格局向"统一领导、分散经营、政企分开"的多元化管理格局转变。这期间,旅游产业规模和产业业绩有比较明显的提高,尤其是入境旅游接待调入有很大发展,为旅游业的进一步发展奠定了基础。"七五"期间,开始贯彻党的"国家调控市场,市场引导企业"的原则,市场功能逐步释放,日益重视旅游业的经济功能。与此相适应,旅游管理体制由行政管理向行业管理转变,由直接管理企业转变为通过市场间接进行管理和调节。旅游业发展的一些主导观念、产业观念、市场观念及中央和地方两个积极性观念得到认可和加强,产业规模持续扩大。"八五"期间,我国建立了适应社会主义市场经济需要的旅游行业管理体制,按照市场经济规律加强行业管理,管理手段日趋多样,管理方式更加规范。国内旅游业迅猛崛起,旅游业的产业地位进一步提升。"九五"期间,为进一步适应市场经济和机构改革的需要,提升旅游产业的竞争力,激励地方发展旅游业的积极性,国家旅游局机关与直属企业彻底脱钩,旅游法制建设加快步伐,行业管理向"大旅游、大市场、大产业"的方向推进。这期间,入境旅游、国内旅游和出境旅游三个市场平衡发展的局面开始形成。旅游业在国民经济中的作用明显提高,成为国民经济新的增长点。

二、旅游产业发展中市场的积极作用与"市场失灵"(Active Effect and Failure of Market in the Development of Tourism Industry)

市场作为配置旅游资源的基础性手段,是通过供求机制及相应的价格机制发挥作用的。旅游产业的供求决定着旅游价格机制的形成,左右着旅游价格的波动。一方面,如果某种旅游产业的供给超过了当时的客源需求,这一产业的社会劳动时间中就有一部分得不到社会的承认,这一产业的产品必然要按低于它们实际所耗费劳动的市场价值的价格出售;反之,如果某种旅游产业的需求超过了供给,价格就会上升。另一方面,价格也反过来影响旅游产业的供求关系。旅游产业价格下降,客源增加;价格提高,客源减少。旅游产业的供给按照和价格相同的方向变动,旅游产业价格上涨,吸引投资,增加供给;价格下降,投资减少,供给就减少。

在我国旅游产业的发展过程中,市场通过供求机制和价格机制对促进我国旅游产业的发展发挥了积极和重要的作用。旅游各产业主体由于追求效用最大化和利润最大化,便根据价格信号做出生产什么旅游产品,怎样生产和为谁生产的决策,这促进了旅游产业经济效率的提高。其作用集中表现为这样几个方面:第一,优化资源配置。价格的变动,直接决定着各种旅游资源在各旅游产业之间、产业内部之间的流动,决定着旅游投资结构和旅游产业结构,决定着不同消费群体对旅游资源观赏价值购买的适应程度。第二,调节经济利益。价格联结旅游经济活动的全过程,实质是联系着旅游各产业的经济利益关系。在旅游产品交换中,价格直接关系到旅游交易双方的经济利益。任何价格的变动,都会引起不同旅游地区、产业、企业和旅游消费者个人之间经济利益的变化,引起旅游总收入在各旅游产业、各企业之间发生结构性变化,从而引起社会经济利益在不同旅游地区、产业和企业之间的波动。而且,利益机制逼迫旅游产业单位加强管理、改善经营、提高效益。第三,传递经济信息。要使旅游产业运行协调顺畅,关键的问题是要有灵敏传递市场信息的机制。由于价格联结着旅游产业各方的经济活动,因此它的水平和变动也就反映了旅游市场供求和资源稀缺的状况,执行着传递旅游经济信息的职能。在旅游市场中,价格的变化可以反映出各旅游产业提供的产品是否适合旅游消费者,供给和需求是否适应,市场有何变化等信息,还可以反映旅游产业供给方面的盈利、劳动耗费、生产成本与企业经营管理等情况的变化,反映旅游客源需求方面的消费水平、消费结构的变化。

市场所具有的调节资源配置、调节经济利益和传递经济信息的职能,决定了它在旅游经济运行过程中起着配置资源的基础性作用。但市场机制也不是万能的,尤其对于旅游产业这个特殊的行业来说,市场在促进旅游产业发展的过程中也存在着明显的市场失灵现象。

1. 旅游产业对要素的利用在很多方面都存在着外部成本。(The external costs exist in many aspects when the factors are used by the Tourism Industry.)由于市场经济中追求利润的刺激,旅游企业对旅游资源的过度开发,对旅游目的地环境和文化遗产的破坏,削弱了旅游产业可持续发展的空间。旅游企业对旅游资源的滥用和破坏,使得旅游资源的价值在长期来看是下降的。但是这种滥用所带来的成本很大一部分由下代人来承担,从而在本代人和下代人之间形成了代际外部成本。另外,个别旅游企业和游客对旅游目的地环境的破坏,破坏了旅游目的地的整体形象和价值,其所带来的成本由所有的旅游企业和游客所承担,而造成污染和破坏的企业或游客往往不必为这种破坏负责,从而在旅游企业之间,在旅游企业和游客之间形成了外部成本。例如,位于秦岭北麓的太白山自然保护区是陕西省最具特色的风景名胜区之一,由于其独特的自然生态系统和自然历史遗迹而被列入世界环境保护基金会的名单。但是,太白山各县区在发展旅游业时缺乏统一的规划,各自为政,盲目开辟旅游线路,将大量游客输送到保护区的核心地带,使太白山的旅游资源遭到了严重破坏。这种破坏资源、污染环境的现象在桂林漓江、湖南张家界、四川九寨沟等景区也普遍存在,它从另一个角度反映了我国旅游市场在发育过程中的缺陷。

2. 旅游产业中存在的公共产品现象限制了旅游产业的发展。(The phenomenon of the public product existing in the Tourism Industry restrains the development of the Tourism Industry.)在发展旅游产业的过程中所遇到的公共产品问题主要体现在两个方面,一是旅游目的地的整体形象推广,二是旅游基础设施的建设。目的地形象推广和基础设施都具有一定的公共产品特性。目的地旅游企业的形象推广和交通、通信等基础设施的建设会大大增强旅游目的地的吸引力,从而增加旅客流量,但是个别旅游企业不为形象推广和基础设施建设支付任何费用,也可以从增加的旅客流量中获益。这种增加的旅客流量被目的地的所有旅游企业所享用,而无法对其中的个别企业进行排斥。因此,公共产品的存在给市场机制带来了严重的问题:由于收益是由所有旅游企业共同获得,成本自然也应该由所有企业共同承担,但在存在公共产品外部性的情况下,每个企业都会希望别人出资进行形象推广和基础设施建设,因为一旦别人进行了这样的投资,他就可以从中获益而不必支付任何费用,这样就产生了搭便车的现象。因而,市场机制在提供旅游地形象推广和基础设施建设等公共产品的过程中就失效了,由市场所提供的供给量将大大小于产业最优的数量,这极大地限制了旅游产业的发展。

3. 旅游市场中的信息不对称使旅游市场秩序混乱,旅游者权益受损。(The information imbalance in the Tourism Market disorders the market and does harm to the tourists.)旅游业的外向性决定了旅游市场的信息不对称极其严重。现代旅游是一种跨地区、跨国界的广泛的人际交往活动,具有明显的外向性或涉外性。在不同的旅游企业、旅游企业与旅游者之间都存在着信息不对称,这种信息不对称成为旅游企业之间不正当竞争的重要原因,使旅游市场的竞争秩序紊乱,从而使旅游企业无法在良好的竞争环境中发展。因为旅游目的地相对于旅游者来说通常是一个陌生的对象,旅游者所拥有的关于旅游目的地的信息远少于目的地旅游企业,而收集这种信息的成本往往极大,以至于旅游者往往放弃这种努力而接受旅游企业,尤其是旅行社的介绍和旅游目的地的广告宣传所提供的信息。在这样的情况下,劣质的旅游商品因为其成本较低,就会用较低的价格来吸引顾客,而旅游者因为信息不对称的原因,无法完全区分优质旅游产品和劣质旅游产品。这样,提供优质产品的旅游企业将因为劣质产品提供者的削价竞争而在市场竞争中处于不利地位,最终是优质产品的提供者丧失发展的机会,从而损害了整个旅游产业的竞争力。这种现象在一定程度上可以通过市场自身的力量得到解决。例如,优质旅游产品的提供者可以通过长期的努力建立名牌,名牌作为一种信号在消费者心目中往往代表了优质,他愿意支付一定的溢价来取得质量的保证,这样从长期来看优质产品就会在竞争中处于有利地位。但是,劣质产品的干扰往往使得建立名牌的成本极大,因为在建立名牌过程中优质产品的提供者只能以劣质产品的价格销售自己的产品,从而面临亏损的境地。在极端的情况下,优质产品的提供者甚至无法支持到成功建立名牌的时候就不得不从市场上退出。这样,市场自动调节的机制就失效了,整个旅游产业的竞争力将受到严重的威胁。

4. 旅游产业结构失衡,过度竞争导致整体经济效益下滑。(The over-competition resulted from the imbalance of the Tourism Industry structure declines the overall economic benefits.)过度竞争通常发生在集中度较低的竞争性行业,尽管这些行业的平均利润率很低,很多企业甚至陷于赤字状态,但生产要素仍然不能从该行业退出,从而使低利润或亏损在该行业长期存在。在较长的一个时期,由于旅游市场体系和市场机制不完善,导致了旅游产业规模的急剧扩张,这种状况在旅游饭店业和旅行社业尤为突出。一些主管部门没有发挥应有的宏观调控作用,反而推波助澜,盲目上部门工程或首长项目,加剧了整个旅游产业和某些旅游行业的过度竞争。

三、旅游产业发展中政府干预行为的有效性与有限性(The Effectiveness and Limitations of Government Interference in the Development of the Tourism Industry)

政府具有垄断性和强制性的政治权力和公共权力,与市场行为相比较,政府行为有垄断性和强制性的特点,也更有权威性。当市场机制失效时,政府的干预行为便成为方便的选择。即使在成熟的市场经济体制下,"市场失灵"和政府干预也是普遍现象。按照最初的认识,政府的干预范围是市场失效范围,主要是公共物品的供应、外部性现象、自然垄断行业、信息不完全和信息不对称等。随着社会发展进程,政府的职能向社会公平职能、经济稳定职能甚至经济发展职能扩张。由此说来,政府干预经济的范围有扩张的倾向,且对社会经济稳定和产业经济健康增长意义重大。在旅游产业中,政府的积极作用主要表现为:

1. 解决旅游产业的外部性、公共产品和信息不对称问题(To Resolve the Problems of the Externality of the Tourism Industry, the Public Products and the Information Imbalance)

首先,在旅游市场存在广泛的外部性的情况下,必须由政府干预制定严格的法律法规,对旅游目的地的破坏和污染者征收一定数量的税收或罚款,从而使其减少以至停止对旅游目的地的破坏和污染。其次,旅游产品的公共物品属性导致了拥挤、污染等外部不经济性的产生。在旅游基础设施建设、旅游产品各环节的协调、旅游促销、环境保护等方面,显然要由政府来推动。政府对旅游目的地的整体形象推广和旅游基础设施的大规模投资,可以改善旅游产业的需求条件和支持性产业状况,对于提高旅游产业的竞争力意义重大。最后,由于旅游产业是一个综合性、系统性、依托性很强的产业,旅游信息的传递过程较为复杂,仅靠市场机制难以保证旅游信息传递的有效性。完善其信息传递机制,改善旅游市场信息集散系统状态,需要政府进行干预。政府通过建立公正权威的旅游产品信息系统,向消费者提供关于旅游产品的正确的信息,同时通过立法和司法过程对劣质商品提供者的削价竞争等不正当竞争行为进行遏制,这样就可以使旅游企业在公平的竞争环境中进行竞争,从而实现优胜劣汰,提高旅游产业的经济效率和经济效益。

2. 促进旅游产业经济增长(To Promote the Economic Growth of Tourism Industry)

中国是一个发展中国家,发展经济的任务相当繁重。到20世纪末,旅游产业作为新的经济增长点,拉动国民经济发展的作用日益显现出来。但中国的旅游产业缺乏资金积累,企业规模小、旅游产品的质量及国际竞争力较低,单纯依靠市场体制下的自发生长需要较长的时间,无论是政府还是旅游产业本身,都希望缩短这一历史过程。吸取日本等东亚国家的经验,政府应在旅游产业发展过程中发挥更积极的作用。首先,政府可以利用行政体制动员所掌握的经济资源,迅速形成旅游产业较大的产业规模和供给能力。其次,政府可能通过颁布出台一系列法规和条例,如旅行社管理条例、旅行社质量保证金制度、饭店星级评定制度、旅游从业人员培训上岗和资格考试制度等,对我国旅游业的健康运行起到良好的推动作用。另外,政府在协调社会各方面力量,进行国家整体形象宣传,改善旅游大环境等方面更是起着无可替代的作用。

3. 保证旅游产业相关领域的社会公平与稳定(To Ensure the Fairness and Stability in the Fields Concerned)

如果只依靠市场来发展经济,往往会出现社会收入分配不公、贫富差距悬殊等社会公平问题,因此政府在这方面应该发挥积极作用,如促进旅游社会化进程,满足人们休闲、度假的需求,提高人民生活质量,提高人的基本素质;扩大对外开放,增进中外交流;协调旅游产业发展中的利益分配,保证社会公平与社会稳定;开展地区间旅游产业交流,促进区域间经济与社会平衡发展,通过旅游开发带动经济与社会全面发展。

政府的广泛干预是中国旅游产业发展的一大特征,也是中国旅游产业能够迅速发展的重要原因。不过,在我国旅游产业的发展过程中,"政府失灵"即政府行为无效率的现象也比较明显,并产生了相当严重的负面影响。如何正确认识和评价"政府失灵",进而采取相应措施提高政府行为效率,是未来中国旅游产业发展无法回避的问题。关于"政府失灵",经济学文献中已有大量的讨论。"政府失灵"大体有几种情况:一是政府行为未达到预期目标;二是政府行为的低效率、高成本;三是政府行为损害了市场效率。我国旅游产业发展过程中,"政府失灵"是由多方面原因造成的:旅游相关信息的分散性,使得政府并不能掌握完全信息;政府本身的能力不一定完全符合旅游发展的需要;还有政府本身利益的影响等,都在或多或少地影响着政府职能的行使过程。政府干预在很多情况下都没有更好地保证社会公平与旅游经济发展的效率,而是成为发展的阻力。

1. 旅游行业的过度投资(The Over-investment of Tourism Industry)

政府有关部门为了取得政绩,就有可能违背市场经济规律,利用所掌握的资源进行过度投入。由于决策失误造成的"面子工程"、"赔钱工程"劳民伤财,造成行业迅速发展与企业经济效益不高的矛盾现象。以饭店业为例,20世纪80年代初旅游产业起步时,饭店数量与效益是同步增长的。而到了90年代,旅游产业渐受各级政府重视,投入增加,但饭店的利润率却一直不高。由于政府毕竟没有利润压力,一旦环境适宜,政府直接投资企业经营的现象屡见不鲜。

2. 政府干预企业经营,严重抑制和削弱了旅游企业的市场竞争力(The Government Interferes the Operation of the Enterprises Which Seriously Weaken the Competitive Market of the Tourism Industry)

在市场经济环境下,企业与消费者是市场的主体。只有旅游企业生产的高效率,才能更好地满足旅游者的消费需求,使旅游产业得到健康稳定的发展。政府过度干预旅游产业的发展,出发点可能是好的,但政府干预往往会使企业丧失应有的经营自主权,压抑企业生产经营的积极性与创造性。

3. 政府的不恰当干预造成旅游市场的不正当竞争(The Improper Interference of the Government Resulted in the Unjustice Competition in the Tourism Market)

政府本应是公平竞争的保障者,但有时因过分强调发展的任务,政府的政策便会导致旅游产业各构成部分之间的不公平竞争。要促进本部门、本地区旅游企业的发展,就会有一些差别性的政策,就产生了地方保护与行业保护,必然会在不同所有制企业间形成不平等竞争,在一定程度上加剧了中国旅游市场某些领域的混乱现象。

4. 旅游产业发展与环境保护、社会公平之间的不平衡(The Imbalance among the Development of Tourism Industry and Environment Protection and Social Justice)

一般情况下,旅游企业的经营目标与保护环境、消费者利益之间存在着一定的矛盾。在几方面的关系中,政府应该引导旅游企业合理利用旅游资源,注意保护自然及社会环境,保护消费者利益。不过,旅游企业的发展对经济的拉动作用相当明显。对于政府有关部门来说,促进企业发展的冲动比较强烈,而约束企业保护环境和保障消费者权益的动力则相对较弱。因此,政府的干预未必就能有效地保障消费者利益,防止资源过度利用及环境破坏。

由此看来,对市场失灵的领域,政府职能并不必然起作用,因为政府也要受各种因素的影响,将政府完全理想化是不现实的。因此,只要政府干预行为存在,"政府失灵"在某种程度上就是不可避免的。政府对旅游产业的干预通常是全局性的,如旅游规划与旅游产业政策的制定等。一旦出现失误,其影响是广泛的,政府失灵通常是对旅游发展全局的危害。因此,政府干预旅游市场应采取谨慎的态度。

四、旅游产业发展中市场导向与政府职能的实施(The Execution of Market Direction and Government Function in the Development of Tourism Industry)

政府主导与市场规律存在内在矛盾,提倡政府主导型旅游发展战略将不利于按市场经济规律办事,而纯粹的市场经济同样行不通,市场规律不能超出自身发挥作用的范围。在旅游产业中,我们不能因为存在政府失灵就否定政府在发展市场经济过程中的作用,更不能因为存在市场失灵就简单地用政府替代市场。关键应该是科学确定政府与市场的关系及提高政府行为的有效性。根据中国旅游产业的现实情况,恰当的选择是在充分发挥市场机制作用的基础上,实行积极而有限的政府职能。

1. 在处理市场与政府之间关系时,必须遵守市场优先的原则。作为扩展秩序的市场扩展到哪里,政府的职能范围就应该收缩到哪里(Observing the Principles of Prioritizing the Market while Dealing with the Relation between the Market and Government. As the Market Expands Order, the Range of the Government Function Should Shrink in Conformity to the Expanding Range of the Market.)

也就是说,政府的职能即政府对市场的干预范围是有限的,有限的政府行为才是有效的。政府部门应当切实尊重市场在旅游产业资源配置中的基础地位,转变观念、放松管制,从竞争性领域退出,不与民争利。企业的创新能力得以充分发挥,市场促进发展的能量才能充分释放。政府的作用主要是在市场机制不能有效发挥作用的领域,如保护环境及促进社会公平方面。在旅游基础设施建设、旅游资源的开发利用等领域,传统的政府职能行使方式容易出现权力寻租、效率低下等问题。为改善这种状况，可使用"市场机能扩张性"政策，在进行政策干预的领域引入市场机制。由于技术进步及管理理论的发展，公共物品的提供及许多天然垄断行业已经越来越多地引入竞争机制，制约政府权力，防止腐败，提高效率。政府也可以摆脱过多的旅游基础设施建设及资源开发利用的具体任务，在宏观的旅游管理层面更好地发挥作用。

2. 培育旅游市场，建立健全市场体系，完善市场秩序，充分维护市场的竞争性和规则（Developing the Travel Market, Establishing the Entire Market System, Perfecting the Market Order and Preserving the Competitiveness and Rules of the Market.）

在旅游产业中，国与国之间，地区与地区之间，乃至同一地区内部各微观经营单位之间的竞争愈演愈烈。在中国进入WTO后，这种竞争将更加国际化。同时，人们闲暇时间和收入的增加，使旅游的队伍急剧膨胀，价廉物美的旅游地成为人们的首选目标，旅行社昔日的招徕功能慢慢隐退，市场成熟、知名度高的景点或旅游地成为游客向往的地方。因此，我们必须迅速适应这一新的旅游市场发展态势，加强旅游经济立法，建立市场规则和实施反垄断法。这是保证市场机制充分发挥作用的关键。成熟市场生产要素和产品价格都由市场竞争决定，这样企业可以根据价格信号和比较优势信息进行投资决策。因此，政府的作用这时就是要保护这种竞争，让价格机制发挥最充分的资源配置作用。而在当前，旅游市场的价格机制并未完全建立，政府还在严格限制价格的升跌，这大大束缚了市场和企业的发展，不利于提高旅游服务质量。另外，作为一个公认的竞争性产业，除了某些确实具有自然垄断特性的环节和领域仍需加强政府管制外，其他环节和领域都应该尽快引入市场竞争机制，要求各活动主体严格遵循统一的游戏规则，从而促使对原有的自身规则作适应性调整。

3. 继续深化旅游管理体制改革，切实提高和拓展管理机构的服务，激励和监督功能与运行效率（Deepening further the Reform of the Travel Management System, Improving and Expanding the Management Organizations' Function of Service, Encouragement, Supervision and Operational Efficiency Conscientiously.）

旅游管理体制的演进实际上是尊重和实现旅游企业、各级地方政府及相关利益者利益的过程。旅游业体制改革的深化，把旅游企业更大地推向了市场。相关的政策转变包括：（1）转变政府职能，实现政企真正分开。当前我国仍有相当一部分旅游企业依然和管理机构保持着千丝万缕的关联,与各级行政机关"明脱暗钩",依靠行政权力形成行业垄断,缺乏竞争意识和有效管理,其运作机理大多与市场经济特性相悖。因而,明晰企业产权,明确资产责任,使企业真正成为自主经营、自负盈亏、自我发展、自我约束的市场主体是政府职能转变的重要内容。(2)强化管理机构的产业规划功能。加快制定各旅游发展区域的开发规划、旅游业利用外商投资的专门规划,分门别类地提出我国旅游业的优先发展项目。(3)制订和完善旅游产业管理的法规。按照明文规定的、与国际惯例接轨的旅游产业法规行事,是规范旅游市场的"游戏"规则和营造公平公开的旅游市场环境与依法维护旅游市场的竞争秩序的基本保证。而这种规章制度的设计与制定必须保证管理机构的利益中性,应该较好地顾及相关主体的利益损益变化,否则很难发挥制度的激励与约束功能。

4. 精心选择旅游产业发展战略,合理开发与保护当地的旅游资源,走可持续发展旅游的路子(Choosing the Development Strategy of Travel Industry Preparedly, Developing and Protecting the Local Tourist Resources Reasonably and Taking the Sustainable Way in Which Tourism Develops.)

旅游业在地区经济运行中的地位和作用以及旅游产业本身所具有的特点,决定了政府在旅游业发展中要扮演重要的角色。所谓旅游产业政策是指在市场经济条件下,政府为实现旅游业在一定阶段的经济目标而制定和实施的促进旅游业发展的主导性和综合性政策体系。其主要内容是以发展为目标,通过政府的经济计划、经济措施、经济立法的扶持和指导,并借助于政府宏观的调控手段,实现产业内各部门在动态下运作中的结构平衡、资源最优配置和效益最大化。政府在主导旅游规划发展的方向上,更多是战略性的。首先要明确旅游在本地经济社会发展中的战略地位、战略目标、战略措施、战略重点和战略步骤等。在规划指导上,各级政府还必须十分重视旅游业的可持续发展。旅游发展要以不破坏其赖以生存的自然资源、文化资源及其他资源为前提,并能对生态环境保护给予资金支持,使其得到可持续利用,动态满足旅游者日益增加的多样化需求,并能保持对未来旅游者的吸引力。还必须能满足当地居民长期发展经济、提高生活水平的需要。

复习思考题：
1. 什么是旅游产业发展模式？
2. 旅游产业发展模式具有哪些类型和特征？
3. 试分析我国旅游产业政府主导型发展模式制定的背景和实施的效果？
4. 在现阶段如何处理市场和政府在我国旅游产业发展过程中的关系问题？

参考文献

1. Abreu, D., External Equilibrium of Oligopolistic Supergames, *Journal of Economic Thoery* 39: 191—225, 1986.
2. Bain, J. S, *Barries to New Competition*, 1st edition, New York: Harvard University Press, 1956.
3. Bain, J. S, *Industrial Organization*, 1st edition, New York: Harvard University Press, 1959.
4. Drew Fudenberg, Jean Tirole, *Game Thoery*, 1st edition, Cambridge: MIT Press, 1991.
5. Robert Gibbons, *A Primer in Game Theory*, 1st edition, New York: Harvester Wheatsheaf Press, 1992.
6. David Kreps, *A Course in Microeconomics*, 1st edition, New York: Harvester Wheatsheaf Press, 1990.
7. Jean Tirole, *The Theory of Industrial Organization*, 1st edition, Cambridge: MIT Press, 1988.
8. Harsani, J., Game with Randomly Distributed Payoffs: A New Rationale for Mixed Strategy Equilibrium Points, *International Journal of Game Theory* 2: 21—23.
9. Schelling, T., *The Strategy of Conflict*, 1st edition, New York: Harvard University Press, 1960.
10. Stigler, G. J., A Thory of Oligopoly, *Journal of Political Economy* 72: 44—61.
11. 陈才,《区域经济地理学》,北京:科学出版社,2001。
12. 陈淮,《日本产业政策研究》,北京:中国人民大学出版社,1991。

13. 陈安泽、卢云亭、陈兆棉,《旅游地学的理论与实践》——旅游地学论文集第七集,北京:中国林业出版社,2000。
14. 陈建斌,"区域旅游竞争力分析",广东商学院学报,2001,3:51—53。
15. 曹宁、郭舒,"城市旅游竞争力研究的理论与方法",社会科学家,2004,5:85—88。
16. 戴斌,《中国国有饭店的转型与变革研究》,北京:旅游教育出版社,2003。
17. 戴伯勋、沈宏达,《现代产业经济学》,北京:经济管理出版社,2001。
18. 丹尼斯·卡尔顿、杰佛里·佩罗夫,《现代产业组织》,上海:上海人民出版社,1998。
19. 丁敬平,《产业组织与产业政策》,北京:经济管理出版社,1991。
20. 杜江,《旅游管理硕士论文文库——2000》,北京:旅游教育出版社,2001。
21. 杜江,《旅游企业跨国经营研究》,北京:旅游教育出版社,2002。
22. 多纳德·海、德理克·莫瑞斯,《产业经济学与组织》,北京:经济科学出版社,2001。
23. 古诗韵、保继刚,"城市旅游研究进展",旅游学刊,1999,14:15—20。
24. 霍利斯·钱纳里,《结构变化与发展政策》,北京:经济科学出版社,1991。
25. J.卡布尔,《产业经济学前沿问题》,北京:中国税务出版社,2000。
26. 里昂惕夫,《投入产出经济学》,北京:中国统计出版社,1990。
27. 李悦,《产业经济学》,北京:中国人民大学出版社,1998。
28. 刘伟,《工业化进程中的产业结构研究》,北京:中国人民大学出版社,1995。
29. 刘峰,《中国西部旅游发展战略研究》,北京:中国旅游出版社,2001。
30. 罗明义,《旅游经济学》,北京:高等教育出版社,1998。
31. 金碚,《产业组织经济学》,北京:经济管理出版社,1999。
32. 钱纳里、鲁宾逊、塞尔奎因,《工业化和经济增长的比较研究》,上海:上海人民出版社,1996。
33. 苏东水,《产业经济学》,北京:高等教育出版社,2000。
34. 孙钢,《新世纪这个区域旅游发展大思路》,北京:中国旅游出版社,2001。
35. 申保嘉,《旅游学原理》,上海:学林出版社,1999。
36. 泰勒尔,《产业组织理论》,北京:中国人民大学出版社,1997。

37. 唐留雄,《现代旅游产业经济学》,广东:广东旅游出版社,2001。
38. 田孝蓉、李峰,《旅游经济学》,郑州:郑州大学出版社,2002。
39. 哈尔·R.范里安,《微观经济学:现代观点》,北京:经济科学出版社,1997。
40. 杨公仆、夏大慰,《现代产业经济学》,上海:上海财经大学出版社,1999。
41. 张辉,《旅游经济论》,北京:旅游教育出版社,2002。
42. 张维迎,《博弈论和信息经济学》,上海:上海人民出版社,1996。
43. 张超,《可持续发展旅游目的地竞争战略研究》,南开管理评论,2002,4:69—73。
44. 朱丽萌、刘镇,《区域经济理论与战略》,南昌:江西人民出版社,2001。